The Cambridge English Course

NAN de watashi ga ...

1
Teacher's Book

Michael Swan and Catherine Walter

Cambridge University Press

Cambridge

New York　　New Rochelle　　Melbourne　　Sydney

*The right of the
University of Cambridge
to print and sell
all manner of books
was granted by
Henry VIII in 1534.
The University has printed
and published continuously
since 1584.*

Published by the Press Syndicate of the University of Cambridge
The Pitt Building, Trumpington Street, Cambridge CB2 1RP
32 East 57th Street, New York, NY10022, USA
10 Stamford Road, Oakleigh, Melbourne 3166, Australia

© Cambridge University Press 1984

First published 1984
Eighth printing 1988

Designed by John Youé and Associates, Croydon, Surrey
Typeset by Text Filmsetters Limited, London
Origination by Vyner Litho Plates Limited, London
Printed in Great Britain by The Eagle Press Plc, Glasgow

ISBN 0 521 28910 6 Teacher's Book 1

ISBN 0 521 28908 4 Student's Book 1
Split edition: ISBN 0 521 31028 8 Part A
             ISBN 0 521 31029 6 Part B
             ISBN 0 521 31030 X Part C

ISBN 0 521 28909 2 Practice Book 1
ISBN 0 521 27865 1 Test Book 1
ISBN 0 521 24703 9 Cassette Set 1
ISBN 0 521 26223 2 Student's Cassette 1

Author's acknowledgements

A book like this necessarily owes a great deal to a great many people. Our thanks to:

Alan Maley, for the splendid seminar programme which he organized at the British Council, Paris, in the 1970s. This was an unparalleled source of information, ideas and inspiration.

Donn Byrne, Alan Duff, Alan Maley, Heather Murray, Penny Ur and Jane Wright, for specific ideas and exercises which we have borrowed.

The many other people — too many to acknowledge — whose ideas have influenced our work, including all the colleagues and students from whom we have learnt.

Those institutions and teachers who were kind enough to work with the Pilot Edition of this course, and whose comments have done so much to shape the final version. (A full list of the institutions involved is given on the Acknowledgements page.)

Peter Roach and Ian Thompson for their expert and sensible help with the phonetic transcription.

John Youé, Steve Williams, Gillian Clack, Richard Child, Chris Rawlings, Clifford Webb and Diana Dobson of Youé and Spooner Limited, our designers, for their unfailing understanding, good humour and expertise.

John and Angela Eckersley, and the staff of the Eckersley School of English, Oxford, for making it possible for us to try out parts of the book in their classrooms.

Steve Dixon, Lorna Higgs, John Peake, Pat Robbins, Fran Searson, Ann Swan, Ruth Swan, Heather and Paul Teale, Sue Ward, Adrian Webber, and Susan Webber, for agreeing to be quizzed and questioned within earshot of our microphones.

Judy Haycox, Joanne Haycox, Susan Webber and Helen Walter, for invaluable domestic support during a trying period.

Mark, for patience and good humour beyond the call of duty.

And finally, to Adrian du Plessis, Peter Donovan, Barbara Thomas and Peter Ducker of Cambridge University Press: few authors can have been so fortunate in their publishers.

Contents

Doshi = (verb)

noun = (meishi)

preposition (zenchi-shi)

vocabulary (goi)

vowels = (boin)

consonants = (shiin)

adjective = (keiyō-shi)

Map of Book 1*

In Unit	Students will learn to	Students will learn to talk about
1	Ask and give names; say hello; ask and tell where people are from.	Numbers.
2	Say hello formally and informally; ask about and give personal information.	Jobs; age.
3	Describe people; tell the time.	Family relationships.
4	Describe places; give compliments; express uncertainty; confirm and correct information.	Geography; numbers to 1,000,000.
5	Describe houses and flats; make and answer telephone calls.	Home: furniture, addresses; telephones.
6	Express likes and dislikes; ask about and describe habits and routines.	Habits and routines.
7	Ask and tell about quantity.	Food and drink; shopping; quantification.
8	Ask for and give directions; ask and tell about physical and emotional states.	Finding your way in a town.
9	Express degrees of certainty; talk about frequency.	How people live; how animals live; weather and climate.
10	Describe people's appearances; give compliments; write simple letters.	Colours; parts of the body; clothing; resemblances.
REVISION 11	Use what they have learnt in different ways.	Physical description.
12	Ask for and give information.	Personal history; differences between past and present; recent past.
13	Make and grant requests; say where things are; check information.	Shopping; travelling.
14	Ask for and give information.	Abilities; comparison; similarities and differences.
15	Ask for and give information; narrate.	Change; history.
16	Ask for and give opinions; agree and disagree; ask follow-up questions.	Weights and measures; appearances; professions; personality types; dates.
17	Order meals; make and reply to requests; borrow; make and reply to offers.	Food; restaurants; differences in formality; having guests at home.
18	Express guesses; write postcards.	Temporary present actions and states; holidays; change; economics and demography.
19	Plan; make, accept and decline invitations and suggestions.	Travel; distance; going out.
20	Initiate conversations, express interest; ask for, express and react to opinions.	Meeting strangers; frequency; likes and dislikes; being in love; duration.
21	Ask for and give reasons.	Physical qualities; composition of objects; personal possessions; production; imports and exports.
REVISION 22	Describe; ask for and give personal information; use what they have learnt in different ways.	Comparison; shopping; people's appearance and behaviour.
23	Give instructions and advice.	Sports; position, direction and change of position; cooking.
24	Make requests; ask for and give information.	Hotels; public transport; air travel; place and direction.
25	Talk about plans; make predictions.	Plans; small ads; travel.
26	Talk about problems; express sympathy; make suggestions; express and respond to emotions; describe relationships.	Common physical problems; personal relationships.
27	Narrate.	Ways of travelling; speed; how things are done.
28	Describe objects; narrate.	Education systems; quantity; shapes; parts of things; position; structuring of time-sequences; daily routines.
29	Predict; warn; raise and counter objections.	Danger; horoscopes.
30	Classify; make and accept apologies; correct misunderstandings; complain.	Need; importance; use and usefulness; shopping.
31	Make, accept and decline offers; ask for and analyse information.	Reciprocal and reflexive action; self and others; social situations; possession.
REVISION 32	Express obligation and opinions; other functions dependent on your choice of activities.	Correctness; other areas depending on activities chosen.

*This 'map' of the course should be translated into the students' language where possible.

VOCABULARY: Students will learn about 1100 common words and expressions during the course.

Students will learn these grammar points	Students will study these aspects of pronunciation
Present of *to be* (singular); possessive adjectives.	Word-stress; weak forms.
A/an with jobs; subject pronouns.	Rhythm; intonation; linking; stress pattern recognition.
Noun plurals; *'s* for possession; present of *to be* (plural); *have got*; adjectives; adverbs of degree.	/ð/; *o* in *mother*, etc.; stress; intonation; linking /r/.
A/an contrasted with *the*; adjectives before nouns; *on/in/at* with places; *Isn't that. . .?*	/θ/ and /ð/; /ðə/ and /ði:/; word-stress and resultant /ə/; intonation of answers; intonation for contrast; linking.
There is/there are; simple present affirmative, *this/that*; *Can/Could I. . .?*; *tell* + object + *that*-clause; formation of noun plurals.	Weak forms; linking and rhythm with *there is/there are*; contrastive stress; rising and falling intonation; plural endings.
Simple Present; omission of article; *like* + *-ing*; *neither. . . nor*; object pronouns; *at* with times; *by* (*bus*); *from. . . until*.	Stress and rhythm; decoding fast speech.
Countables and uncountables; expressions of quantity; omission of article; *was/were*; *some* and *any*; *much* and *many*.	Word-stress; weak forms.
For + expressions of distance; *to be* with *hungry, thirsty*, etc.	Intonation of polite questions; stress and rhythm; weak form of *at*.
Complex sentences; text building; frequency adverbs; impersonal *it*.	Stress and /ə/; /i:/ and /ɪ/.
Have got; *both* and *all*; *look like*; *What (a). . .!*	
(Revision) *Be* contrasted with *have*; *there is/there are*; questions with noun-phrase subjects.	Perceiving weak forms and unstressed words; /θ/ and /ð/; intonation; pronunciation of words with misleading spellings.
Simple Past; *do* as pro-verb; subject and object questions with *who*.	Regular Simple Past endings; stress in negative sentences; rhythm and stress in questions.
One(s) as substitute word; *would like*; *much* and *many*.	Rising intonation in *yes/no* questions; falling intonation in answers; rhythm.
Can; *good at* + noun/*-ing* word; comparative and superlative of adjectives; *a bit/much* + adjective.	/kn/, /kæn/, /kɑ:nt/; pronunciations of the letter *a*, weak forms of *as* and *from*.
Ago; *a* contrasted with *the*; past of *to be*; Simple Past; sequencing devices.	Linking; strong and weak forms of *was* and *were*; rhythm.
Be with ages and measures; *look like/be like*; dates; *with* for possession; *a/any*.	/θ/; pronunciations of the letter *i*.
A little/a few; *I'll have*; *Could you. . .?*; *give/bring/lend/show* + two objects; object pronouns; indirect object with *to*; *something to eat/drink*.	Politeness through intonation; pronunciations of the letter *o*.
Present Progressive; *the girl in jeans*; *the man with a beard*; *get* + comparative; spelling *-ing* forms; contrast of two present tenses.	Pronunciations of the letter *e*.
Present Progressive with future meaning; coordination with *so*; *each* + singular; *who* as object; *How far is . . . from . . .?*; *Let's*; *Why don't we. . .?*	Pronunciations of the letter *u*; decoding fast colloquial speech.
Do you mind if. . .?; reply questions; adverbs and adverbials of frequency; *So do/can/am/have I*; Present Perfect; *since* and *for*.	/i:/ and /ɪ/.
Why + negative verb; *too* + adjective; adjective + *enough*; *made of*; Simple Past and Present Perfect; Passives; relative *which*; *to* and *from*.	Linking final consonants to initial vowels; linking between adjacent vowels.
(Revision) *more. . . than*; *as. . . as*; *not as. . . as*; *less. . . than*; (*not*) *the same as*; *different from*; *but*; revision of tenses.	
Imperatives; *if*-clauses; prepositions of place and movement; *should* + infinitive; grammar of written and spoken instructions.	Letter *o* pronounced /ɒ/ and /ʌ/.
Have to; infinitive of purpose; preposition + *-ing* form; prepositions of place and direction.	Devoicing of /v/ in *have to*.
Going to; connectors in paragraphs; paragraph-structuring adverbials; infinitives and *-ing* forms.	Spellings of /ɜ:/; pronunciation of *going to*.
It + Simple Present + *me*; *It makes me* + adjective.	'Long' and 'short' vowels.
Superlatives; different meanings of *get*; adverbs of manner; adjectives and adverbs.	Decoding fast speech.
Quantifying expressions; fractions; *at the top/bottom* etc.; *in* and *at* for time; structuring with adverbs and conjunctions.	Identifying unstressed words; word-stress and /ə/.
Will + infinitive; *get lost/killed/married*.	Pronunciation of *w*, *'ll*, *won't*.
X uses y to do z (with); *x does y with z*; words having more than one grammatical function.	Use of stress for emphasis and contrast.
Reflexive/emphatic pronouns; *each other, somebody else*; *Shall I. . .?*; *I'd love/prefer/like*; *to* as pro-verb; *whose*; *somebody/anybody* etc.	Strong and weak pronunciations of *shall*; decoding unstressed words in fast speech.
(Revision) *have to*; *should*; verb tenses; question forms; adjectives; and other structures dependent on students' choice of activities.	

Introduction

The nature and purpose of the course

This is Book 1 of *The Cambridge English Course*, a four-level course designed for adult students who are learning English for general practical or cultural purposes. Book 1 is for complete beginners and false beginners. The Student's Book contains about 100 hours' classwork for an 'average' group (though of course the time taken to work through it will depend on the students' mother tongue, the way their classes are organized, where they are studying, how strong their motivation is, and various other factors). The book will take students up to a point where they can begin to use English to achieve a certain number of simple practical aims (a level between 'Threshold' and 'Waystage', in the Council of Europe's terminology).

The course is different in some ways from most beginners' courses. For example, its organization is not simply 'structural' or 'functional', but 'multi-syllabus': it is based on a combination of eight different syllabus-inventories. There is very considerable variety of lesson design and activity types; students often participate actively in choosing exactly what language they will learn; great importance is given to the systematic teaching of vocabulary; dictionary use is an integral part of the course; some reading and listening material is deliberately pitched well above the productive level of the learners.

For a more detailed description of the principles underlying the design of the course, see the following section.

Basic principles

The principles which have guided us in writing the course can be summarized as follows:

1. The language-learning process
Very little is known about how languages are learnt. However, our knowledge is growing and two things seem clear:
a) Most adults learn a foreign language more effectively if it is 'tidied up' for them to some extent, so that they are exposed especially to high-frequency items which correspond to their particular learning needs, and so that they can more easily perceive the regularities of the language structure.
b) However, learners also need to be exposed to a certain amount of 'untidy' natural language (even if this seems too difficult for them). Without this unstructured input, the individual's unconscious ability to acquire languages probably cannot operate effectively.
It is important to provide material which caters for both of these ways of approaching a language (sometimes called 'learning' and 'acquisition' respectively).

2. Preview
In natural language learning, children or adults usually hear or see an item several times before they are ready to remember and use it. They are exposed to a great deal of language which they do not fully understand, but which enables them to 'preview' words and structures which they will learn later. Teaching materials should therefore introduce learners from the beginning to some language which is beyond their productive capacity; there should be training in techniques (such as 'scanning') which help learners to cope with such material; key learning items should be 'previewed' whenever possible.

3. Respecting the learner
Adult beginners are people of normal sensitivity and intelligence, with a wealth of personal experience and knowledge. Language course materials should respect the learner, involving as much of his or her personality as possible. People learn languages best when they are interested in both the material they are learning and the activity they are engaged in; when they are saying things they really wish to say; and when they are required to use their intelligence to carry out learning tasks.

Different individuals have different learning strategies and different aims. Some students learn better through practice in which they express their own ideas and feelings; others when dealing with impersonal, factual material; others when playing a role of some kind. All of these learning styles should be catered for.

Students have views about what they want to learn and how they can best achieve their aims. Even beginners can take some of the responsibility for making decisions about the content and nature of their course.

4. Fiction and humour
Fiction and humour are both good in their places, but neither should be allowed to dominate teaching materials. In courses which rely heavily on fictional input, students do not usually get enough opportunity to talk about things outside the 'pretend' world of the story-line or dialogues, and so learning is impoverished. Beginners' course humour can be very childish and patronizing; the best classroom humour generally comes from the students, not from the textbook.

5. The syllabus: formal or communicative?
Until recently, courses have almost always taken the forms of the language as their starting point. A typical beginners' course of this kind will work systematically through a list of basic structures and common words, often devoting the bulk of each lesson to the presentation and practice of a new structure. Such courses do not usually neglect

meaning (though they are sometimes accused of doing so). However, since they do not work from a systematic semantic syllabus, there is no guarantee that all the most important meanings are in fact covered by the course. A student might complete three or four years' work, learn all the basic structures of the language, acquire a working vocabulary of 5,000 words, and still not know which of his words and structures he should choose in order to give a warning, ask a favour or make a complaint.

Recent work in linguistics has made it easier to draw up a 'syllabus of meanings' – to look systematically at the things we do with language ('functions') and the ideas we express ('notions'). Some newer language courses have taken these meaning categories as the basis for their syllabus. Instead of working through a list of structures, students will work through a list of functions (for example *asking for information, offering help, agreeing*), notions (for example *point of time, duration, doubt*) and skills (for example *listening for gist, speaking fluently, writing personal letters*). This approach is exciting, but it, too, has its drawbacks. For instance, only structures and words which are obviously relevant to the functions, notions and skills that have been chosen are certain to get into the syllabus. There is no guarantee that other important 'general-purpose' items will be covered. So a student may work through a complete beginners' course, achieve an impressive mastery of a whole battery of communicative skills, and still not learn the names of the basic colours, the use of the verb *have*, or the correct position of prepositions in spoken questions.

In fact, neither a formal progression nor a 'communicative' syllabus is adequate as a basis for a language course. Several intertwined syllabuses (lexical, structural, phonological, thematic, functional, notional, situational, skills) are required if we are to capture the complete range of language items and language uses which our students will need to master.

6. Vocabulary
Vocabulary acquisition is the largest and most important task facing the language learner. It is essential to make sure that all the most common words and expressions of the language are included in a course, and that they are taught in such a way that students will learn, retain and be able to use them.

7. Practice
Quantity and quality of practice are both important. Students must have plenty of opportunity to engage in communicative activities, including group work and pair work.

8. Setting realistic standards
At elementary level, students should aim for comprehensibility in their speech and writing; teachers should not require perfect accuracy (this can easily give students a sense of failure and destroy their motivation). In pronunciation work, the features that contribute most to comprehensibility in English – stress and rhythm patterns and linking – should receive the most emphasis.

9. Regularity and variety
If all the lessons are constructed in the same way, a course is easy to use but tends to be monotonous. Variety of approach makes lessons more interesting, but also makes the material more difficult for teachers to prepare and students to get used to. It is important to achieve a reasonable compromise between regularity and variety.

10. Variations of level
There will always be variations of level and ability inside one class, and some students will inevitably learn faster than others. The pace of the class should neither be kept down to that of the slowest students nor constantly held at that of the quicker students. There should be some variation in difficulty (for example, more or fewer new words to learn) from lesson to lesson, in order to accommodate these different speeds of learning.

11. The mother-tongue
Used in moderation and with common sense, the students' mother-tongue is a valuable aid if the composition of the class allows it to be used – for instance, in helping to make explanations faster and more precise. The same is true of bilingual dictionaries, and students should be taught to use them intelligently from the beginning.

12. Study and memorization
Effective language learning must involve some effort of study and memorization on the part of the learner. Students should be expected to spend some time every week, outside class, consolidating what they have learnt.

Organization of the course

Overall structure
The course consists of 32 units, each divided into four sections. Each section (which takes up one page of the Student's Book) contains adequate material for a lesson of around forty-five minutes with learners of average ability, so a unit will take roughly three hours of class time.

Each unit is organized around a thematic or functional area – for example *Houses* or *Where is it?* In choosing the subjects of the units, we have tried for a balance between those dealing with the students' own lives and those concerned with the 'outside world'. Some fiction is introduced, and language material is presented with the aid of fictional characters and dialogues where this suits our purposes. However, there is not a standard 'cast of characters' or story-line running through the Student's Book. Much of the work is based on non-fictional material; for some of the activities imaginative input comes from the students themselves.

Each third of the course ends with a revision unit and a detailed revision test, which can be used to see how effectively students have assimilated the new material.

There are four books: the Student's Book, the Practice Book, the Teacher's Book and the Test Book. (The Teacher's Book contains reproductions of all the Student's Book material, interleaved with notes for each lesson.) The course is accompanied by a set of cassettes for classroom use and a student cassette for self-study.

A British English model is used throughout, but attention is sometimes drawn to important differences between this and other varieties of English, and you will notice American and Commonwealth accents in some of the listening exercises.

The Student's Book
The Student's Book contains presentation material (introducing and demonstrating new language) and exercises. For some of the exercises, reference to the Teacher's Book is necessary. At the end of the Student's Book there are summaries of each unit, containing lists of the structures and vocabulary which students are expected to learn.

The Practice Book
This is intended for individual work at home or in the classroom. It will make a great difference to the students' learning if they can do at least some of the Practice Book work after each lesson.

The Teacher's Book
We have provided detailed step-by-step guides to each lesson. These are intended particularly as a support for less experienced teachers, and for teachers who have little time to prepare. More experienced teachers, and teachers with ample time available, will probably prefer to approach the lessons in their own way, and will have less need for detailed instructions (though they will probably find it useful to look over the Teacher's Book before each lesson). Some lessons cannot be done without the Teacher's Book.

An introductory section in the instructions to each lesson lists the new language items introduced, mentions any special materials that may need to be prepared, and gives notes on language points that may present problems.

The cassettes
These contain recordings of presentation materials, listening exercises, pronunciation exercises, and some practice examples. Much of the material can be demonstrated directly by the teacher if preferred, but the cassettes are desirable for dialogue material and essential for most listening exercises.

Recorded material is indicated in the Teacher's Book by one of two symbols. The heavy symbol ▣ shows that the exercise cannot easily be done without the recorded material; the light symbol ▢ means that the material is recorded for the teacher's convenience, but can simply be read out in class if desired. Ⓐ indicates a piece of authentic listening material.

Using the course: general notes

The detailed teacher's notes for each unit should give all the guidance that is necessary for the efficient use of the materials during the course. However, teachers may find it helpful to read through these notes before starting the course, so as to familiarize themselves in advance with the general approach and the main activity types.

1. Preparing the students for the book
If you speak the students' own language(s), you may want to tell them before you begin using the book that it is likely to be different from other language teaching textbooks that they have had, and to explain briefly why and how it is different. The 'map' of the course on pages 4–5 of the Student's Book and pages IV–V of the Teacher's Book shows in slightly simplified form how the course is constructed and how the several syllabuses interrelate. It is useful to show and explain this to students before the course begins, as well as referring to it from time to time so that students can see how they are progressing. An ideal approach, if this is feasible, is to translate the 'map' into the students' language and provide them with copies to paste into the front of their books.

2. Classes in English-speaking countries
Most of the teachers using this book will be working in countries where English is not the native language. If you are teaching in Britain or another English-speaking country, however, you may wish to bring forward the teaching of some lessons and points that are important for your students' 'survival needs'. Examples are lessons 5B, 5C, 8A, 8B.

3. Mother-tongue explanations and dictionary use
Several years ago the use of the first language in a foreign language classroom was looked on with consternation and horror. Fortunately, most teachers are no longer so dogmatic, and the value of sensible use of the mother-tongue, where possible, is widely recognized. We expect that in some cases teachers will want to give quick vocabulary explanations in the students' first language, for example, rather than spending a much longer time demonstrating the meaning of a word by using only English. It is generally more efficient to give grammar explanations in the mother-tongue, where this can be done. And in

some classes (especially those with few contact hours per week) teachers may want to use the students' language for giving some of the instructions in the classroom.

Of course, if you do not speak the students' language, this option will not be open to you, and you can certainly get along perfectly well without it. Teachers in this situation are usually very expert at techniques like demonstration, mime, paraphrase, and using the help of the other students in the class to communicate new meanings.

The bilingual dictionary can be an extremely useful aid in learning a language, particularly when used under the supervision of a teacher. For some of the exercises in the course, students must have access to bilingual dictionaries: encourage them to buy suitable dictionaries (not pocket editions), and advise them on their choice if possible. As students work with dictionaries they will become more skilled in autonomous work outside the classroom. In the early stages, you may want to help students in order to ensure that they are making effective use of their dictionaries. Show them, if necessary, how the entries are organized and what kinds of information they can provide. Make sure students understand that words have different translations in different contexts, and that they can only discover meanings with a dictionary if they learn to select the appropriate translation from among the several that are offered.

At a later stage, you will want to introduce the use of an English–English dictionary such as the *Oxford Advanced Learner's Dictionary of Current English* or the *Longman Dictionary of Contemporary English*.

4. Problems specific to particular mother-tongues

Speakers of different languages approach English in different ways, determined by the similarities and differences between English and their various mother-tongues. Designed to be used with students from a range of first-language backgrounds, this book cannot deal exhaustively with the special problems which English presents to the speakers of specific languages. Occasional mention will be made, in the Language Notes at the beginning of lesson instructions, of a particular difficulty for speakers of one language (or language group) or another, but the remarks are usually more general. Teachers will therefore need to supplement the book with occasional information and practice on important first-language-specific problems.

5. Grammar

Recent functionally-oriented courses sometimes give the impression that grammar is unimportant, or that it can be learnt 'in passing' in the course of communicative practice. This may be true of many points of grammar, but certain structures are necessary, must be mastered more or less

accurately, and are difficult to learn. In this course we teach all the points of grammar which are normally regarded as necessary for an elementary command of the language. Most of this grammar is presented and taught in a communicative framework, but we have not hesitated to devote special lessons to questions of grammatical form where this seems necessary. Such lessons will inevitably look less attractive than others which are more directly communicative, but they are an important part of the course.

For students who do not speak Western European languages, the English articles present special problems. Some extra explanations and model exercises on the use of the articles, designed for such students, will be found in an appendix on pages 160-162.

6. Vocabulary

We have established a 'core' syllabus of around 1100 of the most common and useful words in the language. These are carefully presented and practised, and listed in the language summaries at the back of the Student's Book. Students should be told to study these words and memorize them (see note below on using the summary).

7. 'Notional' lessons

Much attention has been paid in recent years to organizing teaching on the basis of 'functions' such as *making requests, apologizing, eliciting information, narrating* or *complaining*, and most courses now have a functional component. Less effort has been made to ensure that students are taught the language associated with the most common concepts or 'notions', such as *movement, distance, speed, grief, texture* or *sound*. This course contains a certain number of notional lessons, dealing with areas of language that students must master if they are to be able to express essential concepts and communicate about topics of general interest. These lessons are of necessity largely concerned with vocabulary teaching, and do not contain new structural or functional material. Students and teachers who are not used to this kind of lesson may feel uncomfortable with it; feeling that it does not 'teach anything useful'. But unless students can master the words and expressions that are needed to refer to common concepts, and can learn to use them appropriately and fluently, they will not be able to speak English, however much time they have spent on structures and communicative functions.

8. Pronunciation

Pronunciation exercises are a regular feature of the book. At elementary level it is important to get students used to the fact that English is a stress-timed language (see note below). This will determine their success in listening comprehension skills as well as in making themselves understood. So we put a good deal of emphasis on hearing stress in words, remembering how words are stressed, identifying unstressed vowels, etc. Another area that is dealt with in some detail in both listening and production exercises is the question of linking between words: this, too, is a feature of English that can give big rewards to the learner in exchange for a relatively modest input of practice time. There are also exercises on intonation, on certain vowel and consonant problems, and on the relationship between spelling and pronunciation.

Teachers should be warned not to try for perfection in pronunciation from the start. Students' pronunciation will improve with work, and as their ability to hear English gets better. If students and teachers aim for comprehensibility at this level, it will be more satisfying and provide confidence that will encourage improvement later on. Few students will ever be mistaken for native speakers, but most can be brought to a level of comprehensibility that is adequate for their needs and desires.

How much work students need to do on phonology will of course depend very much on the nature of their mother-tongue. English is difficult to pronounce for Spanish, French or Japanese speakers, for example, and they will need to work hard to achieve an adequate standard of understanding and pronunciation. On the other hand, Scandinavians, Germans or Arabic-speakers usually find the sound system of English easy to master, and they will need to spend less time on this aspect of the language.

Note: stress-timed rhythm
Many languages have what is called 'syllable-timed' rhythm. In this kind of language, each syllable takes roughly the same length of time to say: a sentence with ten syllables will take twice as long as one with five.

English, in common with German, Dutch and Scandinavian languages, has 'stress-timed' rhythm. In this kind of language, some syllables are heavily stressed, and these stressed syllables follow each other at roughly equal intervals (regardless of how many unstressed syllables come in between). A sentence with ten syllables and one with five syllables may take about the same time to say if each has five stressed syllables.
Compare: 'Ann 'Grant 'lives 'near 'Bath.
　　　　 'Ann and 'Martin 'settled 'near
　　　　　 Dun'fermline.

When speakers of syllable-timed languages learn English, they tend to adopt a 'staccato' pronunciation, giving equal value to each syllable. They often have great difficulty perceiving unstressed syllables and weak forms (which are not prominent enough to fit in with their preconception of what a syllable should sound like). They need a good deal of practice in these areas.

9. Preview
As explained in the section on 'Basic principles', language items are often 'previewed' before being

formally taught. This may come as a surprise to students (and teachers) who are used to other kinds of courses where nothing is presented without being explained on the spot. Preview often takes the form of a casual occurrence of a new word in an exercise instruction, sample sentence, listening exercise or reading text. Students should learn not to worry about items of this kind, which will be dealt with in more detail later in the course.

10. Presentation devices
These vary greatly from one part of the book to the next: there is no one standardized 'listen and repeat' format. Students may be taught vocabulary through a prose text, a dialogue or a labelled illustration; they may discover words and expressions by pooling their collective knowledge, by asking the teacher, or by looking up words in a dictionary; in some cases the 'model sentences' may be sentences of the students' own construction. This is not only for the sake of variety; different learning styles and personal interests require different approaches, and not all language items can be best demonstrated in the same way. Suggestions for dealing with each presentation device will be found in the corresponding Teacher's Book lesson.

11. Listening practice
For many students, understanding the spoken language is a major source of difficulty. We provide two kinds of training in listening:
a) 'perception' exercises, which train students to 'decode' sounds into words
b) 'interpretation' exercises, which train students to make sense of the words they hear.

12. Reading
There are a variety of reading activities in the book. One text may be used for presenting a grammatical structure or a lexical set, and the next for developing specific reading skills; this will of course lead to very different treatments in each case. We have not set 'comprehension' questions on each text, but have varied our approach according to what students are learning or practising each time.

13. Extensive reading and listening
From very early on, students are presented with material to read and listen to which they would not be able to produce themselves, and which contains language items they may not understand. Some of this material is 'authentic' (not written for language-teaching purposes); some is adapted or specially written. In most cases students are given specific tasks to carry out which they will be able to do, provided they keep their heads and concentrate on understanding what is within their grasp. In this kind of exercise, it is important to resist the temptation to explain everything; students must get into the habit of coping with material that is beyond their level (as they will have to do in

they are used. You will probably need to help them do this at the beginning. Words in the summaries often come in 'lexical sets' (e.g., the names of articles of clothing, or pieces of furniture). This sort of grouping is often an aid to remembering. Brighter students should be encouraged to extend these lists for themselves with their dictionaries.

We have included phonetic transcriptions for the vocabulary lists. We realize that some teachers or students will not want to refer to them, especially if the students are not used to Roman script and are learning this as they learn English. But for those who do use them, transcriptions are a useful reference to pronunciation, and can make students more independent in their learning. The transcription system used is that found in the *Longman Dictionary of Contemporary English*, with one or two minor modifications. (In particular, we have transcribed final *-al*, *-le* or *-ul* as /ʊl/ in cases where it is necessary to show a vowel: this corresponds better to phonetic reality than the standard transcription /əl/.) We have only marked primary stress.

22. Adapting the course
It is nearly always a mistake to go systematically through a textbook from left to right, without deviating from the list of activities prescribed by the course designer. No textbook can meet all the needs of one group of individuals, and classes work in such different circumstances that the role of the book cannot possibly be the same in each case. The same course may be used with equal success with a full-time class of twelve adults in London, a part-time class of eighteen in an evening institute in Brazil, or a class of thirty-five adolescents in a Greek secondary school. But it will not be used in the same way. Teachers should not hesitate to adapt and supplement the material so as to fit the approach which their experience and instinct tells them is right for their students, and for themselves as teachers.

Where time allows, students should start regular work on easy supplementary reading material from an early stage. This will make a great difference to the speed and breadth of their learning. It is a good idea to set up a circulating class library of simplified readers, containing one copy of each of twenty or thirty books. Lists of suitable reading material can be found in the catalogues of the main ELT publishers; the books are easily obtainable.

23. Validation and feedback
The Cambridge English Course has been extensively piloted before publication, and everything in it has been tried out successfully in a variety of teaching situations. Nonetheless, improvements are still possible, and we should be delighted to hear from any teachers who would like to send us suggestions, criticism, or other comments on their experience with the book. Letters can be sent to us c/o Cambridge University Press (English Language Teaching), The Edinburgh Building, Shaftesbury Road, Cambridge CB2 2RU, Great Britain.

Michael Swan   Catherine Walter   January 1984

Hello

A What's your name?

1 1. Listen to the conversations.
2. Put the sentences into the pictures.

What's your name?   Hello. My name's Mary Lake.
No, it isn't.   Catherine.
Hello. Yes, room three four six, Mrs Lake.
What's *your* name?   Is your name Mark Perkins?
John.   Thank you.   It's Harry Brown.

2 Say your name.

'Hello. My name's ....'

3 Ask other students' names.

'What's your name?'

4 Ask and answer.

'Is your name Anne?' 'Yes, it is.'
'Is your name Alex?' 'No, it isn't. It's Peter.'

5 Pronunciation. Say these words and expressions after the recording.

what   what's   your   my   name   it
it's   isn't
Yes, it is.   No, it isn't.

6 Learn:

1 one	2 two	3 three	4 four	5 five
6 six	7 seven	8 eight	9 nine	10 ten

Unit 1: Lesson A

Students learn to ask people's names and to give their own. They learn to count up to ten.
Structures: third person of *to be*: affirmatives; negatives; questions with *what*; *yes/no* questions; short answers. Contractions.
Words and expressions to learn[1]: *hello*; *my*; *your*; *it*; *is*; *what*; *not*; *thank you*; *yes*; *no*; *name*; numbers *one* to *ten*.

Language notes and possible problems

1. Name In English, *name* can be used to mean 'first name', 'surname' or 'full name'. Some students may assume that it means only one or the other.
2. 's The contracted *'s* is difficult to handle at first: look out for **What your name's?*[2] and *My name Maria.
3. Vocabulary Make sure students know which words they are expected to learn and remember. (See summary.)

Optional extra materials
Name-cards for each student (see Optional activity).
Flashcards for numbers 1–10 (Exercise 6).

1 Listening and matching[3] [4]
● This can be done before or after the personal exchanges in Exercises 2–4.
● Tell students to look at the illustrations.
● Play the three conversations through once or twice.
● Ask students to look at the sentences in Exercise 1.
● Ask what sentence goes into the first speech-balloon.
● Write the answer on the board:
  1. Hello. My name's Mary Lake.
● Do the same with the second speech-balloon.
● Then let students continue by themselves, writing the numbers and sentences on a piece of paper.
● Go over the answers and play the recording again.

Alternative Exercise 1 for 'false beginners'
● If your students already know some English, ask them to try the exercise *before* hearing the conversations.

Tapescript for Exercise 1
1. Hello. My name's Mary Lake.
2. Hello. Yes, room three four six, Mrs Lake.
3. Thank you.

4. What's your name?   5. Catherine.
6. What's *your* name?   7. John.

8. Is your name Mark Perkins?   9. No, it isn't.
10. It's Harry Brown.

---

[1]Words and expressions listed are those which the students are expected to learn and remember now. Other items (i.e. *room, Mrs*) are previewed here, but do not need to be learnt until later.
[2]An asterisk marks an unacceptable utterance.
[3]Explicit exercise instructions are given in the Student's Book from the beginning, for two reasons: to accustom the student to the language used in the instructions, and to make it easier for the teacher to see what is going on. Obviously complete beginners will not understand the instructions, and will need to be told (by demonstration, gesture, or mother-tongue explanation) what to do.
[4]For the meaning of the recording symbols, see Introduction page VIII.

2 Saying your name
● This can be done with books closed. Say:
  My name is … (giving your name). *My name's …*
● Write both forms on the board.
● Try to point out that we normally use the contraction in speaking and the uncontracted form in writing.
● Ask students *What's your name?* and get them to answer *My name's …*

3 Asking people's names
● Write on the board:
  What is your name?   What's your name?
● Practise *What's your name?*
● Tell students to walk round the room asking everybody's names. (If this is difficult, students can just find out the names of their near neighbours.)

4 Yes/no questions; short answers
● Ask a student *Is your name … ?*, and teach *Yes, it is.*
● Ask another student *Is your name … ?* (wrong name) and teach *No, it isn't.*
● Show the examples in the book. Practise the pronunciation (*isn't* is difficult). Note that *it is* and *it isn't* should be linked (pronounced like single words).
● Explain that *isn't = is not*.
● Practise with a walk-round exercise (or ask students to check up on the names of their neighbours). Work on first names and surnames.

Optional activity
● Prepare cards or slips of paper with various names (e.g. *William Shakespeare, Jane Fonda, Mickey Mouse*).
● Shuffle the cards and give them out to students.
● Do further practice on *What's your name?* and *My name's …* , using the new names.
● Alternatively, give students English first names.

5 Pronunciation
● This is an opportunity to work on problem sounds. Don't be too perfectionist at this stage.
● In a small class, get everybody to say each word in turn. In a larger class, ask students to repeat each word in chorus, and then pick out one or two individuals.

6 Numbers *one–ten*
● After teaching the pronunciation, you can:
1. Count forwards, then backwards round the class.
2. Say numbers and ask students to write the figures. Get students to dictate numbers to each other.
3. Write figures on the board (or use flashcards) and get students to say the numbers.
4. In a monolingual class, give mother-tongue numbers for translation.
5. Give simple oral addition sums, such as *What's four and three?* (The total must be less than ten.)
   Continue the exercises in pairs or small groups.

Practice Book
The Practice Book is an important part of the course, and students should consolidate their learning by doing the Practice Book exercises, in class or for homework. During the early part of the course you will probably want to go over homework exercise instructions in class to make sure that the students understand what to do.

Unit 1: Lesson B

Students learn to talk about other people's names, and to spell.
Structures: no new structures.
Words and expressions to learn: *his*; *her*; *first name*; *surname*; *I don't know*; *that's right*; *the alphabet*.

Language notes and possible problems

1. *His* and *her* Speakers of Romance languages, and some others, will need to work hard on the difference between *his* and *her*. (French, for example, uses the same word for both; the word varies in form according to the gender of the *thing possessed*, not the possessor.)

2. *First name*, *surname* Some students may already have learnt expressions such as *Christian name*, *given name*, *family name*. We use *first name* and *surname*, but you can of course teach other terms if you wish. (Note that Chinese family names come before other names, so *first name* may give Chinese a false impression of the meaning of *first*.)

Optional extra materials

Pictures of well-known people (cut from magazines, for example), and separate cards with their names on.
Flashcards with letters of the alphabet.

1 First names and surnames

● This can be done by general discussion in the whole class or in small groups.

2 Matching names and photos: *his* and *her*

● Go through the photos in order and ask for the names. Make sure students get *his* and *her* right.
● Do further practice (and revise numbers) by asking for the names of 'number six', 'number three', etc. Students answer in complete sentences.

The people in the photos are:

1. Paul McCartney
2. Indira Gandhi
3. Brigitte Bardot
4. Jane Fonda
5. Sebastian Coe
6. Robert Redford
7. James Bond
8. Billie Jean King
9. Jacqueline Onassis
10. Karel Wojtila (Pope John Paul II)

Further practice is possible with pictures of well-known people cut out of magazines.

3 Writing

● Ask students to write several sentences about the pictures, like those in the examples.
● Point out that contracted forms are more common in speech, and full forms in writing.

4 Personalization

● Practise the examples.
● Ask a few questions about students' names, using the third person as in the examples. Call on selected students to answer.
● Get volunteers to ask questions. You or other students answer.

● Continue the work in small groups.
● Finally, get students to test *your* knowledge by asking *What's his/her name?*

5 The alphabet: names of the letters

● Run through the alphabet with the students (you may like to use the recording).
● Say (or play) each group of letters several times and get students to practise them.
● Look out for confusions between *G* and *J*, *A* and *R*, *V* and *W*, *A* and *E*, *E* and *I* (depending on nationality).
● Use flashcards (or write letters on the board) for further practice. This can be continued in groups.
Note that students will need to know the alphabetical order of letters by heart in order to work properly with dictionaries.

6 Letter-by-letter dictation

● Play the recording (on which words are spelt out) or spell the words. Stop after each word and check the answers.
● **The words are:** *name, your, hello, right, what, is, yes, no, my, one, eight, three.*
● Continue the exercise with other words, or get students to continue in groups.

7 Students spell their names

● Make sure each student learns to spell his or her own first name and surname.

Practice Book

● Tell students which exercises you want them to do.

B His name's Robert Redford

1 Put the right first names with the right surnames.

First names: Paul   Sebastian   Billie Jean
Jacqueline   Karel   Robert   James   Indira
Jane   Brigitte

Surnames: Wojtila   Bond   Fonda
McCartney   King   Onassis   Coe   Bardot
Gandhi   Redford

2 Put the right names with the photos.

'1. His name's Paul McCartney.'

3 Write sentences. Examples:

1. His first name is Paul.
1. His surname is McCartney.
4. Her name is Jane Fonda.

4 Ask about other students.

'What's his surname?' 'I don't know.'
'Is her first name Anne?' 'Yes, that's right.'
'Is her name Barbara?' 'No, it isn't.'
Is his first name ___ ?

ABCDEFGHIJKLMNOPQRSTUVWXYZ
abcdefghijklmnopqrstuvwxyz

5 Listen to these letters and practise saying them.

B C D G P T V   H Q R W Y Z   A E I O U
F L M N S X   J K

6 Listen and write the words.

name   yo___   h___   r___

7 Spell your name.

C How are you?

1 Listen, and practise the conversation.

2 Close your books. Can you remember the conversation?

3 Listen to the recording and complete the conversations.

ALICE: Excuse me. ....
Fred Andrews?
JAKE: ...., I'm sorry, ..., It's
Jake Barker.
ALICE: .... sorry.

ALICE: Excuse me. Are .... Fred Andrews?
FRED: ...., I am.
ALICE: Oh, ... Alice Watson.
FRED: Oh, yes. How do you do?
ALICE: ....?

4 Practise the conversations.

5 Listen to the recording and answer.

6 Say these numbers.

1 6 3 4 8 9 2 7 5 10

7 Learn these numbers.

11 eleven   12 twelve   13 thirteen   14 fourteen   15 fifteen   16 sixteen   17 seventeen
18 eighteen   19 nineteen   20 twenty

Unit 1: Lesson C

Students learn simple ways of greeting and saying goodbye. They learn to count from eleven to twenty.
Structures: first and second persons of *to be* (*I am, I'm, are you?*).
Words and expressions to learn: *Hi; How are you?; and; Fine, thanks; How do you do?; Excuse me; I'm sorry; Goodbye; Bye; See you; Oh; here's;* numbers *eleven* to *twenty*.

Language notes and possible problems

1. *How do you do?* Students are likely to confuse *How are you?* and *How do you do?* unless the difference is made clear.

2. *Excuse me.* They may also confuse *Excuse me* (used in British English mostly when interrupting people or asking strangers for help etc.) and (*I'm*) *sorry* (used for apologizing).

Optional extra materials

Flashcards for numbers 11–20 (Exercise 7).

1 Presentation of new material

● Play the recording while students follow in their books.
● Explain any difficulties.
● Practise the sentences with the students. Note the 'linking' in *How are you?*
● Get them to practise the conversation in pairs.

2 Recall

● Ask students to close their books and see how much of the conversation they can remember. Build it up on the blackboard.

3 Listening practice

● Play the first sentence (two or three times if necessary) and ask students to write the missing words.
● Tell them to compare notes with their neighbours.
● Tell them the answer. (*Is your name . . . ?*)
● Play the rest of the first conversation (stopping for students to write).
● Let them compare notes.
● Tell them the answers (see below).
● Explain any difficult points.
● Do the second conversation in the same way.
● Point out the relationship between *I'm* (unstressed) and *I am* (stressed).

— interrupting people

Tapescript for Exercise 3
ALICE: Excuse me. Is your name Fred Andrews?
JAKE: No, I'm sorry, it isn't. It's Jake Barker.
ALICE: I'm sorry. *Apologizing*

ALICE: Excuse me. Are you Fred Andrews?
FRED: Yes, I am.
ALICE: Oh, hello. I'm Alice Watson.
FRED: Oh, yes. How do you do?
ALICE: How do you do?

4 Speaking practice

● Get students to write out the complete conversations.
● Practise the pronunciation, paying careful attention to intonation and rhythm.
● Get students to practise the conversations in pairs, changing the names if they wish.

Optional activity
● The dialogues in Exercise 1 and Exercise 3 can be practised further by a 'walk-round' activity, in which students stop when they meet somebody else and improvise brief conversations like the ones in the exercises.

5 Conversational responses

● Play the recording, stopping after each sentence to give students time to answer.
● Repeat the exercise several times until students are fluent.

Tapescript for Exercise 5
Hello. (Answer 'Hello' or 'Hi'.)
Is your name Margaret? (Answer presumably 'No, it isn't'.)
What's your name?
How do you do? (Answer 'How do you do?')
How are you? (Answer 'Fine, thanks'.)
Goodbye. (Answer 'Goodbye', 'Bye' or 'See you'.)

6 Revision of numbers

● Go through the list several times until all students have said two or three numbers.

7 Numbers *eleven* to *twenty*

● These can be taught and practised in the same way as numbers *one* to *ten* (see instructions for Lesson 1A Exercise 6).
● Make sure students stress the last syllable of *thirteen, fourteen,* etc.

Practice Book
● Tell students which exercises you want them to do.

Greetings and goodbyes
● From this lesson onwards, you may like to make a habit of getting students to greet each other in English at the beginning of the class and say goodbye in English at the end.
● When you greet students yourself, make it clear that *you* (in *How are you?*) can refer to one or more people.

Unit 1: Lesson D

Students learn to say where they come from, and to ask where other people are from.
Structures: third person of *to be*.
Words and expressions to learn: *he; she; where; from; speak; a little;* countries; nationalities.
Phonology: weak and strong forms of *from;* introduction to word-stress.

Language notes and possible problems

1. Places of origin Exercise 2 will not work if students all come from the same place. (But see Optional activity.)
2. *England* and *Britain* Many students are likely to think that *England* and *English* refer to the whole of Britain.
3. Gender In Exercise 3, you may need to point out to some students that English adjectives do not have different masculine and feminine forms.
4. Stress Not all languages have stressed and unstressed syllables: Exercise 5 will be difficult (and important) for some students.
5. Dictionaries (Exercise 3) Intelligent use of bilingual dictionaries for self-access learning is an important feature of the course. (See Introduction page IX.) Make sure students are familiar with the basic techniques of dictionary use, and that they know the order of letters in the English alphabet. Students not used to dictionaries will need help.

Optional extra materials
Pictures of famous people from different countries. (Pictures of) things from different countries (e.g. a Swiss watch).
Flashcards with the names of countries on them.

1 *Where's he from? Where's she from?*
● Practise the pronunciation of the names of countries, and of *he* and *she*.
● Practise *Where's he from?* and *Where's she from?*
● Ask students to make questions for the other pictures.
● Then go through the pictures getting them to say where the people are from.
● They should say *He's/She's from* ... Encourage them to pronounce *from* as /frəm/ here, and not as /frɒm/.
● Consolidate by asking them to write about one or two of the pictures, using uncontracted forms (*he is; she is*).

Optional activity
● Use pictures of famous living people from different countries to get more examples of *He/She's from...*

2 Personalization
● Practise the question and answer. *From* is pronounced /frɒm/ (stressed) in the question and /frəm/ in the answer. Practise the linking in *Where are* (/'weərə/).
● Get students to walk round asking others where they are from.
● If students all come from the same place, give them new nationalities for this exercise (see below – Optional activity).

Optional activity
● Give students cards with the names of countries.

● Get them to say, in turn, *I'm from...* (with the name of their 'new' country). Do this twice.
● See how well the class can remember people's new nationalities, by asking *Where's he/she from?*

3 Dictionary work (national adjectives)
● Tell students to use dictionaries to fill in the two lists.
● Then let them compare notes with their neighbours.
● When you give them the answers, point out that national adjectives always have capital letters.
● Ask students if they know (or want to know) any more words to add to the lists, but don't add too many.
● They can look up more nationality words at home.

Optional activity
● (Pictures of) things from different countries can give additional practice in using national adjectives.

4 Languages
● Get students to say sentences like Susie's. (You may need to teach the names of one or two languages.) Notice the pronunciation of *and* (/ənd/).
● Consolidate by asking them to write their sentences.
● Point out that in many cases the name of the language is the same as the national adjective.
● Teach the formula *Do you speak...?*

5 Word-stress
● Play the recording, or say the words for the students; get them to repeat with the correct stress.
● There are no simple rules for word-stress in English. However, this exercise will help to sensitize students to the existence of stress differences.

6 Revision of numbers and letters
● The numbers on the recording are: 8, 4, 1, 3, 2, 6, 16, 9, 11, 5, 12, 20, 13, 7, 17.
● The letters are: A, E, I, O, U, G, H, K, Q, J, V, W, E, I, A, R, J, G, W, V.
● Play them (or say them) in groups of five. Let students compare notes before going on.

7 Summary (page 134)
● At the end of each unit, students should study the summary (in or out of class) and memorize all the prescribed vocabulary. (See Introduction page XII.)
● This unit has a rather high vocabulary load (mainly because the numbers are introduced). Students shouldn't worry too much: the vocabulary will come up again.
● However, as a general rule the vocabulary listed in the summaries is a minimum. Quick learners and well-motivated students should be encouraged to learn more. (In this unit, for instance, they could add to the list of names of countries and national adjectives by working at home with a dictionary.)
● As students learn vocabulary, they should look back at the lessons to see how the words are used.
● Go over the summary in class and make sure students understand its purpose. Explain any difficulties.

Practice Book
● Tell students which exercises you want them to do.

9

color hana= sumire
violet=murasaki   diplomat=gaikokan   Specifically =toku ni

D Where are you from?

France	Scotland
Russia	The United States
England	Poland
India	Italy

1 Where's he from? Where's she from?

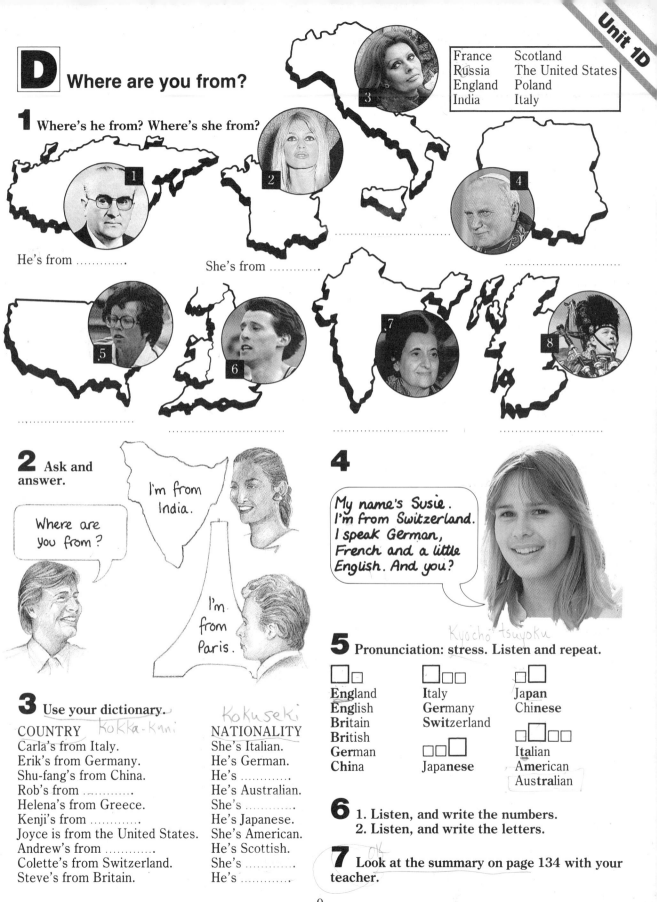

He's from ....

She's from ....

2 Ask and answer.

Where are you from?

I'm from India.

I'm from Paris.

3 Use your dictionary.

Kokka-Kuni

COUNTRY	NATIONALITY
Carla's from Italy.	She's Italian.
Erik's from Germany.	He's German.
Shu-fang's from China.	He's ....
Rob's from	He's Australian.
Helena's from Greece.	She's ....
Kenji's from	He's Japanese.
Joyce is from the United States.	She's American.
Andrew's from	He's Scottish.
Colette's from Switzerland.	She's ....
Steve's from Britain.	He's ....

Kokuseki

4

My name's Susie. I'm from Switzerland. I speak German, French and a little English. And you?

Kyocho" tsuyoku

5 Pronunciation: stress. Listen and repeat.

☐▫ ☐▫▫ ▫☐

England   **It**aly   **Ja**pan
English   **Ger**many   Chi**nese**
Britain   **Swit**zerland
British
German   ▫▫☐   ▫☐▫▫
China   Japa**nese**   I**tal**ian
    A**mer**ican
    Aus**tral**ian

6 1. Listen, and write the numbers.
2. Listen, and write the letters.

7 Look at the summary on page 134 with your teacher.

9

Unit 2
Jobs

A What do you do?

doctor   secretary   electrician
housewife   shop assistant   artist

1 Complete the sentences.

1. He's an *artist*.

2. He's a ....

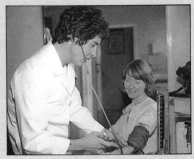

3. She's a ....

4. She's a ....

5. He's an ....

6. She's a ....

2 Say what you do.

'I'm an engineer.'
'I'm a medical student.'
'I'm a photographer.'
'I'm between jobs.'

3 Ask and answer.

A: *What do you do?*
B: *I'm a dentist.*
C: *I'm an artist.*
D: *I'm a housewife.*

4 Say what other students do.

'She's a doctor.'
'He's an electrician.'

5 Pronunciation. Listen and practise.

Are you a photographer?

Yes, I am. Are you an artist?

No, I'm not. I'm a doctor. He's an artist.

No, I'm an artist. She's a doctor.

Are you a doctor?

I'm a secretary.

What do you do?

6 Ask and answer.

'Are you a doctor?'
'Yes, I am.' / 'No, I'm not.'

'Is she an artist?'
'Yes, she is.' / 'No, she isn't.'

'Is he an engineer?'
'Yes, he is.' / 'No, he isn't.'

10

Students learn to talk about professions.
Structures: *a/an* with professions.
Words and expressions to learn: *What do you do?*; *a/an*; names of some professions.
Phonology: rhythm, intonation and linking in questions and statements.

Language notes and possible problems
1. Gender   You may need to tell students that English does not have 'masculine' and 'feminine' nouns, articles, etc.
2. Articles   Students whose languages do not have articles will need extra help and explanations. See Appendix page 160.

Optional extra materials
Five or more pictures of people cut out of magazines (Exercise 1).
Cards or slips of paper with professions written on them (Exercise 6).

1 Matching (vocabulary presentation)
● Get the students to look at the six pictures in Exercise 1.
● They try to match words and pictures.
● Students can work in small groups.
● When they have finished, try to elicit the difference between *a* and *an*. Then write on the board:

an	*a*
a, e, i, o, u	*b, c, d, f, g, h, j, k, l, m, . . .*

Optional activity
● You can do further practice by asking students to guess the professions of people in suitably chosen pictures cut out of magazines.

2 *I'm a teacher*
● Say *I'm a teacher*; write on the board:
I am a teacher.
I'm a teacher.
● Ask students *What do you do?* and help them with answers.
● Aid with pronunciation, stress and rhythm.
● Don't let them forget *a/an*.
● Unemployed people can say *I'm between jobs*.

3 Practice (walk-round)
● Practise *What do you do?*; write it on the board.
● Get students to walk round asking one another's occupations and answering.

4 *He's/She's a student*
● Choose a female student; say *She's a student*.
● Write on the board:
She is a student.
She's a student.
● Demonstrate *He* with a male student. Make sure the students notice that *She's a* and *He's a* are linked so as to sound like single words.

● Point at a few students and ask the class what they do, to check that they have understood and are linking the words properly.
● Put the students in pairs and get them to tell each other what everyone else in the class does; walk round to help when needed.

5 Pronunciation
● Get the students to look at the conversation while you play the recording.
● Help them to practise the pronunciation.
● Points to remember (you may want to write them up):
– **Intonation:** Rising in *yes/no* questions, falling in the answers.
Are you a doctor? No, I'm not.
– **Rhythm:** articles are unstressed.
Are you a doctor?
– **Linking:** *you a* and *I am* are pronounced almost like *you wa* and *I yam*.

6 Guessing: questions, short answers
● Write the names of the professions learnt on cards or pieces of paper.
1. Students work in pairs.
Give each student a card/slip of paper with a profession written on it.
Partners must not look at each other's cards.
They try to guess each other's occupations by asking *Are you a . . .?* and answering *No, I'm not* or *Yes, I am*.
When students have finished they can exchange cards with other students (or change partners) and start again.
2. Use the same cards. Students are in threes.
A shows his/her card to B.
C asks B *Is he/she a . . .?*
B answers *No, he/she isn't* / *Yes, he/she is*.
Help students with linking: almost like *he yis, she yisn't*, etc.

Practice Book
● Tell students which exercises you want them to do.

Shinjiraranai   I don't believe

*Shaberisugi   talks too much
ni panasai*

Unit 2: Lesson B

Students revise and extend the language of self-Identification.
Structures: no new structures.
Words and expressions to learn: *married*; *single*; *different*.
Phonology: recognizing stress patterns.

Possible problems
Two new exercise types are introduced: 'Which word is different?' (to revise vocabulary) and dialogue completion. Care should be taken to help students through these the first time.

Optional extra materials
A few old magazines for students to cut up (Exercise 5).

1 Listening for information
● Get the students to copy the table on a separate sheet.
● Use the examples to show what *nationality* and *occupation* mean. Explain *married* and *single*.
● Play the first section (Bill) once or twice.
● Make sure all students have written correct answers.
● Play the rest, more than once if necessary.
● Allow students to compare notes before giving them the answers.

Tapescript and answers to Exercise 1
Hello. My name's Bill. I'm British. I'm a doctor.

She's an artist. She's American. Her name's Lucy. She's married.

Hello. Come in and sit down. What's your name?
John Webb.
And where do you come from, Mr Webb?
I'm British.
Are you married?
No, I'm not.
And what's your job, Mr Webb? What do you do?
Well, I'm a teacher.
I see. Now, tell me, how do you think...?

He's a French electrician. His name's Gérard. He's single.

I'm a photographer. I'm Greek. My name's Annie.

Hello. What's your name?
Philip.
What's your job, Philip?
I'm a secretary.
Are you American?
No, I'm not. I'm Australian. But I'm married to an American.

NAME	NATIONALITY	OCCUPATION	MARRIED/SINGLE
Bill	*British*	*doctor*	don't know
Lucy	*American*	*artist*	married
John Webb	*British*	*teacher*	*single*
Gérard	French	*electrician*	*single*
Annie	*Greek*	photographer	*don't know*
Philip	*Australian*	*secretary*	*married*

2 Odd-word-out (vocabulary revision)
● Start putting a list of jobs on the board; get students to help you.
● When you have three or four jobs up, add *name* to the list; students should object.
● Get them to look at the first item in Exercise 2, and do the other items in the same way.
● They can compare answers before you correct the exercise.

3 Which stress?
● Put the 'boxes' on the board.
● Play or say the first word and ask students to decide which column it goes in. Write it in.
● Play the next word and do the same.
● Tell students to draw the boxes. Play the rest of the words, with pauses, and let them continue the exercise.
● Let them compare notes before you tell them the answers.

Answers

□ □	□ □	□ □ □	□ □ □
Hello	thirty	Canada	engineer
thirteen	married	secretary	Japanese
Chinese	chemist		
Goodbye	doctor		

4 Dialogue completion (revision)
● Get the students to read the sentences Virginia says.
● They should ask you or consult their dictionaries for new words (*actress, interesting*).
● Write Virginia's first line on the board.
● Ask the students for suggestions for the first reply, writing up the one you decide on.
● Write up Virginia's second line, and point out that they must now supply two sentences – one following the question and one preceding Virginia's next answer.
● Continue until the entire dialogue has been constructed on the board.
● Play the recording, which has gaps for the student's lines, and let them answer.
● You may want to clean the board and try the recording again.
● Follow up the exercise by practising *married* and *single* (talking about the students themselves or people they know).

5 Writing
● If you have brought some magazines, students can cut or tear pictures out to write about.
● They should try to use as many as possible of the words and expressions they have learnt so far.
● If you speak their language, you may want to tell them the sentences do not have to be true.
● Students who finish fast can exchange pictures.
● If you have not brought magazines, students can write about people they know of; you can suggest famous people.
● If time is tight, this can be done for homework.

Practice Book
● Tell students which exercises you want them to do.

11

B I'm an actress. And you?

1 Listening for information. Listen, and complete the table.

NAME	NATIONALITY	OCCUPATION	MARRIED/SINGLE
Bill			*don't know*
Lucy			*married*
John Webb			
Gérard	*French*		
Annie		*Photographer*	
Philip			

2 Which word is different?

1. doctor (name) artist secretary
2. her my (he) your
3. from two four seven
4. Britain France Germany Mary
5. are is not am
6. Excuse Russian Chinese Italian

3 Which stress? Listen and decide.

thirty   Canada   engineer   married   chemist
Hello   thirteen   Chinese   Japanese
secretary   doctor   Goodbye

□▢   ▢□   ▢□□   □□▢

Hello   ....

4 Complete the dialogue and practise it.

VIRGINIA: Hello, I'm Virginia. What's your name?
YOU: ....
VIRGINIA: Is that an English name?
YOU: *No, it's Japanese*
...................................?
VIRGINIA: No, I'm not. I'm Argentinian.
YOU: ...., Virginia?
VIRGINIA: I'm an actress. And you?
YOU: ....
VIRGINIA: That's interesting. Are you married?
YOU: ....
...................................?
VIRGINIA: Yes, I am.

5

1. Think of a person

OR cut a picture
out of a magazine.

This is Jane Brown
She is a model.
She lives in

2. Write about the person.

C I'm very well, thank you

morning afternoon NOON -... evening 6 p.m. — night

1 Morning, afternoon, evening or night? Example: 1. *morning or night*

2 Listen. Learn the new words from a dictionary or from your teacher. Listen again and practise.

WOMAN: Good morning, Mr Roberts. How are you?
MAN: Oh, good morning, Dr Wagner. I'm very well, thank you. And you?
WOMAN: I'm fine, thank you.

MAN: Hello, Mary.
WOMAN: Hi, Tom. How are you?
MAN: Fine, thanks. And you?
WOMAN: Not bad – but my daughter's not well today.
MAN: Oh, I'm sorry to hear that.

3 *Good morning* or *Hello*?

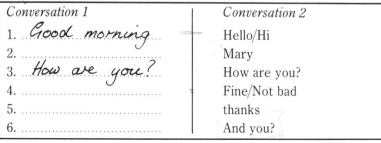

4 Differences. Read the conversations again and complete the table.

Conversation 1	Conversation 2
1. *Good morning*	Hello/Hi
2.	Mary
3. *How are you?*	How are you?
4.	Fine/Not bad
5.	thanks
6.	And you?

5 Stand up, walk around if you can, and greet other students.

Unit 2: Lesson C

Students learn formal and informal ways of greeting.

Structures: no new structures.

Words and expressions to learn: *morning; afternoon; evening; night; good morning; good afternoon; good evening; good night; I'm very well, thank you; not bad; not well; or.*

Phonology: intonation of greetings and replies.

Possible problem

Register Some of the exercises concentrate on the difference in level of formality between the first and the second dialogue. Presenting this concept in a class where you do not speak the students' language(s) requires care.

Optional extra materials

A set of cards or slips of paper (one per student plus a few extras) with names of well-known people on them (extension of Exercise 5).

1 Times of day (presentation, practice)

● Get the students to look at the labelled pictures before Exercise 1. If you think it will be clearer for them, write times on the board to define the four parts of the day.

● Then let them do the exercise, preferably in small groups.

● Practise the pronunciation of the words with them, paying special attention to stress in **mor**ning, after**noon** and **eve**ning.

● When they have finished, call for the answers, paying attention to pronunciation once more.

Answers: 1. morning or evening 2. afternoon or evening 3. night 4. afternoon or morning 5. morning 6. morning or afternoon

2 Greetings (presentation, practice)

● Get the students to look at the two pictures.

● Get them to notice that the same woman is in both pictures. They might be able to tell you where she is each time if they have a little English from before the course.

● Establish that the woman is about 35, the man in the first picture 60+, and the man in the second picture about 35.

● Then get the students to close their books and listen to the recording. Stop after the first dialogue and see if they can remember any words. Do the same with the second dialogue.

● Play the recording again with books open. Explain or demonstrate new words or let students find them in their dictionaries.

● Play the recording once more, stopping after these phrases to let the students practise them (pay special attention to intonation):

Good morning.	*Hello.*
How are you?	*Hi.*
I'm very well, thank	*Fine thanks.*
you. And you?	*Not bad.*
I'm fine, thank you.	

● Try to get the students saying the phrases from the first dialogue in a formal or respectful way. (It will help if you demonstrate.) The phrases from the second dialogue should sound (and look) much more informal.

3 Differences in formality

● Ask students to decide (preferably in small groups) which greeting is probably being used in each picture.

● Check the answers with the whole class.

● Follow up by asking how they would greet people they know or have heard of (another student; a pop star; the Pope; etc.).

● If you speak the students' language, you may want to talk about the different factors which cause British people to choose between formal and informal language (familiarity, age, social class, relative status).

4 Formality (continued)

● Now that students have understood the difference between the two dialogues, they can complete the table giving formal and informal equivalents. The completed table will look like this:

Conversation 1	Conversation 2
1. Good morning	Hello/Hi
2. *Dr Wagner*	Mary
3. How are you?	How are you?
4. *I'm fine/I'm very well*	Fine/Not bad
5. *thank you*	thanks
6. *And you?*	And you?

While going over the table with the students, teach *Good afternoon, Good evening* and *Good night*. Note that *Good morning/afternoon/evening* can mean 'Hello' or 'Goodbye'; *Good night* is only used to say 'Goodbye'.

5 Practising greetings

● If possible, get students to walk round the room greeting as many other people as they can.

● Alternatively, get them to stand up and turn to greet as many others as possible.

● You will presumably want them to use informal greetings.

● To extend the exercise, hand out cards with names of famous people on them. The students hold their cards in front of themselves and go around greeting once again, deciding whether to be formal or informal.

Practice Book

● Tell students which exercises you want them to do.

12

Unit 2: Lesson D

Students learn more numbers and revise various points.
Structures: *to be* in questions and statements about age.
Words and expressions to learn: numbers 20 to 100; *old*; *How old are you?*; *How do you spell…?*; *write*; *divorced*; *nationality*; *Mr*; *Mrs*; *Ms*; *Miss*.
Phonology: the contrast in stress between *thir**teen*** and ***thir**ty*, etc.

Optional extra materials
Flashcards for counting exercises.

1 Presentation: numbers 20 to 100
- Students should have their books closed.
- Write the numbers from the book on the board, getting students to repeat each one after you as you do so.

2 Teens and tens
- Practise the difference between *thir**teen*** (stressed at the end when in isolation) and ***thir**ty* (stressed at the beginning).
- Then say the following numbers (or play the recording) and get the students to write what they hear.
- Let them compare notes before giving them the answers.

thirteen   fifty   seventy   fourteen   forty   nineteen
seventeen   sixteen   ninety   eighty

3 Ages
- In classes where nobody is likely to be embarrassed about their age, this exercise can be made more interesting by asking students to guess each other's age (and yours).
- Ask them to begin *I think you're* …

4 Practice with numbers: counting
- Get students to do the four counting tasks as quickly as they can, each student saying a number in turn.
- If you go around the class once or twice for each task, this should give ample practice – no need to count all the way down to 1 from 99!

5 Group and pair work on numbers
- Call one student to the board and dictate a few numbers to write. Get volunteers from the class to dictate a few more.
- Then divide the class into pairs or small groups and let them dictate numbers to one another.
- Write *38 + 7 = ?* on the board.
- Say *Thirty-eight and seven?* and let the class answer.
- Call out a few more sums, and then put the students back into their pairs/groups to do the same.
- Write *6 × 7 = ?* on the board and say *Six sevens?*
- Once again, call out a few more multiplications and put students back into group/pair work.

6 Spelling: recognition
- Write *Russian* on the board and spell it aloud: '*capital R-u-double s-i-a-n*'.
- Make sure students notice 'capital' and 'double'.
- Get a volunteer to spell *stress* and *English* to check the students have understood.
- Play the recording or spell the words, more than once if necessary, pausing after each word to give students the time to write.

Tapescript
1. answer	7. John
2. Chinese	8. seventeen
3. two	9. assistant
4. engineer	10. Germany
5. actress	11. spell
6. married	

7 Spelling: production
- Call a volunteer to the front to demonstrate the two examples.
- Then divide the class into groups or pairs and let them quiz one another for a few minutes.

8 Filling in a form
- Go over the form explaining new vocabulary.
- Practise pronunciation (note *Ms*: /mɪz/ or /məz/).
- Get students to copy the form before filling it in with their own details.
- Meanwhile write your own form on the board and fill it in.
- If students are likely to be unhappy about revealing personal information, tell them that they don't have to show what they have written to you or anyone else.
- Walk around to check they have understood.

9 Role-play
- Get the students to copy the form again and invent a new identity to complete it with. You may want to demonstrate on the board first, inventing a far-fetched identity for yourself.
- Get students to question one another on their new identities, if possible walking round the room to interview a maximum number of other students.

10 Summary
- Go through the summary on page 135 of the Student's Book with your class.
- You need not go over all the new words, but remind the students that they should try to learn all the words and that they should ask you if they have any problems.
- Make sure they understand that they are to learn three or more of the names of professions. (See summary.)

Practice Book
- Tell students which exercises you want them to do.

Answers to Practice Book Exercise 4
1. name   2. Hi   3. Japan   4. Good morning (formal)
5. good (not an answer to 'How are you?')   6. seven (odd number)   7. eighty-two (not divisible by five)

D How old are you?

1 Listen and practise.

20 twenty	30 thirty	40 forty
21 twenty-one	34 thirty-four	50 fifty
22 twenty-two	35 thirty-five	60 sixty
23 twenty-three	36 thirty-six	70 seventy
24 twenty-four	37 thirty-seven	80 eighty
25 twenty-five	38 thirty-eight	90 ninety
26 twenty-six	39 thirty-nine	100 a hundred

2 Thir*teen* or *thir*ty? Four*teen* or *forty*? Listen and write what you hear.

3 Say your age, or the age of somebody you know.

'*I'm twenty-three.*' '*My mother's fifty.*'

4 Practise with numbers.

1. Count: '1, 2, 3, . . .'
2. Count in twos: '2, 4, 6, 8, . . .'
3. Count in fives: '5, 10, 15, . . .'
4. Count backwards: '99, 98, 97, . . .'

5 Work in groups or pairs.

1. Say numbers for other students to write.
   '*Fifty-six.*' 56
2. Say numbers for other students to add.
   '*Thirty-eight and seven?*' '*Forty-five.*'
3. Say numbers for other students to multiply.
   '*Six sevens?*' '*Forty-two.*'

6 Spelling. Listen and write the words.
Example: 1. *answer*

7 Spelling. Work in groups or pairs.

'*How do you spell* her?' '*h–e–r.*'
'*Write C–h–i–n–e–s–e.*'

Chinese

Unit 2D

Harris & Sanders
Photographic Supplies
13 Old High St, Wembley.

JOB APPLICATION
Shigoto no moshikomi

Mr/Mrs/Miss/Ms

First name ....

Surname ....

Age ....

Marital status: single ☐
married ☐
divorced ☐
separated ☐
widow(er) ☐

Nationality ....

8 Fill in the form.

9 Copy the form and fill it in with a new identity. Then work with a partner. Ask each other these questions.

1. Mr, Mrs, Miss or Ms?
2. What's your first name?
3. How do you spell it?
4. What's your surname?
5. How do you spell it?
6. How old are you?
7. Where are you from?
8. Are you married?

10 Look at the summary on page 135 with your teacher.

People

A I've got three children

1 Look at the 'family tree' and complete the sentences. Use your dictionary.

his	her	wife	husband	brother	sister

1. John is Polly's .... Polly is John's ....
2. Andrew is Joyce's .... Joyce is Andrew's ....
3. Polly and John are Joyce's parents. Polly is her mother, and John is .... father.
4. Andrew and Joyce are John's children. Andrew is his son, and Joyce is .... daughter.

John   Polly

Andrew   Joyce

2 Now look at this family tree. Read the sentences and put in the names.

Eric	Lucy	Ann	Harry
Pat	Fred	Alice	

1. *Joe* ....
2. ....
3. ....
4. ....
5. ....
6. ....
7. ....
8. ....

Joe's wife's name is Ann. Joe and Ann have got three children: two daughters and a son. Their daughters' names are Alice and Lucy, and their son's name is Fred. Fred and Lucy are not married. Alice's husband's name is Harry. Harry and Alice have got two children: a boy and a girl. Their daughter's name is Pat, and their son's name is Eric.

3 Listening. Look at the family tree in Exercise 1. Listen to the sentences and say *Yes* or *No*.
Make some sentences yourself.

4 Listening. Look at the family tree in Exercise 2. Listen and answer the questions. Examples:

'Who is Joe's wife?' 'Ann.'
'Who is Eric?' 'Pat's brother.'

Then ask some questions yourself.

5 Talk about your family. Examples:

'I've got one child (son/daughter/brother/etc.). His/her name's ....'
'How old is he/she?' 'Sixteen.'

'I've got two (three etc.) children (sons/ daughters/brothers/sisters).'
'What are their names?'

'I've got no children (brothers or sisters).'

'My husband's (wife's/mother's/etc.) name is .... He/she's thirty-five.'

Unit 3: Lesson A

Students learn to talk about family relationships.
Structures: noun plurals; 's genitive; *to be* with plural subjects; questions with *who*; have got.
Words and expressions to learn: *wife; husband; brother; sister;* some other kinship terms (see summary); *son; parent; child; boy; girl; family; who; their.*

Language notes and possible problems

1. -s Two functions of the -s suffix are introduced here: plurality and possession ('s genitive). Students may need a little time to sort this out in their minds. The dual function of 's (genitive and contraction of *is*) may also cause some temporary confusion. See Practice Book 3A Exercise 3.

2. Word order Students often have difficulty with the word order in genitive expressions. (A typical mistake is **father's John* instead of *John's father*.) False beginners may also add articles (**The John's father*).

3. No It is common in English to use a plural noun after *no* (e.g. *no children*). This may cause difficulty.

4. Have got This is introduced as an unanalysed item.

1 Vocabulary learning

● Ask students to use their dictionaries to fill in the first blank. Check the answer.
● Let them continue individually or in groups.
● Get students to read out their answers.
● Note that some students may need help in learning to use dictionaries effectively. (See Introduction page IX.)

Grammar points in Exercise 1

● Explain the three new points of grammar.

1. Plurals Write on the board:

1	2, 3, 4...	1	2, 3, 4...
brother	brothers	son	sons
sister	sisters	daughter	daughters
parent	parents	child	children

Practise the pronunciation of the plurals.

2. The 's genitive Write on the board:

I	–	my brother
you	–	your brother
he	–	his brother
she	–	her brother
John	–	John's brother
Joyce	–	Joyce's brother

Practise the pronunciation of *John's* and *Joyce's*; help students to see why 's is pronounced /ɪz/ in *Joyce's*.

3. Third person plural of to be Write on the board:

John is   Polly and John are
Andrew is   Andrew and Joyce are

Practise *are* alone (/ɑː/) and in sentences (/ə/).

2 Comprehension practice

● Copy the family tree onto the board. Read the first sentence and ask students where you should put *Ann*.
● Ask students to carry on by themselves. Let them compare notes before you put the answers on the board.

Answers: 1. Joe 2. Ann 3. Fred 4. Lucy 5. Alice
6. Harry 7. Eric 8. Pat

● Explain the contrast between 's and s':

his son	his son's name
his sons	his sons' names
their daughter	their daughter's name
their daughters	their daughters' names

● Finally, ask students to close their books and see if they can remember any of the sentences from the text.

3 Listening: true or false?

● Tell students to look at the family tree.
● Play the recording or say the following sentences:

Andrew is Joyce's sister. (*No*)   John is Polly's son. (*No*)
Polly is John's wife. (*Yes*)   Joyce is Andrew's sister. (*Yes*)
Joyce is John's father. (*No*)   Polly is Andrew's mother. (*Yes*)
Andrew and Joyce are John and Polly's parents. (*No*)
John is Polly's husband. (*Yes*)

● Students should answer *Yes* or *No*.
● Ask them to try to correct the false statements.
● Finally, ask them to make up 'true or false' statements and try them on each other.

4 Listening: answering questions

● Play the recording or ask the questions yourself.

Who is Joe's wife? (*Ann*)   Who is Harry's son? (*Eric*)
Who is Ann's husband? (*Joe*)   Who is Ann's son? (*Fred*)
Who is Eric? (*Pat's brother / Harry and Alice's son*)
Who is Fred? (*Alice and Lucy's brother / Joe and Ann's son*)
Who is Pat's father? (*Harry*)   Who is Lucy's brother? (*Fred*)
Who is Alice? (*Lucy and Fred's sister / Joe and Ann's daughter*)

● Give students plenty of time to answer. They can look at the family tree or the text, as they wish.
● Get them to ask you similar questions. See if you can answer them without looking at the family tree.

5 Guided conversation

● Practise the pronunciation of the example sentences.
● Get students to make similar statements about their own families, and to ask each other questions.

Optional activities

1. Give students some interesting listening practice by talking about your own family.
2. Two students give information about their families (as in Exercise 5). They repeat the information. The rest of the class then have to remember what they were told. (Teach *He's got* and *She's got*.)
3. Students work in groups. One tells the others about his/her family. The others try to draw the speaker's family tree. Revise *How do you spell...?* so that they can ask about the spelling of names.
4. Students bring family photos to class and tell each other about them. (Teach *This is...*)
5. Vocabulary extension. Students will probably want to know words such as *grandmother, cousin.* You can teach these in class or leave them to look them up in their dictionaries at home. (But note that kinship terms don't always have exact translations.)

Practice Book

● Tell students which exercises you want them to do.

14

Unit 3: Lesson B

Students learn to give simple descriptions of people.
Structures: *we/you/they are*; modification by adverbs of degree.
Words and expressions to learn: some of these (see summary): *tall; fair; dark; pretty; good-looking; strong; young; intelligent; fat; slim; friend; boyfriend; girlfriend; boss; we; you* (plural); *they; very; fairly; not very.*
Phonology: /ð/; pronunciation of letter *o* in *mother, brother*; pronunciation of *'s* (revision).

Language notes and possible problems

1. Are The weak pronunciation of *are* (/ə(r)/) will need attention.
2. Pretty Students will need help to realize that *pretty* is used for women but not for men, while *good-looking* can be used for both sexes.
3. Fairly The exact meaning of *fairly* is difficult to explain in simple terms. For the moment, just let students use it as an adverb of degree midway between *very* and *not very*.
4. We In English, *we* can mean *you and I, he/she and I,* or *they and I*. Some languages have different pronouns for these different cases.
5. Vocabulary This lesson has a heavy vocabulary load. If students find it too much, tell them not to learn the adjectives from Exercise 3 for the moment.

Optional extra materials
Pictures of people for additional descriptions (Exercises 1 and 3).

1 Guided composition
• The descriptions of Sam and Eric can be done on the board with the students suggesting words for the gaps.
• Get them to write the description of Alicia. Let them compare notes before you give them your version.

2 Descriptions (oral)
• Get students to give brief descriptions in turn, using the words and expressions they have learnt.
• They can continue in groups or pairs if you wish.

3 More adjectives
• This gives students a chance to learn a few more common adjectives. Drop the exercise if they are getting overloaded with vocabulary.

4 We and plural *you*
• Demonstrate the meaning of *we*. (It may be important to show both the inclusive meaning (*you and I*) and the exclusive meaning (*he/she/they and I*) – see 'Possible problems'.)
• Practise the pronunciation of *we are* and *we're* (/wɪə/).
• Start the exercise by talking about yourself and a student with whom you have something in common (e.g. height, hair colour, age, nationality, profession). Make at least one untrue statement, and get the class to say *No, you aren't* (as in the example).
• Point out the plural meaning of *you* here.

• Put the students in pairs and get them to continue making examples in turn (including one or two untrue examples). Encourage them to use *fairly* and *(not) very*.

5 They
• Make a few examples with *they*. If possible, make one example about two men and one about two women, so that it's clear that *they* is the plural of both *he* and *she*.
• Practise the pronunciation of *they are* and *they're* (/ðeə/).
• Ask for more examples from the class.
• Pick out two students who have several things in common and ask students to talk about them.

Optional activities
1. You can bring in pictures of suitable-looking people to give further practice in the adjectives from Exercise 1 and Exercise 3. Show the pictures and ask students to describe them.
2. Give more listening practice by chatting about some of your friends or relations. Describe them, using the adjectives that are taught in the lesson. Ask students to try to recall what you have told them.
3. Describe a student without saying who it is. Ask the class to guess. Get them to do the same thing.

6 Pronunciation
• This gives students a chance to practise /ð/ and to revise the pronunciation of *'s*.
• Play the recording or say the words, working on one line at a time.

Practice Book
• Tell students which exercises you want them to do.
• Note that room is not provided in the Practice Book for students to write longer continuous texts or lists of sentences. Warn them that they should do Exercise 3 in a separate exercise book.

- onagi mono erabinasai
- hiteki surumono (match)

Keyoushi - adjective
Huusai - appearance
takumashi - muscular
miwakuteki - glamorous
futsuu
Kangaeru Koto = thought
ugly - yokunai

specfic tokubetsu no
detail - Kuwashiiku hanish te kuda

describe · noberu
explain · sestume

15

B This is Judy

JUDY	SAM	ERIC	ALICIA
This is Judy.	This is Sam.	.... Sam's friend, Eric.	.... Eric's girlfriend, ...
She is tall and fair.	He is Judy's boyfriend.	He is	....
She is very pretty.	He is <u>not</u> very	and	....
	.... dark.	He is .... good-	....
	He is fairly	looking.	
	good-looking.		

irónico (handwritten next to JUDY)

He is fairly (handwritten in SAM column)

1 Look at the pictures and complete the descriptions.

2 Describe your mother/father/wife/husband/boyfriend/girlfriend/brother/sister/teacher/boss/...

3 Use your dictionary. Match the words and the pictures.

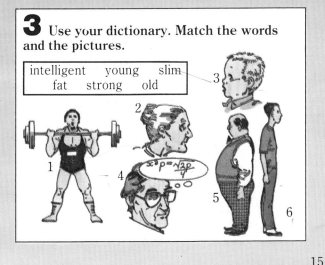

| intelligent | young | slim |
| fat | strong | old |

4 Work with another student. Make sentences about the two of you. Tell the class.

We're fairly tall.

They're (handwritten)

We're English.

No, you aren't. You're Mexican.

5 Talk about two other students. Example:

'Mario and Carla are Italian. They're tall and dark.'

6 Pronunciation revision. Say:

mother   brother   father
Joe's   Harry's   Andrew's   John's
Joyce's   Alice's
who*se*

who's (handwritten)
whom (handwritten)

C An interview

BANK MANAGER: Good morning, Mr Harris.

CUSTOMER: Good morning.

BM: Please sit down.

C: Thank you.

BM: Now, one or two questions...

C: Yes, of course.

BM: How old are you, Mr Harris?

C: Thirty-two.

BM: And you're Canadian, aren't you?

C: Yes, that's right.

BM: Are you married?

C: Yes, I am.

BM: What is your wife's name?

C: Monica.

BM: And your wife's age, Mr Harris?

C: Pardon?

BM: How old is Mrs Harris?

C: Oh, she's thirty.

BM: Thirty. I see. And is she Canadian, too?

C: No, she's British.

BM: British, yes. Have you got any children?

C: Yes, three. Two boys and a girl.

(phone rings)

BM: Excuse me a moment. Hello, Anne. Yes? Yes? Yes, I am. No. Yes. No, I'm sorry, I don't know. No. Yes, all right. Thank you. Goodbye. I'm sorry, Mr Harris.

Now, two girls and a boy, you said?

C: No, two boys and a girl.

BM: Oh, yes, I'm sorry. And what are their names?

C: Alan, Jane and Max.

BM: And their ages?

C: Twelve, ten and six.

BM: I see. Now one more question, Mr Harris. What is your job?

C: I'm a university teacher.

BM: A university teacher. Right. Thank you. Now, you want £50,000 to buy a house.

C: That's right.

BM: And what sort of security...

1 Listen to the conversation. Then see how much you can remember.

2 Pronunciation. Practise these expressions.

one or two questions   Yes, of course.
How old are you?   How old is Mrs Harris?
What is your wife's name?   Yes, I am.
two boys and a girl   What are their names?
Twelve, ten and six.

3 Practise part of the conversation.

4 Ask and answer. Examples:

Have you got any brothers or sisters?

Yes, I have. I've got two brothers.

No, I haven't.

Unit 3: Lesson C

Students practise understanding conversational spoken English.
Structures: preview of infinitive of purpose; *Have you got...?; Yes, I have; No, I haven't.*
Words and expressions to learn: *sit down; please; question; of course; aren't you?; age; pardon; too; a moment; What does...mean?*
Phonology: stress, intonation and linking.

Possible problems
Real beginners will find this lesson more difficult than the work they have done so far. They should not try to learn all of the new material if they find this too hard. False beginners should learn all or most of the new vocabulary.

Extra materials
Role-cards for dialogues (see Optional activity).

Prediction exercise (before Exercise 1)
● If your class are 'false beginners' with some knowledge of English, ask them to look at the picture (while covering up the conversation) and to try to guess what is going on.
Possible questions:
Where are the two men?
Whose office is it? How do you know?
What does the man on the left want?
What do you think the other man will say?
● Real beginners will not be able to do this, and should go straight on to Exercise 1.

1 Presentation
● Play the recording twice, while the students listen with their books closed.
● Ask them to tell you what they can remember (any words or expressions at all from the dialogue).
● Tell them to open their books; replay the recording.
● Go through the text explaining words and expressions that students don't know. This is a good moment to teach the formula *What does... mean?* With real beginners you may wish to explain selected items only.
● You may wish to draw students' attention to the following points:
1. The form of the article (*a* not *an*) in *a university teacher* (/ə juːnɪ'vɜːsəti/).
2. The use of *aren't you?* etc. to ask for confirmation of something the speaker is not sure of.
3. The contrast between *Excuse me* and *(I'm) sorry* (already seen in Lesson 1C).

2 Rhythm and linking
● Practise the expressions – perhaps in chorus first of all and then individually round the class.
● Pay special attention to rhythm – the alternation between slow stressed syllables (printed in bold type) and quicker unstressed syllables.
● Pay attention, also, to linking – where the symbol ‿ is printed, students should join words together so that each phrase sounds like one word.

● Note that the customer's sentences are recorded in a Canadian accent.

3 Dialogue practice
● Divide the dialogue into short sections of between four and eight lines.
● Work on one or more of these sections (depending on students' level, interest and time available) as follows.
● Practise the section together. Pay attention to rhythm and linking, and to intonation.
● Get students to practise the section in pairs, working simultaneously. They should act it, not just say the lines.
● If this works well, get them to memorize the section so that they can act it out without the book.

4 *Have you got...?*
● Students do more preliminary practice on *have got.*
● In older classes, you may want to add *Have you got any children?*
● *Some* and *any* are studied in detail in Unit 7.

Optional activity
● Prepare a number of role-cards (suggestions below).
● Divide the students into pairs: one is a bank manager, the other is a customer.
● Give the customers each a role-card.
● Tell the bank managers to interview the customers, asking more or less the same questions as in the dialogue.
● Demonstrate yourself first with a good student if necessary.

Suggested role-cards:
MR CARTER Age: 22. Married.
Wife's name: Anne. Wife's age: 20.
One child: a boy (John, age 1).
Job: shop assistant.
You want £25,000 to buy a house.

MRS BULL Age: 40. Divorced.
One child: a girl (Jane, age 15).
Job: secretary.
You want £35,000 to buy a house.

DR ALLEN Age: 27. Single.
Job: doctor.
You want £70,000 to buy a house.

MR ROBINSON Age: 34. Married.
Wife's name: Helen. Wife's age: 36.
Four children: three girls and a boy (Sally, age 12; Mary, age 10; Margaret, age 5; Joe, age 3).
Job: businessman.
You want £45,000 to buy a house for your mother.

MRS LANE Age: 27. Married.
Husband's name: Peter. Husband's age: 29.
Two children: a boy (Robert, age 4) and a girl (Emily, age 3).
Job: writer of children's books.
You want £7,000 to buy a car.

Practice Book
● Tell students which exercises you want them to do.

Unit 3: Lesson D

Students learn to tell the time in English.
Structures: *our* completes the set of possessives.
Words and expressions to learn: *half; a quarter; past; to; o'clock; time; What time is it?; short; our; but.*

Language notes and possible problems

1. *Three fifteen*, etc. Some students may be familiar with the other way of telling the time (*three fifteen*, etc.). If necessary, explain that this is less common in conversation.

2. 24-hour clock You may also need to explain that the 24-hour clock is not normally used except in timetables.

3. *Half six* etc. In certain languages (such as German), *half six* means *half past five, half seven* means *half past six,* and so on.

4. Pronunciation *Half* and *quarter* need practice.

5. Pronouns Personal pronouns and possessives are confusing, and the test on these (Exercise 6) may well prove difficult. You may like to return to it and try it again after a few more lessons.

Optional extra materials

A toy clock is useful for practice in telling the time.

1 Telling the time ('past')

● Practise the pronunciation of the five examples. Then ask students to tell you what time it is on each of the eight small dials.
● Consolidate by asking them to write the times.

2 Telling the time ('to')

● Do this in the same way as Exercise 1.

3 Listening practice

● Play the recording (or read the text at normal speed) more than once if necessary.
● Tell students to write down *only* the times they hear in each extract. (They won't understand much else, but this is *not* important.)
● Let them compare notes before giving the answers.
● If necessary, explain that *four twenty* means 'twenty past four' and *seven twenty-five* means 'twenty-five past seven'.
● Don't explain everything in the conversations (see Introduction page X).

Tapescript for Exercise 3

1. 'Excuse me. I wonder if you could tell me the time.'
   'Er, yes. It's half past ten.'
   'Thank you very much.'

2. 'Got the time?'
   'Yeah. Twenty to eleven.'

3. 'What time is your train?'
   'Pardon?'
   'I said, what time did you say your train was?'
   'Oh, just a second. It's, . . . er . . . twenty-five past seven.'
   'Oh, that's all right, then. Adrian can take you.'

4. 'What time do you think you'll be getting home?'
   'Well, it depends on how long the play lasts, but I should

think about eleven o'clock. Is that all right?'
   'Oh yes, that's fine. I just wanted to have an idea.'

5. 'When are the meetings?'
   'Well, we meet on Thursdays at a quarter to eight officially, but things don't really get started until eight o'clock.'

6. The next train from Platform One will be the four twenty for Hereford, calling at . . .

7. At the third stroke, it will be seven twenty-five precisely. EXACTLY

4 Asking the time

● Practise the question.
● Get students to ask several other people the time.
● To add variety, ask the class to set their watches to new times, and do a 'walk-round' exercise. Half the class ask, the others answer; then change over.

5 *We* and *our; and* and *but*

● Go through the text. Students have already learnt *we* and *and*; explain *our* and *but* if they are not sufficiently clear from the context. Explain *all, both* and *short*.
● Do the second text as a blackboard composition with the students suggesting answers; or ask them to do it individually.

Optional activities

1. You can give further practice in telling the time by using a toy clock or drawing clockfaces on the board.
2. In international classes, you might try asking students what time it is in their countries.
3. Follow up this lesson by asking students to tell you the time at odd moments during the next few lessons.

6 Revision of subject pronouns and possessives

● This is probably best done as a test, with students writing the answers individually.
● If they have difficulty, list the pronouns and possessives on the board:

I	–	my	she	–	her
you	–	your	we	–	our
he	–	his	they	–	their

● Give quick demonstrations of the meanings (including the plural use of *you, your*) and try the exercise again.

7 Summary

● Look through the unit summary on page 136 with the students and explain any problems.
● Point out that they do not need to learn all of the kinship terms and adjectives (see instructions in summary).

Practice Book

● Tell students which exercises you want them to do.
● Exercise 3 is the beginning of a serial story for students to read with their dictionaries. There is an episode in Lesson D of each unit. The story is recorded on the cassette in dramatized form, and can be used for additional class work if you wish. Note, however, that it contains a number of 'preview' items (words and structures which students are not expected to study systematically until later).

D What time is it?

1

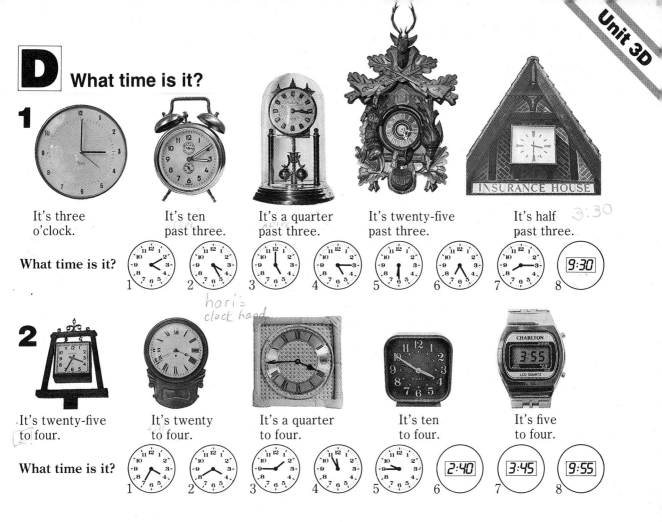

It's three o'clock.

It's ten past three.

It's a quarter past three.

It's twenty-five past three.

It's half past three. 3:30

What time is it?

1 2 3 4 5 6 7 8 9:30

haris clock hand

2

It's twenty-five to four.

It's twenty to four.

It's a quarter to four.

It's ten to four.

It's five to four.

What time is it?

1 2 3 4 5 6 2:40 7 3:45 8 9:55

3 Listening for information. Listen and write down the times you hear.

4 Ask another student the time.

'Excuse me, what time is it?'

5 Grammar revision. Read the text.

Janet and I are both thirty-six. Our children are fourteen, twelve and six. We are tall, and our daughters are both tall for their ages too, but our son is short. We are both fair, but our children are all dark.

Now read this text. Put in *we, our, and, but, are*.

John .... I .... from Scotland, ...
.... live in London. ....
both forty. .... have got three children.
.... daughter, Caroline, is tall ....
fair, ... two sons, Nicholas
and Thomas, ... short .... dark.

6 Grammar revision. Put in *I, my, you, your, he, his, she, her, we, our, they, their*.

1. 'I've got two sisters.' 'How old are ....?'
   'Eighteen and fourteen.'
2. Harry and Catherine are tall, and all ....
   children are tall, too.
3. Polly is fair, but .... sister is dark.
4. Hello. My name's Diego. ....'m Spanish.
5. My wife and I are tall, but .... children are
   short.
6. 'Is that .... sister?' 'No, it's my mother.'
7. 'Excuse me, how old are ....?' 'I'm
   twenty.'
8. John and .... father are both doctors.
9. Robert isn't very good-looking, but ....'s
   very intelligent.
10. 'This is Alice. ....'s a photographer.'
    'How do .... do?'
11. .... husband and I are American, but
    .... live in England.

7 Look at the summary on page 136 with your teacher.

17

Places

A Glasgow is an industrial city…

Newcastle, Maryport and Birkby are in the north of England. Newcastle is a large industrial town in the north-east, and Maryport is a small town in the north-west. Birkby is a small village near Maryport.

Dumfries is a small town. It is near Maryport, too, but not in England: it is in the south of Scotland. Crieff, Glasgow and Aberdeen are in Scotland, too. Crieff is in central Scotland, Glasgow is an industrial city on the west coast, and Aberdeen is a large town in the north-east.

Edinburgh is the capital city of Scotland, and a tourist centre. It is on the east coast.

1 Read the text with help from your teacher.

2 Pronounce these words.

1. thank   thirty   north   south
2. the   their   that
3. the doctor   the secretary
   the receptionist   the west
4. the artist   the electrician
   the engineer   the east

3 Practise reading the text aloud. Then close your book and remember what you can.

4 Make more sentences about places on the map. Examples:

'Dundee is a city in the east of Scotland.'
'Arbroath is a town near Dundee.'

5 Talk about places in other countries. Examples:

'Acapulco is a tourist centre. It is in the south-west of Mexico.'
'Milan is an industrial city in the north of Italy.'

WICK

INVERNESS

ABERDEEN

FORT WILLIAM

SCOTLAND

ARBROATH

OBAN   CRIEFF   DUNDEE

PERTH

GLASGOW   EDINBURGH

DUMFRIES

STRANRAER   BIRKBY   NEWCASTL

MARYPORT   CARLISLE

LANCASTER   ENGLAND

○ VILLAGES
● TOWNS
◎ CITIES

6 Write about places in your country. Example:

Bilbao is an industrial city in the north of Spain, on the Atlantic coast. Madrid is the capital city of Spain. It is a tourist centre. Barcelona

18

Unit 4: Lesson A

Students learn to talk about places.
Structures: a/an in definitions/descriptions; the before a clearly identified noun; position of adjectives before nouns.
Words and expressions to learn: north; south; east; west; north-east; north-west; town; village; city; coast; large; small; industrial; capital; tourist centre; on; in; near; of.
Phonology: /θ/ versus /ð/; two pronunciations of the (/ðə/ versus /ði:/).

Language notes and possible problems

1. The vocabulary load in this lesson is rather heavy. However, students need not remember all the words now; they will come up again later in the unit.

2. Articles The definite article is introduced here. It is used to signal the fact that a noun has a precisely defined reference (**the** north of England; **the** west coast (of Scotland); **the** capital city of Scotland. It contrasts with the indefinite article, which is used here in descriptions and definitions (**a** large town; **a** tourist centre). Students who speak Western European languages will have little difficulty with this; others will probably need extra help at some point (see Appendix page 161).

3. Adjectives You may wish to point out that adjectives come before nouns (a small village, not *a village small), and that and is not usual with adjectives used before a noun (a large industrial town, not a large and industrial town).

4. City Note that in Britain a city is, strictly speaking, a town with a cathedral, but that most people simply use the word to mean a very large town.

1 Presentation: describing a country
● Get the students to look at the map for a minute or two.
● Go through the text with them, explaining new words and expressions where necessary.
● Alternatively, you may want to let them use their dictionaries.

2 Pronunciation
● Write the first list of words on the board, getting the students to repeat each one after you.
● Do the same with the second list; point out the difference between voiced and unvoiced th.
● Point randomly to words in the first and second lists and get students to pronounce them until you feel they have mastered the difference.
● Treat the third and fourth lists in the same way, making sure the students master the difference between /ðə/ and /ði:/, and that they know that the second one is used before vowels.

3 Practice
● Get the students to say the sentences in the text after you or the recording.
● Divide longer sentences if necessary.

● Work on intonation and linking: pay special attention to sentences like *Glasgow is...*, *Aberdeen is...*, *it is on...*: these should be pronounced without pauses, as if each expression was one word.
● Get the students to read through the text again silently.
● Ask them to close their books and tell you anything at all that they can remember – a word, an expression or a whole sentence – from the text.
● Don't be critical of mistakes; simply repeat correctly what students have said.
● When students can't remember any more, get them to open their books and cover the text. See if they can say some more as they look at the map.

4 Freer practice: more about Scotland
● Get the students to volunteer sentences about the map.
● You will probably have to supply some vocabulary, e.g. *south-east, south-west*.
● Do not let this exercise go on too long or it will become boring.

5 Other countries
● Ask for sentences about other countries (not the students' own country/ies). Be quick to stop the exercise when students seem to be running out of ideas, so they are not made to feel ignorant.

Optional extra exercise: guessing
● In classes where students share common geographical knowledge (if they are all from the same country or educational system themselves), try this:
● One student describes a place, e.g.
  It's a tourist centre in the south of Germany.
● The other students have to guess the name, e.g.
  Is it Heidelberg?

6 Writing
● Use this exercise for supervised writing in class, or give it for homework if the students can do it without help.
● Ask them to base their writing on the text in the book.
● Discourage the use of dictionaries.
● For added interest you may want to ask them to write as if to a penfriend in another country.

Practice Book
● Tell students which exercises you want them to do.

England, Ireland, Scotland + Wales = Great Britain United Kingdom

Unit 4: Lesson B

Students learn to ask for and use identifying expressions, ask for supplementary information, make complimentary remarks.
Structures: use of *on*, *in*, and *at* with places; *isn't it?*
Words and expressions to learn: *that*; *mountain*; *beach*; *nice*.
Phonology: word-stress and resultant /ə/.

Language notes and possible problems

1. Isn't it? is introduced as an unanalysed item. Question-tags will be studied in detail later in the course.
2. Prepositions Contrasting uses of *in*, *at* and *on* will be treated again, more completely, in a later unit. They are introduced here in fairly clear-cut situations: *in* for a city or country (considered as having three dimensions); *on* for beaches and mountains (surfaces); and *at* for position near buildings (shape and dimensions not important to speaker).

---

1 Identifying places: presentation
• Ask the students to cover the text and look at the picture.
• Try to elicit as much as you can about the picture, so they will begin to have some idea what the conversation is about.
• Then ask them to close their books and listen to the recording.
• Ask for any words or phrases they remember. Gradually build the dialogue up on the board, playing it again if necessary.
• Explain or demonstrate the new vocabulary.
• Help the students to practise the dialogue, paying special attention to stress and intonation.
• As they do so, start erasing one word after another until only the first word of each line is on the board.
• Then let them practise the dialogue in pairs, changing partners once or twice.
• Finally let them open their books and listen once again.

2 Further practice
• Get students to take a piece of paper and draw a picture of a place on it.
• If you demonstrate by drawing a picture yourself, make sure it is simple so they are not intimidated.
• Get a volunteer to come up to the front and show you his or her picture. Say, *Oh, that's nice. Where's that?* and follow up whatever the answer is.
• Ask the class to stand up and walk round the room, showing one another their pictures and talking about them.

3 Word-stress and resultant /ə/
• Write the word *England* on the board.
• Ask the students where the stress is. When they answer, draw a ⌣ under the syllable: Eng*land.
• Ask them to do the same for the rest of the words in the book. (They should copy them out.)

• Then play the recording or read the words yourself so they can check the answers.
• Point out the pronunciation of /ə/ in *England* (/'ɪŋglənd/). Show them that it is a neutral, weak sound.
• If you speak the students' language, say it is weak because it isn't stressed.
• Get them to listen to you or the recording again, circling the vowels that are pronounced /ə/.
• Check their answers.
• Let them practise pronouncing the words themselves, reading them from their books.

4 In, at or on?
• Get the students to look at the three illustrative pictures. You may want to demonstrate the three prepositions with gestures as well.
• Then either work through the exercise with the students or let them work in groups and check their answers afterwards.

5 Second dialogue
• Get the students to look at the picture and mask their texts.
• Write *A:* on the board and ask for suggestions as to the first line of the dialogue.
• Accept any plausible suggestion that comes up with *Yes* or *OK*, but encourage them to continue until someone comes up with *Who's that?* and write it up.
• Write *B:* on the board and proceed in the same fashion, accepting all reasonable suggestions, but only writing when they get a bit of the dialogue as in the book.
• They will probably need a little guidance from you, but try to avoid actually giving them the words.
• When they have completed the dialogue, play the recording, help them with pronunciation, and let them practise in pairs.

6 Further practice
• Get them to take their pictures from Exercise 2 and add one or more people to them. Show them the pictures in the book or demonstrate with stick figures on the board.
• Get them to walk round once more, talking to one another about their pictures.
• Walk round yourself to give any help that is needed, but try not to correct any mistakes in the form of the language at this time: just let them practise fluency.

Practice Book
• Tell students which exercises you want them to do.

zenchishi = preposition

19

B

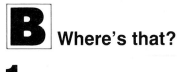

Where's that?

1 Listen and practise.

A: Oh, that's nice. Where's that?
B: It's Acapulco.
A: That's in Brazil, isn't it?
B: No, it's in Mexico.
A: Oh, yes, of course.

2 Draw a picture of a place.

Talk to other students about the picture. Use sentences and expressions from Exercise 1.

3 Pronunciation.

England	India	Japanese
Brazil	Italy	American
Morocco	the west	Italian
centre	Russia	Cyprus

1. Copy the list. Under each word
   draw a ~~~ for stress. Example: England
2. Listen and check your answers.
3. Listen again. Circle ⬭ the vowel where
   you hear /ə/. Example: England
4. Pronounce the words.

4 Prepositions and places. These people are...

at the Kremlin.

on a mountain.

in Paris.

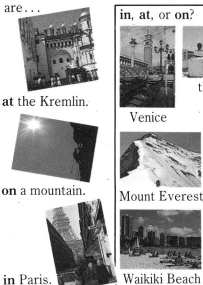

in, at, or on?

the Acropolis

Venice

Spain

Mount Everest

Waikiki Beach   the Eiffel Tower

5 Listen and practise. Be careful to pronounce *h* correctly.

A: Who's that?
B: It's my husband on the beach in Spain.
A: He's good-looking!
B: Oh, thank you.
A: And the beach is nice, too.
B: Mm.

6 Add a person from your family to your picture.

Talk to other students about the picture. Use sentences and expressions from Exercise 5.

C Where's Stockholm?

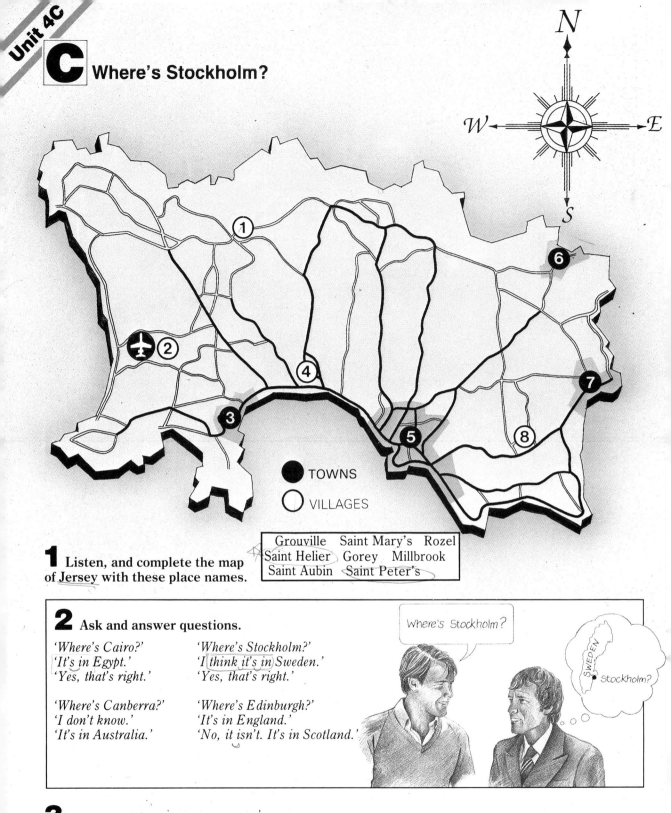

● TOWNS
○ VILLAGES

1 Listen, and complete the map of Jersey with these place names.

Grouville	Saint Mary's	Rozel
Saint Helier	Gorey	Millbrook
Saint Aubin	Saint Peter's	

2 Ask and answer questions.

'Where's Cairo?'
'It's in Egypt.'
'Yes, that's right.'

'Where's Canberra?'
'I don't know.'
'It's in Australia.'

'Where's Stockholm?'
'I think it's in Sweden.'
'Yes, that's right.'

'Where's Edinburgh?'
'It's in England.'
'No, it isn't. It's in Scotland.'

Where's Stockholm?

SWEDEN
● Stockholm?

3 Listen to the recording and answer. Examples:

'Montreal's in Canada.' 'That's right.'
'Berlin's in France.' 'No, it isn't.'
'Is Athens in Greece?' 'Yes, it is.'

Unit 4: Lesson C

Students learn to express doubt and uncertainty and to confirm or correct information; they practise listening for information about location.
Structures: structures from Lesson 4A are revised.
Words and expressions to learn: *I think*.
Phonology: intonation of answers; intonation of contrast.

Possible problem

Exercise 2 may present a problem if your students share little common knowledge of geography. In this case you may wish to use the lists given in the alternative to Exercise 2: one student in each pair gets list A, the other list B, and they exchange information using the forms from the exercise.

1 Listening and locating

- Get students to look at the map of Jersey.
- If necessary, tell them where Jersey is (in the Channel Islands, near the north-west coast of France; these islands are part of Great Britain).
- Read out the names of the places as the students read them in their books, to demonstrate the pronunciation.
- Play the recording right through from beginning to end, or read it yourself at normal speed.
- Play it again, stopping after each bit of information so that students can write the names of the places on the map (or write them next to the numbers on another piece of paper).
- Let the students compare notes in groups.
- If there is a lot of disagreement, play the recording again before giving them the answers.

Tapescript and answers to Exercise 1

Rozel and Saint Mary's are in the north of Jersey: Rozel is a town on the north-east coast and Saint Mary's is a village in the north-west.

Gorey is a town on the east coast of Jersey; Grouville is a small village near Gorey.

Grouville is near Saint Helier, too. Saint Helier is the capital of Jersey; it is a town on the south coast.

Millbrook is a small village in the south, near Saint Helier and Saint Aubin.

Saint Aubin is a small town on the south coast, near Saint Peter's in the west. Saint Peter's is the airport of Jersey.

Answers: 1. Saint Mary's 2. Saint Peter's 3. Saint Aubin 4. Millbrook 5. Saint Helier 6. Rozel 7. Gorey 8. Grouville

2 Doubt and certainty

- Get the students to look at the illustration. Make sure they understand the conventions of the speech balloon and the thought bubble.
- Play the recording while they look at the picture.
- Make sure they have understood what *I think* means.
- Get them to practise the four dialogues quickly. Emphasize the falling intonation both in questions and in answers; and point out the higher intonation curve on *Scotland* in the last example.
- Note linking in *It's in*; *I think it's in*; *It isn't*.
- Then let them quiz each other, in pairs or teams; or hand out copies of the lists which follow and let them work in pairs.

Alternative to Exercise 2

- Students work in pairs. One has list A, the other has list B.
- The student with list B asks *Where's Montreal?*, and enters the answer in his or her list.
- The other student asks *Where's Tehran?* and notes the answer.
- Student B's next question is *Is Caracas in Venezuela or Mexico?* and so on.

List A	List B
Montreal – Canada.	Montreal – .....
Tehran –	Tehran – Iran.
Caracas – Venezuela.	Caracas – Venezuela? Mexico?
Copenhagen – Sweden? Denmark?	Copenhagen – Denmark.
Santiago – Chile.	Santiago – .....
Heidelberg – Germany? Austria?	Heidelberg – Germany.
Bilbao – Spain.	Bilbao – Spain? Portugal?
Sydney –	Sydney – Australia.
Sofia – Bulgaria.	Sofia – .....
Oslo –	Oslo – Norway.
Delhi – India.	Delhi – India? Pakistan?
Buenos Aires – Argentina.	Buenos Aires – Argentina? Brazil?
Baghdad	Baghdad – Iraq.
Nicosia – Cyprus? Greece?	Nicosia – Cyprus.

3 Listening and answering

- Look through the examples with the students.
- Tell them to close their books, say the three example sentences yourself, and get them to answer.
- When they can do this, play the recording or read the sentences, and get them to give appropriate answers.
- If necessary, repeat the exercise until students can understand the recording easily and answer fluently.

Tapescript and answers to Exercise 3

Montreal's in Canada. (True)
Berlin's in France. (False)
Buenos Aires is in Argentina. (True)
Australia is near Brazil. (False)
Peking is in China. (True)
Madrid is in Peru. (False)
Copenhagen is in Norway. (False)
Chicago is in Canada. (False)
Tehran is in Iran. (True)

Is Athens in Greece? (Yes)
Is Moscow in Russia? (Yes)
Is Rome in Spain? (No)
Is Lisbon in Portugal? (Yes)
Is Oslo in Denmark? (No)
Is Caracas in Venezuela? (Yes)

Practice Book

- Tell students which exercises you want them to do.

Unit 4: Lesson D

Students learn to describe towns and cities.
Structures: more practice with adjectives.
Words and expressions to learn: *exciting*; *noisy*;
quiet; *place*; *Where in (Texas)?*; *about*; numbers
101 to 1,000,000; *population*.
Phonology: linking /r/.

Language notes and possible problems
Some of the conventions concerning large numbers may
differ from those in the students' language(s).
1. You may wish to point out the use of commas (not full
stops) to separate thousands and millions.
2. Note that we say *four thousand, three million*, etc., not
**four thousands*, *three millions*.
3. Note that *and* is not used after hundreds in standard
American English (GB *three hundred and seven*; US *three
hundred seven*).

Optional extra materials
Copies (enough for each student to have a list) of the two
lists for the alternative version of Exercise 6.

1 Describing cities: presentation
• Ask the students to read the first dialogue.
• Help them with the new words or encourage them to
use their dictionaries.
• Get them to try to complete the second dialogue; you
may wish them to work in pairs or small groups for this.
• Get the students to practise saying the dialogues (the
first dialogue is recorded).
• Pay special attention to stress and intonation.
• Practise 'linking /r/' in *Where are you from?*
and *Where in Texas?*

2 New vocabulary: personalization
• Teach the students the new words, or let them look
them up in their dictionaries.
• Get one student to ask you, *Where are you from?*, and
answer truthfully, modelling your answers on the
conversations in Exercise 1.
• Put the students into pairs and get them to ask and
answer questions about their villages/towns/cities.
• Let them change partners as many times as you feel it
is necessary to practise the forms.

3 Reporting
• Ask one or two students to tell the class about the
city, etc. of one person they interviewed.
• Then get the students to walk round again telling one
another what they found out in Exercise 2.

4 Guessing game
• Make a two-sentence description of a town or city
that your students will know, like the one in the book.
• Let them guess until they find the name of the place.
• Practise the linking in *Yes, it is* and *No, it isn't*. (*No, it*
is linked with a very light *w*, almost like *no wit*.)
• Divide the class into pairs and get each pair to write
two sentences about a city or town.

• When they have finished, get each pair to read out
their sentences in turn (each partner reads one of the
sentences) and let the rest of the class guess the place.

5 Numbers 101 and up
• Get the students to repeat the numbers in the book
after you (or after the recording).
• Write some numbers on the board and get students to
pronounce them.
• Say some numbers and get students to write them
(pay attention to the commas separating thousands and
millions).

6 Practising large numbers
• Explain the words *population* and *about*.
• Ask one student, *What's the population of Lagos?* and
wait for the answer.
• Ask for the population of some places which are not
on the list, so as to elicit answers with *about* and
I think, as well as *I don't know*.
• Divide the class into pairs and get them to ask one
another and answer.

Optional alternative to Exercise 6
• Begin as above.
• Instead of getting students to read answers out of the
book, divide the class into pairs and give out the
following lists: one student in each pair has list A and
the other has list B.
• By asking questions, students complete their lists.
• They then check with each other to see if their
answers are correct.

LIST A	LIST B
Accra – 564,194	Accra –
Buenos Aires –	Buenos Aires – 2,976,000
Calcutta – 3,148,746	Calcutta –
Geneva –	Geneva – 159,200
Karachi – 3,498,634	Karachi –
Liverpool –	Liverpool – 539,700
Madrid – 3,520,320	Madrid –
Moscow –	Moscow – 7,819,000
New York – 7,481,613	New York –
Peking –	Peking – 7,570,000
Rome – 2,868,248	Rome –
Stockholm –	Stockholm – 661,258

7 Summary
• Go through the summary on page 137 with the
students.

Practice Book
• Tell students which exercises you want them to do.

D It's an exciting place

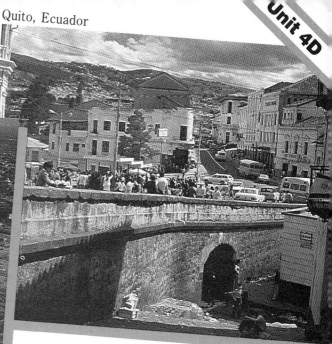

Quito, Ecuador

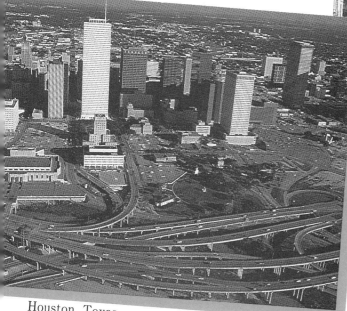

Houston, Texas

1 Read the first dialogue, and complete the second one.

A: Where are you from?
B: Texas.
A: Where in Texas?
B: Houston.
A: Oh, the astronauts' city!
B: Yes, it's an exciting place.
    But it's very polluted.

A: Where .... ?
B: Ecuador.
A: ....Where is........ Ecuador?
B: Quito..
A: ...Is it very.......... nice?
B: Yes, ...it's... a pretty city,
   ..and it's..very exciting, too.

2 With another student, ask and answer questions about your village/town/city. Here are some words to help you:

| quiet | pretty | noisy |
| nice | polluted | exciting |

3 Tell the class (or another student) about your partner's village/town/city. Example:

'Marianne is from Vézelay, near Avallon, in France. It's a small village, and it's very pretty. It's quiet, and it's not very exciting.'
But

4 In pairs: choose a town or city. Write two sentences about it. Read them to the other students. Example:

'It is a city on the east coast of the United States. It is polluted and noisy, but it is exciting.'
'Is it Boston?' 'No, it isn't.'
'Is it New York?' 'Yes, it is.'

5 Say the numbers after your teacher.

101	a hundred and one
132	a hundred and thirty-two
300	three hundred
354	three hundred and fifty-four
1,000	a thousand (one thousand)
1,400	one thousand four hundred
1,000,000	a million (one million)

6 Ask and answer.

What's the population of Tokyo?

I don't know.

About 9 million, I think.

About 2 million.

What's the population of Toronto?

Six hundred and thirty-three thousand, three hundred and eighteen.

1984

Cairo	8,500,000
London	7,028,200
Mexico	8,591,750
Rio de Janeiro	5,157,000
Singapore	2,147,400
Lagos	1,060,848
Munich	1,314,865
Toronto	633,318

7 Look at the summary on page 137 with your teacher.

Home

A   A house

(Handwritten labels on picture: sink, Clothes hamper, nts, hikidashi)

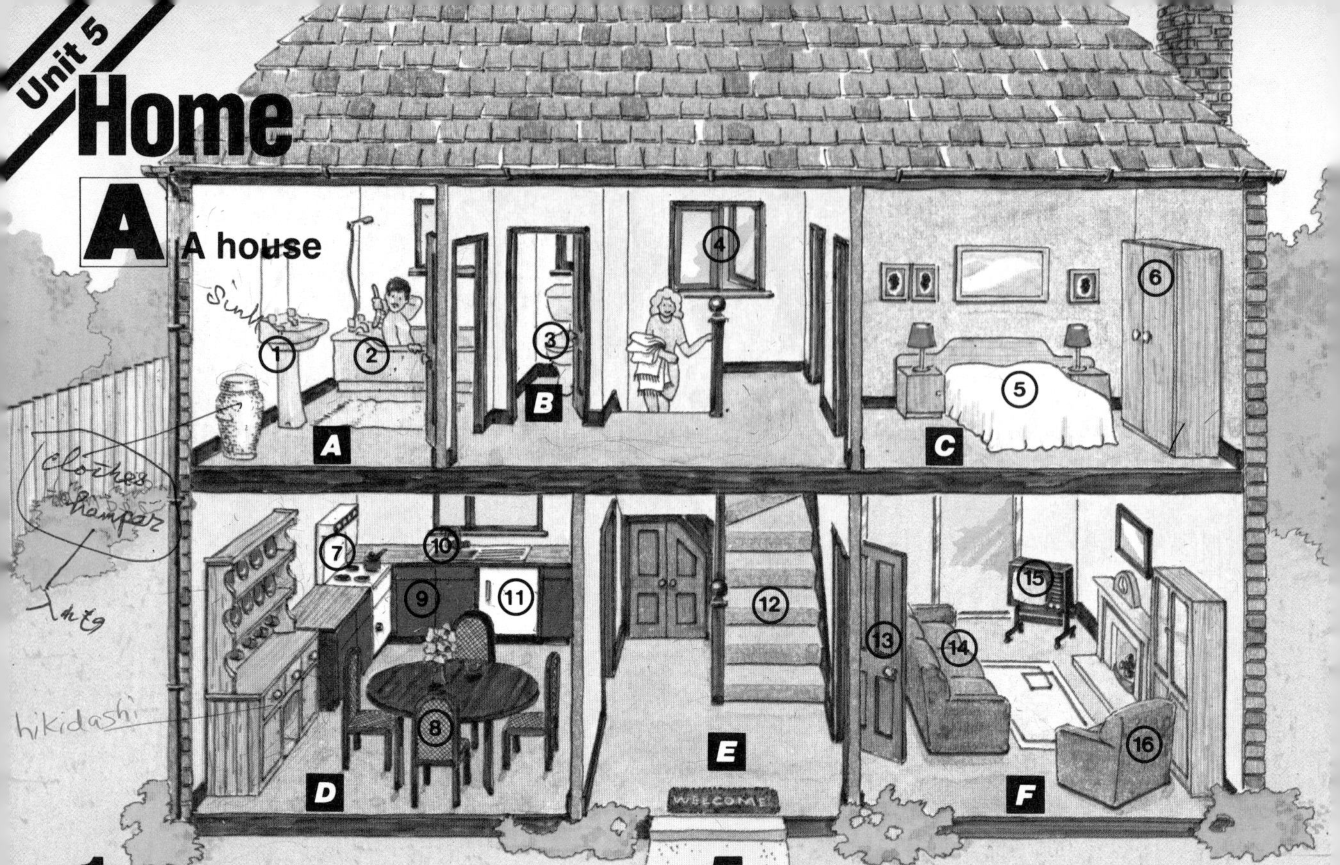

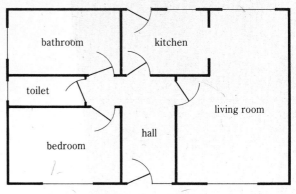

1
Look at the picture, and put the words with the right letters. Use your dictionary or work with other students. Example:

A. *bathroom*

bedroom   kitchen   bathroom   living room
hall   toilet

2
Now put these words with the right numbers.

chair   bed   toilet   door   window   stairs
cooker   sofa   fridge   armchair
television (TV)   cupboard   wardrobe   sink
washbasin   bath

3
The teacher's home.
Listen to the description.

4
Complete the sentences, and make some more sentences about the house in the picture.

1. There are .... bedrooms in the house.
2. There is (There's) an armchair .... the living room.
3. .... (is not) a garage. *isn't*
4. There .... bathroom.
5. There .... two toilets.
6. .... fridge in the kitchen.

5
Work in pairs.

1. Both students copy the plan.
2. One student furnishes his or her rooms.
3. The other asks questions beginning
   Is there a...? or *Are there any...?*
4. He or she listens to the answers and tries to put the right furniture etc. into the rooms.

Examples:
'Is there a fridge in the kitchen?'
   'Yes, there is.' (Or *'No, there isn't.'*)

'Are there any chairs in the bathroom?'
   'No, there aren't.' (Or *'Yes, there are two.'*)

(House plan with labels: bathroom, kitchen, toilet, living room, hall, bedroom)

6
Draw a plan of your house (or your 'dream house') and write five sentences about it.

22

Unit 5: Lesson A

Students learn to talk about houses and flats.
Structures: *there is/are*.
Words and expressions to learn: *there*; *house*; *window*; *door*; *stairs*; names of rooms; names of pieces of furniture; *room*; *furniture*; *garage*.
Phonology: weak forms, linking and rhythm in sentences with *there is/are*.

Language notes and possible problems
1. Articles   Students whose languages do not contain articles may need help to understand the contrast between *a* and *the* in sentences like *There's a big table in the kitchen.* See Appendix page 161.
2. Any is introduced in passing (it may be needed in Exercise 5), but it need not be explained at this stage.
3. Vocabulary   Real beginners will find the vocabulary load in this lesson rather heavy. They should only learn some of the words now – help them decide what is most important.

Optional extra materials
Pictures of rooms and/or furniture would be useful.

---

1 Presentation of vocabulary: rooms
● False beginners can do the exercise in groups, pooling their knowledge. Let real beginners use dictionaries.
● When students are ready, give them the answers and practise the pronunciation of the new words. Note *house*/haʊs/ but *houses*/ˈhaʊzɪz/.

2 More vocabulary: furniture
● This can be done in the same way as Exercise 1.
● Students will probably want to ask for more vocabulary. This is a good opportunity to teach them to say *What's this?* and *How do you say . . . in English?*
● But don't let this go on too long, or students will write down a lot of words which they will not learn.

3 Describing your own home (*there is/are*)
● Start by sketching a plan of your house/flat on the board (or the house/flat of somebody you know).
● Tell the students whose home it is, and where it is – this makes the exercise more interesting.
● Go on to describe the house/flat in a few simple sentences. Include some examples of *there is/are*. Use a chatty conversational style. Students don't need to understand every word.
● Here is an example:
'This is my flat. It's in Via Marconi, and it's small but nice. There are two rooms: there's a living room and a bedroom. And oh, yes – there's a kitchen, and there's a bathroom. The living room is pleasant: there are two big windows; there's a comfortable sofa, and there are three armchairs.'
● Don't ask questions – just let students enjoy understanding a piece of real communication in English.

4 *There is*: practice
● Do the first two example sentences with the class.

● Practise the pronunciation. Work on:
Weak-forms and linking.
there's a = /ðəzə/   *there is* = /ðərɪz/
there are = /ðərə/
Rhythm.
There are **two bed**rooms in the **house**.
There's an **arm**chair in the **living room**.
● Do the exercise orally. Make sure that each student makes at least one sentence.
● After a minute or two, ask students to close their books and continue from memory.

5 Information-gap work
● You will probably need to demonstrate what is wanted by doing the exercise first with a student. Make sure students realize that they should not see each other's sketches. Students who can't draw can write the words (*bed* etc.) in the various rooms.
● The exercise will work best if each student draws *two* plans – one to fill in with furniture, and one to use when it is his or her turn to ask questions.
● You can save time by handing out copies of the plan, if this is feasible.
● Before starting, practise the pronunciation of *Is there a . . . ?* (/ˈɪzðərə/).
● When students have finished, they should compare plans to see if the questioner has got an accurate copy of his or her partner's plan.

6 Writing
● This should be done individually. Help students with extra vocabulary if necessary, but don't let them try to write anything too ambitious.

Optional activities
1. You can use magazine pictures of rooms for extra practice in description.
2. Hand out pairs of pictures showing rooms which are similar but not the same. (Advertisements are a good source of material.) Get students to try to say what is different.
3. Exercise 6 can be extended as follows:
   Students draw plans of their homes or dream homes, without writing their names.
   On a separate paper, they write their names and five sentences about the homes.
   Collect plans and descriptions.
   Shuffle and number the plans; put them on the class notice board or lay them out on tables.
   Shuffle the descriptions and give them out again.
   Students come and look at the plans and try to find the one that matches their description.
   When they find one, they note the name and number and exchange descriptions with somebody else.
   After five minutes or so, compare notes and see how accurate the guesses were.
4. Students sit round a big sheet of paper and draw a flat in which they each have a room. They talk to decide where doors, toilet, telephone, living room etc. are. Then they tell each other about their own rooms. Can be done in groups of four to six.

Practice Book
● Tell students which exercises you want them to do.

Unit 5: Lesson B

Students learn to exchange addresses.
Structures: Introduction to Simple Present affirmative of lexical verbs; prepositions of place in addresses.
Words and expressions to learn: live(s); work(s); address; big; flat; floor; ground floor, first floor etc.; ordinal numbers first to ninth; street; road.
Phonology: contrastive stress; /θ/.

Language notes and possible problems

1. Word order Students may be worried by the word order in the question *What floor do you live on?* You can point out the parallel with *Where are you from?*, and explain (if possible) that prepositions often come at the end of spoken questions. The point will be thoroughly dealt with later in the course.

2. Simple Present Simple Present verb forms will be dealt with in the next unit. For the moment, just make sure that students understand the use of *-s* on the third person of *lives* and *works*.

3. Ground floor, etc. Note that the British *ground floor* is the American *first floor*, the British *first floor* is the American *second floor*, and so on.

4. Foreign addresses Students may want to translate their home addresses into English. Point out that we usually leave foreign addresses untranslated (e.g. *He works at 9 rue de la Paix*, not ** . . . at 9 Peace Street*).

5. Street and **road** can be treated as synonyms for the moment.

Optional extra materials

Cards with British or American-type addresses on (Exercise 3).

---

1 Presentation

● Explain the first sentence to the students. Ask where it should go in the picture.
● Give them a few minutes to decide where the other sentences should go.
● Ask what sentence goes with each number. Practise the pronunciation and explain any problems.
● Practise the pronunciation of the ordinal numbers, but don't be too perfectionist: *fifth* and *sixth* are very difficult.
● You may also like to practise the vowel /ɪ/ in *live*.

2 Prepositions in addresses

● Do the exercise orally, then consolidate in writing.
● In this and the following exercises, pay attention to linking in *live at, live in* and *live on*.
● Help students to see the rules:
 – *at* is used before exact addresses
 – *in* is used before the names of streets and larger places
 – *on* is used before *the first/second/ . . . floor*
● The order of elements in addresses is 'smallest first' (house number, then street name, then town).

3 Exchanging addresses

● Practise the example sentences. Students can ask

What's your address? or *Where do you live?*
● Help them to get the rhythm right: **What's your address? Where do you live?**
● Note the contrastive stress in the answer *Where do you live?*
● Give out cards or slips of paper with English-language addresses on if you want to. Tell students to learn their new addresses by heart.
● Tell students to close their books and find out as many addresses as possible without leaving their seats. They must write down the addresses. Put on the board:
 How do you spell that?
and encourage them to use this question if necessary.

4 On the first floor, etc.

● Ask students the questions. Get them to answer orally and consolidate in writing.
● Make sure they don't forget the article *the*.
● For further practice, do a walk-round exercise in which students have to find out what floor everybody else lives/works on.
● They should note the names of the other students, together with their answers.
● When they have finished, they can report some of their findings back to the class (so as to practise third person forms).

5 Listening for information

● Students will not understand everything they hear. This does not matter; their job is just to listen for specific information and fill in the table.
● They will hear six pieces of conversation or monologue (not in the same order as the names in the table). In each, there is an address; in three, there are telephone numbers.
● Their task is to pick out the addresses and phone numbers they hear from the lists in their books, and enter the letters in the table.
● Note that there are too many addresses and phone numbers: they don't all occur in the recording.
● Tell students to copy the table from their books.
● Play the recording once without stopping. (Students don't write this time.)
● Play the first conversation again, and ask students to fill in the answer. Check that it's right.
● Play the other extracts, pausing after each for students to write the answer.
● Let them compare notes.
● Play the recording once more.
● Give them the answers.

Tapescript for Exercise 5: see page 180

Answers to Exercise 5

NAME	LIVES	PHONE NUMBER
John	D	X
Peter Matthews	F	–
Alice's mother	C	–
Mr Billows	E	–
Mrs Webber	G	Y
Mrs Simon	A	W

Practice Book

● Tell students which exercises you want them to do.

B Where do you live?

ninth (9th) floor
eighth (8th) floor
seventh (7th) floor
sixth (6th) floor
fifth (5th) floor
fourth (4th) floor
third (3rd) floor
second (2nd) floor
first (1st) floor
ground floor

1 Look at the pictures. Put the words in the right places.

> The Prime Minister lives at 10 Downing Street.
> My sister works in Edinburgh.
> 'Where do you live, Mary?' 'In Aston Street.'
> 'What's your address?' '39 Morrison Avenue.'
> We live in a small flat on the fourth floor.
>
> Mrs L. Williams
> 17 Harcourt Road
> Coventry
> West Midlands CY2 4BJ

2 *At, in* or *on*?

1. I live .... 37 Valley Road.
2. 'Where do you work?' '............ New York.'
3. My office is .... the fourteenth floor.
4. Jake lives .... a big old house .... Washington.
5. 'Where do you live?' '............ 116 New Street.'

3 Ask the addresses of some other students and write them down.

'Excuse me. What's your address?'
'16 Grange Road. Where do you live?'
'At 17 Queen's Drive.'

4 a) What floor do you live/work on?
 Examples: *'I live on the third floor.'*
   'I work on the seventh floor.'
 b) Where are you now?
 Example: *'We're on the first floor.'*
 c) What floor does your father/mother/ brother/boss etc. work/live on?
 Example: *'My mother lives on the fourth floor.'*

5 Listening for information. Listen to the conversations, and write the correct letters after the names. (There are only three phone numbers.)

NAME	LIVES	PHONE NUMBER
John		X
Peter Matthews		
Alice's mother		
Mr Billows		
Mrs Webber	G	
Mrs Simon		

A at 16 Norris Road, Bedford.   V 314 6928
B in a small flat in North London.   W 41632
C in Birmingham.   X 314 6829
D at 116 Market Street.   Y 41785
E in New York.   Z 41758
F on the fourth floor.
G at 60 Hamilton Road, Gloucester.

C What's your phone number?

1 Listening. The same or different?

A	472 1067	F	444 6704
B	668 6154	G	238 1176
C	831 7541	H	781 8254
D	374 6522	I	904 0799
E	551 0723	J	235 1600

4703167?

SORRY, WRONG NUMBER.

2 Listen again. Answer 'Yes, hello' or 'No, sorry, wrong number.'

3 What's your phone number? Ask the phone numbers of the students sitting near you. Example:

'Excuse me. What's your phone number?'
'Three one four double two oh seven.'
'Three one four double two oh seven?'
'Yes, that's right.'
'Thanks.'
'What's your phone number?' etc.

WHAT'S YOUR PHONE NUMBER?

FOUR THREE EIGHT DOUBLE TWO NINE OH.

4 Listen to the two conversations and study them. Then make similar conversations and practise them with a partner.

MARIA: Hello. Oxford 49382.
ALICE: Hello. Could I speak to Maria, please?
MARIA: Speaking. Who's that?
ALICE: This is Alice.
MARIA: Oh, hello, Alice. How are you?
ALICE: Fine, thanks. Listen, Maria, I...

JOE: Hello.
BILL: Hello. Could I speak to Sally, please?
JOE: One moment, please...I'm sorry. She's not here. Can I take a message?
BILL: Pardon?
JOE: Can I take a message?
BILL: Yes. Could you tell her that Bill called?
JOE: Yes, of course.
BILL: Thanks very much. Goodbye.
JOE: You're welcome. Goodbye.

Unit 5: Lesson C

Students learn to make phone calls in English.
Structures: *Can I...?* and *Could I...?*; *tell* + object + *that*-clause.
Words and expressions to learn: difference between *this* and *that*; *speak to*; *speaking*; *telephone*; *phone*; *telephone (phone) number*; *wrong number*; *one moment*; *can*; *could*; *Can I take a message?*; *You're welcome*; *double*.
Phonology: contrastive stress; rising and falling intonation.

Language notes and possible problems
1. *Can* and *could* are both introduced in the dialogues. If possible, explain that *Could I...?* is more polite than *Can I...?*, and is more common when one is asking a favour.
2. Demonstratives The lesson introduces the difference between *this* and *that*. Speakers of British English use *this* on the phone to identify themselves, and *that* when asking who the other person is. (In American English, *this* is used in both cases.)

Optional extra materials
Cards or slips of paper with phone numbers for Exercise 3.

Pre-teaching: phone numbers
- Write a phone number on the board. Ask students what it is; practise *telephone number* and *phone number*.
- Point out that the figures are said separately, not in groups (e.g. *one oh six seven*, not *ten sixty-seven*).
- Tell students that *zero* is called *oh* (/əʊ/) in phone numbers.
- Write some more numbers and teach *double* (British English only). *33420* is *double three four two oh*.
- The intonation movement (rise or fall of the voice) is on the last figure. Look out for this in the first two exercises.

1 The same or different?
- Play the recording (or say the numbers below) and ask students to note whether each number is the same as the one in their books or different. (They can write *S* or *D*.) When they have finished, get them to compare notes and discuss the answers. Insist on the article in *the same*.

2 Sorry, wrong number
- This time the students hear the same numbers, but in sentences as follows:
  Hello, is that 472 1067?
- They should answer *Yes, hello* or *No, sorry, wrong number* as appropriate.

Tapescript for Exercises 1 and 2
The numbers are:

A. 472 1067 (S)	F. 444 6784 (D)
B. 668 6152 (D)	G. 438 1176 (D)
C. 831 7549 (D)	H. 781 8254 (S)
D. 374 6522 (S)	I. 924 0799 (D)
E. 551 0623 (D)	J. 235 1600 (S)

3 Personalization
- Give out slips of paper or cards with phone numbers on, or get students to use their own phone numbers if everybody has one.
- Practise the sample conversation. Note the difference in intonation between the statement in the second line (falling intonation) and the question in the third line (rising).
- Note also the contrastive stress in *What's **your** phone number?*
- Tell students to find out the numbers of as many people as they can without moving from their seats.
- They should follow the pattern given in the example: student A asks for B's number, writes it down and checks it; B then gets A's number in the same way.

4 Dialogues
First dialogue
- Tell students to close their books and then play the first dialogue twice.
- Ask them how much they can remember. See if they can help you reconstruct the dialogue on the board.
- Give any necessary explanations; for instance:
  – *Could I...?* used for polite requests.
  – Preposition in *speak to*.
  – Meaning of *Speaking*.
  – Difference between *this* and *that*.
  – British people usually answer the phone by giving their number (or the name of their firm).
- Practise the dialogue, erasing words progressively from the board until students can remember it easily. Continue practice in pairs. Work hard on rhythm and intonation.

Second dialogue
- This is recorded by American speakers. It is more difficult than the first dialogue, and may be too hard for real beginners.
- It can be used for a prediction exercise: play the recording, stopping at suitable points and asking the students what they think comes next.
- Open books and give explanations. Note:
  – Difference between *Can I...?* (offering a service) and *Could I...?* (asking a favour: more polite).
  – *You're welcome* is more common in American English than British.
- Practise together and in pairs, paying attention to rhythm and intonation.

Making up dialogues
- Get students to make up and practise their own conversations, changing the names and numbers but keeping the rest more or less the same.
- Real beginners may just use material from the first conversation.
- With fluent false beginners this can develop into a role-playing improvisation, with students 'telephoning' each other across the classroom, asking to speak to their friends and so on.

Practice Book
- Tell students which exercises you want them to do.

Unit 5: Lesson D

Structures: Rules for formation of noun plurals.
Words and expressions to learn: *Well; food; clean; next; Love; man; woman; person; people.*
Phonology: pronunciation rules for plural endings.

Language notes

This lesson gives complete rules for the pronunciation of regular plurals. You may wish to simplify at this stage, and just teach students how to know when the ending is pronounced /ɪz/. The difference between /s/ and /z/ is less important, and need not be mastered by students who are not aiming at a very high standard of pronunciation.

Rules for formation of noun plurals

Spelling rules:
1. Most nouns form their plural in -s.
2. Nouns ending in a consonant + -y (like *secretary*) form their plurals in -ies. Nouns ending in -ay, -ey, -oy or -uy just add -s (like *boys*).
3. Nouns ending in -s, -ch or -sh add -es (like *glasses*).

Pronunciation rules:
1. After a *sibilant* sound (/s/,/z/,/ʃ/,/ʒ/,/tʃ/,/dʒ/), -es is pronounced /ɪz/. Examples: *glasses*; *matches*. But -es is not pronounced /ɪz/ after other sounds (e.g. *tables*).
Note the pronunciation of *houses* (/ˈhaʊzɪz/, not /ˈhaʊsɪz/).
2. After other sounds (not sibilants), the plural ending is pronounced /z/ or /s/, depending on whether it follows a voiced or unvoiced sound.
/z/ is pronounced after vowels:
   boys /bɔɪz/
   sofas /ˈsəʊfəz/
and after the voiced consonants /b,v,ð,d,g,l,m,n,ŋ/:
   rooms /ruːmz/
   tables /ˈteɪblz/
/s/ is pronounced after the unvoiced consonants /p,f,θ,t,k/:
/p,f,θ,t,k/:
   flats /flæts/
   banks /bæŋks/
   shops /ʃɒps/

Presentation

• Get students to look at the lists of singular and plural words. (Explain the meaning of the words *singular* and *plural* if necessary).
• Note that the list of irregular nouns includes the important new words *man, woman, person, people.*
• Practise the pronunciation of the words in each list, using the recording if you wish.
• Get students to try to see the rules for themselves.
• If you can give mother-tongue explanations, this will help.

1 Pronunciation practice

• Get several students to try each word. Correct if necessary and practise in chorus.

2 Spelling of plurals

• This will help students to see that they can form the plurals of words they don't know.
• When they have written the plurals, get them to pronounce them.

3 Plural expressions

• This can be done orally round the class, with students writing one or two examples for consolidation.

Optional activity

• Further practice on plurals can be done with a simple game, played in two teams.
• Call out singular nouns followed by the names of students (from each team in turn) who must give the plurals.
• Give points for correct answers and correct pronunciation.
• Alternatively, seat students in groups of six to eight. One student in each group gets a ball made of a crumpled-up sheet of paper. He or she says a noun, at the same time throwing the ball to another student, who must give the plural before testing somebody else in the same way.

4 Semi-controlled composition

• Go through the text, explaining difficulties.
• Then ask students to write their own postcards or letters in pairs. They must decide where they are and who they are writing to. (It can be another student.)
• They can decide themselves which of the words and expressions from the original text they are going to use. They should include plenty of these, but change enough to make the postcard interesting and different. They must use *we* and *our* at least once each.
• Help with vocabulary where necessary.

5 Summary

• Look over the summary on page 138 with the students.
• If they find the vocabulary load heavy, tell them that they need not learn everything now.

Practice Book

• Tell students which exercises you want them to do.

D More than one

SINGULAR	PLURAL /z/
room	rooms
table	tables
chair	chairs
boy	boys
family	families
secretary	secretaries

SINGULAR	PLURAL /s/
bank	banks
flat	flats
artist	artists
parent	parents
bath	baths
shop	shops

SINGULAR	PLURAL /ɪz/
address	addresses
watch	watches
dish	dishes
place	places
village	villages
fridge	fridges

SINGULAR	PLURAL (irregular)
man	men
woman (/'wʊmən/)	women (/'wɪmɪn/)
child (/tʃaɪld/)	children (/'tʃɪldrən/)
person	people
wife	wives
house (/haʊs/)	houses (/'haʊzɪz/)

1 Study the pronunciation of the plural nouns. Can you say these words?

rooms   tables   flats   watches   chairs
places   afternoons   toilets   tourists
windows   centres   garages   beds   cities
cookers   messages   sofas   sisters

2 Write the plurals of these words.

field   book   bus   bully   day   trip
try   ash   tree   toy   diary   tiger
sock   match   boss

3 Make the following expressions plural.

a good-looking artist

good-looking artists

a French student

French students

her teacher

her teachers

a tall man
a nice person
our friend
a shop assistant
a nice accountant
my aunt
an intelligent girl
a Spanish village
their secretary
a fair woman
his child
a small job
a large city
a dark room

4 Read the postcard. Work with a partner and write a similar holiday postcard to a friend.

Dear Mary,
Well, here we are at Premiere Miami Beach. At last! Our hotel is very nice and the food's good. We're on the 14th floor! Our room is small, but it's clean and quiet. There are some nice people from Manchester in the next room.
love, Carol and Jim

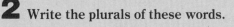

Mrs Mary Anderson
14, Windrush Road
Cartmel
Cumbria
GREAT BRITAIN

5 Look at the summary on page 138 with your teacher.

Habits

A What do you like?

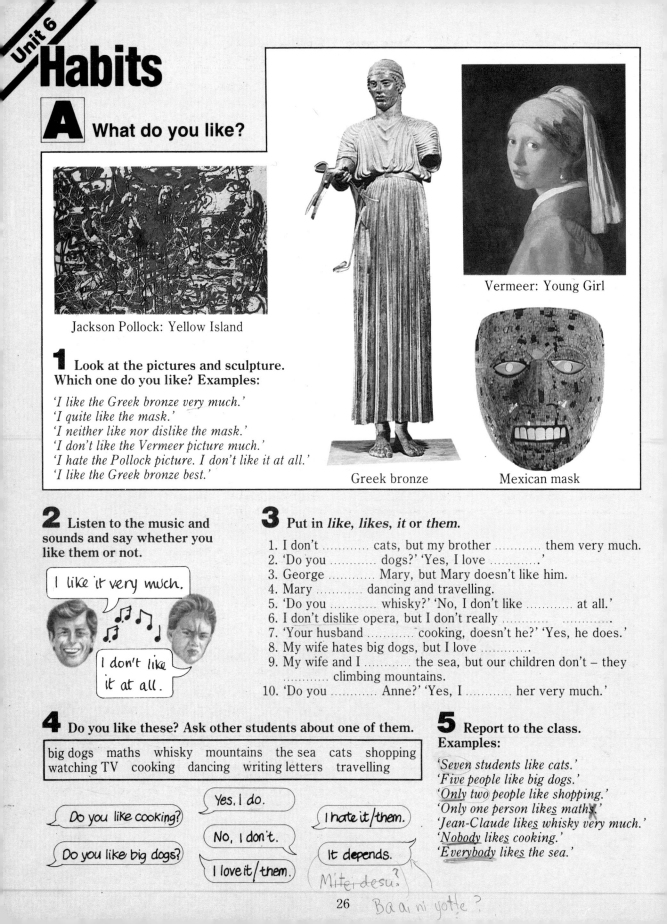

Jackson Pollock: Yellow Island

Vermeer: Young Girl

Greek bronze

Mexican mask

1 Look at the pictures and sculpture. Which one do you like? Examples:

'I like the Greek bronze very much.'
'I quite like the mask.'
'I neither like nor dislike the mask.'
'I don't like the Vermeer picture much.'
'I hate the Pollock picture. I don't like it at all.'
'I like the Greek bronze best.'

2 Listen to the music and sounds and say whether you like them or not.

I like it very much.

I don't like it at all.

3 Put in *like*, *likes*, *it* or *them*.

1. I don't .... cats, but my brother .... them very much.
2. 'Do you .... dogs?' 'Yes, I love ....'
3. George .... Mary, but Mary doesn't like him.
4. Mary .... dancing and travelling.
5. 'Do you .... whisky?' 'No, I don't like .... at all.'
6. I don't dislike opera, but I don't really ....
7. 'Your husband .... cooking, doesn't he?' 'Yes, he does.'
8. My wife hates big dogs, but I love ....
9. My wife and I .... the sea, but our children don't – they .... climbing mountains.
10. 'Do you .... Anne?' 'Yes, I .... her very much.'

4 Do you like these? Ask other students about one of them.

big dogs maths whisky mountains the sea cats shopping
watching TV cooking dancing writing letters travelling

Do you like cooking?

Do you like big dogs?

Yes, I do.

No, I don't.

I love it/them.

I hate it/them.

It depends.

5 Report to the class. Examples:

'Seven students like cats.'
'Five people like big dogs.'
'Only two people like shopping.'
'Only one person likes maths.'
'Jean-Claude likes whisky very much.'
'Nobody likes cooking.'
'Everybody likes the sea.'

Unit 6: Lesson A

Students learn to talk about likes and dislikes.
Structures: Simple Present tense; no article with nouns used in a general sense; *-ing* form after *like* for activities; *neither...nor*; object pronouns *it* and *them*.
Words and expressions to learn: some of these (see summary): *like; dislike; love; hate; music; dog; maths; whisky; the sea; cat; shopping; watching TV; cooking; dancing; writing letters; travelling; it depends; only; nobody; everybody; quite; not...much; him; her; not...at all.*

Language notes and possible problems

1. Simple Present tense   Here students use mainly forms that they have met: affirmatives, second person singular interrogative and first person singular negative.
2. Articles   In Exercises 3 and 4, point out the use of plural and uncountable nouns without articles when the meaning is 'general' (e.g. *mountains, whisky*). But note *the sea* (singular countable noun).
3. -ing forms   Note also the use of *-ing* forms to refer to activities after *like, dislike, love, hate.*
4. Object pronouns   *It* and *them* are practised.
2. Word order   Note the position of *very much* in, for example, *I like whisky very much.*
6. Maths   Note that this word is singular (Exercise 4).
7. Vocabulary   Real beginners should not try to learn all the vocabulary that comes up in the lesson.

Optional extra materials

Postcards (reproductions of works of art, or pictures of singers or film stars) for Exercise 1.
Short pieces of recorded music for Exercise 2.

1 Reacting to pictures
● Ask students to look at the pictures for a minute or two.
● Try to get spontaneous reactions: refer to a picture and help students to say *I like it* or *I don't like it.*
● Then look over the different ways of expressing likes and dislikes in the examples. Explain any difficulties.
● Ask for more sentences about the pictures. Give help with pronunciation of the artists' names as needed.
● Ask students to tell you about other artists they like or dislike.
● Get students to ask you (and each other) questions about your artistic preferences (e.g. *Do you like Picasso?*). Practise *Do you...?* (/djʊ/), *Yes, I do* (not *Yes, I like*), *No, I don't.*
● Finally, ask them to write one or two sentences about their reactions to the pictures.

Alternatives to Exercise 1
● Instead of using the pictures in the book, bring in art postcards, pictures of singers, or anything else about which students can express likes and dislikes.

2 Music and sounds
● This is a similar activity, but this time students react to things they hear.

● Play the recording, stopping after each item to ask for reactions. Students will need to use the pronoun *it* (e.g. *I like it*).
● If reactions are strong, teach *love.*

Students will hear:
1. Several short extracts from pieces of music in very different styles.
2. a pneumatic drill; traffic; birdsong; church bells; children playing; a jet.

3 Grammar
● Before starting the exercise, put on the board:
I like	*we like*
you like	*you like*
he/she likes	*they like*

● Remind students about the *-s* on the third person singular.
● Put on the board:
I like music.	*I like it.*
I like dogs.	*I like them.*

● Practise the pronunciation, being careful not to stress *it* and *them* (/ðəm/).
● Do the exercise, explaining vocabulary as you go along.
● You may like to get students to do some sentences orally and others in writing.
● Practise the pronunciation of *do, don't, does* and *doesn't* as they come up.
● Point out the two object forms *him* and *her*, and tell students to learn them.
● Students may want to ask you about the structure of the third person negative (*doesn't like*), which is previewed in Question 3.

4 Class survey
● Run over the vocabulary, and practise the pronunciation of the questions and answers in the examples.
● Ask some students whether or not they like some of the things in the list. Get them to ask you. (Note that *maths* is singular – they will need to say *I like/don't like it*).
● Then ask each student to choose one thing from the list, and to walk round asking the others whether they like it or not. They must keep a record of the answers, perhaps by writing down a list of the expressions from Exercise 1 (*like, quite like,* etc.) and putting ticks beside them as people answer.

5 Reporting the survey
● When students have finished their survey they should report to the class (or to members of a group) saying how many people love/like/dislike/etc. their item.
● Before starting, look at the examples: remind students that third person singular subjects (including *everybody* and *nobody*) take a verb form with *-s.*
● You may need to teach *doesn't* for singular negative examples like *Maria doesn't like cats.*

Practice Book
● Tell students which exercises you want them to do.

A they like

26

Unit 6: Lesson B

Students learn to talk and ask about daily work routines.
Structures: Simple Present: third person singular interrogatives; *at* with times; *by bus, car* etc.; *from...until...*; *has.*
Words and expressions to learn: some of these (see summary): *clothes; shop; sell; garage; job; after; go; work* (noun); *start; open; have* (lunch etc.); *stop; get up; breakfast; lunch; supper; tennis;* the days of the week; *at the weekend; (At) What time...?; both.*

Language notes and possible problems

1. Simple Present tense: forms   Here, students have to learn that the third person singular has -s on the main verb in affirmatives, but on the auxiliary in questions and negatives. This will be likely to cause problems for some time. The pronunciation and spelling rules for the third person ending are the same as those for plurals.

2. Simple Present tense: use   Students will now have learnt two characteristic uses of the Simple Present: to talk about states (e.g. likes and dislikes) and routines. Until they have learnt the Present Progressive, however, they are likely to over-generalize the Simple Present: look out for mistakes like **Do you work now?*

3. Have   The 'dynamic' use of *have* (as in *have breakfast, have a rest*) is peculiar to English, and students may find it difficult to learn at the beginning. It shouldn't be confused with *have got.*

4. (At) What time...?   Note that the preposition is normally dropped.

1 Text completion
● This is a suitable exercise for 'false beginners', or for others who know a little more English than they have learnt from the lessons.
● Put the students in groups of five or six, and let them pool their knowledge to complete the text.
● Get groups to compare notes before giving them the answers.
● Teach *supper*, to complete the list of meals.
● With complete beginners who don't know any of the new words, you will of course have to tell them which words to put where.
● Give whatever explanations are necessary.

2 Guided composition
● In order to write the text about Karen Miller, students have to ask you for information.
● And in order to do this they must be able to ask third-person questions.
● Start by practising the pronunciation of the first two questions in the list.
● Tell students the answers and get them to start writing the text. They should work individually.
● As they need more information, they will ask you the rest of the questions. The facts about Karen are as follows:

– Karen gets up at half past six.
– She doesn't have breakfast. (Write *does not* on the board.)
– She goes to work by car.
– She starts work at eight o'clock.
– She stops work at a quarter to six.
– She has lunch at twelve o'clock.
– She doesn't work on Saturdays. (Write *does not* on the board.)
– At the weekend she goes to see friends or plays tennis.
– She likes her job.
● Finish by putting an agreed version of the text on the board.

3 Things in common
● They both stop work at a quarter to six; they both play tennis.

4 Grammar
● Before doing the exercise (orally or in writing, as you think best), explain the grammar of Simple Present questions and negatives.
● Put on the board:

I work	*do I work?*
you work	*do you work?*
he/she works	*does he/she work?*
we work	*do we work?*
you work	*do you work?*
they work	*do they work?*

● Point out how the third-person -s appears on the auxiliary verb in questions, not on the main verb.
● Practise the pronunciation of *does.*
● Ask students to make the interrogative forms of a few third-person verbs – for example, tell them to turn *he lives, she gets up, she has breakfast, my mother goes to work* into questions.
● Put the negative forms on the board:

I do not work	*I don't work*
you do not work	*you don't work*
etc.	

● Practise the pronunciation of *don't.*
● Ask students to make a few negatives in the same way.
● Mention the irregular forms *has, goes.*
● Remind students that *be, can* and *have got* form questions (and negatives) without *do* – as in *Are you married?   Can I take a message?   Have you got any children?*

5 The days of the week
● These can be learnt by practising round the class, and then by asking questions like *What day is after Tuesday? What's today?   What's tomorrow?   What was yesterday?*
● Note the pronunciation (/'mʌndi/, /'tjuːzdi/ etc.).

Practice Book
● Tell students which exercises you want them to do.

27

B Work

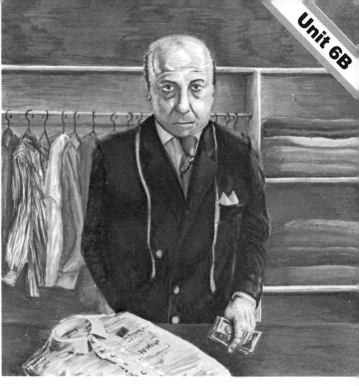

1 Put the words into the text.

Stan Dixon is a shop assistant. He sells men's clothes in a small shop. It is a tiring job.

Stan .... at seven o'clock. After ...., he .... to work by .... He .... work at a quarter past nine; the shop .... at half past. Stan .... lunch at twelve, and then .... from 12.45 until 5.45.

On Saturdays, Stan .... work at one o'clock. On Sundays he .... cycling or .... tennis.

Stan does not .... his job much.

has	like	breakfast	goes
works	bus	gets up	opens
stops	plays	starts	goes

2 Do it yourself. Ask the teacher questions, and write the text about Karen Miller.

Karen Miller is a mechanic. She repairs cars in a garage. . . .

What time does she get up?
Does she have breakfast?
How | go to work?
What time | start work?
What time | stop work?
What time | have lunch?
| work on Saturdays?
What | do at the weekend?
| like her job?

3 Stan Dixon and Karen Miller both have lunch at twelve. Find out two more things that they both do. What are they?

4 Put in the correct verb forms.

1. Stan .... breakfast at half past seven. (have/has)
2. Karen does not .... breakfast. (have/has)
3. How does Karen .... to work? (go/goes)
4. Stan .... to work by bus. (go/goes)
5. My father .... in Cardiff. (work/works)
6. He does not .... travelling. (like/likes)
7. He .... at six o'clock every day. (get up/gets up)
8. He does not .... on Saturdays. (work/works)
9. My parents .... in a big flat. (live/lives)
10. What does your father ....? (do/does)

5 Learn the days of the week.

MARCH

Monday		5	12	19	26
Tuesday		6	13	20	27
Wednesday		7	14	21	2
Thursday	1	8	15	22	2
Friday	2	9	16	23	3
Saturday	3	10	17	24	3
Sunday	4	11	18	25	

27

C What **news**paper do you read?

are you interested in?
are your interests?

NEWSPAPER	I read ....
BOOKS	I read ....
	I don't read ....
FOOD	I like ....
	I don't like ....
DRINK	I like ....
	I don't like ....
SPORT	I play ....
	I don't play ....
	I watch ....
MUSIC	I like ....
	I don't like ....
	I play ....
INTERESTS	I'm interested in ....
LANGUAGES	I speak ....
	I don't speak ....
HOLIDAYS	I often go (to) .... on holiday.
ACTIVITIES	I like .... ing.
	I like .... ing.
	I don't like .... ing.

1 Fill in the table. The teacher will help you.

2 Listen to the recording and answer the questions. Examples:

'Are you married?' 'Yes, I am.' / 'No, I'm not.'
'Do you like music?' 'Yes, I do.' / 'No, I don't.'
'What sort of music do you like?' 'Rock.'

3 Interview the teacher. Ask him or her questions about his or her day, interests etc. Possible questions:

What time do you get up?
Do you have breakfast?
How do you travel to work?
What time do you start work?
      have lunch?
      stop work?
What do you do in the evenings?
      at the weekend?
What newspaper do you read?
Do you like reading?
What sort of books do you like?
Do you like science fiction?
Do you like fish?
What sort of food do you like?
Do you like beer?
Do you play tennis?
Do you like skiing?
Do you watch football?
Do you like music?
Do you play an instrument?
Are you interested in politics?
What languages do you speak?
Where do you go on holiday?

4 Interview another student. Spend five minutes with him or her, and try to find:

1. Five negative facts (for example, *'He doesn't play tennis.'*).
2. Five things that you both have in common (for example, *'We both like the sea.'*).

5 Write about the student you interviewed.

Unit 6: Lesson C

> **Students learn** to talk about their leisure occupations and interests.
>
> **Structures:** more practice on Simple Present forms, especially interrogatives, negatives and short answers.
>
> **Words and expressions to learn:** *newspaper; book; What sort of...?; read; play; interested in; language; on holiday.*

1 Students' interests

- Ask students to copy the form.
- Ask them to fill in the first entry.
- Then ask what sort of books they read; supply vocabulary as necessary. Make sure they tell you about a *category* of book – they shouldn't give you the name of a particular book they are reading at the moment. Try to bring the term *science fiction* into the discussion; this will be needed for the next exercise.
- Ask students to continue filling in the form, asking you for more words or using their dictionaries as necessary.
- The exercise will probably generate a good deal of new vocabulary. This is *preview* vocabulary (see Introduction page VI), and students don't need to learn it now.
- Make sure the words *fish, beer, football* and *politics* come up – students will need to recognize these in the next exercise.

2 Interrogation

- In this exercise, the tape-recorder 'interrogates' the students, asking them a number of questions about themselves.
- Explain vocabulary in advance if necessary.
- Alternate between chorus and individual replies. You may like to get written answers to three or four of the questions. There is a pause after each question, but you will need to stop the recording when you want written replies.
- You may like to go through the exercise twice or more so that students can increase their fluency.
- Check that short answers (*Yes, I do, No, I'm not* etc.) are correct.

Tapescript for Exercise 2
Hello. How are you?
What's your name?
Where are you from?
What do you do?
Are you married?
Have you got any brothers or sisters?
Where do you live?
What's your address?
What's your phone number?
How old are you?
Pardon?
Do you speak English?
What newspapers do you read?
Do you like music?
What sort of music do you like?
Do you play football?
Do you watch football?
Do you like reading?

Do you read science fiction?
What sort of books do you like?
Do you like fish?
Do you like beer?
What drinks do you like?
Where do you go on holiday?
Are you interested in politics?
Are you interested in maths?

3 Interviewing the teacher

- A list of questions is given in the Student's Book for reference, but it is much better if students can make up the questions for themselves.
- Ask them to close their books and work in groups to prepare a list of questions to ask you about yourself. (Like the questions the recording has just asked them.)
- When they are ready, they can open their books and compare their lists against the list in the book, making any corrections or adjustments that they wish to.
- Get them to ask you their questions. They don't need to note the answers.

4 Interviewing another student

- Put students in pairs. Each student has five minutes to interview the other – give a signal when it's time to change over.
- They can use the same questions as they used for Exercise 3.
- When they have finished, ask them to report some of the negative facts and things in common that they have found out, either to another student or to the class. This gives practice in third person forms (e.g. *Mario doesn't like fish*). *neg. dislikes*

Optional activities
1. Exercise 4 can be done as a role-play, with students taking parts such as Cleopatra, the President etc., and answering appropriately.
2. False beginners who have some extra vocabulary can play a variant of 'Twenty questions' called 'Who am I?' A volunteer student is a famous person. The others have to find out his or her identity by asking questions; the only answers that are allowed are *Yes* and *No*.

5 Writing

- If time allows, this can be done as a supervised class writing exercise. Otherwise students can do it for homework.
- Encourage students to join sentences with *and* and *but*.

Practice Book
- Tell students which exercises you want them to do.

Unit 6: Lesson D

Students consolidate what they have learnt so far in the unit.
Structures: revision of Simple Present forms.
Words and expressions to learn: *tea; coffee; beer; wine; drink.*
Phonology: stress and rhythm; decoding fast speech.

1 Listening to authentic speech

- This will seem difficult at first: some native English speakers were asked to talk about their likes and dislikes, and some of the language used is advanced.
- However, students will discover that they can complete the task (filling in the table) without understanding more than a part of what is said.
- Ask them to close their books and listen to the first section (Lorna's). Then ask them to tell you any words or phrases they remember from the recording. This will encourage them to realize that they have understood quite a lot.
- Get them to open their books. Play the first section again.
- Discuss the answers.
- Play the rest of the recording, stopping occasionally to give students time to mark their answers.
- Tell the students to write *?* if a drink is not mentioned.
- Don't go over the whole text, or waste time answering questions about words and expressions that they have not understood. (For an explanation of the purpose of this kind of exercise, see Introduction page X.)

Tapescript and answers to Exercise 1

LORNA
'Hot drinks, I think I prefer (a) good cup of strong coffee with cream.'
'Do you like wine?'
'Yes, I love wine, especially white wine.'
'Yeah. Gin?'
'Gin, yes, I like gin. I don't get a chance to drink, you know, that much, so I've just tried a bit of everything, and so I like most things really.'

KATY
'Um, well, um, I like, um, I like coffee, coffee with cream in the morning and cof... black coffee later on in the day. I'm not crazy about tea but I'll drink tea occasionally. Um, I drink a lot of water, actually, um, occasional glass of wine, I like gin and tonic, um, I like beer occasionally, um, I guess that's about it.'

PAT
'I like tea, most of the time. And, uh, coffee I like, pure coffee only, just after an evening meal. Um, it's mainly the hot drinks I like. Cold drinks, I like, well in summer I like soft drinks, you know, orange, lemon, whatever's going. I like any beers, and I'll develop a taste for most things. That's me.'

RUTH
'Hot drinks, tea and coffee, both equally; coffee has to be strong and very milky or creamy. Umm, I like wine, I like beer, uh, ah, it's a ... great drink.'

	Coffee	Wine	Gin	Beer	Tea
Lorna	√	√	√	?	?
Katy	√	√	√	√	√
Pat	√	?	?	√	√
Ruth	√	√	?	√	√

2 Pronunciation (rhythm)

- Get students to mark where they think the stresses are.
- Play the recording (or say the sentences) and let students make any corrections they want to.
- Get the students to practise saying the sentences.

3 Listening to fast speech

- This exercise trains students to hear unstressed words in fast natural speech.
- Play the first sentence, and ask everybody to decide how many words there are in it.
- Count contractions (*Edinburgh's, they've*) as two words.
- Then ask what the words are. Put the correct sentence on the board.
- Do the other sentences in the same way.

Tapescript for Exercise 3
Excuse me. What's your address?
Where are you from?
Do you like mountains?
Yes, I love them.
There are two bedrooms in our house.
There are two chairs and a table in the bedroom.
Do you like your work?
Edinburgh's in the south of Scotland.
They've got two children.
A boy and a girl.
Maria and her mother are both doctors.

4 Grammar revision

- You may like to do this exercise, or part of it, as a test, with everybody writing the answers, so that you can see if any students are having problems with the grammar of this unit.

5 Summary

- Look over the summary with the students and make sure there are no problems.

Practice Book
- Tell students which exercises you want them to do.

---

[1]Authentic recording of spontaneous speech.

D What does Lorna drink?

1 Listening for information. Listen to the recording and complete the table. Put a ✓ for the things each person drinks. Part of Lorna's table is done for you.

	Coffee	Wine	Gin	Beer	Tea
Lorna	✓	✓			
Katy					
Pat					
Ruth					

2 Pronunciation. Where are the stresses?

1. What does she do? Where does she work? How does she go to work?
2. Where do you live? What time do you stop work? Do you work on Saturdays?
3. Yes, I do. No, I don't. Yes, he does. No, he doesn't.

3 Listening to fast speech. How many words are there? What are they? Contractions like *what's* count as two words.

'No thanks – I don't drink.'

4 Grammar revision.

A. Put in *do, don't, does* or *doesn't*.
1. '............ you like fish?' 'Yes, I ....'
2. Where .... Sally live?
3. I'm sorry, I .... know.
4. '............ your mother work?' 'No, she ....'
5. What newspaper .... you read?
6. What newspaper .... your father read?

B. Make questions.
1. you | tired? *Are you tired?*
2. Lucy | like beer? *Does Lucy like beer?*
3. Where | your father | work?
4. they | work on Saturdays?
5. Alex and Jimmie | like skiing?
6. she | German?
7. What time | you | stop work?
8. your sister | pretty?

5 Look at the summary on page 139 with your teacher.

29

Food and drink

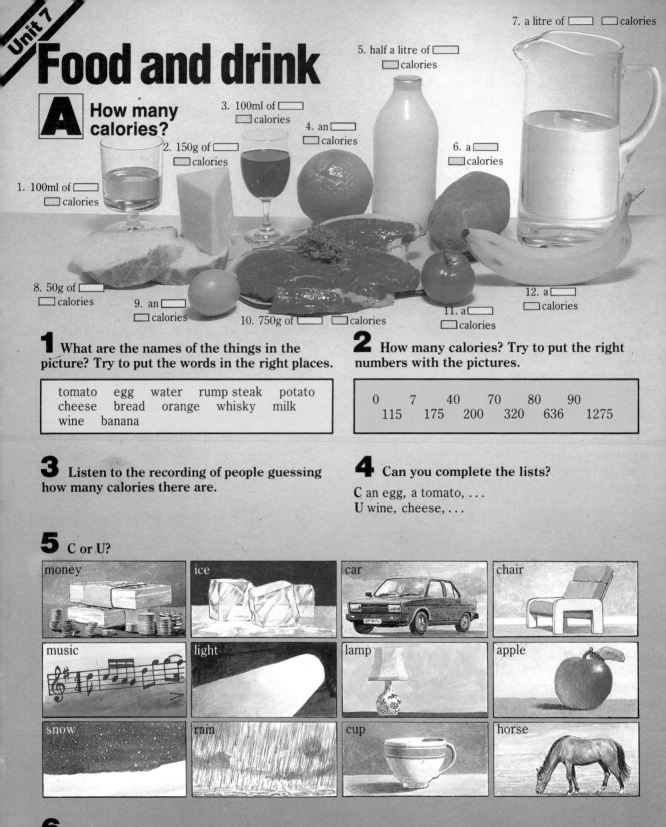

A How many calories?

1. 100ml of ☐ ☐ calories
2. 150g of ☐ ☐ calories
3. 100ml of ☐ ☐ calories
4. an ☐ ☐ calories
5. half a litre of ☐ ☐ calories
6. a ☐ ☐ calories
7. a litre of ☐ ☐ calories
8. 50g of ☐ ☐ calories
9. an ☐ ☐ calories
10. 750g of ☐ ☐ calories
11. a ☐ ☐ calories
12. a ☐ ☐ calories

1 What are the names of the things in the picture? Try to put the words in the right places.

> tomato   egg   water   rump steak   potato
> cheese   bread   orange   whisky   milk
> wine   banana

2 How many calories? Try to put the right numbers with the pictures.

> 0   7   40   70   80   90
> 115   175   200   320   636   1275

3 Listen to the recording of people guessing how many calories there are.

4 Can you complete the lists?

C an egg, a tomato, . . .
U wine, cheese, . . .

5 C or U?

money
ice
car
chair
music
light
lamp
apple
snow
rain
cup
horse

6 Pronunciation. Try to say these words with the right stress.

tomato   potato   orange   whisky   banana   calorie   family   bathroom   television
wardrobe   furniture   intelligent   boyfriend   eleven   thirty   thirteen

Unit 7: Lesson A

> **Students begin** work on quantification, in the context of food and drink.
> **Structures:** the difference between countable and uncountable nouns; no indefinite article with uncountables; *of* in expressions of quantity; *half a ....*
> **Words and expressions to learn:** *gram; litre; money; listen to; try;* names of some foods and drinks (students choose how many to learn).
> **Phonology:** practice of word-stress.

Language notes and possible problems
Countable and uncountable nouns   This terminology is adopted (in preference to 'count and mass nouns') because of its widespread use in standard dictionaries.

The distinction between countable and uncountable nouns is important for correct use of articles and quantifiers. It is, however, a difficult and abstract concept, and some students may take time to grasp it, especially if it does not correspond to a grammatical distinction in their languages. Even where a student's language does have the same distinction, certain nouns may be countable in English and uncountable in another language, or vice versa (the word for *hair* is plural in many languages, for instance).

The distinction is often arbitrary (compare *lentils* and *rice*, or *soot* and *ashes*, or *wheat* and *oats*). Note also that many nouns have both countable and uncountable uses (e.g. *paper, potato, glass*).

Optional extra materials
You may wish to bring concrete examples of countable and uncountable things into the classroom, for additional practice. Suggestions: salt, sugar, tea, polish, make-up, a brush, a stamp, a toy, a photo, a ring. Avoid 'grainy' things like rice, peas, grapes, unground coffee – usage here is inconsistent.

1 Presentation of vocabulary
● Ask students to look at the picture and to try to write the answers. They can do this in groups, pooling their knowledge – or it can be a dictionary exercise.
● Give the answers and practise the pronunciation.

2 Guessing the number of calories
● Make it clear that students are not expected to *know* the number of calories – they have to see how many they can guess right. They may get some surprises.
● The exercise can be done individually, or in groups (with each group giving an agreed group answer after discussion).

Answers
water 0	bread 115
tomato 7	potato 175
orange 40	whisky 200
wine 70	milk 320
banana 80	cheese 636
egg 90	rump steak 1275

3 Listening: other people's guesses
● This is a recording of some native speakers of English trying to do what the students have just done – guess how many calories there are in various items of food and drink.
● Just play the recording once or twice for the students' entertainment – there is no task.

4 Countable and uncountable nouns
● Don't tell students what is meant by 'C' and 'U'. Ask them what words from Exercise 1 they think can be put in each list.
● If they have trouble in deciding, put on the board:
  Is... C or U?
and get them to ask you questions about the various words they have learnt.
● They should see sooner or later that the top list contains words with *a/an*, and the other has words with no article.
● Explain that the words with *a/an* are the names of things you can count; the other words are the names of things you can't count – they have no plurals. (You can say *three tomatoes* but not **three milks*.)
● Tell them that *a/an* means *one*.
● Teach *countable* and *uncountable*.

5 C or U?
● Get students to tell you what they think.
● Then tell them to write the words in two lists – countable words with *a/an* added, and uncountables.
● Ask if they know any more countable or uncountable words.
● You may like to show some other examples of countable and uncountable things.

Optional activities
● Additional conversation practice can be provided as follows:
1. Teach *I (don't) like* and ask students to tell you which of the foods in the illustration they like and which they don't.
2. Ask them to choose a meal by putting together some of the things in the illustration.

6 Word-stress
● Ask students to try to decide (individually or by group discussion) where the stress comes on each word.
● Correct them if necessary and practise saying the words.

Practice Book
● Tell students which exercises you want them to do.

Hanetsuki Game
Hane
wooden ball
Hagoita – paddle
paint brush

30

Unit 7: Lesson B

Students learn to talk about prices.
Structures: non-use of indefinite article with plural nouns; no article with nouns used in a general sense; *to be* used for prices; *80p **a** kilo*, etc.; *I was, they were*.
Words and expressions to learn: *price; terrible; Do you know?; pound (£); pence (p); I know; yesterday; kilo*.
Phonology: practice in rhythm, stress, linking and intonation.

Language notes and possible problems

1. Money You may want to explain the British monetary system. Note the common use of *p* (/piː/) instead of *pence*.

2. Improvisation Exercise 4 involves some simple improvisation. If your students are not yet able to manage this sort of work, let them prepare their conversations instead.

Optional extra materials

A few shopping bags will add realism to the improvisation in Exercise 4.

---

1 Listening for information

- Ask students to close their books, and play the conversation while they listen.
- Play it again, and ask them to write down the names of any items of food or drink they recognize.
- Play it again, and ask them to listen for the prices of potatoes (two prices), tomatoes (two prices), milk, rump steak, oranges, cheese and bananas.
- Play it one more time, and ask students to note down any uncountable nouns they hear.
- Tell students to open their books. Go through the dialogue checking the answers and explaining any difficulties.
- Point out the irregular spelling of the plurals *tomatoes* and *potatoes*.
- You may also want to point out that *a/an* is not used with plurals, and that *the* is not used with plurals when they have a general sense.

2 Rhythm, stress and linking

- Practise the words and expressions.
Note:
1. Weak pronunciation of *a*, *are* and *was* (/wəz/).
2. Pronunciation of *Do you know?* (/djə'nəʊ/).
3. Syllables in bold type are stressed.
4. Words beginning with a vowel should not be separated from preceding words in the same phrase.

3 Intonation practice

- Get students to say some of the sentences after you or after the recording. Concentrate on getting the intonation reasonably correct.
- Then ask them to practise in pairs, going through the dialogue.

4 Improvisation

- Get a volunteer group of good students (four or five), give them shopping bags, and ask them to act out a conversation between shoppers who meet in the street. It doesn't need to go on longer than 30 seconds.
- Put the other students in groups and get them to try the same.
- Real beginners may find this too difficult. They could prepare conversations of between six and eight lines in groups of three.

5 *a/an* with countable nouns

- This can be done orally (if you want a general idea of whether the point has been grasped), or individually in writing if you want to see who is having difficulty.

6 *is/are/was/were*

- When students have done the exercise, you may like to give them all the persons of the past of *to be*.

Practice Book

- Tell students which exercises you want them to do.

B It's terrible

- It's terrible.
- The prices
- Oh, dear.
- Do you know potatoes are eighty pence a kilo?
- Eighty pence a kilo? In our supermarket they're eighty-five.
- It's terrible.
- Oh, dear.
- Everything's so expensive.
- Do you know tomatoes are £1.20 a kilo?
- £1.20? In our supermarket they're £1.30.
- No!!!
- Yes!
- It's terrible.
- Milk's seventy-five pence a litre.
- Half a kilo of rump steak is £7.50.
- An orange costs 20p. One orange!
- And cheese!
- I know!
- Do you know, yesterday I was in Patterson's
- Were you?
- Yes, and cheese was £6.30 a kilo.
- £6.30?
- Yes, and bananas were £2.25.
- It's terrible.

1 Listen to the conversation (books closed) and answer the teacher's questions.

2 Say these words and expressions.

It's terrible
eighty pence a kilo
Potatoes are eighty pence a kilo.
In our supermarket
they're eighty-five.
expensive
Everything's so expensive.
tomatoes are one pound twenty
one pound twenty a kilo
half a kilo
an orange
I was in Patterson's
Do you know?
bananas were two pounds twenty-five

3 Practise the conversation.

4 Make short conversations in groups of four or five.

5 Put in a/an where necessary.

1. A .... kilo of rump steak is very expensive.
2. There are 424 calories in 100g of .... cheese.
3. .... potatoes are not very expensive.
4. .... orange is 20p.
5. There are 7 calories in .... tomato.
6. There are no calories in .... water.
7. 'How much are .... bananas?' '£2.25 a kilo.'
8. .... wine is expensive in Britain.

6 Put in is, are, was or were.

1. Yesterday I .... in London.
2. Steak .... very expensive.
3. Yesterday my mother and father .... in Manchester.
4. Oranges .... £1.40 a kilo
5. In 1960, oranges .... 20p a kilo and a bottle of wine .... 60p.

C Have you got a good memory?

1 Find out the names of the animals etc. (Ask your teacher.)

2 Talk about the picture.
Examples:

'There's some water in the big field.'
'There are some pigs in the small field.'
'There are some sheep on the mountain.'

3 Have you got a good memory?
Close your book, listen and answer the questions.
Examples:

'Is there any grass on the mountain?'
'Yes, there is.'

'Are there any chickens in the big field?'
'No, there aren't.'

'I don't remember.'

4 Write five questions about the picture. Close your book. Ask another student your questions, and answer his or her questions.

5 Listen to the questions. Answer:

'Yes, there is.'   'No, there isn't.'
'Yes, there's one.'   'No, there aren't.'
'Yes, there are.'

6 Make sentences.

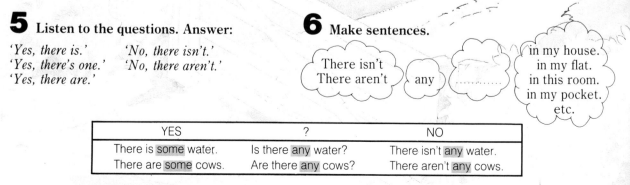

There isn't / There aren't — any — .... — in my house. / in my flat. / in this room. / in my pocket. / etc.

YES	?	NO
There is some water.	Is there any water?	There isn't any water.
There are some cows.	Are there any cows?	There aren't any cows.

Unit 7: Lesson C

Students learn more about quantification.
Structures: *some* and *any* with uncountables and plurals.
Words and expressions to learn: *memory*; *tree*; *grass*; *I don't understand*; *I don't remember*. If students are interested, some of the following as well: *cow*; *pig*; *chicken*; *sheep*; *horse*; *duck*.
Phonology: practice of weak forms (e.g. *There are some* . . . /ðərəsəm/).

Language notes and possible problems

1. Some/any The meaning of *some/any* may be difficult to get across (they are used to talk about a limited but indefinite quantity or number).
2. Singular countables Some students may try to make examples using *some* or *any* with singular countable nouns (e.g. **There isn't any TV in my house*). Get them to keep to uncountables and plurals for the moment.
3. There is/are Students' command of *there is/are* is probably still precarious.
4. People, sheep Note the irregular plurals *people* and *sheep*.
5. Unstress Students will find it hard to pronounce a string of unstressed weak forms as in *There are some* . . . Don't be too perfectionist about this.

1 Asking about vocabulary

● Don't start by telling students the names of the animals etc. – get them to ask you. (This is good training for 'real-life' use of English.)
● Remind them how to say *What's this in English?* and *How do you say . . . in English?*
● They will probably use mime and animal noises to help them – this or any other useful strategy should be encouraged.

2 Some

● Practise the pronunciation of the example sentences. Encourage weak forms (*There are some* is pronounced /ðərəsəm/).
● Explain *field*.
● Get at least one example from everybody, but don't let it go on too long, or the exercise will become boring.

3 Presentation of *any*: memory test

● Practise the short answers in the examples.
● Tell students to close their books.
● Play the recording.
● Pause long enough after each question for students to answer.

Tapescript and answers to Exercise 3
Is there any grass on the mountain? (Yes)
Are there any chickens in the big field? (No)
Are there any dogs in the small field? (No)
Is there any water in the big field? (Yes)
Are there any ducks on the mountain? (No)
Are there any people in the small field? (No)
Are there any sheep on the mountain? (Yes)
Are there any chickens on the mountain? (No)
Are there any trees on the mountain? (Yes)
Is there any water in the small field? (No)

4 Practice of *any* (questions)

● Point out that *any*, not *some*, is usually used in questions.
● When students write their questions they should note the answers.
● Make sure they use plural or uncountable nouns.
● After they have questioned each other, you can get them to question you and test your memory.

5 Personalization

● This is a more difficult exercise, because students don't know what to expect.
● Play each question more than once if necessary, but don't 'translate' the questions into slower English. It is important for students to practise understanding natural speech.
● Students should answer or say *I don't know* or *I don't understand* (write these on the board) if they can't answer.
● When the exercise is over you can write the questions on the board if you wish.

Tapescript for Exercise 5
Is there any water in this room?
Is there any cheese in your house?
Are there any Americans in this room?
Are there any doctors in the class?
Is there any money on your table?
Is there any wine in your fridge?
Are there any eggs in your fridge?
Are there any chairs in your bedroom?
Are there any dogs in your house?
Is there any bread in your kitchen?

6 *Any* in negative sentences

● Before starting, point out that *any*, not *some*, is used in negative sentences.

Grammatical summary

● Finish by looking at the table at the bottom of the page.
● Make sure all students understand the difference between *some* and *any*.

Practice Book

● Tell students which exercises you want them to do.

Unit 7: Lesson D

Students continue their work on quantification.
Structures: *how much* and *how many*; *too much* and *too many*; *not much*, *not many* and *a lot of*; *enough*.
Words and expressions to learn: *toothpaste*; *shaving cream*; *perfume*; *light*; *chips*; *hair*.

Language notes and possible problems
1. *Much* and *many* Students will easily see that *much* and *many* are used with uncountable and plural nouns respectively.
2. *A lot of* Note that *much* and *many* are unusual in affirmative sentences in an informal style (except after *too*, *so* and sometimes *very*). Students should be encouraged to say, for instance, *I've got a lot of friends* or *There is a lot of noise* rather than *I've got many friends* or *There is much noise*, which sound unnatural.
3. *Hair* may cause problems – the equivalent in some languages is a plural countable, so students will be tempted to say **too many hairs*.

1 Presentation of *how much/many*
● Students learn to distinguish the two expressions at the same time as they do a simple general knowledge quiz.

Answers
1. 50 (though European atlases often count the District of Columbia, making a total of 51)
2. 75cl
3. 110 million bottles
4. Nine (Mercury, Venus, Earth, Mars, Jupiter, Saturn, Uranus, Neptune, Pluto)
5. 60%
6. Usually 88
7. After breathing in, between one and a half and two litres
8. Four

● After doing the quiz, students may like to try to make up their own general knowledge questions to ask the rest of the class, using *how much* and *how many*.
● You will need to help with vocabulary.

2 Authentic listening
● Students may be interested to listen to this short recording of some English people trying to answer some of the questions in the quiz.
● They will not understand every word, but will have no difficulty in following the gist of what is said.

3 Listening: *not much/many; a lot of*
● Students will hear a series of conversations and sounds – their job is to say or write appropriate phrases to describe what they hear.
● Before starting, practise the pronunciation of *a lot of* (/ə'lɒtəv/).
● Explain that it means the same as *much/many*, but that *a lot of* is more common in affirmative sentences in spoken English.

Answers to Exercise 3
Suitable descriptions of the situations are:
1. not many people
2. a lot of people
3. not much money
4. a lot of cats
5. a lot of food
6. not much time
7. not many students
8. a lot of girlfriends
9. a lot of money
10. a lot of water
11. not much food

4 The classroom
● Students should be able to think of several examples (you may need to help with vocabulary).
● The exercise can be extended by looking out of the window; thinking about the whole building; about the students' homes; about the town.
● Encourage correct pronunciation of *a lot of*.

5 *Not enough; too much/many*
● Translate or demonstrate *not enough*, *enough*, and *too much/many*.
● Practise the pronunciation of *enough*.
● Do the first two or three examples together.
● Get students to do the exercise individually or in small groups, comparing notes when they have finished.

6 Personalization
● Ask students to write one or two sentences first.
● Get them to tell you what they have written, and see if they can make more examples orally.

7 Summary
● Look over the summary with the students and see if there are any problems.

Practice Book
● Tell students which exercises you want them to do.

D Not enough money

1 Quiz. Put *how much* or *how many*; answer the questions. Make some questions yourself.

1. .... states are there in the USA – 36, 49, 50 or 60?
2. .... wine is there in a normal bottle – 75cl, 85cl or 95cl?
3. .... Coca Cola is drunk in the world in one day – one million bottles, 11 million bottles or 110 million bottles?

4. .... planets (Mercury, Venus etc.) are there – 7, 9, 11 or 13?
5. .... of a person is water – 40%, 60% or 90%?
6. .... keys are there on a piano – 70, 82 or 88?
7. .... air is there in our lungs – half a litre, one and a half litres or two and a half litres?
8. .... Beatles were there – 3, 4 or 5?

2 Listen to the recording of people trying to do the quiz.

3 Listen, and choose the right words for each situation.
Example: *1. 'not many people'*

> not much
> not many
> a lot of

> people cats cigarettes
> students food money
> time water girlfriends

4 Talk about the classroom. Begin:

'There isn't much...'
'There aren't many...'
'There is/are a lot of...'

5 Look at the pictures and choose the right words.

> not enough
> too much
> too many

> people toothpaste
> hair perfume light shaving cream money
> cars toilets children chips hair numbers

6 Talk about yourself.

'I've got enough/too much/too many...'
'I haven't got enough...'

7 Look at the summary on page 140 with your teacher.

33

Where?

A Where's the nearest post office?

1 Put the words with the correct pictures.

> phone box   supermarket   bank   post office
> police station   car park   bus stop   station

2 Listen and practise these dialogues.

A: Excuse me. Where's the nearest post office, please?
B: It's over there on the [right ⟩ / ⟨ left.]
A: Oh, thank you very much.
B: Not at all.

———◇———

A: Excuse me. Where's the nearest bank, please?
B: I'm sorry, I don't know.
A: Thank you anyway.

3 Complete these dialogues and practise them.

A: .... the manager's
   office, ...?
B: .... by the
   reception desk.
A: ....

———◇———

A: .... the
   toilets, ...?
B: Upstairs .... the first floor, first
   door .... left.
A: .... much.

4 Make up similar conversations and practise them.

1. *post office*

2. ....

3. ....

4. ....

5. ....

6. ....

7. ....

8. ....

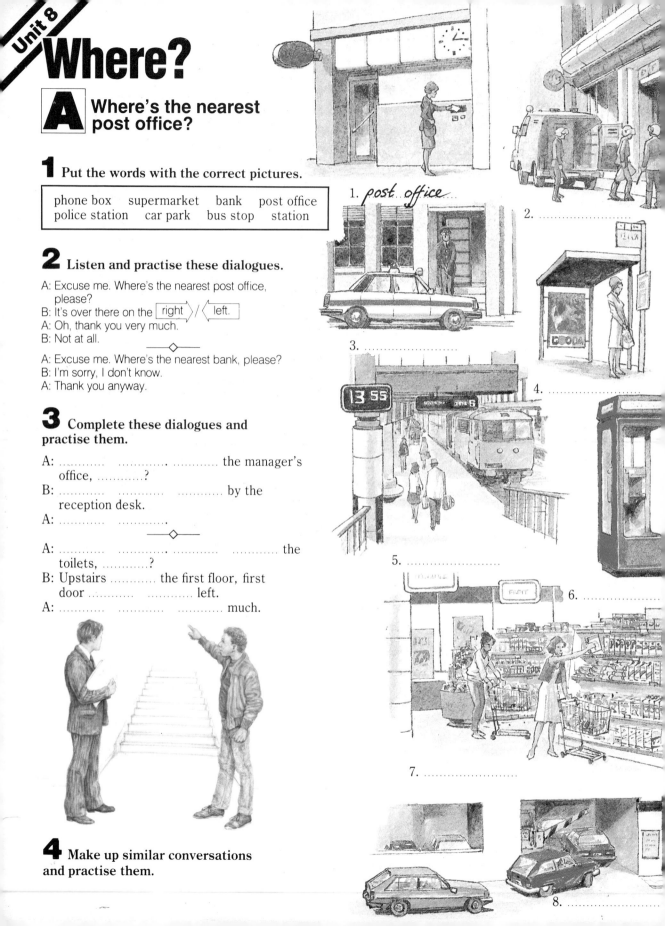

Unit 8: Lesson A

Students learn to ask for and give directions.
Structures: no new structures.
Words and expressions to learn: *phone box; supermarket; bank; post office; police; police station; car park; bus stop; station; there; over there; on the right/left; thank you anyway; not at all; by* (place); *upstairs; downstairs.*
Phonology: intonation of polite questions.

Language notes and possible problems

1. Intonation   Intonation is difficult to describe by precise rules. It is best to teach it by imitation exercises in well-defined situations. In Exercise 2 help students to hear how the question-word *where* is pronounced on a high pitch, and how the voice falls and rises at the end of the sentence. It is this (even more than the use of *Excuse me* and *please*) that makes a question or request sound polite.

2. Answer to *Thank you*   Students should realize that *Not at all* is not an automatic answer to *Thank you* – it doesn't come in all of these dialogues. People often make no reply when they are thanked for small things.

3. Additional vocabulary   Students may want to learn the words for some more of the places that one might ask one's way to (e.g. *swimming pool, pub, restaurant*). Teach more words at your discretion, but don't allow the students to become overloaded with vocabulary.

Optional extra materials
Cards with names of places for Optional activity, Exercise 4.

1 Presentation of vocabulary
● This can be done in small groups, with students pooling their knowledge. (With real beginners who don't know any of the words, and who don't have cognate words in their languages which would help them to guess, tell them the answers.)
● Practise the pronunciation of the new vocabulary.

2 Dialogues
● Play the dialogues once or twice while students listen with their books closed.
● Ask them to recall words and expressions.
● Get the class to help you build up the dialogues on the board.
● Open books and play again while students follow the text.
● Explain new words and expressions.
● Practise the sentences, paying special attention to intonation, linking and rhythm.
● Ask students to practise in pairs until they can do it without the books (changing over so that each student plays both parts).

3 Dialogue completion
● Students can do this in groups – the missing expressions can be found in the dialogues in Exercise 2.
● Explain any difficulties. Teach *downstairs*.
● Get students to practise the new dialogues once or twice.

Answers to Exercise 3
A: Excuse me. Where's the manager's office, please?
B: It's over there by the reception desk.
A: Thank you.

A: Excuse me. Where are the toilets, please?
B: Upstairs on the first floor, first door on the left.
A: Thank you very much.

4 Extension and improvisation
● Ask students (working in pairs) to make up similar conversations, using words and expressions from the dialogues they have just studied, but varying and combining elements so as to make something a little different.
● You might like to do one on the board with the students first of all to give them the idea.
● Tell them to practise their conversations.
● Finally, do a 'walk-round' exercise with the class divided into two groups: 'strangers' and 'natives'.
● Tell them to imagine that they are in a particular well-known place (e.g. the town centre; the entrance to the school).
● Strangers stop natives and ask them the way to various places; natives improvise their answers.
● After a time, change over roles.

Optional activities
1. If possible, develop Exercise 4 by taking students out into the street or into other parts of the building – this gives much more realistic practice.
2. If necessary, give 'strangers' cards with the names of places that they have to ask the way to.
3. Another approach is to draw a simple town plan on the board and ask students to copy it, filling in the station, car park etc. where they want to. Then do a 'walk-round' exercise as above; 'natives' use their maps to work out their answers.

Practice Book
● Tell students which exercises you want them to do.

Unit 8: Lesson B

Students learn more ways of giving and asking for directions.
Structures: *for* with expressions of distance.
Words and expressions to learn: *near; nearest; opposite; straight on; then; yard; how far?; swimming pool; next to; take.*

Language notes and possible problems

1. Vocabulary   Exercise 5 introduces some new vocabulary which might overload weaker students. Drop the exercise if you think they will find it too daunting.

2. Yards occurs in Exercise 1 – this is the word students will hear if they ask for directions in Britain, and they must know it. (For practical purposes, a yard is close to a metre.) Students may prefer to use *metre* in their own practice (for instance in Exercise 4).

Optional extra materials

Photocopies of the local town plan, or of a plan of some other place that students know, would be useful. (See Alternative to Exercise 4.)

1 Separating dialogues

● This is quite a demanding exercise. It can be done in groups, or (with weaker classes) as a whole-class activity.
● Get students to put words in all the blanks before attempting to separate the two conversations and put the sentences in order.
● Students will need to ask you about the meaning of some of the new words and expressions as they do the exercise. Remind them to say *What does... mean?*
● When they are ready, let them compare notes and check their answers. (Note that *Not at all* can come at the end of either conversation.)
● You may like to get students to practise the conversations in pairs – standing up and acting out the situations if possible.

Answers to Exercise 1

'Excuse me. Where's the nearest car park, please?'
'First on the right, then second on the left. It's next to the post office.'
'How far is it?'
'About five hundred yards.'
'Thank you very much.' (OR: 'Thanks very much.')
('Not at all.')

'Excuse me. Is there a swimming pool near here?'
'Yes. It's opposite the car park. Go straight on for about three hundred yards.'
'Thanks very much.' (OR: 'Thank you very much.')
('Not at all.')

2 Memory test

● Give students a couple of minutes to memorize the map. Then put them in groups of four or so. One questions the others, looking at the map if necessary.

Alternative to Exercise 2

● As a variant, you can get students to test each other on their knowledge of the town where they are studying.

3 Listening practice

● Before playing the first section (which starts 'You are at A'), point out A, B, C and D on the map.

Tapescript for Exercise 3

1. You are at A. Go straight on, take the second street on the left and the first on the right. Where are you? (**Answer:** in Wood Street.)
2. You are at C. Go down Park Road, turn right, turn left into Station Road, go straight on for about 200 yards. Where are you? (**Answer:** by the railway station and the police station.)
3. You are at D. Take the first left, second right and first left. Where are you? (**Answer:** near the bus stop in Wood Street.)

4 Giving directions

● This can be done in small groups, with students taking turns to give directions. The others follow on the map, as in Exercise 3.

Alternative to Exercise 4

● A variant of this exercise can be done with copies of the local town/city map.
● Give students fixed starting points (e.g. 'You are at the end of rue Leblanc facing north'); this avoids confusion.

5 Extension

● This exercise introduces some new vocabulary (which will need explaining).
● In each pair, one student should take list A and the other list B.
● Each student should fill in the new places where he or she wants to (on a copy of the map if you don't want students to write in their books).
● Then students work in pairs as in the example.

Optional activity

● If there is room, pretend the classroom is a central place in a town or city the students know.
● Divide them into tourists and natives.
● Students walk round.
● Tourists stop natives and ask them the way to various places.
● (It is advisable to make sure that everybody knows which way the classroom is supposed to be facing – for instance, the blackboard could be the north side of the square.)

Practice Book

● Tell students which exercises you want them to to.

B First on the right, second on the left

1 Put in the missing words, separate the two conversations, and put the sentences in the right order.

'Yes. It's .... the car park. Go ....
for about three hundred ....,'
'Excuse me. .... the nearest car park,
..........................?'
'Thank you very much.'
.... on the right, then second ....
It's next to the post office.'
'.......................... is it?'
'..........................,'
'........................... Is there a .... near here?'
'Thanks very much.'
'About five hundred yards.'

first	please	not at all	opposite	where's
on the left	how far	straight on	excuse me
yards	swimming pool

2 Look at the map. Then work with another student and test his or her memory.

'Where's the police station?' 'Opposite the railway station.'
'Where's the car park?' 'I don't remember.'

3 Listen and follow the directions on the map. Then say where you are.

4 Give directions to other students. Example:

'You are at A. Take the first left, second right, first right, second right, and go straight on for about three hundred metres. Where are you?'

5 Copy the map. Then put in *either* the places in list A *or* the places in list B.

A. a supermarket   B. a church
   a swimming pool   a good restaurant
   a bookshop   a good hotel *drug store*
   a phone box *(booth)*   a chemist's *(pharmacy)*
   a cheap restaurant   a public toilet
   a cheap hotel

Work in pairs. Ask and give directions (you are at A on the map). Example:

'Excuse me. Is there a bookshop near here, please?'
'Yes. First left, second right, in Station Road.'
'Thank you.'

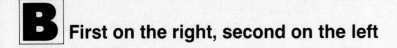

metres
0 ⊢—┼—┼—┼—┤ 300
yards

scale

35

C Where are they?

1 Listen to the conversation.
Where is Simon's house?

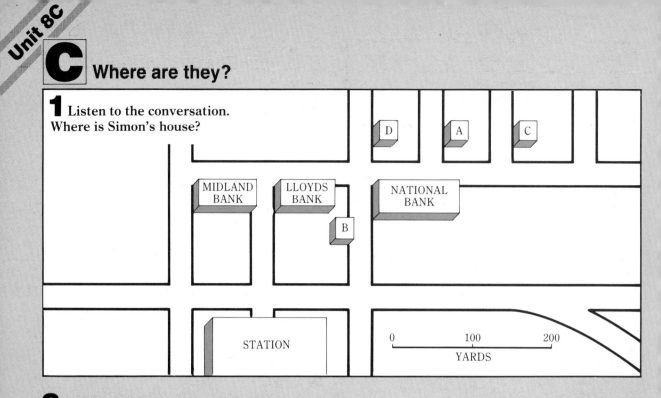

2 Listen to the conversation. Which flat is Sally's?

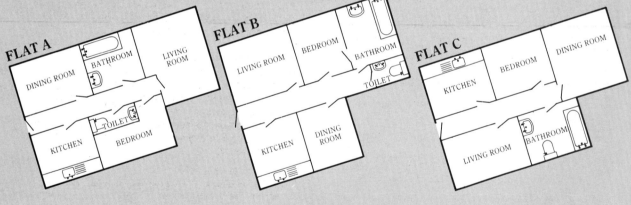

FLAT A

FLAT B

FLAT C

3 Listen to the conversations.
Where are the people?

Nelly	
Mrs Jackson	
Jane	
Alice	E
John	

A   at the station
B   at the supermarket
C   at the bank
D   at home
E   we don't know
F   at the swimming pool

4 Listen to the recording of somebody asking
the way. Do all the people give the same answer?

5 Pronunciation. Mark the stresses in these
sentences and practise saying them.

How do you do?
Where are you from?
Polly and John are Joyce's parents.
My mother and I are both tall.
Two boys and a girl.
What are their names?
There are two bedrooms in my flat.
What's your address?
I live at twenty-two New Street.
A litre of water.
A kilo of potatoes.
Everything's so expensive.
My birthday is on March the twenty-first.
First on the right, second on the left.

Unit 8: Lesson C

Students carry out a number of tasks designed to give practice in listening comprehension.
Structures: no new structures.
Words and expressions to learn: none.
Phonology: rhythm (sentence-stress).

Language notes and possible problems

1. Listening   Some students may find the four listening exercises rather too much. If so, drop or postpone one or more of them.

2. Rhythm   Exercise 5 is a difficult and important one for students whose languages do not have the same kind of 'stress-timed' rhythm as English. They must learn to perceive 'weak forms' (such as *and* /ənd/, *of* /əv/), which they find difficult to hear. They also need to learn to speak with proper alternation between slower stressed syllables and faster unstressed syllables – this is much more important for comprehensibility than mastering individual sounds.

1 Where is Simon's house?

- In this exercise and the next two, students are not expected to understand everything they hear (as they will not when they listen to English in real life).
- If they listen carefully, they will understand the information they need in order to do the exercise.
- Point out A, B, C and D on the map. Simon's house is at one of these.
- Play the recording one or more times (depending on the level of the class). Let students compare notes before giving the answers.

Tapescript for Exercise 1
SIMON: (on the phone) OK, Bill. So we'll see you about eight o'clock.
BILL: OK, Simon. That's fine. Oh, by the way, where's your house?
SIMON: Oh, yes, of course, sorry. When you come out of the station, turn right, take the first left, go straight on for about 100 yards, turn right at the bank, and it's the second street on your left. Third house on the right.
BILL: Third house on the right. Great. OK, see you about eight. Bye.
SIMON: Bye, Bill.

(Answer: C)

2 Which flat is Sally's?

- Give students a minute or two to look at the floor plans. If you want to make the exercise easier, get students to describe the flats (seen from the front door) before they listen to the recording.

Tapescript for Exercise 2
My new flat's very comfortable. There's a good kitchen, a small dining room, a living room, a bathroom, a separate toilet, and a bedroom. As you come in the front door, the kitchen's on your right, the dining room's next to the kitchen, the living room and bedroom are opposite the kitchen and dining room, and the bathroom and toilet are at the end of the passage next to the bedroom.

(Answer: B)

3 Listening for information

- Do the exercise in the same way as Exercise 1.

Answers

Nelly	C
Mrs Jackson	D
Jane	F
Alice	E
John	A

Tapescript for Exercise 3: see page 180

4 Authentic listening

- This is an authentic recording of somebody asking for directions.
- There is no specific task for students to carry out – the aim of the exercise is simply to give them practice in listening to natural speech – but ask them to see if there are any differences between the directions given by the different people.
- (In the fourth conversation, the woman is told to go straight on over the crossroads. The first three people tell her – correctly – to turn right at the crossroads. The last person doesn't know where the library is.)

5 Rhythm

- These are all sentences that the students have already met.
- Get them (singly or in groups) to try to mark the stresses with a wavy underline. (Do one or two sentences together on the board so that they get the idea.)
- Go over the answers, and practise saying the sentences. (Use the recording if you wish.)
- Important: note that unstressed syllables tend to be said faster than stressed syllables (this is partly what gives English its characteristic rhythm). Many unstressed syllables are pronounced with the vowel /ə/: for instance, *A kilo of potatoes* is pronounced /ə'ki:ləʊ əv pə'teɪtəʊz/.

Answers to Exercise 5
Typical ways of pronouncing the sentences are as follows (stressed syllables marked in bold type).
How do you **do?**
Where are you **from?**
Polly and **John** are **Joyce's parents.**
My **mother** and **I** are **both tall.**
Two boys and a **girl.**
What are their **names?**
There are **two bed**rooms in **my flat.**
What's your **add**ress?
I **live** at **twenty-two New Street.**
A **litre** of **water.**
A **kilo** of **potatoes.**
Everything's so expensive.
My **birthday** is on **March** the **twenty-first.**
First on the **right,** **second** on the **left.**

Practice Book
- Tell students which exercises you want them to do.

Answers to Practice Book Exercise 2
1. go 2. orange 3. travel 4. this 5. duck (the only bird)
6. home 7. floor 8. bath (the others begin with *th*) 9. four (the others begin with *t*) or three (the only odd number)

36

Unit 8: Lesson D

> **Students learn** to talk about some physical and emotional states.
>
> **Structures:** *to be* with adjectives like *hungry, cold*; more work on *at* with places; preview of *when*-clauses.
>
> **Words and expressions to learn:** some of these (see summary): *hungry; happy; bored; thirsty; tired; cold; unhappy; hot; wet; dirty; disco; cinema; the doctor's; the dentist's: in bed; at home; at school.*

Language notes and possible problems

1. Hungry, cold etc. For some students it may be surprising that the verb *to be* is used to express these ideas.

2. To, at and in It may be necessary to explain the difference between *to* (movement) and *at* or *in* (position).

The difference between *at* and *in* is not easy to explain in simple terms. Get students to note which preposition is used in which expression. Note that *at* is pronounced /ət/ unless stressed.

3. Mime Mime can be a useful device for stimulating speech. However, students need time to get used to it. Start Exercise 3 by demonstrating yourself and calling on volunteers.

1 Matching

• False beginners can try this exercise in groups, pooling their knowledge.
• With real beginners who don't know any of the words, you will have to tell them what each one means.
• Practise the pronunciation of the adjectives.

2 Personalization

• Get students to tell you how they feel. Say how you feel, too.
• Ask a few questions and elicit short answers (*'Are you hungry?' 'No, I'm not.'*).

3 Mime (adjectives)

• Start by miming one of the adjectives yourself and getting students to say, for instance, *You're cold.*
• Ask for volunteers to mime one or two of the other adjectives.
• Continue the work in small groups.

4 Mime (places)

• This can be done by groups. Each group chooses a phrase and mimes it collectively; the rest of the class say where the group is.
• Encourage correct rhythm and stress (e.g. *at a cinema* /ət ə ˈsɪnəmə/).

5 Memory test

• The purpose of this exercise is threefold: to preview *when*-clauses, to give further practice in the adjectives that have just been taught, and to revise the Simple Present tense.
• Note also the useful expressions *have a drink, have a bath, have a wash.*

• Ask students to look over the sentences for just two minutes (time them carefully), and then tell them to close their books.
• Ask them to write (or tell you) the answers to the following questions:
– What does Lucy do when she's thirsty?
– What does Fred do when he's unhappy?
– What does Fred do when he's hot?
– What does Lucy do when she's bored?
– What does Fred do when he's hungry?
– What does Lucy do when she's hungry?
– What does Lucy do when she's unhappy?
– What does Lucy do when she's happy?
– What does Fred do when he's bored?
– What does Lucy do when she's hot?

6 Summary

• Go over the summary with the students.

Practice Book

• Tell students which exercises you want them to do.

D I'm hungry

1. She is ....

2. He is ....

3. She is ....

4. He is ....

5. She is ....

6. He is ....

7. She is ....

8. He is ....

9. She is ....

10. He is ....

1 Put the adjectives with the right pictures.

> hungry tired wet happy cold dirty
> bored unhappy thirsty hot

2 Say how you feel now.

'I'm hungry.' 'I'm thirsty.' 'I'm fine.'

3 Mime one of the adjectives for the class.

You're unhappy.

4 You're in one of these places. Do a mime; the class will say where you are.

> at a swimming pool at a disco at a cinema
> at a pub at a restaurant in bed
> in the bathroom at a car park at the doctor's
> at the dentist's at a supermarket at home
> at school at a bus stop

5 Have you got a good memory? Look at the sentences for two minutes. Then close your books and answer the teacher's questions.

When Fred's hungry he goes to a restaurant.
When Lucy's hungry she has bread and cheese.
When Fred's thirsty he goes to a pub.
When Lucy's thirsty she has a drink of water.
When Fred's bored he goes to the cinema.
When Lucy's bored she watches TV.
When Fred's hot he goes to the swimming pool.
When Lucy's hot she has a drink of water.
When Fred's dirty he has a bath.
When Lucy's dirty she has a wash.
When Fred's happy he sings.
When Lucy's happy she dances.
When Fred's unhappy he goes to bed.
When Lucy's unhappy she has a bath.

6 Look at the summary on page 141 with your teacher.

The World

A How people live

1 Separate the two mixed-up texts. Work in groups. Use dictionaries, but not too much.

AUSTRALIAN ABORIGINES
AMAZON INDIANS

The Karadjere people live in the desert of Western Australia,
These people live in the Amazon Basin, in Brazil,
where the climate is very hot.
where the climate is hot and wet:
and the rest of the year is dry.
It rains from January to March,
it rains for nine to ten months of the year.

They travel by canoe.
They do not live in one place,
They live in villages;
but travel around on foot.
They sleep in shelters made of dry tree branches.
and the roofs are made of palm leaves.
their houses are made of wood,
Several families live in each house.

Their food is fruit, nuts and kangaroo meat,
They eat fruit and vegetables, fish, and meat
   from animals and birds
and they eat fish in the wet season;
(for example monkeys, wild pigs, parrots).
they also make bread from grass seeds.
The Karadjere like music, dancing and telling
   stories.
They like music, dancing and telling stories.
Water is often difficult to find.
They do not wear many clothes.
They do not wear many clothes.

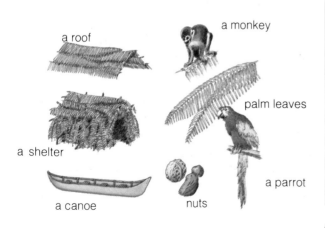

a roof

a monkey

palm leaves

a shelter

a canoe

nuts

a parrot

2 What do you know about the Eskimos' traditional way of life? Write what you know in a short text.

a dog-sledge

a seal

an igloo

a kayak

3 How do you think most Eskimos live today?

Unit 9: Lesson A

Students begin to look at how sentences and texts are put together. They learn some facts about two primitive cultures.
Structures: more work on the Simple Present and its use to refer to regular actions and events. Introduction to complex sentences.
Words and expressions to learn: some of these (see summary): *rain; the rest; dry; on foot; sleep; make; made of; fruit; meat; difficult; wood; wear; fish.*

Possible problem

Vocabulary The texts in Exercise 1 contain a lot of unknown vocabulary. It is important for students to realize that they do not need to understand every word in order to grasp the meaning of the texts and carry out the task. (In 'real-life' reading of English, later on, they will rarely understand every word in a text; this will not usually matter.)
They should only be asked to learn a small number of the new words and expressions (see list above and summary page 142).

Optional extra materials

A copy of the text, cut into strips, for every four or five students (see Exercise 1).

1 Mixed-up texts

● You may like to start by pre-teaching *climate* and *rain*, and by asking students what they know about the climate in Australia and the Amazon basin.
● Start the exercise collectively. Write on the board:

AUSTRALIAN   AMAZON
ABORIGINES   INDIANS

● Write the first sentence of the text under AUSTRALIAN ABORIGINES, the second under AMAZON INDIANS, and ask students where the next sentence should go.
● Then get them to continue the exercise in groups.
● Tell them to use dictionaries only for essential words; they should not look up more than ten words.
● The aim of the exercise is to produce two separate texts. Note that the sentences in the mixed-up version are almost, but not quite, in the correct order.
● A good way to make the exercise work well is to copy the text in advance (one copy for each group), cut the text up into separate strips, and give a set of strips (in an envelope) to each group.
● This makes the exercise a little more difficult (but also more interesting), because students must first separate the strips into two piles (to go with the two pictures) and then arrange each set of strips in a logical order to make a sensible text.
● This is a good opportunity to teach a few appropriate expressions for the group discussion: *this is first; I think this is next; this is/goes after that; this is/goes before that; I think this goes here.*
● If you want to make the exercise easier, number the sections 1, 2 or 3 (corresponding to the three blocks of text in the Student's Book) before you copy and cut out the text. This will help students to work out the order more quickly.

● If you don't want to copy the text yourself, get each group to divide up the task of copying the sentences by hand and dividing them into separate strips.
● In order to do the exercise successfully, students need to pay attention to punctuation, capitalization and the use of conjunctions. As they work, you can walk round helping them to notice signals of this kind.
● Encourage them to use dictionaries only to look up essential words which prevent them from understanding the sense of what they are reading.

Texts for Exercise 1
(Slight variations are possible in the order of sentences.)

Australian Aborigines
The Karadjere people live in the desert of Western Australia, where the climate is very hot. It rains from January to March, and the rest of the year is dry. They do not live in one place, but travel around on foot. They sleep in shelters made of dry tree branches. Their food is fruit, nuts and kangaroo meat, and they eat fish in the wet season; they also make bread from grass seeds. Water is often difficult to find. The Karadjere like music, dancing and telling stories. They do not wear many clothes.

Amazon Indians
These people live in the Amazon basin, in Brazil, where the climate is hot and wet: it rains for nine to ten months of the year. They travel by canoe. They live in villages; their houses are made of wood, and the roofs are made of palm leaves. Several families live in each house. They eat fruit and vegetables, fish, and meat from animals and birds (for example monkeys, wild pigs, parrots). They like music, dancing and telling stories. They do not wear many clothes.

2 Guided composition

● This can be done as a class composition on the board, or as an individual exercise (perhaps for homework) as you prefer.
● The most important thing is that students should use the first two texts to help them write the third. Most of the things they know about the Eskimos can be expressed using sentence-frames they have just seen:
    These people live...; where the climate is...; Their food is...; etc.
● Help with vocabulary as necessary.

3 Discussion

● This can be done as a brief follow-up to the reading and writing work.
● As students will probably imagine, most Eskimos today live in houses, travel by car and bus, and so on. (The large majority of Eskimos have never seen an igloo.)

Practice Book
● Tell students which exercises you want them to do.
● Exercise 2 is a writing exercise related to the texts in the Student's Book. It should be done as a guided composition, using sentence-patterns and vocabulary from the Student's Book texts.
● Exercise 3 gives practice in extensive reading. Students will need to look up some words in their dictionaries. They should try to understand the text at first without looking up every word. Key words are marked.

Unit 9: Lesson B

Students practise replying to statements and learn to express degrees of certainty. The subject-matter is animal behaviour.
Structures: interrogative short answer (*Do they?*); omission of conjunction *that*; position of *certainly*, *perhaps*; transferred negation (*I don't think* + affirmative).
Words and expressions to learn: *that* (conjunction); *I'm sure*; *certainly*; *perhaps*; names of some wild animals and foods.
Phonology: relationship between stress and the vowel /ə/; /iː/ and /ɪ/.

Language notes and possible problems

1. Vocabulary   Students may see this as a vocabulary lesson. In fact, of course, the subject-matter is mainly a vehicle for practising tense usage, ways of replying to statements, and ways of expressing degrees of certainty. (Though it is hoped that most students will find the subject-matter reasonably interesting.) Students who wish to learn the names of the animals should of course do so, but this should not be made compulsory. Some students may want to ask for the names of large numbers of other animals; they should probably be tactfully asked to do this work with a dictionary at home.

2. *That*   The conjunction *that* is often omitted in informal usage after common verbs such as *say*, *think*, *know*. You may wish to tell students (in Exercise 3) that this is more frequent in speech than in writing.

3. Transferred negation   Note that we normally say, for instance, *I don't think cats eat insects*, and not **I think cats don't eat insects*. Not all verbs that introduce *that*-clauses behave in this way (compare *I hope (that) she won't be late*).

1 Matching

● This should be done in groups, with students pooling their knowledge and guesses.
● When they have finished, get them to compare notes between groups; then give them the right answers.
● Practise the pronunciation of the animals' names.
● With complete beginners, you may need to give them the answers straight away (perhaps asking, for each picture, *Does anybody know . . . ?*).

2 Replying to statements

● Practise the various possible replies to an affirmative statement given in the example. You may wish to add others (e.g. *Oh, yes?*).
● Pay attention to linking in *live in*.
● Note the rising intonation on *Do they?*
● *Sure* is normally pronounced /ʃɔː(r)/ (and not /ʃʊə(r)/ as shown in many standard dictionaries).
● Get volunteers to make statements which may be true or false. The other students can reply as they wish.
● If the exercise goes well, continue it in groups.

3 Degrees of certainty

● Practise the examples.
● Draw students' attention to the position of *perhaps* (at the beginning of the sentence) and *certainly* (just before the verb).
● Ask students to make as many examples as they can (you might ask them to write one or two, to make sure that everybody contributes).
● They can probably remember the names of some other animals from Unit 7 (e.g. *horses*, *sheep*).
● This could be done as a walk-round exercise.

4 Unstressed syllables and /ə/

● Students have already learnt (in Lesson 4B) that unstressed syllables are often pronounced /ə/. This exercise will remind them of the point (which is crucial for students who want to achieve a good standard of pronunciation).
● Tell students to copy the words.
● Let them find the stresses for themselves.
● Then play (or say) the words so that they can check. If you say the words yourself, make sure you pronounce them naturally at normal speed, so as not to change /ə/ into the 'written' vowel.
● Play or say the words again, and get students to circle the examples of /ə/.
● They should see that these are always unstressed vowels.
● Put the words, correctly marked, on the board (see below).
● Pronounce the words with the class.

Answers
goríllə   párrət   pólər   tígər   éləphənt
Austráliə   Brəzíl   Áməzən   Əmérikə
Gérmənə   Ítələ   Chínə   Jəpæn   Cánədə

5 /iː/ and /ɪ/

● Students have now learnt a number of words with one or other of these vowels.
● Before starting pronunciation work, you may like to try the following ear-training exercise.
● Write on the board:

   leaves   lives
   eat   it

● Say one of the words and ask students which side it is on, left or right.
● Do this a few times, then add some more pairs such as *Jean/gin*; *feet/fit*; *sheep/ship*.
● Ask students to choose words and say them; you and the rest of the class will say which side of the board they are from.
● Finish by dictating some of the words, chosen at random.
● Then practise the two lists in the Student's Book.
● Apart from pronunciation practice, students will learn a relationship between spelling and pronunciation (that *ea* and *ee* are usually pronounced /iː/, and that *i* is often pronounced /ɪ/.

Practice Book

● Tell students which exercises you want them to do.

B What do parrots eat?

1 Put these words with the correct pictures.

gorilla   camel   parrot   snake   polar bear
tiger   penguin   elephant

2 Make true or false sentences about where animals live.
Examples:

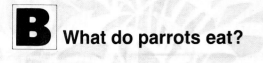

Penguins live in the Arctic.

I know.   Do they?   Are you sure?   No, they don't. They live in the Antarctic.

3 How sure are you? Make sentences about what animals
eat. Use *I know (that); I'm sure (that); certainly; I think (that);
perhaps; I don't think (that).* Examples:

*'Penguins certainly eat fish. I think (that) parrots eat nuts. Perhaps
snakes eat grass. I don't think (that) cats eat insects.'*

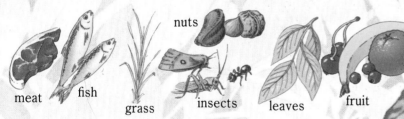

nuts

meat   fish   grass   insects   leaves   fruit

4 Pronunciation.

gorilla   parrot   polar   tiger   elephant   Australia
Brazil   Amazon   America   Germany   Italy   China
Japan   Canada

1. Underline the stressed syllable in each word.
   Example: <u>go</u>rilla
2. Listen and check your answers.
3. Listen again. Circle the vowel (*a, e, i, o* or *u*)
   where you hear /ə/. Example: g(o)rilla
4. Pronounce the words.

5 Pronunciation. Say these words.

eat   meat   leaves   sleep   these   people
seeds   peanuts

it   village   fish   live   in   pig   this
difficult   women   think

39

CD The weather

THE WEATHER IN EAST TEXAS

In East Texas, near the Gulf of Mexico, the climate is hot and often very humid. Temperatures in summer are between 30° and 40°C; 25°C is a normal winter temperature. It is sometimes cold, but only for two or three days at a time; it snows perhaps once every twenty years. It quite often rains heavily for two or three days or more, but most of the time it is sunny with bright blue skies. Occasionally there are droughts – periods when there is no rain for a long time. It is not usually very windy, but there are hurricanes every few years.

1 Read the text about the weather in East Texas. Use a dictionary or get your teacher to help you.

2 Now read the text about the weather in Britain. Fill in the blanks with these words and expressions.

skies	but	fairly
temperature	short	Kawadi yasu
rains	know	changeable
people	winters	
sometimes	long	at a time
often	weather	does

THE WEATHER IN BRITAIN

In Britain, the .... is very ....: it .... a lot, but the sun often shines too. .... can be .... cold, with an average .... of 5°C in the south; there is often snow.

 Summers can be cool or warm, but the temperature .... not usually go above 30°C. It is .... cloudy, and there are .... grey .... for days or weeks ....

Days are .... in summer and .... in winter. There is sometimes fog, ... not so often as foreigners think. British .... never .... what tomorrow's weather will be like.

Reports for the 24 hours to 6 pm on August 3				
	Sun-shine hrs.	Rain in	Max. Temp. C F	Weather (day)
			25 77	Sunny
London	11.2	—	25 77	Sunny
Birmingham	10.5	—	26 79	Sunny
Bristol	10.2	—	24 75	Sunny
Cardiff	9.8	—	20 68	Rain pm
Anglesey	3.2	—	21 70	Bright
Blackpool	5.8	—	24 75	Sunny
Manchester ..	8.3	—	26 79	Sunny
Nottingham ..	10.9	.03	21 70	Drizzle pm
	1.6		73	Bright

Celsius

Unit 9: Lesson C/D

Students learn to talk about the weather, and to express ideas relating to frequency. Note that this is a double lesson.

Structures: frequency adverbs; preview of *will*-future; impersonal *it* for weather.

Words and expressions to learn: some of these (see summary): *weather; temperature; spring; summer; autumn; winter; day; week; year; snow; sky; rain* (noun); *sun; fog; cool; warm; cloudy; windy; between; few; tomorrow; once; usually; often; sometimes; never; occasionally; once every twenty years; quite often.* tamani

Language notes and possible problems

1. Frequency adverbs In Exercise 6 students see two of the rules governing the position of frequency adverbs (and many other adverbs):

   a) these adverbs follow *am/are/is/was/were*
   b) they come before other main verbs.

A fuller study of this subject will come later in the course.

2. Word formation Also in Exercise 6, students look at the relationships between the noun, adjective and verb forms of word groups such as *rain/rainy, fog/foggy*. Exercises of this analytic kind will come occasionally in the course; some students like to 'see how the language works'.

3. Tenses The *will*-future is previewed briefly in Exercise 8; it will be taught in detail later. Students may well want to talk about the weather they are having at the moment. There is no harm in teaching a few present progressive forms like *It's raining, It's snowing, The sun's shining*, but it is probably better to postpone detailed discussion of this tense until it comes up in Unit 18.

4. It Note the use of *it* as a subject in sentences about the weather. This may be a little difficult for students whose languages don't have the same structure.

---

1 Intensive reading

● Give students some time to read the text. Most of the vocabulary is useful, either for this lesson or for later work, and it is worth students spending time looking words up or asking about them.

2 Text completion

● This will take less time. Students can do the exercise either individually or in groups, comparing notes afterwards.

● Alternatively, you may wish to do it as a whole-class activity.

● Complete the list of the seasons by teaching *spring* and *autumn*. Mention *fall* (the American equivalent of *autumn*).

Answers to Exercise 2
The weather in Britain

In Britain, the *weather* is very *changeable*: it *rains* a lot, but the sun often shines too. *Winters* can be *fairly* cold, with an average *temperature* of 5°C in the south; there is often snow.

Summers can be cool or warm, but the temperature *does* not usually go above 30°C. It is *often* cloudy, and there are *sometimes* grey *skies* for days or weeks *at a time*. Days are *long* in summer and *short* in winter. There is sometimes fog, *but* not so often as foreigners think. British *people* never *know* what tomorrow's weather will be like.

➡

40

3 Frequency adverbs

● This can be done by class or group discussion.
● Obviously there is no 'right answer'. The order of the words and phrases should be as follows, from left to right:

never, once every twenty years, not very often, occasionally, sometimes, quite often, often, very often, all the time.

But not all students will put each expression in exactly the same place on the scale.
● As students discuss the problem, they should be encouraged to use *between* and *at* (e.g. 'I think *very often* is at 8.').

4 Using frequency adverbs

● This exercise requires students to interpret and transfer information from the texts.
● Do the first line or so together, and then let students continue individually or in groups.
● When you discuss the answers, ask them to tell you the sentences which gave them the information they needed.

Answers to Exercise 4

WEATHER	GB	TEXAS
sun	*often*	*very often*
rain	*(very) often*	*quite often*
snow	*often*	*once every twenty years*
fog	*sometimes*	*don't know*
hurricanes	*don't know*	*once every few years/occasionally*
droughts	*don't know*	*occasionally*
temperatures above 30°C	*occasionally*	*very often*

5 Talking about the climate

● Tell students to close their books and ask them to talk about the climate in their own countries.
● When they have run out of things to say, ask about other countries they know about.

6 Word formation; position of adverbs

● This is probably best done as a whole-class activity.
● Put the three columns on the board, with their example sentences.
● Ask students where to put *sunny*, and get them to make a sentence.
● Continue in the same way with the other words.
● Students should notice two things:
  a) some words can function as nouns and verbs (*rain, snow*)
  b) some adjectives are formed by adding *-y* to nouns (*rainy, windy, cloudy, foggy*).
● Point out the position of *often*: after parts of *to be*, and before other verbs. Other one-word frequency adverbs (*sometimes, occasionally, never*) tend to come in the same position as *often*.

7 Listening for information

● This is a piece of difficult speech – an extract from a radio weather forecast.
● The purpose is to help to bridge the gap between classroom English and real English, showing students that they can pick out some words and expressions from fast difficult unclear material, even with their present level of English.
● Explain what is going to happen.
● Play each part of the recording once, with pauses (at the places shown in the tapescript) for students to circle the words and expressions they identify.
● Do this again once or twice.
● Let students compare notes with their neighbours.
● Go through the recording pointing out the expressions which actually occur (they are circled in the text below).
● Don't give students the whole text – this is a waste of time at this level, as the material is far too advanced to be suitable for intensive study.

Tapescript for Exercise 7

'What's actually going to happen today, then?'
  'Well, today is another good day. Much the same as yesterday, with the mist and foggy patches clearing in the next hour or so, and then everywhere should have prolonged sunshine throughout the day...' (PAUSE)
'Tomorrow morning bright and dry, but it'll cloud over gradually during the day, and there is a threat tomorrow evening and tomorrow night of some showery outbreaks of rain. I think it'll be mostly small amounts, but one or two of the showers could be a bit heavy tomorrow night. Temperatures a little bit cooler, but not much, probably about 26–27 maximum tomorrow, with a light southerly wind.' (PAUSE)
  'Briefly, Sunday and Monday?'
  'Sunday, a rather cloudy day in this area I think, with a few showers, not much sunshine, much cooler, maximum 23, (PAUSE) but dry on Monday I think with a fair amount of sun, but again rather cool with, well, normal temperatures 22 or 23 centigrade.'
  'Still, not bad, not bad at all. OK, Harry, thanks very much indeed. Bye now.'
  'Bye-bye.'

8 Forecasting the weather

● Write on the board:
  It often rains.
  It will rain tomorrow.

  It is cloudy.
  It will be cloudy tomorrow.

  There is fog.
  There will be fog tomorrow.
● Ask students to try to say what they think the weather will be like tomorrow, using one of the patterns on the board and inserting appropriate vocabulary.
● Get each student to write his/her prediction and see whether it comes true.
● Check next time you meet the students.

9 Summary

● Go over the summary.

Practice Book
● Tell students which exercises you want them to do.

41

3 How often? Put these expressions on the line between NEVER and ALL THE TIME.

> not very often   quite often   sometimes
> occasionally   often   once every twenty years
> very often

NEVER   *quite often*   ALL THE TIME

0	1	2	3	4	5	6	7	8	9	10

4 Fill in the table with information from the two texts. Use the following words and expressions: *very often, often, quite often, sometimes, occasionally, once every ... years, never, don't know.*

WEATHER		GB	TEXAS
sun	☀		
rain	🌧		
snow	❄		
fog		*sometimes*	
hurricanes	🌴		
droughts	H_2O	*don't know*	
temperatures above 30°C	🌡 35°c		

5 Say some things about the weather in your country. Use the words *often, sometimes, occasionally, never* in some of your sentences.

6 Look at these three ways of talking about the weather.

WITH A VERB	WITH A NOUN	WITH AN ADJECTIVE
It often **rains**.	There is often **rain**.	It is often **rainy** (or **wet**).

Put these words into the correct columns: *sunny, sun, hot, snows, snow, wind, windy, cold, cool, cloud, cloudy, warm, foggy, fog.*

7 Listening for information. Copy the table. Listen to the recording and circle the expressions which you hear.

TODAY:	⟨another good day⟩ not a good day
	sunshine rain drought
TOMORROW:	it'll cloud over tomorrow evening showers
	today warm temperatures 36–37 maximum
SUNDAY:	rather cloudy a few showers
	not much cooler
MONDAY:	sun very hot normal temperatures

8 What will the weather be like tomorrow? Say what you think. Write your forecast and check tomorrow. Examples:

'It will rain.'
'It will be cloudy.'
'There will be snow.'

9 Look at the summary on page 142 with your teacher.

'I'm afraid it's the weather.'

Appearances

A Sheila has got long dark hair

1 Put the right names with the pictures.

Sheila has got long dark hair and brown eyes.
Helen has got long red hair and green eyes.
Mary has got long fair hair and green eyes.
Lucy has got short grey hair and blue eyes.

2 Ask the teacher questions.

What's this?

It's your mouth.

What are these?

Ears.

3 Test other students. Do they know these words?

hair   eyes   nose   ears   mouth   face
arm   hand   foot   leg

TOUCH YOUR RIGHT EYE.

TOUCH YOUR LEFT EAR.

4 Talk about yourself and other people.
Examples:

'I've got small hands. My mother has got pretty hair.'

5 Write three sentences with *and*, and three with *but*. Examples:

I've got blue eyes, and my mother has, too. I've got straight hair, but my brother's got curly hair.

6 Listening for information. Listen to the recording and fill in the table.

	height	hair colour	face	eyes	good-looking?
Steve's wife	5ft 8				don't know
Lorna's mum			pale		
Ruth's friend					
Katy's son					
Sue's husband					

Unit 10: Lesson A

Students learn to describe people's physical appearance.
Structures: *have got* (affirmative).
Words and expressions to learn: some of these (see summary): *long; short; blue; brown; red; green; grey; eyes; nose; ears; mouth; face; arm; leg; hand; foot; head; finger; beard; moustache; tooth; touch.*

Language notes and possible problems

1. Have got Students have already used some forms of *have got*. In this unit they learn more about the verb.

The forms of *have* are very complicated, and are not the same in British and American English. In spoken British English, the *have-got* forms are generally used in speech to talk about possession and related ideas, and forms without *got* are often unnatural in the present tense.

2. Hair Remind students that *hair* is uncountable (and has a singular verb). Note also that 'red' hair is not really red; students may find this use of the word confusing.

3. Vocabulary Students will probably want to ask for words referring to parts of the body and physical description. Use your discretion about how long to spend on Exercise 2 – there's no value in students noting words which they won't have time to learn. Real beginners will in any case find the vocabulary load heavy in this lesson.

1 Presentation

● Give students a minute or two to look at the pictures, work out their answers and compare notes.
● Go over the answers. Practise the pronunciation of *eyes*; pay attention to the unstressed weak forms of *has* (/həz/) and *and* (/ənd/).

2 Learning vocabulary

● Practise the two questions *What's this?* and *What are these?* (/'wɒt ə 'ðiːz/).
● Let students ask you questions.
● Put the new words on the board and practise their pronunciation.
● Teach both singular and plural of *tooth, foot.*
● Give students a minute or two to consolidate their knowledge of the words.

3 Testing vocabulary

● Start by testing the students yourself.
● Practise the pronunciation of *touch* and let the students continue in groups.

Alternative to Exercise 3: 'Simon says'

● This is a (rather childish) game which can make the practice more amusing.
● Give commands as in Exercise 3, but put the words *Simon says* before some of them. (For example: *Simon says touch your nose.*)
● Students must only do what 'Simon says'; if they hear a command without these words they should do nothing.
● Give the commands more and more quickly.

4 Descriptions

● Put the affirmative of *have got* on the board:

I have got	*I've got*
you have got	*you've got*
he/she/it has got	*he's/she's/it's got*
we have got	*we've got*
you have got	*you've got*
they have got	*they've got*

● Give students a moment or two to take it in.
● Tell students that *have got* means the same as *have*, but that *have got* is much more common in spoken British English.
● Then ask them for descriptions of themselves and other people. Get examples from everybody.

5 Written descriptions

● Go over the examples with the students. Make sure they understand the structure of the first one, with *has* used elliptically for *has got blue eyes.*
● When students read you their sentences, help them pronounce the weak forms of *and* (/ənd/) and *but* (/bət/).

6 Listening for information

● Tell students that they are going to hear a recording of five people describing people they know well.
● Get them to copy the table from the book; make sure they understand all the words.
● Explain that all the heights except one are given in feet and inches: 'five foot eight' or 'five feet eight' means five feet eight inches. (An inch is about 2½ cm; a foot is about 30 cm.)
● Students will not understand every word they hear, but they should be able to pick out most of the information necessary to complete the table.
● Play the recording right through once.
● Then play it again, stopping after each description so that students can fill in their tables.
● They may not have met the words *thin* and *round*, which come in the descriptions of people's faces, but encourage them to try to write the words anyway.
● You will probably need to play the recording again.
● Let students compare notes; then go over the answers with them.
● Play the recording one more time if you wish, but don't waste time going over the text in detail.

Tapescript for Exercise 6: see page 180

Answers to Exercise 6

	height	hair colour	face	eyes	good-looking?
Steve's wife	5ft 8	*fair*	*thin*	*don't know*	don't know
Lorna's mum	5ft 5	*dark brown*	pale	*dark brown*	*fairly pretty*
Ruth's friend	5ft 10/11	*dark brown*	*nice*	*blue*	yes
Katy's son	105 cm	*fair*	*don't know*	blue	*yes (very)*
Sue's husband	5ft 8	*fair/white*	*round*	blue	*don't know*

Practice Book

● Tell students which exercises you want them to do.

Lesson 10D Advance warning

In the last lesson of Unit 10, students will need to bring photos of themselves and their families to class.

Unit 10: Lesson B

Students learn to talk about clothing and colours.
Structures: preview of Present Progressive tense.
Words and expressions to learn: names of articles of clothing; colour-words; *these*; *What's this called in English?*; *What are these called?*; *How do you say . . .?*; *colour*.

Language notes and possible problems

1. Present Progressive tense You may like to explain that we say something *is happening* when it is a present action, rather than a habitual or repeated one. If you prefer, however, explanations can be left until Unit 18.

2. Vocabulary problems Students may take a little time to grasp that *trousers*, *jeans*, *tights* and *pants* are plural.

Note: we don't say somebody *is wearing* a beard.

3. Colours Unlike most other adjectives, colour-words are used with *and* before nouns (*a red and white dress*). They come after most other adjectives (*a long red dress*).

Purple may be a 'false friend': in many European languages there is a similar-looking word which refers to a kind of dark red; *purple* is close to *violet*.

4. Vocabulary load A lot of new words are introduced in this lesson. Don't insist on students learning more than they can easily manage.

Optional extra materials

Pictures cut from magazines (showing people wearing appropriate clothes) can be a useful practice stimulus.

1 Colours

- Look at the colours on the right-hand side of the page.
- Practise the pronunciation of the words.
- Get students to find examples of coloured things.
- A good way for them to give their examples is to say *This is red* or *That's red*, etc. This gives you a chance to practise the difference between *this* and *that*.

2 Descriptions

- Go over the names of the articles of clothing with the students (either using the illustration, or demonstrating meanings by showing students' and your own clothing).
- Practise the pronunciation of *is wearing*.
- Ask students to say what Keith and Annie are wearing in the pictures.
- Ask them to write down what Robert is wearing.
- Let them compare notes and check the answers.
- Use pictures from magazines for more practice.

3 Memory test

- This can be done in various ways.
1. A student comes to the front. The others observe him/her. He/she goes to the back and the others try to remember what he/she is wearing.
2. A student comes to the front and observes the class for a minute or two. He/she closes his/her eyes and somebody asks *What am I wearing?* The student tries to give an accurate description.
3. Students stand in pairs observing each other for a minute or so. They then close their eyes, or stand

back to back, and each says what the other is wearing.

4 Eight questions

- Demonstrate yourself first of all with a volunteer.
- Make sure that the person who answers starts by saying *It's a man* or *It's a woman*; otherwise the questioner doesn't know whether to say *he* or *she*.
- This can be done in small groups rather than pairs.

5 Vocabulary extension

- Students will already have asked for more vocabulary in earlier exercises. If you feel they've learnt enough new words, drop this exercise.

6 Answering questions

- The questions follow each other quickly, and the tape-recorder will not wait for somebody who is slow to answer; so students must think fast in order to keep up.
- The *yes/no* questions can be answered by everybody simultaneously, or by selected individuals.
- You may like to play through the recording two or three times until students can answer fluently.

Tapescript for Exercise 6

Are you wearing a sweater?   Who's wearing a green dress?
Who's wearing brown shoes?   Are you wearing a red shirt?
Are you wearing jeans?   What colour are your shoes?
Are you wearing a skirt?   Are you wearing a white sweater?
Are you wearing glasses?   Are you wearing a yellow blouse?
Are you wearing blue socks?   Who's wearing glasses?
Who's wearing boots?   Who's wearing a grey jacket?

Optional activity   Observation game

- Get two teams of students (six to eight in each team) to stand facing each other about ten feet apart. Tell the students that they have three minutes to observe the opposite team without speaking. Each student must try to memorize the appearance of all the people opposite – clothes, appearance and position.
- Separate the teams. If possible, put one team outside the classroom or in another room. One person in each team acts as secretary; with everybody's help, he or she writes down everything the team can remember.
- Tell each team to make as many changes to their appearance as possible, exchanging glasses, jewellery and articles of clothing.
- Tell teams to come back and stand opposite each other again, but to line up *in a different order*.
- Students now speak in turn. Each student tries to get one thing put right. He/she might say, for instance:
  Juan, go and stand next to Fritz. Alice, that's Rosita's watch. Yasuko, where's your scarf? Brigitte, you've got Olga's shoes on.

Put a few examples on the board (using these structures) to help students make their sentences.
- If possible, students should get the opposite team back in the original order, dressed as before.

(This game is taken from *Drama Techniques in Language Learning*, by Alan Maley and Alan Duff, Cambridge University Press, second edition published 1982.)

Practice Book

- Tell students which exercises you want them to do.

43

densen = a run in nylons.
shita

B A red sweater and blue jeans

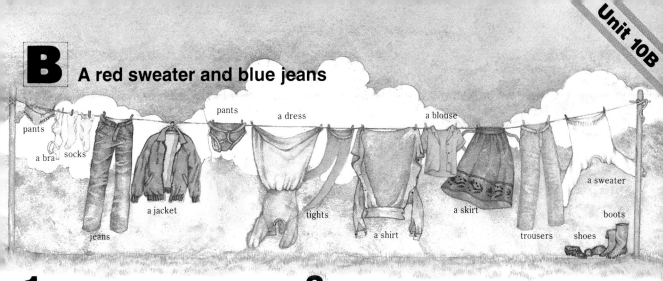

pants
a bra
socks
a jacket
jeans
pants
a dress
tights
a shirt
a blouse
a skirt
trousers
shoes
a sweater
boots

1 Can you find something red in the classroom? Something blue? Something orange?...

2 Look at the pictures.
Pat is wearing a white sweater and a red and black skirt.

Make some more sentences about Pat, Keith, Annie and Robert.
'*Keith is wearing...*'

Pat   Keith

Robert   Annie

3 Look at another student. Then close your eyes and describe him/her. Example:

'*Carlos is wearing blue jeans and a black shirt. I can't remember the colour of his shoes.*'

4 Work with another student. One of you thinks of a man or woman in the class.
The other tries to find out who it is, in eight questions beginning '*Is he/she wearing...?*'. Example:

'*It's a man.*' '*Is he wearing jeans?*'
'*No, he isn't.*' '*Is he wearing glasses?*'
'*Yes, he is.*' ...

5 Ask the teacher questions.

 '*What's this called in English?*'

 '*What are these called?*'

'*How do you say* boucles d'oreille *in English?*' '*Ear-rings.*'
'*How do you say* rosa?' '*Pink.*'
'*How do you pronounce* b-l-o-u-s-e?'

6 Listen to the recording and answer the questions.

'*Are you wearing a sweater?*'
 '*Yes, I am.*'
'*Who's wearing brown shoes?*' '*I am.*'

RED
PINK
ORANGE
YELLOW
GREEN
BLUE
PURPLE
BROWN
BLACK
WHITE
LIGHT GREEN
DARK GREEN
LIGHT BLUE
DARK BLUE

C I look like my father

1 Cover the text and listen. Look at the pictures. Who is speaking? Put the names with the pictures.

Alice   Ann   Joe   Philip   Alice's father
Alice's mother   Uncle George and family
Uncle Edward

My name's Alice. I've got a sister (her name's Ann), and two brothers, Joe and Philip. We've all got fair hair and blue eyes, and we're all slim except Joe – he's very fat. Ann's very pretty, and she's got lots of boyfriends. I've only got one boyfriend: his name's Kevin, and he's very nice.

I look like my father – I've got his long nose and big mouth – but I've got my mother's personality. Joe and Phil both look more like Mum.

We've got two uncles and an aunt. Uncle George and Aunt Agnes have got three young children. Uncle Edward is only thirteen, so he hasn't got any children, but he's got a rabbit.

2 Who looks like who in your family?
Examples:

'I look like my father.'
'My brother looks like me.'
'I've got my mother's eyes, but I've got my father's personality.'
'I don't look like my mother or my father.'

3

John and Sally have got children; so have Fred and Lucy.
Joe and Mary haven't got any children; nor have Pete and Anne.
The men have all got brothers and sisters; their wives haven't.
John, Joe, Sally and Mary have got green eyes; the others have got brown eyes.

Work with another student. He or she is one of these eight people. Can you find out who? Ask three questions:

Have you got any children?
Have you got any brothers or sisters?
What colour are your eyes?

4 Write sentences with *both* and *all*.
Examples:

In my family we're all tall.
We all wear glasses.
My brothers are both architects.
My brother and I both look like our mother.
Carlos and I have both got dark hair.

5 Look at the pictures again. You are one of these people: Ann, Joe, Philip, Alice's father, Alice's mother.
Write about your family.

Unit 10: Lesson C

Students learn to talk about resemblances between people.
Structures: interrogative and negative forms of *have got*; position of *both* and *all*; inversion with *so* and *nor* (preview); *What colour is/are...?*
Words and expressions to learn: *all*; *except*; *lots of*; *look like*; *more*; *personality*; *the others*.
Phonology: practice in linking.

1 Listening and identifying

● Ask students to cover the text and look at the picture for a minute or so.
● Tell the students they are going to hear one of the people in the picture speaking; they must try to decide which one.
● Play the recording once without stopping. See if the students can tell you which person is Alice.
● Play it again once or twice, and see if they can identify some of the other people, using the names in the box.
● Let students look at the text and finish working out the solution.
● Discuss the answers with them. Go over the text and explain any difficulties.
● Put the negative forms of *have got* on the board:
  I have not (haven't) got
  you have not (haven't) got
  he/she/it has not (hasn't) got
  we have not (haven't) got
  you have not (haven't) got
  they have not (haven't) got
● Practise the pronunciation of *haven't* and *hasn't*.

Answers: 1. Alice's mother 2. Joe 3. Uncle Edward 4. Ann 5. Alice 6. Uncle George and family 7. Philip 8. Alice's father

2 Personalization

● Practise the example sentences.
● Ask students to talk about resemblances in their families, or between people they know.
● If they are interested in the subject, they can go on to talk about resemblances between people in the class.
● You can also talk about what types people fall into (e.g. *Alfonso looks like a teacher; Maria looks like a student*).

3 Problem game

● Demonstrate yourself first of all. Choose one of the names, and say *Who am I?*
● If students ask you the three questions, they should be able to deduce from your answers who you are. (For instance, if you haven't got any children you are one of Joe, Mary, Pete and Ann. If you haven't got any brothers or sisters you are Mary or Ann. If you've got brown eyes you must be Ann.)
● Practise the short answer forms (*Yes I have / No I haven't*) before getting students to work in pairs.
● Put the interrogative forms of *have got* on the board:
  have I got?   *have we got?*
  have you got?   *have you got?*
  has he/she/it got?   *have they got?*

4 *Both* and *all*

● Go over the sentences. Make sure students understand the position of *both* and *all*. It is the same as for frequency adverbs:
– after *am/are/is/was/were*
– before another main verb.
Note the position in the last example (after the first part of a verb with more than one part).
● Get students to write at least two sentences each.
● Ask them to read you the sentences, paying special attention to linking:
  we're all   we all   brothers are   brother and I   etc.

5 Guided composition

● This can be done as a class composition on the board.
● Get students to agree on a person to write about.
● Start *My name's...*
● Ask students what to put next, and build up the composition as they make suggestions.
● Encourage them to use as much material as possible from the text in Exercise 1, and to follow more or less the same structure (or, if they choose a different way of organizing the ideas, to make it reasonably logical and coherent).

Practice Book
● Tell students which exercises you want them to do.

Unit 10: Lesson D

Students learn to pay compliments, and to write simple letters. They practise descriptions by looking at each other's family photos.
Structures: exclamations with *What (a)*.
Words and expressions to learn: *lovely*; *beautiful*; *arrive at*; *a.m.*; *p.m.*; *meet*; *photograph*; *with*; *Dear*; *Yours sincerely*; *those*; *me*.

Language notes and possible problems
1. Exclamations   Students may be inclined to leave out the article when *What...!* is followed by a singular countable noun (e.g. **What pretty dress!*).
2. *Pretty*   Note that *pretty* is not usually used to refer to men's features or clothing (Exercise 1).
3. Letters   Some of the conventions regarding layout of letters are probably different in the students' languages. (For instance, the address may be put on the left-hand side; the writer's name may be put above the address.)

Extra materials needed
Students' (and your) family and childhood photos for Exercise 2.
Optionally, copies of the letter in Exercise 3, with passages to change underlined.

1 Exclamations
• This is a pleasant way to start a lesson, and can be done from time to time as a revision activity throughout the course.
• Look at the illustration and examples in the book, or introduce the structures one by one yourself (complimenting students to show how they are used).
• Point out the use of the article, and the use of *those* before plurals (including *jeans* and *trousers*).
• Get the students to say a few sentences after you or the recording, with as lively and enthusiastic an intonation as possible.
• Then ask everybody to stand up and walk round complimenting as many people as possible.

2 Talking about personal photos
• Students should have been warned in advance to bring photos to class (see note in Lesson 10A).
• If students are studying in their own countries they can probably collect quite a number of family photos, photos of themselves when younger, etc. Even students studying abroad are likely to have some photos with them.
• Before starting, bring out one or two of your own photos and show them around.
• Get students to make comments and ask some questions about them.
• Write the questions (corrected if necessary) on the board.
• Possible questions:
  Who's that?
  How old is he/she?
  Where is it?
  When was that?

• Talk about what else it is possible to say about the photos (people's appearance, what they do, where they live and so on).
• Get students showing their photos in groups – not too many groups, so that you can get round to each one to help with vocabulary.
• If the activity goes well, it can be done more than once, with students showing their photos to several different groups.

3 Letter (guided composition in class)
• Go over the letter with the students, explaining any problems and pointing out features of layout etc.
• When you explain a.m., teach p.m. as well.
• Tell students to write similar letters, changing the address, dates, places and personal details.
• A good approach is to prepare copies of the letter with the things that need changing underlined.
• As an alternative, give the letter as a dictation (after study); then tell students to correct it and underline on their copies what you want them to change.

4 Summary
• With the names of colours, parts of the body and articles of clothing, this unit has a large vocabulary load.
• Use your discretion about how much to tell students to learn – they can always leave some of the words and come back to them later.

Practice Book
• Tell students which exercises you want them to do.

D What a nice shirt!

1 Compliment other students.

What a / That's a — nice / pretty / lovely / beautiful — dress! / shirt! / jacket! / blouse! / etc.

What / Those are — nice / pretty / lovely / beautiful — ear-rings! / trousers! / shoes! / etc.

I like your — dress. / ear-rings. / etc.

That's a pretty dress!

Oh, thank you.

What a nice shirt!

Thank you very much.

What lovely ear-rings!

I like your new glasses!

Thank you!

Oh, thanks.

2 Work in groups. Show the other students photos of your family and friends, and talk about them.

This is my mother.

What nice eyes!

She's very pretty.

Who's that?

This is my brother. He's got blue eyes.

This is my sister - she's 23.

3 You are going on a holiday or business trip to another country. Write a letter to a person you don't know, asking him/her to meet you at the station, and giving a description of yourself. Here is an example.

1609 Burkitt Ave
Chicago, IL 60611

September 12, 1984

Mr G.D. Bell
Monument House
Castle Street
Edinburgh

Dear Mr Bell,

  I am arriving at Waverley Station, Edinburgh, at 11.37 a.m. next Tuesday, September 17th. Can you meet me?

  I am sorry that I have not got a photograph, but here is a description: I am 32, quite short with dark hair and a small beard. I have got blue eyes. I will be wearing a dark blue sweater and light grey trousers and black shoes.

  I look forward to seeing you,

  Yours sincerely,

  Paul Sanders

4 Look at the summary on page 143 with your teacher.

Revision and fluency practice

A Wanted for murder

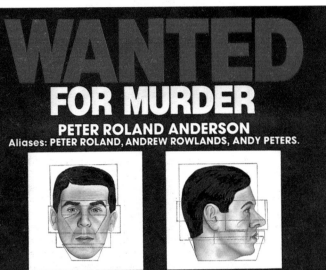

WANTED

FOR MURDER

PETER ROLAND ANDERSON

Aliases: PETER ROLAND, ANDREW ROWLANDS, ANDY PETERS.

DESCRIPTION
Age: 30, but looks younger
Height: 6'2" (1m 90)
Weight: 175 pounds (80kg)
Build: medium
Hair: black
Eyes: blue
Complexion: pale; scar under right eye prominent nose
Nationality: British
Occupation: mechanic

WARNING
This man is armed and dangerous. If you see him, do not approach him, but contact the nearest police station immediately.

1 **Listening for information. Listen to the telephone conversations.**
Who do you think saw Peter Anderson – the first caller (Mrs Collins), the second (Mr Sands), or the third (Mr Harris)?

2 *Be* or *have*? Put in *am, are, is, have got,* or *has got.*

1. My sister .... a very pretty cat.
2. How tall .... you?
3. I don't know if they .... any children.
4. It's very windy today – I .... cold.
5. What colour .... your car?
6. There .... too many people in this room.
7. 'I .... very hungry.'
8. 'I .... some bread and cheese. Would you like some?'
9. You look as if you .... thirsty. Have some beer.
10. You .... beautiful eyes, Veronica.
11. .... you married?
12. You .... Italian, aren't you?
13. What time .... the next train for Dublin?
14. My address .... 13 Church Way, Llangollen.
15. She .... tired after her journey.
16. How far .... it from London to Rome?
17. I think they .... artists. They look like artists.
18. You .... your father's nose and mouth.
19. I .... too much work and not enough free time.
20. 'Would you like a cold drink?' 'Yes, please. I .... hot.'

3 Listen to the recording. What is the *third* word in each sentence? (Contractions like *don't* count as two words.)

46

Unit 11: Lesson A

Students practise listening and revise grammar.
Structures: revision of the difference between *be* and *have*.
Words and expressions to learn: none.
Phonology: perceiving weak forms and unstressed words.

Language notes and possible problems

'Decoding' (Exercise 3) When an English phrase is spoken at natural speed, it often sounds like one word. It can be very difficult for students to 'decode' sound sequences like /ˈwɒtʃəθɪŋk/ (*What do you think?*), /ˈweədʒəlɪv/ (*Where do you live?*) or /ˈsleɪtʃənəʊ/ (*It's late, you know*), and to hear how they are made up. Exercise 3 is the first of a series of exercises which practise this skill.

Some students may react badly to exercises like this, feeling that the fast colloquial pronunciation illustrated is 'not correct'. It is very important for them to realize that educated people commonly speak like this, and that if they want to understand natural spoken English they must work hard at exercises of this kind.

1 Listening to descriptions

● Before starting the exercise, spend plenty of time looking at the illustration and explaining the description of the murderer.
● Tell the students they will hear three telephone conversations with people who *think* they have seen Anderson.
● Only one person has seen the real Peter Anderson. Which one?
● Students will not understand everything that is said, and they should not worry about this. Get them to concentrate on the descriptions, particularly age, hair colour, eye colour and the scar.
● Play the recording two or three times.

Answer: Mrs Collins saw the murderer.

Tapescript for Exercise 1
– North Yorkshire Police.
– Hello. Listen. I've just seen Peter Anderson! In the...
– One moment, please.
– Peter Anderson! The murderer! He's here in Newtown! I saw him in the street! He...
– One moment, please.
– He's a big man, with short black hair and a scar on his face. He's 25 or...
– What is your name, please?
– Mrs Collins. He's 25 or 26. He's got...
– Your address, Mrs Collins?
– blue eyes, I think. And what a big nose he's got! I know it's him. He's wearing a black jacket and green trousers...

– Thames Valley Police.
– Hello. I've seen Peter Anderson.
– One moment, please.
– Hello. Detective Sergeant Callan speaking. Can I help you?
– Yes. I've just seen Peter Anderson. In the post office. Here in Chilton.
– Can I have your name and address, please, sir?
– Robert Sands. 17 High Street, Chilton. I'm sure it was Anderson. He's very tall, with long dark hair, a big nose, green eyes, and a scar on the left-hand side of his face.

About 35 years old.
– What was he wearing?

– ...and can you describe the man, Mr Harris?
– Yes. He's quite tall, about 25 or 30, with long fair hair, big ears, and a scar under his left eye. Oh, and he's got a big nose.
– Colour of eyes?
– I've no idea.
– What was he wearing?
– A blue jacket and brown trousers...

2 Be or have?

● Beginners sometimes confuse these two verbs.
● You may like to do this as a written exercise, so as to make sure that everybody in the class can distinguish them correctly.
● We have avoided contracted forms throughout this exercise so that students will not risk confusing *is* and *has*.

3 What is the third word?

● This exercise makes students concentrate on hearing unstressed words and weak forms.
● Play the recording, stopping after each sentence so that they can write down the number of the sentence and the third word. (For the purposes of this exercise, contracted forms such as *don't* count as two words.)
● You may like to play the recording several times before stopping and letting students compare notes.
● Finally, give them the sentences and practise saying them (but don't insist on students speaking as quickly as the recorded speakers).

Tapescript for Exercise 3
1. Do you think she understands? (*think*)
2. A lot of people work here. (*of*)
3. Where do you live? (*you*)
4. I know some nice people. (*some*)
5. My mother and father are on holiday this week. (*and*)
6. She's a policewoman. (*a*)
7. He's wearing blue jeans. (*wearing*)
8. I think that gorillas eat fruit. (*that*)
9. Sometimes there are too many words to learn. (*are*)
10. Where does her sister work? (*her*)

Practice Book

● There are no Practice Book exercises for this unit; students will want to look back over earlier lessons before the test which follows Lesson 11D (see Teacher's Book page 162).

46

Unit 11: Lesson B

Students practise listening skills and revise vocabulary and pronunciation.
Structure: revision of *there is/are.*
Words and expressions to learn: none.
Phonology: /θ/ and /ð/; intonation.

1 Listening: detecting differences

- There are a large number of differences between the picture in the Student's Book and the description on the recording.
- Tell students to look at the picture for a minute or two.
- Get them to talk about it, as far as their limited vocabulary permits. Make sure everybody understands what is going on.
- Explain the caption (*How would you like it?*) if you wish.
- Play the recording once through without stopping. Ask students if they noticed any differences.
- Play it again; ask students to write down the differences they noticed.
- Play it a third time, stopping at intervals to compare the recording and the picture. Make sure everybody speaks.

Tapescript for Exercise 1

This is a picture of a bank – Barclay's Bank. There are four people in the bank: the cashier, another man, a woman and a small child. The cashier is dark. The other man, who is tall and fair, is taking money from the cashier. The woman is neither tall nor short; she's dark and very pretty. She is on the man's right. She has got two dogs with her. The child is sitting in a chair by the window. There are three doors in the picture. The time is twenty to three in the afternoon; it is Tuesday March 18th.

2 /θ/ and /ð/

- Students have already met the words listed, but they may not really understand that there are two ways of pronouncing *th.*
- It's not difficult to demonstrate the difference.
- Say the words in group 1, exaggerating the 'whispered' quality of the unvoiced *th* (/θ/).
- Then 'switch on' your voice to make the voiced sound (/ð/) in the words in group 2.
- Get students to imitate you, and then ask them to decide which group the other words belong in.
- Get them to compare notes, and then listen to you or the recording, before you tell them the answers; finish by getting them to practise saying the words.
- Tell students that if they learn the phonetic symbols /θ/ and /ð/, they can check the pronunciation of words with *th* in a dictionary.
- Note that /ð/ is much less common than /θ/. It comes at the beginning of a small group of 'grammatical' words (*this, that, these, those, the, there, then, than, that, though, thus, they, them, their, theirs*), and at the end of *with*. Apart from these cases, it occurs mainly in the ending *-ther.*

Answers

Group 1: (/θ/)	Group 2: (/ð/)
thing Thursday thousand think thirty thirteen	father that their other them they there brother these those with

3 Spelling

- If students are hesitant, give them extra practice (spell words for them to write down; ask them to spell other people's names and addresses; etc.).

4 Intonation

- Students should already have some feeling for the difference between rising intonation (common in *yes/no* questions) and falling intonation (common in statements).
- Look over the instructions and examples.
- Demonstrate the two different intonations in the example sentences (using the recording if you wish).
- Tell students to write the ten words and expressions on a separate paper.
- Play the recording. Students should write Q or S after each expression.
- Play the recording again, so that students can change their answers if necessary.
- Let them compare notes.
- Discuss the answers with them.

three o'clock *Q*	at the pub *Q*
London *S*	a cigarette *S*
Michael *S*	two pounds *S*
Tuesday *Q*	Washington *Q*
a girl *Q*	trinitrotoluene *Q*

(The last example will help students to realize that they can understand that a word is a question even if they don't know what it means.)

B One way of getting money

ow would you like it?

1 Look at the picture and listen to the recording. How many <u>differences</u> can you find?

2 Say these words.

1. thank   three   thirsty   third
2. the   this   then   mother

Group 1 or group 2?

thing	Thursday	father	that	their
thousand	other	them	think	thirty
they	there	brother	these	thirteen
those	with			

3 Spell your name and address.

4 Intonation. Look at these two conversations, and listen to the recording.

1. *'Cambridge 31453.' 'Mary?' 'No, this is Sally.'*
2. *'What's your name?' 'Mary.'*

In the first conversation, *Mary* is a question.
The voice goes up. *Mary?*
In the second conversation, *Mary* is a
statement. The voice goes down. *Mary.*

Now listen to the words and expressions on the recording, and decide whether they are questions or statements. Write *Q* or *S* after the words.

three o'clock .....*Q*..... London .....*S*.....
Michael .... Tuesday .... a girl ....
at the pub .... a cigarette ....
two pounds .... Washington ....
trinitrotoluene ....
(TNT)

C A rich 36-year-old dentist

1 Who is who?

Jane, Pete, Joe and Alice are from Birmingham, London, New York and Canberra (not in that order).

One is a doctor, one a dentist, one an artist and one a shop assistant.

Their ages are 19, 22, 36 and 47.

Apart from English, one of them speaks French, one German, one Greek and one Chinese.

Only one of them is tall, only one is good-looking, only one is rich, only one is dark. The tall one is 22.

One of them is a rich 36-year-old dentist from Canberra who speaks Chinese. What are the others?

Ask your teacher questions. He or she can only answer Yes or No. Examples:

'Is Jane a dentist?' 'No.'
'Is the artist good-looking?' 'Yes.'
'Does Joe speak Chinese?' 'Yes.'

		Alice	Joe	Pete	Jane
Appearance	Tall				
	Good-looking				
	Rich				
	Dark				
Age	19				
	22				
	36				
	47				
Profession	Doctor				
	Dentist				
	Artist				
	Shop assistant				
Home	Birmingham				
	London				
	New York				
	Canberra				
Languages	French				
	German				
	Greek				
	Chinese				

2 Vocabulary revision. Add some more words to these lists.

1. chair, sofa, ...
2. mother, brother, ...
3. tomato, cheese, ...
4. bathroom, living room, ...
5. bank, post office, ...
6. Spain, Australia, ...
7. Monday, Friday, ...
8. Italian, Chinese, ...
9. cow, dog, ...
10. I, she, ...
11. my, her, ...

3 Make sentences with *neither... nor*, as in the examples.

I am not tall and I am not short.
'I am neither tall nor short.'
Alex does not speak French and Rose does not speak French.
'Neither Alex nor Rose speaks French.'

1. I am not fair and I am not dark.
2. She is not at home and she is not in her office.
3. John is not fat, but he is not slim.
4. It is not true and it is not false.
5. I do not speak German and I do not speak French.
6. Compton has not got a bank or a post office.
7. John is not married and Peter is not married.
8. My mother does not smoke and my father does not smoke.

4 Make sentences with *neither... nor* about yourself and other people.

5 Pronounce these words.

brother son mother love money some once beautiful fruit usually
young touch cupboard   English women
many any friend sweater weather breakfast
night light right tight write eye quiet
daughter quarter water   half could
orange village   you're sure
child woman people tired wrong watch year
autumn enough aunt listen

Unit 11: Lesson C

Students revise grammar, vocabulary and pronunciation.
Structures: revision of interrogative sentences with noun-phrase subjects.
Words and expressions to learn: none.
Phonology: pronunciation of words with misleading spellings.

1 Problem: who is who?

• Students can work in groups (pooling the information they obtain) or individually. Make sure everybody asks questions.
• To help them keep track of the answers, students may like to copy the grid from the book and fill it in square by square.
• Use the following table to answer their questions.

Alice	Joe	Pete	Jane
good-looking	rich	dark	tall
19	36	47	22
artist	dentist	doctor	shop assistant
London	Canberra	New York	Birmingham
Greek	Chinese	German	French

2 Vocabulary revision

• This will help students (and you) to see if they have been learning enough of the vocabulary listed in the summaries.
• It can either be done as a test (with students working individually), or as a group activity (with each group trying to get the most words in answer to a question), or round the class.
• Perhaps the best approach is to vary the technique through the exercise.

3 Neither...nor

• Practise the examples with the students.
• Note the pronunciation of *neither*. There are two versions: /ˈnaɪðə(r)/ (more common in standard British English) and /ˈniːðə(r)/ (more common in American English).
• Do the exercise orally or in writing, as you prefer.

4 Personalization

• Get students to write at least one sentence each.

5 Difficult pronunciations

• These are all words whose spelling is misleading. They are grouped roughly by sound.
• See how many of them students can pronounce correctly, and practise the others (using the recording as a model if you wish).

Unit 11: Lesson D

Students write and perform small dramatic sketches, using creatively some of the language they have learnt so far.

Introductory note

As this is the first time that students have done full-scale dramatizations, the quality will probably be uneven: some groups will succeed in completing and performing sketches, others may not. This doesn't matter: the purpose is not to put on a polished theatrical performance, but to revise some language points in a new and interesting way.

Not all students will be used to doing this sort of work in school, and there are always one or two students who really dislike acting. Some gentle pressure will be necessary to get everybody working, but once the initial resistance is overcome students will enjoy the activity. (Anybody who is really very shy, however, should not be forced to take part.)

Give lots of encouragement, and be generous with praise for good ideas and successful performances.

If possible, you may like to record the final sketches on tape or video – this encourages students to aim at a high standard.

Presentation

● Divide the students into groups of four to six. Try to mix strong and weak students.
● Go through the instructions with them, helping them to understand what they have to do. (Note that Alex can be a boy's or a girl's name.)
● Tell the students if they are going to be recorded when they perform their sketches.
● Set a time-limit for the work.
● Explain the listed words and expressions where necessary and practise pronunciation.

Preparation

● If necessary, work with one group at the front of the class for a minute or two, demonstrating how to start. ('OK. Mr and Mrs Harris and Alex are going into the bank. Who's Mr Harris? . . . What does the manager say?')
● In groups of less than six, not all the roles need to be included in the sketch.
● Students usually spend the first five or ten minutes in despair because they can't think of anything, and then get going. If a group gets really stuck, help out with suggestions.
● Discourage groups from writing over-complicated material which will be full of mistakes, and which only they will understand. They should use a maximum of material from the previous lessons (tell them to look back in their books) and a minimum of new vocabulary.

Practice

● When groups are ready, ask them to practise their sketches a few times. Correct grammar and pronunciation where necessary.
● Practice should be done with appropriate actions and movements (where space allows), so that when they perform their sketches for the class they will know how to position themselves.

Performance

● When groups perform their sketches, make sure that the others keep quiet and listen. (Groups who have not yet performed will be tempted to discuss last-minute changes to their own sketches.)
● Don't take the best group first (they will make the others feel they can't compete), but start with a group that is likely to do a reasonable job without breaking down (panic is infectious).
● It's nice if the class applauds each performance.
● If time allows, it's good to get students to try to learn their parts so that they can act them without scripts.
● If you have recorded the sketches, don't be over-critical when you play them back – this is a vulnerable moment for students.

Optional activity

● Another good revision activity is a class interview.
● Arrange for some 'outsiders' to come into your class for an hour. (Native English-speakers are ideal; if you can't get in touch with any, use colleagues, or students from a higher class.)
● Before the interviews, spend a lesson in preparation. Get the students to work in groups drawing up a list of questions to ask the visitors. (Possible subjects: personal data, likes and dislikes, daily routine, . . .)
● When the visitors arrive, each one can sit with one group and answer their questions. After five minutes or so they can move round to other groups. Each group should see every visitor.
● Afterwards students can write up what they have found out.

Summary

● There is no summary for this unit.

NOW DO REVISION TEST ONE. (See page 163 and the Test Book.)

D Give me the money!

REVISION EXERCISE: SKETCH

Work in groups of four to six.
Roles: Mr Harris
Mrs Harris
Their child Alex
Bank manager
Wanted man or woman
Policeman or policewoman

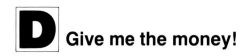

**Write and practise a sketch, using the English
you have learnt in Units 1–10.
In your sketch, you must use five of these
sentences:**

First on the right, second on the left.
It's terrible.
It's foggy.
I'm sorry.
Two boys and a girl.
I quite like Picasso.
Tall, dark and good-looking.
What a pretty dress!
Hands up!
Give me the money!

Personal history

A He was born in London

1 Close your book and listen. Try to remember as much as you can. Then look at the curriculum vitae. Listen again.

```
              CURRICULUM VITAE

NAME:          Philip George Hallow

DATE OF BIRTH: 21.3.47

PLACE OF BIRTH: London

EDUCATION:     Highgate Hill School, London, 1959-1963.
               GCE O level, 5 subjects.

FAMILY:        Father:  George David Hallow, retired
                        bus-driver.
               Mother:  Alice  Emily  Hallow,  nee
                        Tomkins, housewife, died 1979.
               Two sisters.

EMPLOYMENT:    1963-1976  Accounts clerk,
               Imperial Furniture Company, York.
               1976-1978 Unemployed.
               1978-present  Area Manager,
               Hartford Security Services Ltd., Bristol.

MARRIAGE:      Colette Andrews, 1970.

CHILDREN:      Two daughters, one son.
```

2 Match these verbs from the text with their present tense forms.

worked	died	married	went	left	became
marry	work	die	go	become	leave

3 Say these regular past tense verbs.

1. married   died   opened   played   lived
2. worked   liked   cooked   stopped   finished
3. started   hated   depended   painted   assisted

4 Write your own curriculum vitae.

5 Take another student's curriculum vitae and tell the class about it. Don't say the student's name!

> This person was born in Caracas in 1960. His mother worked as a nurse ...

> Is it Jaime?

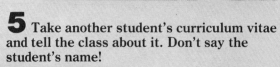

Unit 12: Lesson A

Students learn to speak about people's pasts.
Structures: Simple Past tense of regular verbs (three irregular verb forms are also introduced).
Words and expressions to learn: *was born*; *die*; *marry*; *leave/left*; *become/became*; *retired*; *clerk*; *unemployed*; *manager*; *bus driver*; *education*.
Phonology: pronunciation of regular Simple Past tense endings.

Language notes and possible problems

1. *To be born* is passive in English, but not necessarily in the students' language(s). This may cause problems.

2. GCE O Level You will need to explain the meaning of *GCE O Level, five subjects* (Mr Hallow passed five subjects in the 'General Certificate of Education, Ordinary Level' exam. This is usually taken at age 16.)

3. Pronunciation of -ed In the first line of Exercise 3, -ed is pronounced /d/, because it follows a 'voiced' sound in each case. In the second line, -ed is pronounced /t/, because it follows an 'unvoiced' sound. And in the third line, -ed comes after *d* or *t* and is pronounced /ɪd/.

The most important thing is for the students to know when to pronounce /ɪd/ and when not to. The difference between /t/ and /d/ is less important.

The 'optional preparation' for Exercise 3 helps you to teach your students about voicing, in case you want to work on the difference between voiced and unvoiced -ed.

4. Past narrative In some European languages, the tense used for past narrative is formed like the Present Perfect in English: a 'have' verb + past participle. You will want to point out to speakers of these languages that it is the Simple Past, and not the Present Perfect, which is the normal tense for narrative in English.

1 Presentation: listening 🔲

- The students keep their books closed.
- Explain the meanings of: *retired, bus driver, housewife, clerk, unemployed, manager.*
- Play the recording once, and ask the students to tell you any words or phrases they remember.
- Then get them to open their books and look at the curriculum vitae. Now they should be able to give you quite sizeable chunks of the text; write the correct bits on the board as they do.
- Play the recording again as they look at their books. They may be able to complete the text now. If not, help them by playing the recording again.
- Explain any of the other new words the students ask about.
- Play the recording one final time as they read the text.

Tapescript for Exercise 1

Philip Hallow was born in London in 1947. His father worked as a bus driver before his retirement; his mother was a housewife and died in 1979. He has two sisters. He went to Highgate Hill School from 1959 to 1963, and left after passing GCE O levels. From 1963 to 1976 he worked with the Imperial Furniture Company as an accounts clerk. From 1976 to 1978 he was unemployed, and then in 1978 he became Area Manager for Hartford Security Services. He married Colette Andrews in 1970; they have two daughters and a son.

2 Past tense forms

- Get the students to do the matching exercise.
- When you have checked the answers, point out that the first three verbs all end in *d* in the past. Tell them that these verbs are regular. (If you do not speak the students' language(s), they may not understand exactly what this means at first, but they will gradually realize as they work with the tense.)
- Point out that there is no third-person inflection in past tense verbs.

Optional preparation for Exercise 3: voicing

- Write these two groups of letters on the board:
  oy m v r o d ee   *vibration = Shindō*
  s sh t f p k x
- Get the students to pronounce them after you (without putting /ə/ after any of the consonants).
- Get them to do the same thing again, but with the palms of their hands tight over their ears. They will hear that in the first group there is a loud buzzing vibration which is absent from the second group.
- Explain or demonstrate that the vibration comes from the vibration of the vocal cords in the throat.
- Rub the *d* and the *t* out of the lists and show what happens when *d* or *ed* follows the sounds:
  oy m v r o ee + ed/d = 'd'
  s sh f p k x + ed/d = 't'

3 Pronouncing -ed 🔲

- Go over each line of the exercise, getting students to say the past tense forms after you or the recording.
- Make sure they don't pronounce /ɪd/ in either of the first two lines.
- See if they can tell you why -ed is pronounced /ɪd/ in the third line (because it isn't possible in English to pronounce /dd/ or /tt/).

4 Writing

- Get each student to write his or her own curriculum vitae.
- Walk around the class as they are working to give any help that is needed.
- Make sure they keep reasonably close to the model in the textbook.
- Write down a c.v. for yourself at the same time.

5 A guessing game

- Take up all the papers and shuffle them. Include your own paper.
- Pass the papers back out, making sure that no one has his or her own paper.
- Demonstrate what is to be done by taking the paper you are left with and giving the students the information from it. Begin: *This person was born in...*
Then let the students guess who the person is.
- Afterwards, each student in turn will relate the information on his or her sheet and the others will try to guess who wrote it.
- In a large class, you may want to do this exercise in groups.

Practice Book

- Tell students which exercises you want them to do.

Unit 12: Lesson B

Students learn to talk about differences between the past and the present.
Structures: negative forms in the Simple Past tense; spelling of affirmative Simple Past of regular verbs; *do* as pro-verb.
Words and expressions to learn: *passport*; *paper*; *calculator*; *pocket*.
Phonology: stress in negative sentences.

Language notes and possible problems

1. Exercise 1 Some students may feel that they do not know enough about history to do Exercise 1. A way of modifying the exercise to make it easier for them is given below.

2. Spelling of regular past tense The rules given will permit students to deal with most verbs. You may have to point out that final *y* is considered as a vowel, not a consonant (and so does not fall under rule 3). Verbs like *open* where the last syllable is unstressed do not double the final consonant, but it may be better not to mention this unless students bring it up; they can learn this once they have mastered the basic rules.

3. Past of *have/has got* *Had/didn't have* are the most common past tense forms of *have/has got*.

4. *One* as a substitute word occurs in one of the examples for Exercise 3. You may wish to emphasize it (and the plural *some*) if opportunities come up in the students' own sentences.

5. Long sentences Students may have difficulty with the long sentences in Exercise 3. They can be helped with emphasis on correct stress and rhythm, and with 'back-chaining' (first they repeat only the last stress group of the sentence, then the last two stress groups, etc.).

1 Life in 1440

- Get students to look at the pictures at the top of the page (covering up the rest of the text). Ask them when they think people lived like that.
- One of the students may see the date in Exercise 1; otherwise write the date, *1440*, on the board.
- Ask the class where they think the pictures are of. You will probably get answers like *France, Germany,* etc.; say that it is somewhere in Europe.
- Go over the example sentences with the students, getting them to repeat them after you or the recording. Explain the new meaning of *most* in the phrase *most people*.
- Pay special attention to stress and rhythm, and point out that the word carrying the negative (*didn't, wasn't, weren't*) is usually stressed.
- Divide the class into groups of three or four and ask each group to write fifteen other sentences about the people in Europe in 1440.
- Walk round the room as they are working, and help with any problems that come up. Encourage them to use the vocabulary they know, but give them a few new words if they ask for them.
- When the exercise is finished get each group to read out or write on the board one or two of their sentences.

Alternative Exercise 1 procedure

- If students feel daunted by the task, you can put the following words on the board to help them. They will still get practice using the forms, though the exercise will not be as exciting for them as if they had thought up the examples themselves.

coffee	hospitals	travel
Coca-Cola	banks	read
cigarettes	Australia	write
shaving cream	electricity	supermarkets
toothpaste	telephones	universities
buses	machines	bookshops
cars	central heating	Eskimos
fridges	trousers	jazz
aeroplanes	school	

2 Spelling regular past tense forms

- Go over the rules with the students to make sure they understand.
- Get them to write the past tense forms individually, then compare answers in small groups before you check the answers. (You could get each group to send a representative up to the board to write a few answers.)

3 Personalization

- Go over the examples with the class, explaining how the pro-verbs (*do, does, don't, doesn't*) work.
- Then ask each student to write seven true sentences on the same model.
- Tell them they can ask you for help; give them any vocabulary or irregular past forms they need.
- (You may want to teach them to say, *Is . . . a regular verb?*)
- Ask for volunteers to read out some of their sentences to the class.

4 Authentic listening

- Students must listen for a few specific bits of information in an interview.
- Explain what they are to do and let them read and copy the list of items in the book before playing the recording.
- You may be able to play the recording only once in a fast class, but in most classes at least two run-throughs will be necessary.
- Let students compare answers with each other before checking with you.
- The only items that are not mentioned on the recording are *post office* and *radio*.

Practice Book

- Tell students which exercises you want them to do.
- Exercise 3 trains students to read and understand the gist of a passage without understanding every word. Make sure they understand the instructions for this exercise.

B They didn't drink tea

1 These pictures show life in the country in 1440. Make fifteen sentences about people who lived in Europe then; use *didn't, wasn't* and *weren't*. Examples:

'They didn't eat bananas.'
'They didn't drink tea.'
'They didn't have passports.'
'They didn't know about America.'
'Most people didn't live in cities.'
'Most people weren't very tall.'
'There wasn't any paper money.'

3 Write seven sentences about changes in your life. Read one or two of them to the class. Examples:

I didn't like cheese when I was a child, but now I do.
I played tennis when I was a girl, but now I don't.
We didn't have a colour television then, but now we've got one.
There weren't any pocket calculators then, but now there are millions of them.

2 How do you write regular past tenses? Here's how:

1. Most regular verbs:
   work + ed = worked; listen + ed = listened
2. Verbs ending in *e*:
   live + d = lived; hate + d = hated
3. Short verbs ending in consonant + vowel + consonant:
   stop + ped = stopped; slim + med = slimmed
4. Verbs ending in consonant + *y*:
   study + ied = studied

Now write the past tenses of the regular verbs below.

arrive	live
cook	look
dance	start
shop	marry
remember	watch

4 Listen to two people talking about life in a farming village in England in the 1940s. Which of the following do they talk about?

electric light   heating   post office   car
radio   National Health System   clothes   shop

51

C Danced till half past one

1 Match the present and past forms of these irregular verbs.

go tell get can do come hear (wake) have say know
(woke) could went heard said told came had did got knew

2 Close your book and listen to the dialogue. See how much you can remember. Then read the dialogue and the text. Ask your teacher about new words.

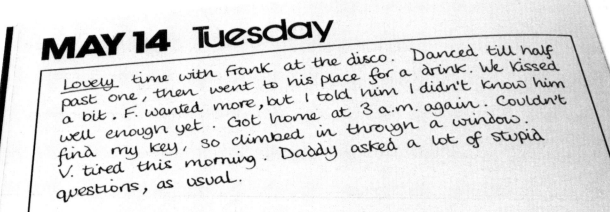

MAY 14 Tuesday

Lovely time with Frank at the disco. Danced till half past one, then went to his place for a drink. We kissed a bit. F. wanted more, but I told him I didn't know him well enough yet. Got home at 3 a.m. again. Couldn't find my key, so climbed in through a window. V. tired this morning. Daddy asked a lot of stupid questions, as usual.

FATHER: What time did you come home last night, then, June?
JUNE: Oh, I don't know. About half past twelve, I think.
FATHER: Half past twelve? I didn't hear you.
JUNE: Well, I came in quietly. I didn't want to wake you up.
FATHER: You didn't go to that damned disco, did you?
JUNE: Disco, Daddy? Oh, no. You know I don't like loud music. No, I went to a folk concert with Alice and Mary. It was very good. There was one singer...
FATHER: Why did you come back so late? The concert didn't go on till midnight, did it?
JUNE: No, but we went to Alice's place and had coffee, and then we started talking about politics, you know. Alice's boyfriend – he's the President of the Students' Union Conservative Club...

3 Find the differences. Example:

June said (that) she went to a folk concert, but actually she went to a disco.
OR: _June told her father (that) she..._

4 Ask some other students what they did _either_ yesterday _or_ at the weekend. Ask as many questions as possible. Examples:

'What time did you get up yesterday?'
'Did you come to school by bus?'
'Did you have a bath?'
'What did you have for breakfast?'

Unit 12: Lesson C

Students learn to ask for information about the recent past.
Structures: Simple Past tense question forms.
Words and expressions to learn: some irregular past tense forms; *tell*; *come*; *want*; *ask*; *kiss*; *midnight*; *late*; *last night*; *till*; *a bit*; *again*; *now*.
Phonology: rhythm and stress in questions.

Language notes and possible problems

1. Reported speech   When we are reporting things that people have said about the recent past, we do not always make all the 'tense changes' that are described in grammars. For instance, instead of 'June said that she *had gone* to a folk concert', it is quite all right to say 'June said that she *went* to a folk concert'. In Exercise 3, students can use this structure; a more detailed study of 'reported speech' will come later.

2. Say and tell   You will need to explain the difference between *say* (which does not need to have an indirect object) and *tell* (which normally must have one).

3. That   Note that the conjunction *that* is often left out after common verbs of reporting in an informal style. You may wish students to practise sentences with and without *that*.

4. Go and come   Students may need to be shown the difference between *go* (movement away from the speaker or unrelated to the speaker) and *come* (movement towards the speaker).

5. Actually   The meaning of *actually* should be clear from the context – it is very often used in this way to correct mistakes or misunderstandings. Note, though, that it is a 'false friend' for many students: similar words in other European languages tend to mean 'at present'.

6. Got is encountered for the first time as the past of *get* (rather than as part of *have got*).

1 Irregular verbs
● Get the students to do the matching exercise. This should not be difficult.
● The exercise will prepare students for the new verb forms in the next exercises.
● Before going on, make sure students know how to find and use the irregular verb lists in their dictionaries. (There is also a list of common irregular verbs at the back of the Student's Book.)

2 Listening
● Set the scene by getting the students to look at the picture.
● Elicit the information that the people are a father and daughter; get the students to guess their approximate ages.
● Then get them to close their books.
● Explain or demonstrate the meanings of *hear*, *concert*, *late*, *midnight* and *disco*.
● Play the recording once.
● Ask questions to see if students have got the gist of the dialogue, e.g.
  What time did June come home?
  Did she go to a disco or a concert?

● You may have to play the recording again if students have not understood much the first time.
● When you are satisfied that they have got the gist of the dialogue, play it again, stopping after these sentences for the students to repeat them:
  What time did you come home last night, then, June?
  Oh, I don't know. About half past twelve, I think.
  Half past twelve? I didn't hear you.
  You know I don't like loud music.
  Why did you come back so late?
● Pay special attention to stress and rhythm.
● Ask the students to open their books and read the dialogue as you play it again.
● Get them to ask you about any words they don't know, using the *What does . . . mean?* form.
● Get them to read the diary entry, once again asking you for the meanings of new words.

3 Find the differences (reported speech)
● Point out the distinction between *say* and *tell*, and the meaning of *actually*.
● Get each student to write down one difference, following the models in the book.
● Ask a few volunteers to read their sentences. Help them with pronunciation, paying special attention to rhythm and intonation. Point out the pronunciation of *said* (/sed/).
● Make sure you have examples of both *say* and *tell*; or you may wish to ask each student to give his or her answer in both forms.
● Ask the class if there are any more differences (i.e. let them complete the exercise orally).

4 Questions about the recent past
● Divide the class into groups of three or four and ask them to prepare questions like the examples.
● Write *yesterday morning/yesterday afternoon/yesterday evening/last night* on the board to help them.
● Walk around while the students are working to help with any problems. Encourage them to try to use words they already know.
● Ask them to write a large number of questions. All members of each group should write all the questions or notes for all the questions.
● When the groups have finished working, get each group to ask you two or three questions. Answer them truthfully. You may want to teach *I pass* or *I'd rather not say* in order to allow students to avoid giving information they'd rather not give.
● Get everyone to walk round and ask as many questions as possible; or get each person to ask as many other people as possible without moving from his or her seat.
● You may want to write a few questions on the board when the students have finished, to leave a written record of the forms.

Practice Book
● Tell students which exercises you want them to do.
● Exercise 4 practises extensive reading skills: students are asked to separate two jumbled stories. Tell them that they need not understand every word in the texts in order to do the task.

> **Students practise** listening for information with four authentic monologues, and revise past tense forms and question words.
> **Structures:** subject and object questions with *Who.*
> **Words and expressions to learn:** *find; hear; answer; through; at the weekend; when?; actually.*

Language notes

Exercise 2 Sentences with personal objects can give rise to two sorts of question with *Who*: questions about the subject of the sentence, and questions about the object. In subject questions, the verb keeps the same form as in an affirmative sentence; in object questions the verb has the same form as in questions with words like *When, How,* etc. Here students will practise both sorts of question.

1 Listening for information

- Students will hear four people speaking about themselves. They will not understand every word, but they will grasp enough to do the exercise.
- Go over the table with the students. Make sure they understand everything.
- Tell them to copy the grid, with the names and headings.
- Tell them that when they listen to the recording, they should write each person's age, the number of his/her brothers and sisters, the place of birth (chosen from the alternatives in the Student's Book), and an appropriate phrase about the person's childhood (chosen from the alternatives given).
- When they are ready, play the recording, pausing after each extract so that students can write their answers.
- Play the recording two or three times if necessary.
- Let students compare notes before going over the answers.
- The tapescript is given for reference, but you will probably not want to spend time going over everything that was said.

Answers to Exercise 1

Steve Dixon: Age 40; a sister (brother died); born in Darlington; quite enjoyed his childhood.
Adrian Webber: Age 42; a sister; born in India; childhood varied and quite happy.
Lorna Higgs: Age 19; two brothers; born in Oxford; childhood 'quite mixed, really'.
Sue Ward: Age not given; three brothers and a sister; born in Tadcaster; very happy childhood.
Tapescript for Exercise 1: see page 180

2 Subject and object questions

- The easiest way to present this exercise is to put the diagram up on the board as you talk your way through it, i.e. write *Jane,* say *Jane wrote to Alice,* draw an arrow to Alice's place in the diagram and write her name there, etc.
- Then point to the diagram as you show how the two sorts of question are formed.
- Let the students practise the two example questions and their answers.

- Ask two or three volunteers questions using the names of some of the other people in the diagram to make sure the class have grasped the point.
- Then get them to work in pairs, each asking their partner all the possible questions from the diagram.

Optional activity

- When the students have finished Exercise 2, erase three of the names from the diagram on the board, leaving only one name and the arrows.
- Get each student to copy the diagram and fill in three new names, without letting his or her partner see.
- Partners must question one another in order to reproduce the new diagram.
- (If you want, you can also introduce a new verb at this stage, e.g. *send a present to,* to make it a bit more complicated.)

3 Revision of question forms

- You can call on individual students to give you questions like those in the example, or you can organize this exercise as a team game.
- For the game, divide the class into two teams.
- Each team gets first try at one sentence in turn, and can make as many questions as it wishes. One point for each correct question.
- When the team has finished, ask the other team if they can think of any other questions, before giving them their own sentence to work on.
- Another possibility is for the whole class to work together, volunteering questions as they wish, and seeing how many questions they can come up with.

4 Matching captions

- Get students to look at the pictures for a moment.
- Go over the captions with them, explaining any difficulties.
- Then ask them to decide which of the five captions goes with each of the three cartoons.
- When they have thought about it, ask them to compare notes with their neighbours.
- The original captions were:
  'He's tired' with the picture of the bar.
  'How was the holiday?' with the picture of the animals.
  'Remember me from last night?' with the picture of the man in a cell.
- Students may, however, find other combinations which work well; don't tell them that they are wrong if they find different solutions from those given.

5 Summary

- Go over the summary with the students.
- Note that the irregular verbs that have come up so far are all listed with their past tense forms.
- Students should learn these as soon as they can.

Practice Book

- Tell students which exercises you want them to do.

D Who wrote to Alice?

1 Listen to the four speakers and fill in the table.

NAME	AGE	BROTHERS	SISTERS	PLACE OF BIRTH	CHILDHOOD
Steve Dixon				Dartington Darlington Parlington	very happy he quite enjoyed it he liked it a lot
Adrian Webber				India England Edinburgh	varied and quite happy very unhappy very happy
Lorna Higgs				Austria Oslo Oxford	quite miserable quite interesting quite mixed, really
Sue Ward				Tadcaster Manchester Hong Kong	very unhappy very happy varied and happy

2 Four friends wrote letters on the same day.

Jane wrote to Alice.
Alice wrote to Mary.
Mary wrote to John.
John wrote to Jane.

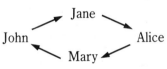

Ask and answer questions about the letters.
Examples:

'Who wrote to Alice?'   'Jane did.' / 'Jane.'
'Who did Alice write to?'   'She wrote to Mary.' / 'Mary.'

3 Make questions about these sentences.

1. Marilyn walked home from school with someone.
   Who *did she walk home* with?
   When *did she walk home from school*?
2. One of my women friends showed me some pictures.
   (When...? What sort...?)
3. They stopped to have lunch. (Who...? When...?
   Where...?)
4. Sandra went to work. (How...? What time...?)
5. There were some children at the party.
   (How many...?)
6. He started work at the same time every day.
   (Who...? What time...?)
7. He went on holiday with someone. (Who...?
   Who... with? Where...? When...?)
8. I heard someone in the street at midnight
   last night. (Who...?)
9. Susan's brother found something strange at
   the weekend. (What...? Where...?)
10. Matthew said he was with Sarah, but actually
    he wasn't. (Where...?)
11. Somebody climbed through a window. (Who...?
    When...?)

4 Choose one sentence for each cartoon.

'How was the holiday?'
'Happy birthday!'
'He's tired.'
'What's today?'
'Remember me from last night?'

5 Study the summary on page 144
with your teacher.

Buying things

A This one?

1 Draw a picture of something. Ask and answer questions with other students.

'What is this/that called in English?'

2 Draw a picture of two things; for example, two cats or two chairs. Ask and answer.

'What are these/those called in English?'

3 Find these in the window.

a ring	a spoon	some ear-rings	a glass	a watch	a box	a lamp	a Buddha	a teapot

4 Work in pairs: ask to see things, and answer.

Could you show me those glasses?
These?
Yes, those.
Of course.

Could I see that ring?
This one?

No, that one.
Here you are.

5 Say where things are in the window.

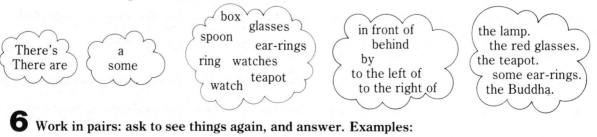

There's
There are

a
some

box
spoon
glasses
ear-rings
ring   watches
watch   teapot

in front of
behind
by
to the left of
to the right of

the lamp.
the red glasses.
the teapot.
some ear-rings.
the Buddha.

6 Work in pairs: ask to see things again, and answer. Examples:

'Could I see that box, please?'
'This one?'
'No, the one behind the teapot.'

'Could you show me those glasses, please?'
'These?'
'No, the red ones.'

Unit 13: Lesson A

Students learn ways of indicating where things are, and making and granting requests.

Structures: *could* + infinitive without *to*; *one(s)*; demonstratives; prepositions of place.

Words and expressions to learn: some of these (see summary): *one(s)*; *Here you are*; *of course*; *buy*; *thing*; *ring*; *spoon*; *glass*; *watch*; *box*; *in front of*; *behind*; *see*; *show*.

Phonology: rising intonation on *yes/no* questions, falling intonation on the answers.

Language notes and possible problems

1. Demonstratives Students have met *this* and *that* before in isolation; here they learn *these* and *those*.

2. One(s) In some languages nouns can be left out after adjectives when the meaning is clear. Students must learn that this is not normal in English, and that they cannot say **I'd like the green* or **I would prefer a blue*. We generally use *one(s)* to avoid repeating a noun:
a) adjective + *one(s)*: *a blue one*; *the little ones*.
b) *the one(s)* + defining phrase (e.g. prepositional expression): *the one in the window*; *the ones by the lamp*.
c) *this one* and *that one*.

3. Could Remind students that *could* is commonly used instead of *can* to make polite requests.

Optional extra materials

Small objects: at least two of each, and at least twice as many objects as students in the class: pairs of ear-rings, rings, pens, pencils, rubbers, watches, spoons...
NOTE: The lesson will be much livelier for your students if they can do Exercises 4 and 6 with real objects. Suggestions are given below. In this case, use the shop window picture only for practising prepositions of place (Exercise 5). You may wish to reverse the order of Exercises 3 and 4, doing the vocabulary work just before Exercise 5.

1 *This* and *that*
● Ask students to take a piece of paper and draw one thing on it. Draw something yourself.
● Hold up your picture and ask: *What is this called in English?*
● When your question has been answered (e.g. *It's a bed* or *I don't know*), practise the pronunciation of the question. Pay special attention to /ð/.
● Get one or two students to show their pictures to the class and ask about them.
● When they have done this, continue the exercise as a walk-round activity.
● Get the students to draw a picture of something else.
● Ask one student to stand up and show his/her picture. Point to it and ask: *What is that called in English?*
● When the question has been answered, show your new picture and ask about it (with *this*); then get the student to ask the two questions, using *this* for his/her picture and *that* for yours.
● Practise the pronunciation of the question with *that*, and get students to walk round, asking each other the two questions.
● This exercise also revises vocabulary.

● It is not important if the students draw things whose names they do not know in English. This will turn their questions into real requests for information.

2 *These* and *those*
● Get the students to take another piece of paper and draw *two* things on it (e.g. two chairs, two eyes).
● Follow the same procedure as before to get them practising: *What are these called in English?* and *What are those called in English?*

3 Vocabulary
(If you are going to use real objects for Exercise 4, it is probably best to delay this exercise until afterwards.)
● Students will know some of the words already.
● Give them a few minutes to work in groups pooling their knowledge, and then tell them the meanings of any words they haven't been able to work out.

4 *One*
● Get a volunteer to come to the front of the class.
● Place one pen near him/her and have another ready.
● Ask *Could I see that pen?* and answer *Thanks* when you get it.
● Then get the student to ask the question.
● In answer, take the other pen from your desk or pocket and ask *This one?*
● The student need only say *No* for you to hand the correct pen over; say *Here you are* as you do.
● Get the students to look at the illustrations for Exercise 4. Make sure they understand the situations.
● Practise the questions and answers, paying special attention to intonation: *This one? No, that one.*
● If you have brought some small objects in to use, divide the class into groups of three or four (or into pairs if you have enough objects).
● Give each group six or more objects (two of each kind of object, e.g. two rings, two pairs of ear-rings).
● Get one student to play the shopkeeper and the others to practise asking him or her for things.
● The customers can move on to another 'shop' after a few minutes.
● If you have not brought objects in to use, divide the class into pairs.
● One student takes the part of the customer (pointing at things in the picture as if it were a shop window); the other acts as the shopkeeper.
● After a few minutes students can change partners.

5 Prepositions of place
● *In front of* and *behind* are the only new prepositions in this exercise. Demonstrate them and then let the students make as many sentences as they can.

6 *Ones*
● This can be done in the same way as Exercise 4.
● Before beginning, go over the sample sentences, pointing out the use of *ones*, and get students to give you a few more examples (e.g. *the blue ones*, *the ones in front of the Buddha*).

Practice Book
● Tell students which exercises you want them to do.

Unit 13: Lesson B

Students learn to buy clothing and shoes.
Structures: no new structures.
Words and expressions to learn: *size; help; look; look for; suit; fit; try ... on; take; other; another; really; anything; I'm afraid ...; larger; just.*

Language notes

1. *Lovely* and *nice*   You may want to point out that *lovely* is a bit stronger than *nice*.
2. *Suit* and *fit*   Students will need to learn the difference between these two words.

Optional extra materials

Copies of the lists given here after Exercise 3, cut into strips – enough so that each student can have at least one strip.

1 Presentation: matching

● Ask students to match the first two sentences to the numbered speech balloons in the first cartoon strip.
● Check that everyone has understood and done the task correctly.
● Then ask them to do the second strip.
● Students can compare notes before you check the correct order with them. (1e, 2c, 3b, 5a, 6d, 7g, 8j, 9h, 10f, 11i; or ... 7g, 8f, 9i, 10j, 11h)
● Write the dialogue on the board as the students give you the correct order.
● Do the third dialogue in the same way as the second. (Correct order: 1a, 2d, 3c, 4e, 5b.)

2 Consolidation and practice

● Work on each dialogue as follows:
● Play the dialogue once while the students look at the strip.
● Allow students to ask questions (*What does ... mean?*) or give them practice in using their dictionaries to look up words and expressions.
● Then wipe the dialogue off the board, ask students to close their books, and get them to recall any words or expressions they can.
● With their help, reconstruct the dialogue on the board, playing the recording again if necessary.
● Get the students to practise the customer's part in the dialogue, using the recording as a model if you wish.

3 Extension

● You have already written the second dialogue on the board.
● Now erase the word *jumper* and ask students to suggest other words that might go there e.g. trousers, skirt etc. Do the same with *fourteen, yellow, blue.*
● Get the students to pair off and make up their own dialogues to practise, reading from the board and changing the words.
● They may want to make use of the size charts at the bottom of the page.

Optional activity

● Before class, copy the following items and cut each item out on a separate strip of paper.

● If there are more than sixteen students in the class, copy the lists twice or more.
● Try to have a few more items than there are students.

a. You've got red, blue and green jumpers, all sizes, £11.
b. You've got blue jumpers and red jumpers, all sizes, £9.50.
c. You've got men's and women's trousers, all sizes, brown or black, £10.99.
d. You've got men's and women's trousers, all sizes, all colours, £12.49.
e. You've got blue, pink and white shirts for men, £9.99.
f. You've got white shirts for men and women, £8.95.
g. You've got shoes, all colours, sizes 3 to 11, £15.45.
h. You've got shoes, all colours, sizes 3 to 11, £19.99.

1. A red jumper; you've got £10.
2. A blue jumper for a friend; you've got £12.
3. Trousers; you've got £12.
4. Blue trousers; you've got £15.
5. A shirt for your mother or father; you've got £10.
6. A white shirt for your uncle; you've got £12.
7. Black shoes; you've got £25.
8. Brown shoes; you've got £20.

● Get half the students to stand on one side of the room.
● Tell them they are shop assistants and give each of them one or more lettered sentences.
● Distribute all the lettered sentences.
● The other students, the customers, each get a numbered sentence.
● Leftover numbered sentences are put in a pile on your desk.
● Customers walk round and try to find what they want at a price they can pay.
● You may wish to demonstrate with one pair before the exercise begins.
● When a student has found the item on the slip of paper, he or she can exchange slips with another customer or with the pile of leftovers.

Practice Book

● Tell students which exercises you want them to do.

B Yellow doesn't suit me

1 Match the sentences to their places in the conversations.

a. Can I help you?
b. I'm just looking.

a. Here's a lovely one.
b. What size?
c. Yes, I'm looking for a jumper.
d. Well, yellow doesn't really suit me. Have you got anything in blue?
e. Can I help you?

f. Can I try them on?
g. Here's a nice one in blue. And here's another one.
h. £13.99.
i. Yes, of course.
j. How much are they?

a. These are a bit small. Have you got them in a larger size?
b. Yes, these fit perfectly. I'll take them, please.
c. No, I'm afraid I haven't. Would you like to try these?
d. I'll just see.
e. Yes, please.

2 Listen to the three conversations. Use your dictionary or ask your teacher about the new words. Then practise the customer's part in each conversation.

3 Change things (clothes, colours, sizes) in the second conversation and practise the new conversation with another student.

International clothing sizes

Women's clothes						
British	10	12	14	16	18	20	22
Continental	38	40	42	44	46	48	50
American	8	10	12	14	16	18	20

Women's shoes						
British	3	4	5	6	7	8	9
Continental	35½	36½	38	39½	40½	42	43
American	4½	5½	6½	7½	8½	9½	10½

Men's clothes			
British	37-38	39-40	41-42	43-44
Continental	94-97	99-102	104-107	109-112
American	38	40	42	44

Men's shoes						
British	7	8	9	10	11	12	13
Continental	41	42	43	44	45½	47	48
American	8	9	10	11	12	13	14

C The next train to Oxford

TICKETS

1 Listen, and complete the dialogues with your teacher's help. Then ask your teacher about the new words, or find them in your dictionary. Listen again.

1. TRAVELLER: .... two
   singles .... Norwich,
   ....
   CLERK: .... £12.40, ...
   TRAVELLER: Let's see, there's twelve, and
   ...., twenty, ..., forty.
   CLERK: ....
   TRAVELLER: ....
   NEXT
   TRAVELLER: Return .... Cambridge,
   ....

INFORMATION

2. TRAVELLER: What time is the next train to
   Oxford, please?
   CLERK: There's one at ...., change
   at Didcot, arriving at Oxford at
   ...., or there's a direct one
   at ...., arriving at ....
   TRAVELLER: Which platform for the ....?
   CLERK: Platform ....
   TRAVELLER: Thank you very much.

BUREAU DE CHANGE

3. CLERK: How would you like it?
   TRAVELLER: ....?

speak	understand
Thank	four fives
slowly	Pardon

   CLERK: How would you like it?
   TRAVELLER: ....
   ....?
   CLERK: How would you like your money?
   In tens?
   TRAVELLER: ....
   CLERK: Fifty, one, two, three and twenty
   pence. And here's your receipt.
   TRAVELLER: ....

2 Practise the traveller's part in each dialogue.

3 In pairs, choose a dialogue and change the places and numbers. Practise the new dialogue.

4 Which platform? Listen to the platform announcements and write the platform numbers.

a. Reading   c. Radley   e. Swindon
b. Oxford   d. Goring

56

Unit 13: Lesson C

Students learn to buy rail tickets, ask for train information, request that information be repeated, and change money.
Structures: *would like.*
Words and expressions to learn: *single; return; next; change; direct; platform; train; which; Please speak more slowly; would.*

Language notes and possible problems

1. At You may want to draw students' attention to the use of *at* in *change at* and *arriving at.*

2. What time Students should notice the very commonly used *What time...?* instead of *At what time...?*

3. The dialogues Each of the three dialogues in this lesson is the object of a different sort of task. You will have to make sure that students understand this, and understand each task clearly.

1 Completing the dialogues

Dialogue 1 is fairly simple, and the students should be able to predict most of the missing words.
● Use the picture to make sure the students understand what is happening and where.
● Then put the students into groups of three or four to try and supply the missing words and phrases.
● When they have done as much as they can, play the recording and give them a chance to write down any other words they hear before checking the answers.
● Allow them to ask about any unknown words or look them up in their dictionaries.
Dialogue 2 is a listening exercise.
● Students listen one or more times with their books open, and try to supply the missing numbers.
● Or they listen a first time or two with their books closed, concentrating only on the numbers. Then they listen with books open.
● In either case, use the picture to establish the situation before the first open-book listening.
● Give the students a chance to ask you about new words or to look them up in their dictionaries.
Dialogue 3 is a bit more difficult.
● Use the picture to establish the situation.
● Point out that this time it is whole sentences that are missing, and not just words or phrases.
● The words in the box are there to help the students.
● Get students to read through the whole dialogue.
● Then write the Clerk's first line on the board and ask if anyone has any ideas for the Traveller's first line.
● Try to give all the students a chance to think about the exercise: so if the right answer comes up right away, ask the rest of the class if they agree.
● Continue building up the dialogue. If the students produce something that is close to the actual text but not exactly the same, write it in.
● If there is any sentence that they cannot get the gist of, just leave it blank.
● Play the recording.
● Discuss any differences.
● Deal with any new vocabulary as in the other two dialogues.

Tapescript for Exercises 1 and 2

1. TRAVELLER: I'd like two singles to Norwich, please.
   CLERK: That's £12.40, please.
   TRAVELLER: Let's see, there's twelve, and ten, twenty, thirty, forty.
   CLERK: Thank you.
   TRAVELLER: Thank you.
   NEXT
   TRAVELLER: Return to Cambridge, please.

2. TRAVELLER: What time is the next train to Oxford, please?
   CLERK: There's one at 3.45, change at Didcot, arriving at Oxford at 5.04, or there's a direct one at 3.49, arriving at 4.50.
   TRAVELLER: Which platform for the 3.49?
   CLERK: Platform 6.
   TRAVELLER: Thank you very much.

3. CLERK: How would you like it?
   TRAVELLER: Pardon?
   CLERK: How would you like it?
   TRAVELLER: I'm sorry, I don't understand. Could you speak more slowly, please?
   CLERK: How would you like your money? In tens?
   TRAVELLER: Oh! Er, four five's and the rest in tens, please.
   CLERK: Fifty, one, two, three and twenty pence. And here's your receipt.
   TRAVELLER: Thank you.

2 Controlled practice

● Play the dialogues again, stopping after the Traveller's sentences to let the students practise them. Pay attention to stress and rhythm.

3 Freer practice

● Depending on the class, you can get them to stick fairly closely to the dialogues, or they can do something approaching an improvisation.
● Put the students in pairs, get each pair to choose one of the three dialogues and change some of the elements in it.
● Walk round as they do so to help with any problems.
● Get them to change partners once they have finished a dialogue or two.

4 Listening for information

● The students listen for the platform numbers corresponding to certain destinations.
● Get them to copy the place names on a piece of paper.
● Then let them listen to the recording, more than once if necessary, until they are satisfied that they have written as many of the platform numbers as they can.
● Check the answers with them and play the recording once again.

Answers: Reading 4, Oxford 3, Radley 3, Goring 4, Swindon 1
Tapescript for Exercise 4: see page 181

Practice Book

● Tell students which exercises you want them to do.
● Exercise 3 is an exercise in reading for information. Make sure the students understand that they are not to read every word, but only try to answer the questions. They should keep dictionary use to a minimum.

Unit 13: Lesson D

Students practise listening for factual detail. They learn to enquire about the pronunciation of English words.
Structures: various uses of *much* and *many*.
Words and expressions to learn: *How do you pronounce* + spelling; *Is this correct* + pronunciation; *expensive*; *without*; *meal*; *OK*; *cigarette*; *hotel*.
Phonology: stress patterns in sentences.

1 Listening for detail

• Ask the students to read the telegram in their books.
• Then tell them that there are some things wrong with the text in the book. They must listen to the telegram being dictated and correct the mistakes.
• (If you do not wish students to write in their books, just get them to write down the correct word when they hear a difference.)
• The correct version is as follows:

Robbins
The *Goddards*
Chilton
Near Didcot
Oxfordshire

Please *give* complete figures for *furniture* imports *1968 to 1972* to James *Polixenes* as soon as possible. Telephone me *Thursday afternoon* at 371 41*99* to discuss *German* visit next *April.*
Regards *Peter*

2 Sentence-stress

• Get the students to look at the first five lines of the dialogue (up to *Cigarette?*) and try to decide where the stresses are.
• They can do this work in groups, marking the stresses by wavy underline (perhaps in pencil at this stage) after copying the sentences.
• Ask them how they decided which words to mark.
• You may be able to elicit the fact that stress usually falls on content words rather than structure words.
• Play the first five lines of the recording and give the students a chance to modify their answers.
• Then play the same portion, stopping after each line.
• Go over the answers with the students. If it has not come up earlier, mention now the content word / structure word distinction.
• Follow the procedure for the rest of the dialogue – letting students try to predict the stress, playing once without stopping and once with stops before checking.

Answers to Exercise 2
A: What would you like to drink?
B: Beer, if you've got it.
A: I think so. Just a minute. Yes, here you are.
B: Thanks.
A: Cigarette?
B: No, thanks, I don't. How's the family?
A: They're OK. Peter's gone to the States for a month.
B: Oh, yes? Holiday?
A: Yes.
B: Isn't that expensive?

A: Not really. Five hundred pounds for a month including air fares and hotels. Without meals.
B: That's not bad.

3 Asking about pronunciation

• Get students to look back through their books.
• When they find a word or expression whose pronunciation they are not sure of, they should check the pronunciation with you to see whether they have got it right.
• (If your students have been using the phonetic transcriptions to help them with pronunciation, they should first of all look the word or expression up in the summary before checking with you.)

4 *Much* and *many*

• Let students do this gap-filling exercise individually before comparing their answers in pairs or small groups.
• When they have checked their answers with you, you might want to ask each group to come up with its own sentences, one with each expression.

5 Summary

• Look over the summary with the students.

Practice Book
• Tell students which exercises you want them to do.

D Five hundred pounds for a month

1 Listen to the recording of a man dictating a telegram over the telephone, and correct the following text.

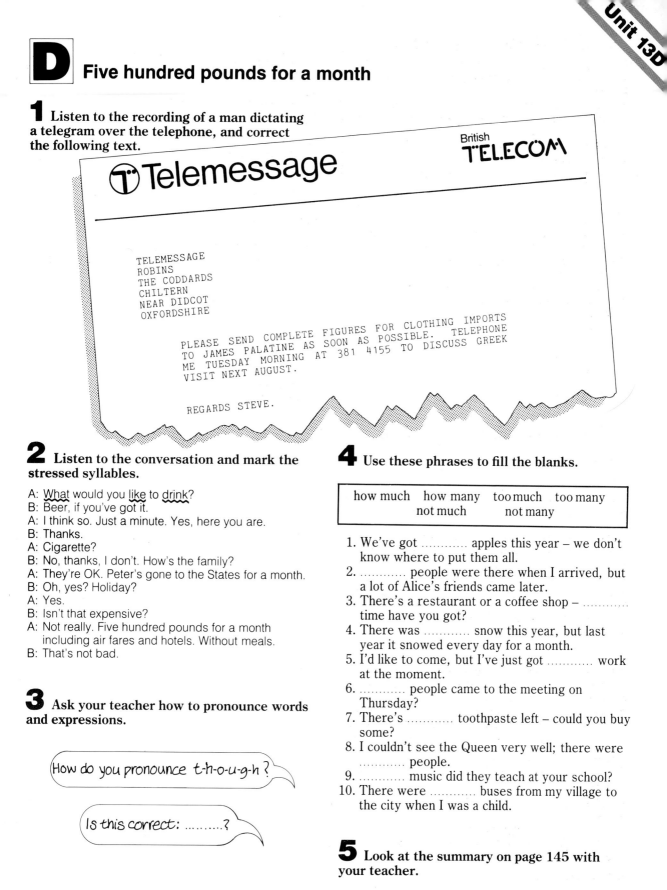

British
TELECOM

ⓣ Telemessage

```
TELEMESSAGE
ROBINS
THE CODDARDS
CHILTERN
NEAR DIDCOT
OXFORDSHIRE

        PLEASE SEND COMPLETE FIGURES FOR CLOTHING IMPORTS
        TO JAMES PALATINE AS SOON AS POSSIBLE.  TELEPHONE
        ME TUESDAY MORNING AT 381 4155 TO DISCUSS GREEK
        VISIT NEXT AUGUST.

        REGARDS STEVE.
```

2 Listen to the conversation and mark the stressed syllables.

A: What would you like to drink?
B: Beer, if you've got it.
A: I think so. Just a minute. Yes, here you are.
B: Thanks.
A: Cigarette?
B: No, thanks, I don't. How's the family?
A: They're OK. Peter's gone to the States for a month.
B: Oh, yes? Holiday?
A: Yes.
B: Isn't that expensive?
A: Not really. Five hundred pounds for a month including air fares and hotels. Without meals.
B: That's not bad.

3 Ask your teacher how to pronounce words and expressions.

How do you pronounce t-h-o-u-g-h?

Is this correct: ....?

4 Use these phrases to fill the blanks.

how much	how many	too much	too many
	not much	not many	

1. We've got .... apples this year – we don't know where to put them all.
2. .... people were there when I arrived, but a lot of Alice's friends came later.
3. There's a restaurant or a coffee shop – .... time have you got?
4. There was .... snow this year, but last year it snowed every day for a month.
5. I'd like to come, but I've just got .... work at the moment.
6. .... people came to the meeting on Thursday?
7. There's .... toothpaste left – could you buy some?
8. I couldn't see the Queen very well; there were .... people.
9. .... music did they teach at your school?
10. There were .... buses from my village to the city when I was a child.

5 Look at the summary on page 145 with your teacher.

57

Differences

A I can sing, but I can't draw

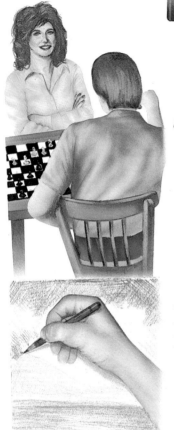

1 Which of these things can you do? Which of them can't you do?

Example: *'I can sing, but I can't draw.'*

> play chess   speak German
> type   play the violin   drive
> draw   run a mile   sing   play tennis

2 Can you swim / cook / play the piano / dance / go without sleep / sleep in the daytime? Ask two other people, and report their answers to the class. Make sentences with *but*.

> *'Can you dance?' 'Yes, I can.'*
> *'No, I can't.'*
> *'Diego can dance, but Alice can't.'*
> *'Diego can dance, but he can't cook.'*

3 In groups: find a person for each job. Tell the class about it. Example:

'Preeda can do the first job. He can't play the guitar, but he can play the flute. He can cook and drive, and he likes children.'

4 Listen, and write *can* or *can't*.

Help us with our children and travel around the world. If you can play the guitar or another instrument, cook, and drive, phone Whitfield at 689 6328.

Travelling companion/driver required for American writer; speaking English, other languages. Chess player appreciated. Excellent pay. Write to Box 492, Newton Tribune.

Typist required, excellent pay, one week nights, 2 weeks days. Musician appreciated. Write to Box 635, Oxford OX6 82J

Take 2 Italian boys, 8 and 10, on holiday in June. Some cooking but no cleaning. Swimming, tennis, windsurfing. Very good pay. Phone Guidotti 278 3440 evenings.

Unit 14: Lesson A

Students learn to talk about abilities.
Structure: *can* (affirmative, negative, question).
Words and expressions to learn: *chess*; *sing*; *go without sleep*; *type*; *drive*; *draw*; *swim*
Phonology: /kən/, /kæn/ and /kɑːnt/ (recognition and production); American /kænt/ (recognition).

Language notes and possible problems

1. Pronunciation   When *can* is followed by another verb (as in *I can swim*), it is normally pronounced like *c'n* (/kən/); the strong pronunciation /kæn/ is mostly heard in short answers (*Yes, I can*). In questions (*Can you swim? What can you see?*), both pronunciations are possible.

In standard British English, the negative *can't* is pronounced /kɑːnt/. The listening exercise also includes some examples of the American pronunciation /kænt/, for the students to recognize.

2. Spelling   You may wish to tell students that *cannot* is written as one word.

3. Grammar   Point out that there is no *-s* on the third-person singular *can*, and that *can* is followed by an infinitive without *to*.

4. Articles   Note the difference between *to play **the** piano* and *to play football/chess*.

Optional extra materials

Cards with *can*-questions (see Optional activity after Exercise 2).

1 *I can / I can't...*

● Let the students look at the words in the box, and ask you if there are any that they don't understand. You may want to use the pictures in the book to help you.
● Then make a true sentence about yourself in the form *I can ... but I can't ...*
● Point out the pronunciations /kən/ and /kɑːnt/ (as in the recorded example), and make sure students notice the stress pattern of the sentence. Correct stress will help them to pronounce /kən/ correctly.
● Then let the students make sentences about themselves, using the words in the box.
● You could do this as a 'ball game': crumple a sheet of paper and roll it into a ball, and say your sentence again: *I can ... but I can't ... And you?*
● At the last words throw the ball to someone else, who must give their sentence and throw the ball again.
● Continue until you think the students are at ease with the sentences.

Optional activity

● Students mime things they can do; the others watch them and say *You can cook*, or whatever they think it is.

2 Survey

● Once again, go over the vocabulary with the students to make sure they understand.
● Demonstrate and help the students practise the pronunciation of the question and answer forms.
● Then divide the class into threes. Each group asks one another the questions, and notes the answers.

● When the questioning is finished, each person should report to the class with at least two sentences about the other people in the group. The sentences should all contain *but*.

Optional activity

● Prepare a large number of cards. Each card should tell students to find a person who can do one thing. Examples:
Find a person who can speak Chinese (or some other appropriate language).
Find a person who can stand on his/her head.
Find a person who can write your name in Arabic.
Find a person who can solve this equation: $3x = 75 - 2x$.
Find a person who can swim well.
Find a person who can dance the tango.
● There should be several times as many cards as students – but some can be duplicated.
● Students take a card from you, and go round asking *Can you...?* When they find a person who can do the thing on the card, they write down his/her name and take another card.
● The winner is the one who collects the most names.

Other optional activities

1. Students tell the class what they can do, but include lies. The others listen, and shout *No, you can't!* if they hear something they don't believe.
2. Two students both tell the class what they can do. The class then have to write down what was said without confusing the two accounts.

3 Small ads

● Divide the class into groups of three or four.
● Let them read the small ads with their dictionaries or ask you for unknown words. (Don't forget to insist on their asking *What does ... mean?*.)
● Each group must find the best person in the group for each job, given the requirements and the abilities and tastes of the people in the group.
● The groups then report to the class, with the reasons for their choices.
● The class can vote on the best candidate for each job.

Optional activity

● Students can write a simple letter of application for the job they have been chosen for.
● Remind them how a letter is set out and suggest something like:
Dear Sir,
    I should like to apply for the job of .... which you advertised in yesterday's paper. I can .... and .... I like ....
    I am looking forward to your reply.
        Yours faithfully,

4 Listening

● Students will hear seven fragments (four of British speech and three of American speech).
● They simply have to note down whether they hear *can* or *can't* in each one.
Tapescript for Exercise 4: see page 181

Practice Book

● Tell students which exercises you want them to do.

Unit 14: Lesson B

> **Students learn** to compare how well things are done.
> **Structures:** *I can ... better than you; good at + noun/gerund.*
> **Words and expressions to learn:** *count; run; ski; better* (adverb); *faster; cheaper; well; now.*
> **Phonology:** different pronunciations of the letter *a*: /æ/, /eɪ/, /ɑː/, /ɔ/.

Language notes and possible problems
Anything is used here in a new sense: 'it doesn't matter what'.

1 True or false?
• Go over the table and explain vocabulary, or let students use their dictionaries.
• Then get them to answer the questions, comparing notes with their neighbours.

2 Listening: true or false?
• Get students to write the numbers 1–10 down the side of a sheet of paper.
• Then play the recording, pausing for them to write *T* or *F* for each sentence.

Tapescript and answers to Exercise 2
1. I'm the Queen. I can spell very well. (T)
2. I can sing better than the Prime Minister. (F)
3. I can cook better than the Foreign Minister. (T)
4. The Minister of Finance can run faster than me. (T)
5. The Minister of Finance can count better than the Foreign Minister. (F)
6. I'm the Minister of Education. I can run very fast. (F)
7. I can sing better than all the others. (T)
8. I can play tennis better than the Foreign Minister. (T)
9. I can speak English better than the Prime Minister. (F)
10. I can count better than all the others. (F)

3 Personalization
• Get at least one sentence from each student.

4 ... when I was younger
• Go over the example sentences with the students, pointing out:
1. the use of *good at* + noun or gerund
2. ellipsis (omission of words) after *than* and *but* ('... than I can (swim) now.' '... but I'm not (good at maths) now.')
• You may wish to write the sentences up on the board and get the students to help you mark the stressed syllables before practising the sentences.
• Then ask each student to write two sentences about now and when he/she was younger.
• You can walk round while students are working to help with any problems.
• Then get each student to say one of his or her sentences to the class.

5 Memory test
• Divide the class into two teams.
• Each team must try to remember what the members of the other team said in Exercise 3.

• The person in question should answer *You're right* or *I'm afraid you're wrong.*
• One point for each correct answer.

Optional activity: boasting and confessing
• Students compete to produce the most impressive piece of boasting or confession.
• *Either* they tell the class what they can do, what they are good at, what they do well;
• *Or* they tell the class what they can't do, what they are bad at, what they do badly.
• Emphasize that they do not have to tell the truth!

6 Pronunciations of *a*: presentation
• Get the students to repeat the words after you or the recording. Point out that each row contains words where *a* is pronounced the same.

7 Discovering pronunciation rules
• Let the students work individually for a few minutes to see if they can classify the words in this exercise according to the pronunciations they practised in the previous exercise.
• Then let them compare answers in small groups.
• Rather than giving them the answers (e.g., 1 or 3) right away, simply play the recording or say the words yourself.
• Then check which numbers they have put, and see if they can offer any rules.
• The rules are:
  /æ/ before final consonant or double consonant;
  /eɪ/ before consonant + *e*, or *i* + consonant;
  /ɑː/ before (mute) *r*, *f*, *s* + consonant, final *th*;
  /ɔː/ before final *w*, double *l*, *lk*.

Answers
a. past 3	e. ball 4	i. law 4
b. page 2	f. part 3	j. tape 2
c. map 1	g. pass 3	
d. bag 1	h. Spain 2	

8 Song
• You may like to play students the song (*Anything you can do I can do better*, from *Annie Get Your Gun*).
• Help them to understand the words. In successive verses, one person tells another that he or she can:
  do anything better; be anything greater; sing anything higher; buy anything cheaper; say anything softer; hold any note longer; wear anything better; say anything faster.
(For copyright reasons, we are not able to give the exact words here.)

Practice Book
• Tell students which exercises you want them to do.

B I can do anything better than you

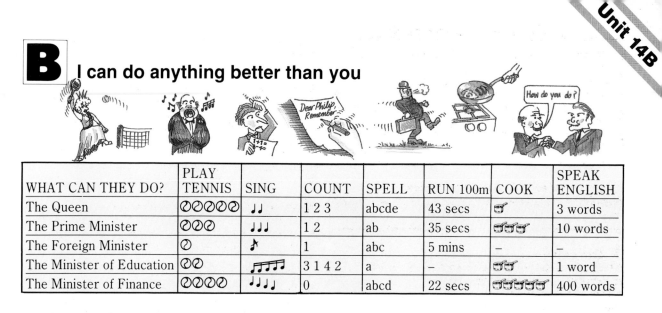

WHAT CAN THEY DO?	PLAY TENNIS	SING	COUNT	SPELL	RUN 100m	COOK	SPEAK ENGLISH
The Queen	⊘⊘⊘⊘⊘	♪♪	1 2 3	abcde	43 secs	☜	3 words
The Prime Minister	⊘⊘⊘	♪♪♪	1 2	ab	35 secs	☜☜☜	10 words
The Foreign Minister	⊘	♪	1	abc	5 mins	–	–
The Minister of Education	⊘⊘	♫♫♫♫	3 1 4 2	a	–	☜☜	1 word
The Minister of Finance	⊘⊘⊘⊘	♪♪♪	0	abcd	22 secs	☜☜☜☜☜	400 words

1 True or false? Look at the table.

1. The Queen can spell very well.
2. The Foreign Minister can count quite well.
3. The Minister of Education can't run.
4. The Minister of Finance can't speak English.
5. The Prime Minister can't count.
6. The Queen can cook better than the Minister of Finance.
7. The Minister of Education can sing better than the Queen.
8. The Prime Minister can run faster than the Minister of Education.
9. The Minister of Education can spell better than the Foreign Minister.
10. The Queen can spell better than all the others.

2 True or false? Listen to the recording.

3 Make some sentences with *better than*. Example:

'I can cook better than my sister.'

4 Talk about now and when you were younger; use *than* and *but*.

'When I was younger I couldn't cook at all, but now I can cook quite well.'
'I was good at maths when I was younger, but I'm not now.'
'I could swim better when I was younger than I can now.'
'My father can speak Spanish better now than he could when I was younger.'
'I'm better at running now than I was when I was younger.'

5 In teams: try to remember other students' sentences. One point for each correct one.

Michel can ski better now than he could when he was younger.

You're right. / I'm afraid you're wrong.

6 Say these words after the recording or your teacher.

1. am   cat   back   hand   bad
2. came   late   wake   rain   made
3. car   last   glasses   bath   half
4. saw   tall   walk   talk   all

7 1, 2, 3 or 4? Decide how to pronounce these and then check with your teacher or the recording.

a. past ...3......   f. part
b. page   g. pass
c. map   h. Spain
d. bag   i. law
e. ball   j. tape

8 Listen to the song.

C I'm much taller than my mother

LONGER

smaller

TALLER

BIGGER

1 Look at the list of adjectives. Can you see any rules? What are the comparative and superlative of these words?

long *longer   longest*
dark   hungry
cold   nice
near   intelligent
big   expensive

2 Compare people you know.

A is (much) taller   than B.
   (a bit)   shorter
             older
             younger
             thinner
             etc.

'I'm much taller than my mother.'
'Mario's a bit older than his brother.'

In your family, who is the oldest / the youngest / the shortest / the best at English?

3 Compare countries (warm/cold/big/small/ cheap/expensive/noisy/quiet) or cars (big/small/ fast/slow/expensive/cheap/comfortable/ economical/good).

'Japan is much more expensive than Greece.'
'A Volkswagen is much cheaper than a Mercedes.'

hikaku   *saijokyu*

ADJECTIVE	COMPARATIVE	SUPERLATIVE
1. old	older	oldest
young	younger	youngest
short	shorter	shortest
tall	taller	tallest
cheap	cheaper	cheapest
cool	cooler	coolest
2. fat	fatter	fattest
thin	thinner	thinnest
3. happy	happier	happiest
easy	easier	easiest
4. late	later	latest
fine	finer	finest
5. good	better	best
bad	worse	worst
far	farther	farthest
6. interesting	more interesting	most interesting
beautiful	more beautiful	most beautiful
difficult	more difficult	most difficult

4 Compare your liking for steak, chicken, trout, pizza and curry. Which do you like best?

'I like steak better than pizza.'
'I like trout best.'

5 Compare Einstein, Chaplin, Cleopatra, Getty, de Gaulle, John Lennon, Samson (intelligent, rich, funny, strong, beautiful, tall, interesting).

'Getty was richer than Einstein.'
'Samson was the strongest.'

60

Unit 14: Lesson C

Students learn to compare people, places and things.
Structures: comparative and superlative of adjectives; *a bit/much* before adjectives.
Words and expressions to learn: *easy; bad/worse/worst; best; comfortable; economical; rich; funny; interesting.*

Language notes and possible problems

1. Pronunciation You will want to point out the pronunciation of *younger/youngest* (/'jʌŋɡə(r)/ /'jʌŋɡɪst/), and remind students that *the* is pronounced /ði:/ before vowels (e.g. *the oldest*).

2. *Than I / than me* Tell the students that *I* and *me* are both correct after *than*; *I* is preferred in a more formal style, and is common in written English. (The same is true of *she/her*, etc.)

3. Topics In Exercises 4 and 5, you may want to choose different foods and people to fit in better with your students' experience and knowledge.

Optional extra equipment

A long ruler or pointer for Exercise 5.

1 Rules for comparing adjectives

● Ask students to look at the table of adjectives and try to see what is special about each group. Do not get them to offer suggestions aloud yet.
● Ask them to do Exercise 1 individually, to check their guesses.
● Get them to compare their answers in small groups before checking them with you.
● Ask them to tell you a rule for each group of words.
  Group 1: normal short adjectives add *-er, -est.*
  Group 2: one-syllable adjectives that end in one vowel + one consonant: these double the consonant and add *-er, -est.*
  Group 3: two-syllable adjectives ending in *y* change the *y* to *i* and add *-er, -est.*
  Group 4: adjectives ending in *e* add *-r, -st.*
  Group 5: irregular.
  Group 6: longer adjectives prefix *more, most.*
● As a working rule, you can tell students to use *more* and *most* with adjectives of more than one syllable, except for two-syllable words ending in *-y.*
● Explain any words the students don't know.

2 Comparing people (age and appearance)

● In a class where this will not cause discomfort, you can get the students to compare people in the class. Teach the use of *much/a bit* and make sure students use them in their sentences.
● One way of making this exercise more interesting is to get each student to make one comparison and then get everyone to try to write down as many as they can remember.
● Point out the use of *in* after superlatives and make sure students say *in my family* or *in the class.*

3 Comparing countries and cars

● You will want to introduce the new adjectives before you begin the exercise, or as you go along.
● According to your students' interests, you may wish to talk about countries or cars or both.
● Point out that the *ow* in *slow* is considered a vowel, not a consonant, so isn't doubled for comparative and superlative.

4 Liking for foods

● Choose different foods than the ones given if these do not correspond to your students' experience and tastes.
● When students have practised the model sentences, put them in pairs. Each student tells his or her partner three sentences with *better* and one sentence with *best.*
● Bring a volunteer up to the board, and get each student to report on his or her partner's favourite of the five foods: *X likes ... best*, while the volunteer keeps score to see which is the best-liked food.

5 Famous people (comparing qualities)

● Choose different people if the ones in the book do not correspond to your students' knowledge and interests.
● Explain or demonstrate the new words.
● One way of varying this exercise is to put the following on the board:

  Einstein Getty   -er   -est   them   all
  funny   sexy   Samson   -ier   -iest
  more   most   intelligent   Chaplin
  the   rich   Cleopatra   than
  strong   was   of   de Gaulle
  beautiful   tall   interesting

● A volunteer comes up to the board and forms a sentence by pointing to one word after another, and the class then says the sentence.
● The pointer is then handed to another volunteer, and so on.
● Make sure that students pronounce unstressed *was* (/wəz/).

Practice Book

● Tell students which exercises you want them to do.

Unit 14: Lesson D

Students learn to talk about similarities and differences.
Structures: *the same as; different from; (not) as...as; as* vs. *than*.
Words to learn: *typewriter; typist; handsome; heavy*.
Phonology: weak forms of *as* and *from*; stress and rhythm recognition.

Language note
Because English is a 'stress-timed' language, some words are pronounced more quickly and lightly than others. Students whose own languages are not stress-timed find this difficult to get used to, and they often have trouble actually hearing some of the words in a sentence, particularly words such as *from, can, and, but, as*, which have a 'weak form' with the vowel /ə/. Exercise 4 will help them to become more sensitive to unstressed words.

Optional additional materials
Sets of brochures on countries, cars, or other things that the students could compare.

1 The same or different?
● Get students to read through the list of pairs, using their dictionaries or asking you questions.
● Run over the exercise orally, asking whether the things in each pair are the same or different.
● Make sure they don't leave out the article in *the same*.
● Then get each student to write three sentences with *the same as* and three with *different from*, like the ones in the examples.
● Get them to read out their sentences; emphasize correct stress, teaching the unstressed pronunciation of *as* (/əz/), and reminding them of the unstressed pronunciation of *from* (/frəm/). These pronunciations will be easier to realize if they say their sentences with a good rhythm, passing quickly over the unstressed syllables.

1. S   2. D   3. S   4. D   5. S   6. S   7. D   8. D   9. D
10. D   11. D   12. D   13. D   14. S

2 *(not) as...as...*
● Practise the pronunciation of the example sentences, paying careful attention to the pronunciation of *as* (/əz/) and to the rhythm.
● Get students to write their sentences; go round helping as necessary.
● When they are ready, ask them to read their sentences to each other or to the class.
● At this stage, it is probably better not to introduce the alternative structure *not so... as...* ; the structure with *not as* is equally correct and less confusing.

3 *As or than?*
● These two words are often confused by foreign learners of English.
● If they can grasp the difference clearly now, they may avoid mistakes later on. Ask students to do the exercise and then compare notes, before checking with you.

4 How many words?
● Play each sentence twice or more, pausing afterwards each time so students can note their answers.
● When you have played the ten sentences, let the students compare notes in small groups and then play the sentences again so they can listen more carefully to those where they differ.
● Then check their answers.

The sentences are:
1. There are some 'men in the 'garden. (7)
2. 'Where are the 'children? (4)
3. I'm from the 'south of the U'nited 'States. (9)
4. He can 'swim as 'well as a 'fish. (8)
5. 'What do you 'think of the 'lesson? (7)
6. I 'asked 'Ann and 'Peter and a 'friend of 'John's. (10)
7. There are some 'glasses of 'wine in the 'kitchen. (9)
8. We have 'dinner at 'seven o''clock. (6)
9. 'What was the 'name of the 'book? (7)
10. I'd 'like a 'cup of 'tea 'better than a 'glass of 'beer. (13)

Optional activity
● After finishing Exercise 4, you can use the same sentences for pronunciation practice if you wish.
● Ask students to say each sentence after the recording or after you.
● Get them to decide how many stressed syllables there are in each case. For example, sentence 1 has seven words, but only two stressed syllables.
● If they pronounce the stressed syllables slowly and clearly, they will find it easier to say the other syllables quickly and lightly.

5 Detailed comparisons
● For this exercise, it will help students if you can collect brochures on countries, cars, or anything else you think they might like to compare. It is not important in a monolingual class if the brochures are in their native language rather than in English, as they are only a starting point for their work.
● If you do have brochures, pass them around after dividing the class into groups of about four.
● If you do not have brochures, tell the groups they must choose two countries or two cars or two famous people. Be prepared to suggest specific ones if they get stuck.
● Tell each group they must decide which two things they are going to compare, and write down as many points of comparison as they can.
● It may be helpful to give a target number of sentences, say eight; enthusiastic groups will always go on if they have reached the target.
● Walk round to give any help that is needed.
● You may need to help with suggestions of points.
● Make sure each group has a secretary noting the sentences down as they produce them.
● The final products can be read out or posted up for the other groups to read.

6 Summary
● Go over the summary with the students.

Practice Book
● Tell students which exercises you want them to do.

61

D The same or different?

1 The same or different? (Use your dictionary.)

1. 7 × 12 and 3 × 28
2. Britain and England
3. Holland and The Netherlands
4. The USSR and Russia
5. Peking and Beijing

6. three o'clock and 15.00
7. a café and a pub
8. handsome and pretty
9. a woman and a wife
10. a pen and a pencil

11. 4,718 and 4.718
12. a cooker and a cook
13. a typewriter and a typist
14. a telephone number and a phone number

Write three sentences with *the same as* and three with *different from.*
Examples:

Three o'clock in the afternoon is the same as 15.00.
A café is different from a pub.

2 Compare some of these people and things. Use *(not) as... as...*
Examples:

I'm as good-looking as Robert Redford.
A Volkswagen is not as quiet as a Rolls-Royce.

I/me Robert Redford a Volkswagen
a Rolls-Royce the President Bach
an elephant a cat Canada
rock music Kenya a piano

tall heavy good-looking
strong old fast economical
cold warm cheap expensive big
noisy quiet comfortable
intelligent nice

COMPANY
DOCTOR

"How d'you mean I'm as fit as a man of thirty—I am thirty!"

3 *As* or *than?*

1. I can sing better .... you.
2. Elizabeth's much taller .... her brother.
3. I'm .... old .... my teacher.
4. Your eyes are the same colour .... mine.
5. Germany is bigger .... Switzerland.
6. Your problems are not .... important .... mine.

4 Listen to the recording. How many words are there in each sentence? What are they? (Contractions like *I'm* count as two words.)

5 Work in groups. In each group, make a detailed comparison between two people, or two countries, or two cars, or two other things. Find as many things to say as possible. Write down all the things you think of.

6 Look at the summary on page 145 with your teacher.

Some history

A 91 million years ago

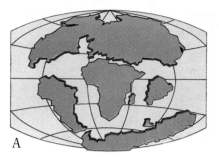

A

1 Put the pictures in order by reading the text. You can use a dictionary or ask your teacher for help.

A long time ago, Africa was not far from South America. In fact, 300 million years ago all the land on earth was only one big continent, called 'Pangaea'.

Very slowly, Pangaea separated into two parts, and the future continents began to move towards their places. But until 160 million years ago South America, Africa, India, Australia and Antarctica were still only one huge land mass ('Gondwanaland'). North America, Europe and Asia together made the other super-continent ('Laurasia').

Then Gondwanaland and

Laurasia also began to divide. Seas started to spread between the new continents. This was a slow process: Africa and South America only finished separating 91 million years ago.

Some strange results of land mass movements:
1. There is a diamond deposit that starts in Africa, stops on the west coast, and begins again in South America.
2. Mountains in Norway, Scotland, Greenland and the north-east US all belong to the same mountain chain.

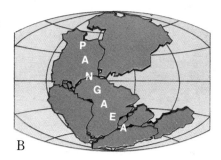

B

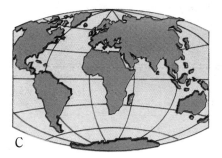

C

2 When did it happen? Match the two halves of each sentence. Example:

'Julius Caesar invaded Britain about 2,000 years ago.'

The last dinosaurs died	about 3½ million years ago.
The French Revolution happened	about 2,000 years ago.
Julius Caesar invaded Britain	about 400 years ago.
The Great Pyramid was built	about 500 years ago.
Columbus discovered America	about 4,500 years ago.
Europeans discovered Australia	about 200 years ago.
The first people lived on earth	about 70 million years ago.

D

3 Ask and answer questions with *ago*. Example:

'How long ago was World War II?' 'About 40 years ago.'

New Year's Day   4.00 a.m.   the beginning of this class   last Tuesday
World War I   your first English lesson   etc.

4 Fill each blank with a word from the text in Exercise 1.

I don't live with my husband now; we .... six months ago. I .... see him occasionally, but we don't want to live together again.

It is difficult to say when our problems .... Slowly, life became more and more uncomfortable; even very small problems looked .... to us. We are both happier now that we have .... living together.

It was not difficult to .... our belongings into mine and his, but I was a bit upset the day I .... my things into my new flat. It meant an important part of my life was really ....

Unit 15: Lesson A

Students learn to situate past events, and to say more about the process of change.
Structures: *ago; How long ago...?*
Words and expressions to learn: *Africa; Asia; Europe; Australia; America; part; begin; move; separate* (verb); *finish; ago; still; a long time; slow; last.*
Phonology: linking in *years ago* and *long ago*.

Language notes and possible problems

1. *Begin* and *start* At this point, it is not useful to teach students the very small, quasi-stylistic differences between these two words; they can be considered as having identical meanings.

2. *Stop* and *finish* You may want to point out to the students that something which has stopped may start again, whereas something which has finished will not.

3. Linking While not essential to intelligibility, correct linking in expressions like *... years_ago* and *How long_ago...?* will make students much easier to understand, and is probably worth a bit of work.

1 Presentation: ordering pictures 🔊

- Tell the students to read the text and try to put the pictures in order as quickly as they can.
- Let them use their dictionaries or ask you about words they have difficulty with; but point out that it is not necessary that they understand every word of the text.
- When they have finished, let them compare answers in groups before checking with you.
- Then read them the text or play the recording, and give them another chance to ask questions.

Alternative approach to Exercise 1

- This is a more explicit way of helping students develop their scanning skills.
- Get them to read the text; they can ask you for words they want to know, or ask you if they can look for them in dictionaries.
- But they must only ask about words which are important to their task. If they ask for words which are not important, tell them so, and don't give the meaning.
- Once the ordering task is finished, let them read the text again and ask you for *any* words they want to know. Then play the recording.

2 *Ago*

- Help students with any new words.
- Get the students to practise the example sentence, paying special attention to linking in *years ago*. Make sure students are pronouncing a /z/ and not a /s/.
- Divide the class into groups of three or four and let them attempt the matching exercise.
- When you check the exercise with the class, get students to read out the complete sentences, once again paying attention to linking.

Answers
last dinosaurs – about 70 million years ago
French Revolution – about 200 years ago

Great Pyramid – about 4,500 years ago
Columbus – about 500 years ago
Australia – about 400 years ago
first people – about 3½ million years ago

3 *How long ago?*

- Get the students to practise the example sentences, paying special attention to linking in *long ago*; make sure the students say /ˈlɒŋəgəʊ/ and not /ˈlɒŋəgəʊ/.
- Get a few volunteers to ask questions with the first two or three cues, and then put the class into pairs to ask and answer questions.
- Encourage them to make questions with *did* as well as *was*.
- In a class that enjoys competing, and where students share a certain amount of historical knowledge, you can set up a team game with points for correct answers and unanswered (or incorrectly answered) questions.

4 Vocabulary work

- This exercise focuses on some of the vocabulary from the first text which is useful in talking about change.
- Tell the students that each blank is for *one* word from the text in Exercise 1. (Verbs may be in a different tense.)
- Let students work individually before comparing their answers in small groups.
- Then go over the answers with them.

Answers (in order)
separated; still; began (or started); huge; stopped (or finished); divide (or separate); moved; finished.

Practice Book
- Tell students which exercises you want them to do.

Unit 15: Lesson B

Students revise a number of points in the context of a discussion about historical personalities.
Structures: *a* vs. *the*; past tense of *to be*; Simple Past tense; question forms.
Words and expressions to learn: *university*; *plane*; *republic*; *across*; *discover*; *walk*.

Possible problems

Multinational classes   In classes where students come from several different cultures, they will not share the same historical knowledge necessary to make Exercises 4 and 5 successful. Alternative exercises are suggested below.

1 Presentation of information

- Get the students to do the matching exercise; let them use their dictionaries to find the new words.
- Make sure they understand that for each person there is one item in list A, one item in list B, and so on.
- If students speak the same language you may wish them to work in groups, so that they can divide up the work of looking up words in dictionaries. Otherwise it may be good to let them compare answers in groups when they have finished working.
- To check the answers, say, *Tell me about Amelia Earhart*, and let volunteers give you one sentence each.
- Insist on full sentences, e.g. *She was born in Atchison, Kansas, in the USA.*
- Aim for correct stress and rhythm, and weak form pronunciation of *was* (/wəz/) and *were* (/wə/).
- Point out the contrast between *a* (B and C) before *student* and the names of professions, and *the* (D) before expressions which define specific people.
- Go through the information about the other people in the same way.

2 Practice

- Ask the students to close their books. Write:
  Who?   Where?   What?   on the board.
- Demonstrate with a volunteer that students are to take turns asking and answering questions on the people they have just read about.
- Divide the class into pairs and let them work, walking round to give any help that is needed.

3 Listening

- Students hear most of the information they have learnt in the lesson, in a slightly modified form.
- Meanwhile, they listen for four specific bits of information.
- Explain the new words. If you do not wish the students to write in their books, get them to copy the two lists on a separate piece of paper.
- Play the recording once through without stopping.
- Let the students compare answers.
- If necessary, play the recording again so they can check on any disagreements.

Tapescript for Exercise 3
Galileo Galilei was born in Pisa, Italy, in 1564. He was a mathematician, astronomer and physicist and made valuable discoveries in all these fields. For example, he discovered sunspots for the first time. Galileo was a student at the University of Pisa when he was young, and later a professor at different universities in Italy. He was famous for his lectures, and students came from all over Europe to hear them.

Amelia Earhart was a famous aeroplane pilot. She was born in Atchison, Kansas in 1898. When she was 22, she stopped her studies at Columbia University, New York, to learn to pilot a plane. Flying lessons were expensive and she took several jobs to pay for them: once she worked as a lorry driver because the pay was good. In 1932 she was the first woman to fly her own plane across the Atlantic, from Newfoundland to Ireland.

Ho Chi Minh was a Vietnamese politician and poet. He was born in Annam in 1892 and studied in Hué and Saigon. Later he visited North Africa, the USA, England and France, working on ships, sweeping snow, and, in Paris, working as a photographer. He was the founder of the People's Republic of Vietnam and worked all his life to liberate and unify his country. It was only after his death that this dream came true.

Marie Sklodowska was born in Warsaw, Poland in 1867. She later went to Paris, where she met and married Pierre Curie. The Curies were both physicists, and became famous for their work. One of their first discoveries was the element radium. They were both professors of physics at the Sorbonne, and they shared the Nobel Prize for physics in 1903.

4 History quiz

- Divide the class into two teams.
- Each team takes a turn asking a question about a historical personality; points are gained for correct answers or unanswered/wrongly answered questions by the other team.

Alternative to Exercises 4 and 5

- Get each student to write four or five sentences about a famous historical personality from his or her country or culture.
- Encourage them to use only the English they know, or at most a couple of new words.
- Divide the class into groups of four or five.
- In each group people take turns reading their sentences, and the others must ask them two or three questions about the person they have described.
- Walk around while the students are working to help with any problems.
- If there is time, you can then change the composition of the groups so that students read their sentences to people who haven't heard them before.

5 Twenty Questions

- Get a volunteer to come to the front of the class and think of a famous person or group of people.
- The student says one affirmative and two negative sentences about the person; pay attention to unstressed *was* or *were* if the affirmative sentence contains these, and stressed *didn't* or *wasn't/weren't* in the negative sentences.
- Tell the other students to ask questions in order to find out who the person is; but the student at the front can only answer *Yes* or *No*.
- Once the person has been guessed, you can divide the class into groups to continue the game.

Practice Book
- Tell students which exercises you want them to do.

B Where was Galileo born?

1 Match four of the phrases with each picture. You can use a dictionary.

A
born in Paris, France and Warsaw, Poland
born in Annam, Viet Nam
born in Atchison, Kansas, USA
born in Pisa, Italy

B
student in Saigon
student at the University of Pisa
student at Columbia University, New York
professors of physics at the Sorbonne, Paris

C
mathematician, astronomer and physicist
politician and poet
physicists and teachers
pilot and writer

D
first woman to fly a plane across the Atlantic
people who discovered radium
founder of the People's Republic of Viet Nam
man who discovered sunspots

Galileo, 1564-1642

Amelia Earhart, 1898-?1937

Ho Chi Minh, 1892-1969

Marie and Pierre Curie, 1867-1934 and 1859-1906

2 Close your book. Ask and answer questions about the four people. Examples:

'Where was Amelia Earhart born?'
  'In Kansas, I think. What did Ho Chi Minh do?'
'He was a politician. Who discovered sunspots?'
  'I don't remember. The Curies?'

3 Listen, and match the names with the phrases.

1. Galileo
2. Earhart
3. Ho Chi Minh
4. The Curies

a. Nobel prize
b. lorry driver
c. famous for lectures
d. photographer

4 Ask and answer questions about famous people in the past. Examples:

'Who was the first man to walk on the moon?'
  'Neil Armstrong.'
'Who was Simon Bolivar?'
  'The founder of Bolivia.'

5 1. One student thinks of a famous person, or a group of famous people, from the past.
2. The student says one affirmative and two negative sentences, for example:
  'This was a woman. She wasn't American. She wasn't a writer.'
3. The other students try to guess who it is by asking questions with yes/no answers; for example:
  'Was she European? Was she married? Did she work in America?'

C America invades Britain!

1 **Put the pictures in the correct order. Only use your dictionary for the important words.**

In 1778 the British had the strongest navy in the world. They laughed at the small navy of their American colonies, who were fighting Britain for their independence.

One American captain decided to show the British that size was not everything. Here is what happened:

On the night of April 24, 1778, Captain John Paul Jones silently brought the American ship *Ranger* into Whitehaven harbour on the west coast of England. As soon as he arrived, he took a group of his men to a local inn, broke into it, and had a drink with them.

Then they went back to the harbour and began their work. Some of them went to the fort and put the guns out of order; others began burning British ships. The British sailors finally woke up, and put up a good fight, but they lost to Jones and his men.

Captain Jones was pleased, but not completely satisfied. So he sailed to the nearby Scottish coast and went to the home of the Earl of Selkirk. Jones and his men put all of the Earl's silverware onto the *Ranger* to take back to America! The British did not laugh so much about America's navy after Jones' visit.

2 **Irregular verbs: match the present and past forms.**

began	made	brought	(took)	broke	put	lost
put	bring	lose	make	(take)	begin	break

3 **Read the text below, and put one of these words or expressions into each blank.**

after	at midnight	finally	as soon as
about	dancing	and then	on the night of
others	sang	so	some
went	began		some of them

.... December 31st, we invited .... friends to a New Year's Eve party. .... the first guests arrived, we offered them drinks, ... we put on some music. .... half an hour there were .... thirty people in our small flat. .... to dance; .... just went on talking, eating and drinking. .... we all joined hands and .... an old Scottish song called 'Auld Lang Syne'; then we went on ....

At seven o'clock in the morning there were still eight people left, ... we had breakfast. .... the last guest went home, and we .... to bed.

4 **Write a story using at least five of the words or expressions from Exercise 3. You can write about a journey, a holiday, a party, a nice birthday, etc.**

Unit 15: Lesson C

Students begin learning to narrate.
Structures: Simple Past tense: sequencing devices.
Words and expressions to learn: *world, lose, laugh; take (someone somewhere); decide; finally; as soon as; on the night of; some of...; break (into); wake (up); back.*

Language notes and possible problems

1. Reading for meaning There are a fair number of new words and expressions in the reading text in this lesson, and this may be daunting to students. However, (1) during their first reading they should look up (or ask you about) only those words they need to put the pictures in order. This should give them confidence in the fact that they can understand the story without understanding every word. (2) Words for special attention are singled out for re-use in Exercises 3 and 4, and these with a few others are included in the summary; they need not worry about the other words. (3) Of course, some students will want to learn all the words in the text, and this is a perfectly legitimate way of acquiring new vocabulary in a foreign language. But one of the aims of the lesson is to show students that word-for-word understanding is not necessary in every case.

2. Sequences In this lesson students learn some of the words and expressions used in English to establish sequences of events, e.g. *then, as soon as.* Since these items are more common in written than in spoken language, the exercises are writing-based. But this need not mean a dull and silent lesson if students work in groups to carry out the tasks.

---

1 Reading for meaning

● Before the students begin to read, look at the pictures with them, eliciting or teaching a few words as you do so (*ship, harbour, fight, gun*).
● Then tell them that the pictures are not in order, and they must read the story to put them in order.
● They can ask you for words they need (and you may wish to decline to give them words which are not important to the gist of the text), or they may work with their dictionaries.
● If they all speak the same language, you may want them to do the dictionary work in groups of about four, dividing the work up.
● Help with the irregular past tenses or refer students to Exercise 2 if their dictionaries do not list irregular past tenses separately.
● If the students have been working individually, get them to compare answers in small groups.
● When you are checking the answers, ask them to give you a sentence for each of the pictures, e.g. *C: Captain Jones brought the 'Ranger' into Whitehaven harbour.*
● Give the students a chance to ask you questions about the text, but do not spend too much time on this.
● Finally, you may like to read the text to the students or play the recording.

2 Irregular verbs

● Students may have done this exercise while working on Exercise 1.
● Otherwise, get them to do it now, to reinforce the forms of the irregular verbs in the text.

3 Focusing on items from the text

● Divide the class into groups of three or four, and get them to try to put one of the words or expressions into each blank.
● Walk round as they are working to give any help they may need.
● To check the answers, you may want to get students to come to the board in turn to write up the sentences.

Answers to Exercise 3
On the night of December 31st, we invited *some* friends to a New Year's Eve party. *As soon as* the first guests arrived, we offered them drinks, *and then* we put on some music.

After half an hour there were *about* thirty people in our small flat. *Some of them began* to dance; *others* just went on talking, eating and drinking. *At midnight* we all joined hands and *sang* an old Scottish song called 'Auld Lang Syne'; then we went on *dancing.*

At seven o'clock in the morning there were still eight people left, *so* we had breakfast. *Finally* the last guest went home, and we *went* to bed.

4 Writing

● Get the students to write their own stories, using at least five of the words or expressions from Exercise 3.
● Students may use the suggestions in the book, or choose another subject.
● If you are really pressed for time, you may want to give this exercise as homework; however, it is much more useful to the students if they can do it in class, with you walking round to give any help that is needed.
● See the note on page XII of this book about correcting written work.

Practice Book
● Tell students which exercises you want them to do.

Unit 15: Lesson D

Students revise ways of talking about the past.
Structures: past of *to be*, Simple Past tense.
Words and expressions to learn: *disagree;*
radio; novel; kill; build.
Phonology: stress patterns in sentences with *was*
and *were*; weak forms of *was* and *were*.

1 History quiz

• This can be done informally, with students
volunteering the answers, or as a team competition.
• If you run it as a competition, divide the class into
two or three teams, give the questions to teams in turn,
and give a point for each right answer.
• Questions can either be answered by the team as a
whole, or by one student in the team, as you wish.
• If a student or team can't answer a question, it can be
offered to another student or team for half a point.
• You will need to explain some vocabulary as you go
along.

Answers: 1. by air (first Channel crossing by aeroplane)
2. Lee Harvey Oswald 3. Mao Tse-Tung 4. elephants
5. six 6. Bethlehem 7. Ptolemy said the sun went round the
earth; Copernicus said the opposite 8. Marconi, in 1901
9. It was the old name for New York City 10. Alexander
Fleming, in 1928 11. Julie Andrews 12. Groucho and Harpo
(the other Marx Brothers were Chico and Zeppo) 13. Ian
Fleming 14. John Lennon, Paul McCartney, George
Harrison, Ringo Starr 15. Vincent van Gogh 16. football
17. running 18. Gustave Eiffel

2 Stress and weak forms: presentation

• This exercise revises correct stress and weak form
use in sentences with *was* and *were*.
• Get the students to practise the sentences with you,
and then put them in pairs and get each student to read
all the sentences to his or her partner.

3 Stress and weak forms: practice

• This exercise requires the students to remember or
discover the rules governing stress in sentences with
was and *were*.
• Ask the students to work through the sentences
individually, deciding whether to mark *was* and *were* for
stress.
• Then let them compare their answers in small groups.
• Finally, play the recording or read the sentences to
them so they can try to hear if they have got the stress
right, and go over the answers with them.
• You may wish to get them to tell you the rules now:
the words are stressed in short answers and negative
sentences, but not in normal affirmative sentences or
questions.
• Get the students to read the sentences to one
another.

4 Past tense verb forms

• Get the students to do this exercise individually,
walking round as they work to see if there are students
who are having trouble.
• (A few irregular verbs and all the categories of
regular verbs are included here.)

• When checking the answers with the students, you
may wish to ask them whether each verb is regular or
irregular, and in the case of regular verbs ask for other
verbs falling into the same category.

5 Listening

• Make sure the students understand the questions
they are to answer.
• Tell them that they need not worry about
understanding the rest of the recording, but only need
listen for the answers to the questions.
• Then play the recording once through.
• Give the students a chance to compare answers with
one another before playing the recording a second time.
• Some classes may want you to play the recording a
third time before checking the answers with you.

Answers: 1. 1557 2. Queen Elizabeth I 3. Shakespeare
4. 1597 5. light music

Tapescript for Exercise 5
This is the third in a series of seven programmes devoted to
the madrigal. Today's programme will explore the work of
Thomas Morley, one of the greatest of English madrigal
composers. Born in 1557, he became organist at St Paul's
Cathedral, London, and, like so many of the great musicians of
the time, a Gentleman of the Chapel Royal. This body of
musicians performed for the Queen and composed church
music for performance at her court. Queen Elizabeth I must
have admired Morley's work, for in 1598 she granted him a
monopoly which allowed him to control printing and
importation of music and music-ruled paper for all of Britain.
This must have represented a considerable financial advantage
for the musician.
    Morley was probably a friend of Shakespeare; he composed
songs for some of the poet's plays. He was also a writer
himself, and his *Plaine and Easie Introduction to Practicall*
Musicke, published in 1597, was popular for two hundred
years. It is now one of our best sources of information about
musical life in the sixteenth century.
    Morley wrote church music, instrumental music, lute songs,
and many of the finest madrigals of the period. Some of his
best madrigals are in the light, rhythmic style called the ballet.
    Our first selection for today is a madrigal from a collection
called *The Triumphs of Oriana*, a collection of twenty-nine
madrigals by twenty-six different composers, generally
thought to have been composed in praise of Queen Elizabeth.
    By Thomas Morley, a madrigal from *The Triumphs of Oriana*.

6 Summary

• Go over the summary with the students, answering
any questions they may have.

Practice Book
• Tell students which exercises you want them to do.

D   Who? How? What? Where? Which?

1 History quiz. Take turns answering the questions.

1. How did Louis Blériot travel from France to England in 1909?
2. Who killed President Kennedy?
3. Who made the 'Long March' in China?
4. What animals did Hannibal take across the Alps on his invasion of Italy?
5. How many wives did King Henry VIII have?
6. Where was Jesus Christ born?
7. Copernicus disagreed with Ptolemy. What about?
8. Who first sent radio signals across the Atlantic?
9. Where was 'New Amsterdam'?
10. Who discovered penicillin?
11. Who starred in the film *The Sound of Music?*
12. Which of these were members of the 'Marx Brothers': Harpo, Karl, Groucho, Choco?
13. Who wrote the James Bond novels?
14. What were the names of the Beatles?
15. Which famous painter cut off his ear?
16. Which sport was Pele famous for?
17. These people were (or are) famous for the same sport. What is it? Jesse Owens, Abebe Bikila, Grete Waitz, Sebastian Coe.
18. Who built the Eiffel Tower?

2 Read these sentences to another student.

1. **Who** was at the **of**fice **when** you ar**rived**? Nobody **was**.
2. Were **Paul** and **Ann** at the **par**ty? **They weren't**, but the **Nel**sons **were**.
3. His **mo**ther and **fa**ther were **both doc**tors.
4. **Ein**stein was American, but he **wasn't born** in America.

3 Stressed or not? Underline *was* and *were* where they are stressed. Then read the sentences to another student.

1. Were **a**ny of the **chil**dren **there**? **Kev**in and **Mat**thew were, but the **others weren't**.
2. **Ann** wasn't at **home** when I **got there**.
3. **Who** was the **first per**son to **swim** the **Eng**lish **Chan**nel?
4. **I** was in **Ja**pan when my **fa**ther **died**.

4 Put the verbs into the past tense.

1. My sister .... me with my homework. (help)
2. The school year .... three months ago. (begin)
3. When I was younger I .... mushrooms. (hate)
4. My brother never .... football when he was a child. (play)
5. It .... us three hours to get home on Friday. (take)
6. I .... my passport in Barcelona once. (lose)
7. She always .... about her weight when she was younger. (worry)
8. The jacket .... him perfectly. (fit)
9. My car .... making a terrible noise two days ago. (start)
10. Her grandmother .... ten children. (have)

5 Read these questions about Thomas Morley, an English musician. Then listen to the recording and try to answer the questions.

1. When was Morley born?
2. Who was the Queen at the time?
3. What was the name of Morley's writer friend?
4. What was the date of Morley's own book?
5. Was Morley's best music dramatic or light?

6 Look at the summary on page 146 with your teacher.

Personal information

 Unit 16

A Ages, heights and weights

1 How old do you think the buildings are? Example:

'I think building 1 is about 400 years old.'

How old is your house?

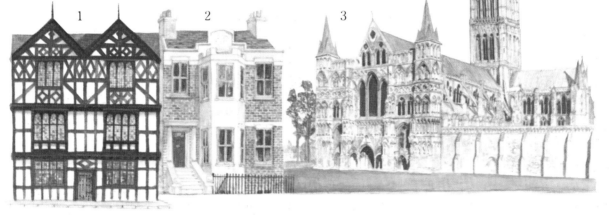

2 How old do you think the people are? Examples:

'I think Mark is six months old.'
'I think Mike is forty (years old).'

| Mark | Thomas | Kate | Stuart | Mike | Ann |

3 Look at the chart and make sentences. Example:

'Thomas is five feet six (inches tall), and he weighs 130 pounds.'

	HEIGHT	WEIGHT
Mark	2ft 1in	14lbs
Thomas	5ft 6ins	130lbs
Kate	5ft 4ins	125lbs
Stuart	5ft 10ins	180lbs
Mike	6ft 2ins	200lbs
Ann	5ft 1in	112lbs

4 Make sentences about yourself and other people. Examples:

'I'm five feet six inches tall.'
'My husband is six feet tall.'
'My father weighs about 190lbs.'
'My mother's sixty-six, but she looks older.'
'I'm thirty-four, and I look my age.'
'I'm over twenty-one.'

5 Ask some other students.

'How old/tall are you?'
'How much do you weigh?'

6 Listen to the recording. Some English-speaking people are trying to guess other people's ages and heights.

7 Describe your dream man/woman. How old is he/she? How tall? How much does he/she weigh? What does he/she look like?

| 1 inch = 2½cm |
| 12 inches = 1 foot (30cm) |
| 1lb = about 450gm |
| 2.2lbs = 1 kilogram |

66

Unit 16: Lesson A

Students learn to talk about weights and measures.
Structures: *be* with ages (revision) and measures.
Words and expressions to learn: *building*; *foot* (measure); *inch*; *pound (lb)*; *height*; *weight*; *weigh*.

Language notes and possible problems

1. Metric and imperial measures It will probably be useful for students to be familiar at least with the basic imperial measurements (foot, inch, pound), and to have a feeling for how much they represent. Rough equivalents will do (see table at bottom of Student's Book page). Tell students that British people calculate their weight in *stones* (1 stone = 14 lbs). Americans calculate their weight in pounds.

2. Ages In talking about people (but not things) we tend to drop the expression *years old*.

3. *Tall* This word is used mostly for people; sometimes for buildings and trees. You may wish to tell students that *high* is used to talk about mountains, rooms etc.

4. Pronunciation *Height* (/haɪt/) and *weight* (/weɪt/) are confusing.

5. People's weights You may wish to avoid personalization exercises in classes where somebody has a weight problem.

Optional extra materials

Pictures of old buildings of various ages. (Exercise 1).

1 Buildings
● Get students to look at the pictures in the book, or those you have brought, and ask them to guess the ages.

Answers
1. Elizabethan house: about 400 years old.
2. Victorian house: about 100 years old.
3. Salisbury Cathedral: about 700 years old.

● Ask students how old their own houses are, approximately. You might also ask about well-known local buildings.

2 People's ages
● Ask students to discuss the people's ages in groups.
● Teach *I don't agree*.

Answers
Mark 4 months, Thomas 13, Kate 19, Stuart 40, Mike 45, Ann 70.

● Follow up by getting students to guess your age and those of some other students (unless this is likely to lead to embarrassment).

3 Heights and weights
● Go over the instructions and example with the students.
● Practise the pronunciation of *height* and *weight*.
● Make sure students understand how the sentence is constructed.
● You may wish to explain the origin of the abbreviation *lbs* (Latin *libra = pound*).

● Get students to make some sentences – at least one in writing.

4 Personalization
● Go over the examples and get students to make similar sentences.
● They will need to refer to the table at the bottom of the page to work out their weights and heights in pounds, feet and inches.
● Follow up by asking students to guess your height and weight (if these are not sensitive areas!), and those of two volunteers.
● Then ask students to guess the heights and/or weights of some things in the room (use *high*, not *tall*).

5 Questions
● You can get students to ask their neighbours, or do a walk-round exercise.
● Avoid the activity if it is likely to embarrass anybody.

6 Authenticlistening
● This is a brief recording of some English-speaking people trying to guess other people's heights and ages.
● Students may be interested to listen to it (there is no task).

7 Dream man/woman
● This can be done orally or in writing, as you prefer.
● Students should try to give detailed descriptions of their dream men/women.
● Anybody who doesn't like the exercise can be asked to describe a real person.

Optional activity
● Mention the name of a friend of yours, and ask students to find out as much as they can about him/her by asking questions.

Practice Book
● Tell students which exercises you want them to do.

Unit 16: Lesson B

Students learn to say more about people's appearances, relating them to professional and personality types.
Structures: *What does X look like?*; *look like* + noun phrase; *look* + adjective; *What is X like?*
Words and expressions to learn: *I don't agree*; some names of professions and adjectives for personality types.

Language notes and possible problems
1. Vocabulary A lot of new words are introduced in this lesson. Students are not expected to learn them all; they should choose a reasonable number of words that they think will be particularly useful to them and learn those. (See summary.)
2. Look like The structures *What does X look like?* and *What is X like?* are complex and not easy for students to master. They may tend to try to use *How?* instead of *What ... like?* to elicit descriptions.

1 What do they do?
● Give students a minute or two to look at the photographs.
● Explain the words and practise their pronunciation. Note *businessman* (/'bɪznɪsmən/).
● Spend a few minutes in general discussion, getting students to use the new expressions in the examples (*I don't agree*; *looks like*; *looks more like*).
● Put students in groups of three or four. Each group *must* draw up an agreed group list, saying what profession each person has.
● When they are ready, see whether all the groups have reached the same conclusions. The people were chosen to represent the following professions: *A poet B politician C businessman D footballer E criminal F scientist.*
● Follow up the exercise by asking students to talk about each other (e.g. *Tomasso looks like a teacher*).

2 Personality types
● Exercise 2 can be done in the same way.
● Explain and practise the vocabulary and the example sentences.
● Start with a general discussion, and then ask for groups to produce lists.
● There are no 'right' answers.

3 Personalization
● Start by getting students to write at least one sentence each about themselves.
● In a friendly class they can read their sentences out to everybody; less confident students might prefer just to show you what they have written.
● Then get students to ask and answer questions as in the example.

4 Signs of the zodiac
● This section looks difficult, but students are usually prepared to do a lot of work to find out more about themselves.

● Let them read their own sections (and others if they wish) with dictionaries, asking questions if necessary.
● When they have done this, ask for reactions.
● You may need to teach the pronunciation of the signs of the zodiac. They are:

Aries /'eəriːz/
Taurus /'tɔːrəs/
Gemini /'dʒemɪnaɪ/
Cancer /'kænsə(r)/
Leo /'liːəʊ/
Virgo /'vɜːgəʊ/
Libra /'liːbrə/
Scorpio /'skɔːpiːəʊ/
Sagittarius /sædʒɪ'teərɪəs/
Capricorn /'kæprɪkɔːn/
Aquarius /ə'kweərɪəs/
Pisces /'paɪsiːz/

Practice Book
● Tell students which exercises you want them to do.

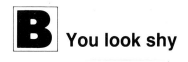

B You look shy

1 What do they do? Look at the pictures. The six people are: *a criminal, a poet, a footballer, a businessman, a scientist* and *a politician*. Discuss who does what.
Examples:

'I think C is a poet.' 'I don't agree. I think he's a criminal.'
'D looks like a scientist.' 'No, C looks more like a scientist.'

2 What are they like? Look at the pictures and discuss the people's personalities.
Useful words:

kind	shy	sensitive
self-confident		intelligent
stupid	bad-tempered	
calm	friendly	nervy

Examples:

'What is A like, do you think?'
'I think she's shy.'
'I think C looks rather friendly.'
'I don't agree. I think he looks very bad-tempered.'

3 Say some things about yourself and other people. Ask about other people. Examples:

'I look shy, but I'm not.'
'What's your sister like?' 'She's rather bad-tempered.'

4 Read your sign with a dictionary. Is it true?

Aries (21/3 - 20/4): energetic, bossy, often bad-tempered, warm, generous, sensitive, artistic.
Taurus (21/4 - 21/5): hardworking, calm, friendly, interested in business, money, friends and family.

Gemini (22/5 - 21/6): clever, witty, very talkative, changeable, interested in books, people and ideas.
Cancer (22/6 - 23/7): humorous, conservative, often happy, anxious, shy. Interested in history.
Leo (24/7 - 23/8): proud, bossy, independent; either very tidy or very untidy; passionate and generous.
Virgo (24/8 - 23/9) practical, punctual, critical, hard-working, perfectionist. Interested in nature.

Libra (24/9 - 23/10): friendly, energetic (but also lazy), pleasant, argumentative. Interested in sport, animals.
Scorpio (24/10 - 22/11): brave, sometimes violent, extremist, possessive, passionate. Often very religious.
Sagittarius (23/11 - 21/12): talkative, self-confident, cheerful. Interested in sport, travel, living dangerously.
Capricorn (22/12 - 20/1): conservative, polite, serious, sociable but shy. Interested in home, politics, people.
Aquarius (21/1 - 19/2): tolerant, sociable but unstable. Interested in sport and politics. Often brilliant or mad.
Pisces (20/2 - 20/3): sensitive, emotional, imaginative, artistic, depressive. Very interested in themselves.

It's not true! I'm not talkative! I'm not talkative! I'm r

C When is your birthday?

1 Listen to the conversation and answer the teacher's questions.

JANET: Happy birthday, Shirley.

SHIRLEY: Oh, thanks, Janet.

JANET: How old are you, then?

SHIRLEY: Never mind. Look at my new ring.

JANET: Oooooh! Shirley! It's beautiful! Is it a birthday present?

SHIRLEY: Yes. David gave it to me.

JANET: What's he like, then?

SHIRLEY: Oh, he's really nice, Jan.

JANET: Yes, but what's he *like*?

SHIRLEY: Well, he's *terribly* shy. But very interesting when he gets talking. And he's tall, dark and very good-looking. *I* think so, anyway.

JANET: What does he do?

SHIRLEY: He works in a bank. Assistant manager.

JANET: Oh, nice.

SHIRLEY: Yes. He's just got a new car.

JANET: Oh, yes? What sort?

SHIRLEY: A big red Mercedes.

JANET: Ooh! How old is he?

SHIRLEY: Twenty-eight. Twenty-nine next Tuesday.

JANET: What does your mother . . .

2 Fill in the missing numbers.

1st first	13th	31st ....
2nd	14th	40th ....
3rd	18th	52nd ....
4th	20th twentieth	63rd ....
5th	21st twenty-first	70th ....
11th	22nd twenty-second	99th ....
12th twelfth	30th	100th ....

3 Pronounce the names of the months.

January **Feb**ruary **March** April **May**
June July **Au**gust Sep**tem**ber October
No**vem**ber De**cem**ber

4 Ask and answer.

'What's the eighth month?' 'August.'

5 When is your birthday? Examples:

'My birthday is on March the twenty-first.'
'My birthday is today.' 'Happy birthday!'

Now listen to some people saying when their birthdays are. Two of them have got the same birthday. When is it?

6 Dates.

Write	Say
Jan 14, 1983	January the fourteenth, nineteen eighty-three
April 5, 1482	April the fifth, fourteen eighty-two
December 9, 1793	December the ninth, seventeen ninety-three

Say these dates:

Jan 14, 1978	May 17, 1936	Dec 30, 1983
Aug 3, 1066	Oct 10, 1906	Mar 3, 1860
Sept 21, 1980	July 20, 1840	April 1, 1900

7 Vocabulary revision. Some students will draw things from Units 1–15. Say what they are. Examples:

I think it's a sofa.

Is it a bed?

Perhaps it's a horse.

I don't know.

Unit 16: Lesson C

Students learn to talk about dates and birthdays.
Structures: article in *January the fourteenth* etc.; preposition in *My birthday is on . . .*
Words and expressions to learn: ordinals *tenth* to *hundredth; month;* names of the months: *birthday; today; date; Happy birthday; new.*
Phonology: more practice of /θ/.

Language notes and possible problems

1. Vocabulary Students probably won't learn the ordinal numbers and all the names of the months in one lesson. Come back to them from time to time.

2. Spoken dates are taught in their simpler form (*March the twenty-first*). Some students may be familiar with the longer form (*the twenty-first of March*).

3. Written dates There are various conventions for writing dates. The simplest is taught here.

4. American usage differs from British in some respects. 11.7.83 is the eleventh of July in Britain and the seventh of November in the United States. Americans leave out the article in phrases like *March twenty-first* (British *March the twenty-first*).

Optional extra materials

Specially prepared parcel for 'pass the parcel' (see Optional activity).

1 Dialogue comprehension

● Tell students to close their books, and write these questions on the board:
  1. What is Shirley's birthday present? 2. How old is Shirley? 3. Is her boyfriend tall or short? 4. Is he dark or fair? 5. What sort of personality has he got? 6. Where does he work? 7. What is his job? 8. What sort of car has he got? 9. What colour is the car? 10. How old is he? 11. When is his birthday?
● Go through the questions explaining difficulties.
● Then play the recording once without stopping.
● Give students a minute or two to write the answers to any questions that they can already deal with.
● Play the recording again, pausing once or twice for students to write the rest of their answers.
● Let them compare notes before discussing the answers with the class.
● (The answer to question 2 should be *I don't know.*)
● Open books. Play the recording again while students follow. Explain any difficulties.

2 Ordinal numbers

● Students have already learnt the first nine of these. The rest can be learnt by self-study.
● Give students five minutes or so to do the exercise and compare notes, then check the answers with them.
● Practise the pronunciation of *twentieth, thirtieth,* etc. – make sure students realize there are three syllables.

3 The months

● Practise the pronunciation of *month* (compare *one, mother, brother, some, money*).
● Practise the names of the months, paying careful attention to stress.
● Close books and see if students can remember them.

4 What's the eighth month?

● Students can test each other in a 'chain'.
● The question is something of a tongue-twister, but gives good practice in pronouncing /θ/.

5 When's your birthday?

● Ask everybody. If it is somebody's birthday, teach *Happy birthday!* (and sing *Happy birthday to you*).
● If you want more practice, do a walk-round exercise.
● For a real tongue-twister, try: *Her birthday's on Thursday September the thirtieth.*
● Then tell students they will hear people saying when their birthdays are. Play the recording.
● Two of the people have the same birthday; students must try to hear what it is (March 12).
● Play the recording more than once if necessary.

6 Complete dates

● Look at the examples and then do the exercise.
● If students are getting tired of figures, drop the exercise for now and come back to it later.

7 Vocabulary revision

● Ask for volunteers to draw things which they have already learnt the names of (they can look back through the book).
● They can either come out and draw things on the board in turn, or draw on sheets of paper and show them.
● The class should try to say what the things are. Teach *I think* and *perhaps* if drawings are not clear.

Optional activity   Pass the parcel

● Before the lesson, prepare a parcel. It must have a number of wrappings, one outside the other; inside *each* wrapping there is a picture of a 'present' (or a card with the name of a present on). Students must know the words.
● Students and teacher sit in a circle and pass the parcel, saying the names of the months in turn.
● The teacher positions himself or herself so as to get the parcel on the month of his/her birthday, and says *It's my birthday!*
● Students say (or sing) *Happy birthday!*
● The teacher opens the parcel, takes out the first picture or word, looks at it and says *Oh! A car!* (or whatever) *How lovely!*
● The teacher passes the parcel on. Whenever a student says the name of his or her birth month, he or she opens a wrapping.
● If there are twelve (or twenty-four) students, the teacher must continue to play to make a thirteenth, so that the months change for each person. Otherwise he/she can drop out.
● In larger classes, the game can be played in groups.

Practice Book

● Tell students which exercises you want them to do.

Unit 16: Lesson D

Students practise asking about possessions. They learn to develop exchanges by asking follow-up questions.
Structures: interrogative and negative of *have got* (revision); distinction between *a* and *any* (revision); use of *with* for possession.
Words and expressions to learn: *bicycle; guitar*.
Phonology: the pronunciations of the letter *i*.

Language note
Any It is unusual in English to use *any* (as in *I haven't got any . . .*) with a singular countable noun. Some students may tend to make mistakes like **I haven't got any car.*

Optional extra materials
A collection of unexpected objects in your briefcase (see Optional activities).

1 *A* and *any*
● Explain or demonstrate the new vocabulary (or let students explain it to each other).
● Practise the pronunciation.
● Ask students to write one question with *a* and one question with *any* (taking the words from the table).
● Check that everybody has made correct sentences.

2 Follow-up questions
● Ask students to work out additional questions to ask when they receive the answer *Yes* to their first question.
● If the examples are not enough to give them the idea, do one or two more on the board with the whole class. Then ask students to work out new follow-up questions for themselves.
● Check that the questions are correctly expressed.

3 Survey
● Do this as a walk-round. Every student should try to ask everybody else his/her two questions, and the follow-up questions where appropriate. (You may like to ask a volunteer to practise on you first.)
● Students should prepare a piece of paper with two columns to record the number of *Yes* and *No* answers (and to make any other notes they wish).

4 Reporting
● Look over the examples with the students.
● Note that they can report their findings in several different ways.
● Ask for reports.

5 Negatives
● Students should be able to produce a fair number of examples spontaneously.
● You may wish to ask for at least one written example with *any*, to check that nobody is using it with singular countable nouns.

Optional activities
1. If students want to learn some more useful everyday vocabulary (while continuing to revise *have got*), they can talk about the contents of their handbags and pockets.

2. A variant of 'Kim's game' is possible using the contents of somebody's handbag or pocket (once the vocabulary is known). (Display the various objects for a minute, put them back, and get students to write down as much as they can remember.)

3. Another vocabulary game is as follows:
   Before the lesson, fill your briefcase or school bag with a variety of things that you would not normally put in it. These should mostly be objects that the students know the names of, or that are easily explained.
   Examples: a picture of a beautiful girl; a few toy objects (dog, elephant, car); a potato; a crystal; a tin of peas; a piece of cheese; a shoe. When you start the game, write up the names of these things on the board, mixed in with the names of things that students would expect to find in your bag (but which this time are not there). So the list might look like this:

a beautiful girl	a potato	a newspaper
a book	a tin of peas	etc.
an elephant	a shoe	

   Then ask the students to write sentences (say, five each) in which they say whether they think items in the list are in your bag. Examples:
   I think you've got a book in your bag.
   I don't think you've got an elephant.
   (Put these examples, or two similar ones, on the board.) When the students have written their sentences, ask them what they have written, and then show them what you've got.
      Note that this kind of game works well with adults, but may not go down well with adolescents (who often resent activities that appear 'childish').

6 Spelling and pronunciation
● Students are probably already aware (consciously or not) of the main ways in which the letter *i* is pronounced.
● This exercise will help them to see the rules more clearly.
● Practise the words in group 1 (making sure students say /ɪ/ and not /iː/).
● Then pronounce the words in group 2. Ask what makes these different.
● Finally, practise the /ɜː/ sound in *first* and *shirt*. Ask when *i* is pronounced /ɜː/.
● Now get students to look at the words lettered (a) to (p). They should be able to pronounce correctly not only the first eight (which they know), but also the last eight (which they probably don't know).

7 Summary
● Look over the summary with the students.

Practice Book
● Tell students which exercises you want them to do.

Answers to Practice Book Exercise 3: 1. chair 2. apple 3. bus 4. fridge (the rest are pieces of living-room furniture) 5. chicken 6. dog (not kept for food) or sheep (irregular plural) 7. Thursday 8. March (doesn't end in *y*) or February (doesn't have 31 days). 9. Japan (not a continent)

D   Have you got a cat?

1 Make two questions: one with *a* and one with *any*.

> Have you got

> a
> any

> English books bicycle
> children piano animals
> British money guitar TV
> calculator cat jazz records
> gold watch perfume
> car American friends

> ?

2 Make two 'follow-up' questions. Examples:

'Have you got a car?' 'Yes, I have.'
'What sort of car? What colour is it?'

'Have you got a guitar?' 'Yes, I have.'
'Can you play it? How often do you play?'

'Have you got a calculator?' 'Yes, I have.'
'Where did you buy it? Was it expensive?'

3 Ask your questions. Make a note of the answers.

4 Report to the class. Examples:

'Four students have got bicycles.'
'Two people have got some jazz records.'
'There are three students with children.'
'Only one student has got an animal.'
'Nobody has got any British money.'
'Maria hasn't got a bicycle.'
'27 per cent of the students have got cars.'
'Heinz has got a guitar. He can't play it.'

5 Have you got everything you want? No?
What haven't you got? Examples:

'I haven't got a raincoat.'
'I haven't got any nice clothes.'
'I haven't got enough books.'

6 Pronunciation. Say these words after the
recording or after your teacher.

1. sit   in   big
2. wine   five   night   right
3. first   shirt

Now decide how to pronounce these words. Are
they in group 1, 2 or 3? Check with your
teacher or the recording.

a. girl	e. white	i. fin	m. bright
b. like	f. skirt	j. bird	n. excite
c. arrive	g. light	k. stir	o. ride
d. tights	h. with	l. slight	p. skip

7 Look at the summary on page 147 with
your teacher.

69

Ordering and asking

A I'll have roast beef

1 Put the sentences in order.

1

'Yes, sir. Over here, by the window.'
'Have you got a table for two?'

2

'How would you like your steak?'
'Oh, all right, then. I'll have a rump steak.'
'I'll start with soup, please, and then I'll have roast beef.'
'I'm sorry, madam, there's no more roast beef.'
'Rare, please.'

3

'Vegetables, sir?'
'Chicken for me, please.'
'A few mushrooms and a green salad, please.'
'And for you, sir?'

4

'Certainly, madam.'
'Could I have a lager, please?'
'Would you like something to drink?'
'I'll have a lager too. And could you bring me some water?'

5

'A bit tough. The vegetables are nice.'
'Not too bad. What about your steak?'
'How's the chicken?'

6

'Is everything all right?'
'Very good.'
'Oh yes, excellent, thank you.'

'Could you bring us the bill, please?'
'No, sir.'
'Can I give you a little more coffee?'
'No, thank you.' 'Yes, please.'
'Is service included?'

2 Listen to the conversation and practise the pronunciation. Then practise the conversation in pairs. Make up your own 'restaurant' conversations.

Unit 17: Lesson A

Students learn how to order meals in English.
Structures: *a little/few; I'll have; no more; Could you...?; give* and *bring* with two objects; object pronoun *us*.
Words and expressions to learn: some of these (see summary): *beef; mushroom; steak; chicken; salad; bring; everything; all right; not too bad; the bill; give; us; for; restaurant; Is service included?*

Language notes and possible problems

The dialogue introduces quite a number of new points. You may want to mention some of the following:

Picture 1
For (to indicate eventual possession) is new (see also Picture 3). Note the weak pronunciation /fə(r)/.

Picture 2
I'll have; I'll start: use of the *will*-future to announce decisions (preview). Pronunciation of *I'll* needs practising.
No more: emphatic way of saying *not any more.*
Then used in two senses (*in that case; after that*).

Pictures 3 and 7
A little and *a few:* not followed by *of.* The distinction is practised in 17C.

Picture 4
Some, something are used in interrogative sentences when these are offers or requests.
Bring is followed by two objects, and the same pronouns are used for direct and indirect objects. You may wish to point out the difference between *bring* and *take.*

Picture 6
Note that *everything* is singular.

Pictures 7–9
Thank you: If the man said *Thank you* instead of *No, thank you* it would indicate acceptance. Note also that *please* is not used when giving things.
Us completes the list of object pronouns.

Optional extra materials

If you are going to finish the lesson with an improvisation, you may like to prepare menus (one for each group).

1 Unscrambling the dialogue

• This can be done in groups.
• Encourage students to use English during their discussion. Useful expressions (put them on the board):

> *Yes, that's right.*   *Then she says...*
> *I don't agree.*   *No, she doesn't.*

• Students should finish up with a correct written version of the dialogue (to use in the next exercise).
• If time is short, just deal with part of the dialogue (and perhaps set the rest for homework).

Answers to Exercise 1
1. 'Have you got a table for two?'
   'Yes, sir. Over here, by the window.'

2. 'I'll start with soup, please, and then I'll have roast beef.'
   'I'm sorry, madam, there's no more roast beef.'
   'Oh, all right, then. I'll have a rump steak.'
   'How would you like your steak?'
   'Rare, please.'

3. 'And for you, sir?'
   'Chicken for me, please.'
   'Vegetables, sir?'
   'A few mushrooms and a green salad, please.'

4. 'Would you like something to drink?'
   'Could I have a lager, please?'
   'Certainly, madam.'
   'I'll have a lager too. And could you bring me some water?'

5. 'How's the chicken?'
   'Not too bad. What about your steak?'
   'A bit tough. The vegetables are nice.'

6. 'Is everything all right?'
   'Very good.'
   'Oh, yes, excellent, thank you.'

7/8/9. 'Can I give you a little more coffee?'
   'No, thank you.' 'Yes, please.'
   'Could you bring us the bill, please?'
   'Is service included?'
   'No, sir.'

2 Explanation and practice

• Go through the dialogue (or part of it) with the recording, practising pronunciation.
• Pay special attention to stress, linking and intonation.
• Explain language points.
• After each section, get students to practise it in groups of three.

Follow-up: students' conversations
• Tell students (in groups of three or four) to prepare and practise short sketches.
• One student is a waiter; the others are customers.
• They should use language from the dialogue.
• Don't let them spend too long in preparation.
• They should act out the sketch as they practise it.
• Ask selected groups to perform their sketches for the class.

Optional activity   Improvisation
• First of all, get three or four volunteers to improvise a restaurant scene.
• Don't correct mistakes unless they really impede communication.
• Then turn the whole classroom into a restaurant (with one waiter for every two tables, more or less), and let students act out the situation as they wish.
• You may like to prepare menus in advance. Alternatively, you can put the menu on the board.

Optional activity   Pronunciation practice
• The text can be used for a pronunciation exercise as follows.
• Tell students to say any sentence from the text that they want to (one at a time).
• Don't comment in any way, but just say the same sentence with a correct pronunciation.
• If a student is not satisfied with his/her pronunciation, he/she can say the same sentence several times, checking against your version each time.

Practice Book
• Tell students which exercises you want them to do.

Unit 17: Lesson B

Students learn to borrow things, and to reply to requests; they study differences of formality.
Structures: *Could you* + infinitive without *to*; more practice on verbs that have two objects (*lend, give, show*).
Words and expressions to learn: *Sorry to trouble you; lend; borrow; Have you got a light?; Could you possibly lend me...?; hour; half an hour; minute; Just a minute; need; smoke; I don't smoke; sugar;* names of some common small possessions.

Language notes and possible problems

1. *Lend* and *borrow* Students may confuse these. If so, concentrate on practising *lend* and leave *borrow* for another time.

2. Requests Make sure students understand the differences of formality (very polite, polite and casual) illustrated in the lesson.

Note that we normally use *yes/no* questions to ask for things (*Could you...?; Have you got...?*). It is the question form (with appropriate intonation) that makes a request polite; an imperative request (even with *please*) generally sounds like a command. Compare:

Have you got a cigarette? (request)
Please give me a cigarette. (command)

3. Pronunciation Point out the pronunciation of *minute* /ˈmɪnɪt/ (Exercise 1) and *hour* /ˈaʊə(r)/ (Exercise 2).

4. Cultural differences Students from some cultures may be taken aback by the situation in this lesson: calling casually on a neighbour one doesn't know in order to borrow something. (In some countries people would be most unlikely to do this; in others they would probably know all the neighbours.) You may need to explain that this is normal behaviour in most parts of the English-speaking world.

1 Completing the conversation 🔊

● Ask students to look at the story for a few minutes. There is no need for you to ask 'comprehension questions'.
● Explain any difficulties. Make sure students understand the exact meaning of *lend* (= 'give for a time').
● Ask for ideas about how the conversation might continue. (There are innumerable possibilities – he might ask her name; he might invite her out; he might talk about himself.)
● Get students to write the end of the conversation in pairs. You will need to supply words and expressions – students will certainly not know the English for everything they think of.
● Go over the text in the picture story, practising rhythm, intonation and linking. Use the recording as a model if you wish.
● Then get students to practise their completed conversations.

2 Requests and replies; formality 🔊

● First of all, look at the requests with the students. Explain any difficulties and practise the pronunciation.
● Ask which requests they think are most formal (or

'polite'), and which they think are more suitable between close friends.
● Practise the pronunciation, paying special attention to intonation – this is important.
● Ask students to suggest possible answers to the first request – there are at least five. They should understand clearly why answers with *them* or *one* are not possible.
● Ask students to continue the exercise alone or in groups.
● Get them to compare notes; go over the answers with them.
● Get them to practise the exchanges in pairs.

3 Vocabulary extension

● Before doing Exercise 4, students need to learn the names of some common possessions.
● Get them to look in their bags and pockets for things to ask you about.
● Before giving the answers, you might ask *Does anybody know?*

4 Borrowing and lending

● Get half the class to become borrowers and the other half lenders.
● The borrowers walk round trying to borrow as many things as they can (using the expressions from Exercise 2). Lenders should answer appropriately.
● Before changing over and letting the lenders become borrowers, teach *Can I have my ... back, please?*

Optional activity Sketch

● If time allows, get students to prepare and perform little sketches based on the situation in the picture story.
● They can work in pairs or groups of three, starting with the idea of borrowing something from the person/people in the next flat, and developing it as they wish.
● (For detailed suggestions about organising this kind of work, see Lesson 11D.)

Practice Book

● Tell students which exercises you want them to do.

B Could you lend me some sugar?

1 Read the story and complete the conversation.
Practise the complete conversation with a partner.

2 Match the questions and answers. You can find more than one answer to each question.

QUESTIONS
1. Sorry to trouble you. Could you lend me some bread?
2. Could you lend me a dictionary?
3. Could you show me some black sweaters, please?
4. Excuse me. Have you got a light, please?
5. Could you possibly lend me your car for half an hour?
6. Could I borrow your keys for a moment?
7. Could I borrow your umbrella, please?
8. Have you got a cigarette?

ANSWERS
a. Yes, of course. Here you are.
b. Yes, of course. Just a minute.
c. I'm sorry. I need it/them.
d. I'm afraid I haven't got one.
e. I'm afraid I haven't got any.
f. Sorry, I don't smoke.
g. Sorry, I'm afraid I can't.

3 Ask the teacher the names of some of
your possessions. Examples:

'What's this?'

'What's this called
in English, please?'

'Is this a pen
or a pencil?'

'Is this a lighter?'

4 Ask other students to lend, give or show you things. Example:

'Could you lend me your watch?' 'I'm sorry, I need it.'

C Something to drink?

1 **Listen to the dialogue and see what you can remember.**

MARY: Hello, John. What a surprise! Come in.

JOHN: Thank you, Mary.

MARY: Sit down. Would you like something to drink? Beer? Scotch? A cup of tea?

JOHN: Yes, thanks. Perhaps some Scotch. With a little water, please. I'm quite thirsty.

MARY: It's a hot day . . . Here you are. Help yourself to water.

JOHN: Thanks.

MARY: Can I give you something to eat? A piece of apple pie? Some biscuits?

JOHN: Er, no, nothing to eat, thanks. I'm not hungry. Mary, can I talk to you for a few minutes? I've got this letter from Sue. She . . .

2 *A little* or *a few?*

1. Could you bring us .... water?
2. Could you possibly lend me .... potatoes until tomorrow?
3. There's .... cheese in the fridge, if you're hungry.
4. Have you got .... minutes? I'd like to talk to you.
5. I need .... money. Can you help me?
6. I'm going to France for .... days next week.

3 Put in *of* if necessary.

1. Would you like a few .... biscuits?
2. Can I give you a piece .... apple pie?
3. Could I have a cup .... tea?
4. I'd like some .... cheese and a glass .... milk, please.
5. Could you give me a lot .... potatoes – I'm hungry.
6. And I'd like a little .... salad, please.
7. I've got too many .... letters to write.
8. I've got about two hundred .... letters to write.
9. Please don't give me much .... Scotch – I just want a little.
10. My sister's got lots .... boyfriends.

4 **Work in pairs. Offer your partner something to eat and something to drink.**

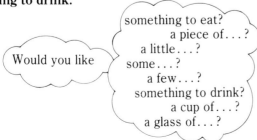

Would you like

something to eat?
a piece of . . . ?
a little . . . ?
some . . . ?
a few . . . ?
something to drink?
a cup of . . . ?
a glass of . . . ?

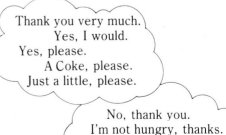

Thank you very much.
Yes, I would.
Yes, please.
A Coke, please.
Just a little, please.

No, thank you.
I'm not hungry, thanks.
I'm not thirsty, thank you.

Unit 17: Lesson C

Students learn to make and reply to offers.
Structures: *something to eat/drink; of* after *piece, cup* etc.; indirect object with *to* (*talk to you*).
Words and expressions to learn: some of these (see summary): *surprise; come in; something; nothing; eat; something to eat/drink; help yourself (to); piece; talk; apple; biscuit; cup.*

Language notes and possible problems

1. *Of* is used after some quantifiers and not after others. (Compare *many people, a lot of people.*) Exercise 3 helps with this.

2. Verbs with two objects   Students will need to learn that not all verbs can have an indirect object without *to*. A preposition is necessary after *talk*.

1 Dialogue work

- Play the dialogue once while students listen with their books closed.
- Ask for any words they can remember (not in order) and write them on the board.
- Play the dialogue again (books closed) and see if students can begin to get some of the words and phrases in order.
- Open books and play again.
- Close books and see if the class can get the complete dialogue on the board.
- Open books and repeat. Pay attention to linking (e.g. to eat – almost 'toweat'); /iː/ and /ɪ/ (*tea, eat, piece, in, sit, drink, it's, biscuits*); /h/ in *Hello, hot, help, hungry.*
- Practise once or twice in pairs.

2 *A little* or *a few?*

- Students have already learnt that *a little* is used with singular (uncountable) words and *a few* is used with plurals.
- Ask students to write the answers and compare notes with their neighbours.
- Repeat the explanation if necessary.

3 Quantifiers with or without *of*

- This should be straightforward, but if students have difficulty with any particular structure you can get them to make a few more examples of its use.

4 Offering and replying to offers

- To make the practice more fluent, give students a minute or two to prepare their questions (two or three each) before they start work.
- Exchange a few questions and answers yourself with selected students, and then divide them into pairs.
- For additional practice, students can change partners several times.

Practice Book

- Tell students which exercises you want them to do.

Unit 17: Lesson D

Students continue to study ways of expressing politeness; they revise pronouns.
Structures: overview of pronouns; possessives.
Words and expressions to learn: *polite*; *rude*.
Phonology: expression of politeness through intonation; sentence-rhythm; pronunciations of *o*.

Language notes and possible problems

1. Subject and object pronouns *Us* and *them* both have strong and weak pronunciations (strong /ʌs, ðem/, weak /əs, ðəm/). The weak pronunciation is normal; the strong form is only used when the word is either alone or stressed.

Terminology is confusing: 'personal' pronouns are used for things as well as people; there are two series of possessive 'pronouns' (*my* etc. and *mine* etc.).

2. Politeness This is a complicated matter. The same utterance can be polite, neutral or rude according to what intonation we use, what words and expressions we use to 'wrap it up' and how well we know the listener.

It is important not to confuse beginners by giving too many details. In Exercises 2 and 3 they are simply asked to study the difference between yes/no questions and imperatives, and between rising and falling intonation.

Optional extra materials

Copies of the drawings on page 183 (or other suitable pictures) should be used for the optional activity.

1 Revision of pronouns

● Look over the table with the students, and clear up any problems they may have.
● Practise the pronunciation of the examples (with the pronouns and possessives unstressed).
● Then do the exercise. Get students to write some or all of the answers individually.

2 Politeness (structures)

● We normally make polite requests with *yes/no* questions (because this gives the person asked the chance to say *No*, at least in theory).
● Some students may not realize that adding *please* to a command does not turn it into a request.
● Look at the first three sentences, and help students to see the importance of the formula *Could you . . . ?*
● Go through the rest of the exercise with them. 4 is rude; 5, 6, 7 and 8 could all be polite requests (depending on the intonation and the situation).

3 Intonation

● Students will probably hear (without analysing the intonation) which sentences sound polite. (1, 3, 4, 6.)
● If they have trouble, demonstrate the polite pronunciation for all of the sentences – voice starts high, drops through the sentence and rises at the end, thus:

Could you lend me a pen, please?

● Then play the recording again.
● Finish by practising all the sentences politely.

4 Rhythm

● Practise the rhythm of the three model sentences.
● Let students do the exercise in groups *before* hearing the recording.
● Play the recording (or say the sentences) and let them change their answers if they wish.
● Go over the answers and practise the sentences.

Answers to Exercise 4

□ □ □ □	□ □ □ □	□ □ □ □
Where do you live?	I like the sea.	These books are cheap.
What do you think?	She drinks a lot.	Green eyes are nice.
First on the right.	He went in May.	Five pounds of meat.
Right at the top.	I've got some wool.	Jane works in Greece.
	A cup of tea.	

5 Pronunciations of *o*

● Get students to say the words in the three groups.
● The second sound (/əʊ/) can be learnt by putting together the /ə/ of *mother* and the /uː/ of *too*. The third sound (/ɔː/) is the same as the *aw* in *saw*.
● Get students to work in groups, trying to see what the rules are and sorting out the second set of words.
● Finish by pronouncing or playing all the words for the students and discussing the answers.
● Students should realize that there are exceptions to these 'rules' – *gone* has a pronunciation which does not correspond to its spelling, and there are words in which *o* is pronounced /ʌ/ (e.g. *mother, come, one*).

Answers to Exercise 5
The complete lists are:
1. (/ɒ/) *not, job, stop, lost, on, got, dog, clock.*
2. (/əʊ/) *home, phone, no, wrote, note, those, hotel, go, road, know, snow, boat.*
3. (/ɔː/) *more, born, short, or, sport, bored, forty, morning.*

Optional activity   Making yourself understood

● This is a good opportunity to give students practice in asking for things whose names they don't know.
● Copy or cut out the drawings on page 183, (or cut out suitable pictures from magazines).
● Students take turns to take a card. They must ask the class for the object in any way they like, but without using its name if they know it. (Make them put their hands in their pockets or behind their backs.)
● The class should say whether they understand.
● Communication is more important than correctness:
1. 'Excuse me. I'm very sorry to trouble you, but could you possibly lend me a . . . a . . . ?'
(Correct English; unsuccessful communication.)
2. 'Excuse me, am sorry, but maybe you can lend one, how you say, thing because shoes are dirty.' 'A shoe-brush?'(Poor English; successful communication.)
● Remind students of the word *thing*, and of the formula *something to . . .* + infinitive.

6 Summary

● Look over the summary with the students.

Practice Book
● Tell students which exercises you want them to do.

D I like Alice; Alice likes me

SUBJECT	OBJECT	POSSESSIVE	EXAMPLES
I	me	my	**I** like Alice. Alice likes **me**. There's **my** house.
you	you	your	Are **you** married? Thank **you**. What's **your** name?
he	him	his	**He** works in London. Give **him** your phone number. **His** wife is American.
she	her	her	**She** is a doctor. I like **her**. **Her** husband travels a lot.
it	it	its	**It**'s raining. I don't like **it**. That's a pretty cat – what's **its** name?
we	us	our	**We** usually get up at seven. Please show **us** some rings. **Our** flat is on the sixth floor.
you	you	your	Do **you** both smoke? Can I help **you**? What is **your** address?
they	them	their	Where are **they**? Can I try **them** on? The children are with **their** aunt in Manchester.

1 Put in the right word.

1. Could you show .... that ring? (I/me/my)
2. I can't remember .... name. (she/her)
3. When is .... birthday? (you/your)
4. I don't want to give .... my name. (he/him/his)
5. Andrew lost .... wallet yesterday. (he/him/his)
6. I like .... very much. (she/her)
7. .... are both tall and dark. (We/Us/Our)
8. So are .... children. (we/us/our)
9. Could you give .... your name? (we/us/our)
10. Can you help ....? (we/us/our)
11. Can I try .... on? (they/them/their)
12. How much are ....? (they/them/their)

2 Is the structure polite or rude? Read these sentences and write: P (polite) or R (rude).

1. Give me your pen. ...*R*......
2. Excuse me. Could you lend me your pen? ...*P*......
3. Please lend me your pen. ...*R*......
4. Give me a light, please.
5. Excuse me. Could you give me a light, please?
6. Excuse me. Could I look at your newspaper?
7. Have you got a light, please?
8. Could you lend me £5 for a couple of days, John?

3 Is the intonation polite or rude? Listen; mark the sentences P or R. Then say them politely.

1. Could you lend me a pen, please?
2. Have you got a light, please?
3. Can you tell me the time, please?
4. Could I look at your newspaper for a moment?
5. Could you send this to my address in Tokyo?
6. Can you show me some sweaters, please?

4 Say these sentences; compare the rhythm.

A. Where do you live?

B. These books are cheap.

C. I like the sea.

Now group these sentences according to their rhythm: A, B, or C.

What do you think?   Jane works in Greece.
She drinks a lot.   He went in May.
Green eyes are nice.   I've got some wool.
First on the right.   Right at the top.
Five pounds of meat.   A cup of tea.

5 Say these words after the recording or after your teacher.

1. not   job   stop   lost
2. home   phone   no   wrote
3. more   born   short   or

1, 2 or 3? Decide how to pronounce these words and check with your teacher or the recording.

a. on   e. bored   i. dog   m. road
b. sport   f. those   j. go   n. know
c. note   g. forty   k. morning   o. snow
d. got   h. hotel   l. clock   p. boat

6 Look at the summary on page 148 with your teacher.

The present

A
What's happening?

Hello, darling...Yes...
Are you having a good
time?...How's your
mother?...What?...What
do you mean, 'what's
happening?'...Oh, the
noise...Yes, it's the TV – I'm
watching something good on
the TV...What?...

1 Who is the man on the phone talking to?
What does she think is happening in the room?
What is really happening? Examples:

'Some people are dancing.'
'A man is lying on the floor.'

2 Memory test. Who is doing what? Work in
pairs: one student closes his/her book, and the
other asks questions about the picture.
Examples:

'What is the woman in the red dress doing?'
'What is the man with glasses doing?'

3 What do you think your wife/husband/
father/mother/boyfriend/girlfriend/boss etc. is
doing at this moment?

*'I think my boyfriend's working. My wife's shopping.
John's probably getting up.'*

4 Mime an action.
The others will try
to say what you're
doing.

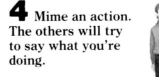

You're drinking.

I don't know
what he's doing.

I think you're shaving.

Unit 18: Lesson A

Students learn to talk about temporary present actions and states.
Structures: Present Progressive (continuous) tense; *the girl in jeans, the man with a beard.*
Words and expressions to learn: *stand; sit; lie; fight; happen; out of; on the phone; probably.*

Language notes and possible problems

1. Present Progressive: forms The tense is easy for students to construct. The only formal problem is likely to be the word order in questions with noun-phrase subjects such as *What is the girl in red doing?* Students may tend to put the subject in the wrong place (*What is doing the girl in red?* or *The girl in red, what is doing?*), because they are reluctant to separate the two parts of the verb.

2. Present Progressive: meaning This is a more difficult problem. Most languages do not have a special verb form for *temporary* present states or actions, so it is difficult for students to get used to the fact that one has to make this distinction when speaking English.

Note that it is important (and not very easy) to practise the tense realistically as far as possible. People generally ask or say what *is happening* in a situation where it is impossible to see or understand what is going on – when talking on the telephone, for instance.

3. *Stand*, *sit* etc. State-verbs like *stand, sit, lie, kneel, lean* may present problems for some students. The equivalent in some languages of, for instance, *he's standing*, might not be constructed with an active verb-form at all, but with a passive, a reflexive, a past participle or even an adjective.

4. Prepositions Note that *in* is used when we talk about clothing and colours (*in jeans, in red*); *with* is used when we refer to hair, beards, moustaches and glasses.

1 Presentation

● Give students time to look at the picture and see what is happening.
● Read through the man's side of the phone conversation with them and make sure they understand everything.
● Ask them who they think the man is talking to, and what they think she says.
● Ask what *she* thinks is happening in the room.
● Get students to say as much as they can about what is happening in the picture. Supply vocabulary as needed.
● To finish the exercise, ask students what they think the man's wife is doing. (Is she *really* visiting her mother?)

Grammar explanation

● Tell the students that we say, for example, *he is talking* or *she is dancing* when we want to say what is happening at this moment (and not *he talks* or *she dances*).
● Write the forms of the Present Progressive on the board:

I am . . . ing   *we are . . . ing*
you are . . . ing   *you are . . . ing*
he/she/it is . . . ing *they are . . . ing*

● The use of the Present Progressive (and the contrast with the Simple Present) will be studied in detail in this unit.

2 Memory test

● Look over the examples with the students and make sure they understand how questions are constructed. Write on the board: *What is/are + subject + doing?*
● Get them to write four or five questions each like the ones in the examples.
● Tell them to work in pairs. One student closes his/her book and the other asks questions. Then they change over.
● Encourage them to say *I don't remember* when necessary.
● Let them open their books again and make up some more questions (orally this time) to test *your* memory of the picture.

3 Personalization

● You may like to remind students of *perhaps* (usually put at the beginning of the sentence).
● Explain *probably.*
● Ask for as many examples as possible – you may have to supply vocabulary.
● If somebody uses the verb *sleeping*, point out that in British English it is more common to say *asleep.*

4 Mime

● Mime creates a natural context for the use of the Present Progressive (because it is not completely clear what is happening, so students need to talk about it).
● Ask individuals (or small groups) to take it in turns to mime an action. The others have to say what it is.
● If students are short of ideas, suggest that they mime playing an instrument or a game (the others say what they are playing); or cooking or eating a particular food (the others say what they are doing).
● Make sure the mime continues while the class are making their guesses, so that students associate the idea of *present* activity with the tense.

Optional activity   Telephone mime

● Put students in groups of three.
● Student A 'telephones' student B, who pretends to answer the phone.
● A says *Can I speak to C, please?* (naming another student).
● As soon as C is named, he or she starts miming an activity which makes it impossible for him or her to come to the phone.
● B decides what C is doing, and says to A:
   I'm sorry, he/she's having a bath / cooking / washing his/her hair / working etc. Can you ring back later?

Optional activity   Revision (clothing)

● This is a good opportunity to revise the names of articles of clothing.
● Get students to say what other students are wearing.
● Games for this are suggested in the teaching instructions for Lesson 10B.

Practice Book

● Tell students which exercises you want them to do.

Unit 18: Lesson B

Students practise writing about temporary present actions and states.
Structures: Present Progressive; spelling of *-ing* form.
Words and expressions to learn: *send; post-card; look at; have a bath; wonderful; boring; bar; café; under.*
Phonology: pronunciations of the letter *e*.

Optional extra materials
Pairs of similar pictures (see Optional activity).

1 Holiday postcards
● Look over the exercise with the students, and help them to understand the system.
● Explain unknown vocabulary in the 'dictionary', or let students look words up.
● In order to write the postcard, they must fill in each blank with a word from one of the columns of the 'dictionary'.
● The letter in the blank shows which column to look in.
● Start off by filling in one or two blanks on the board, and then let students continue on their own.
● They should write out the complete text.
● If you like, they can send their 'postcards' to other students.

2 *-ing* forms
● Let students try the exercise themselves, to see how far they can get without help.
● They should be able to get the first and second sections right, but they may need help to see the rule that applies in the third section.
● Only one-syllable words have been put in, so as to avoid the complication introduced by the fact that we don't double letters at the end of unstressed syllables (compare *be'ginning* and *'happening*). Don't mention this unless students ask about it.

3 Pronunciation of the letter *e* 🔲
● This is an easy exercise, and is perhaps not worth doing in a class which does not contain a number of bad spellers.
● It is, however, useful for students to realize that the three groups of words in the second section all have the same vowel.
● After getting students to say the words in the two sections, ask them to work in groups putting the sixteen words in the right places.
● Note that the last four words have irregular spellings; they are all in group 2.

Optional activity Imagining
● Ask students to close their eyes and spend five minutes imagining themselves (as vividly as possible) in another place – a very beautiful place, where they are having a very good time.
● When they are ready, ask them to tell you about the place, and what they are doing, in as much detail as possible.

Optional activity Similar pictures
● Before the lesson, collect pairs of pictures (e.g. advertisements) which look fairly similar.
● Advertisements for cars and clothes in glossy magazines are a good source of material. You can often get two similar pictures by cutting a full-page advertisement in half.
● Hand out pictures to two volunteers. They should sit face to face (so that they can't see each other's pictures) and describe them in turn. (E.g. *There's a woman. She's wearing a red dress. She's standing by a car.*)
● The students' task is to find some differences (decide in advance how many).
● When the volunteers have finished, hand out pairs of pictures to other students.
● It's worth building up a library of pairs of pictures of this kind. Each pair can be kept in a separate envelope, with the subject and the number of differences to be found written on the outside.

Practice Book
● Tell students which exercises you want them to do.

B The Swan-Walter Universal Holiday Postcard Machine

1 It's easy to write holiday postcards! Write one now and send it to a friend.

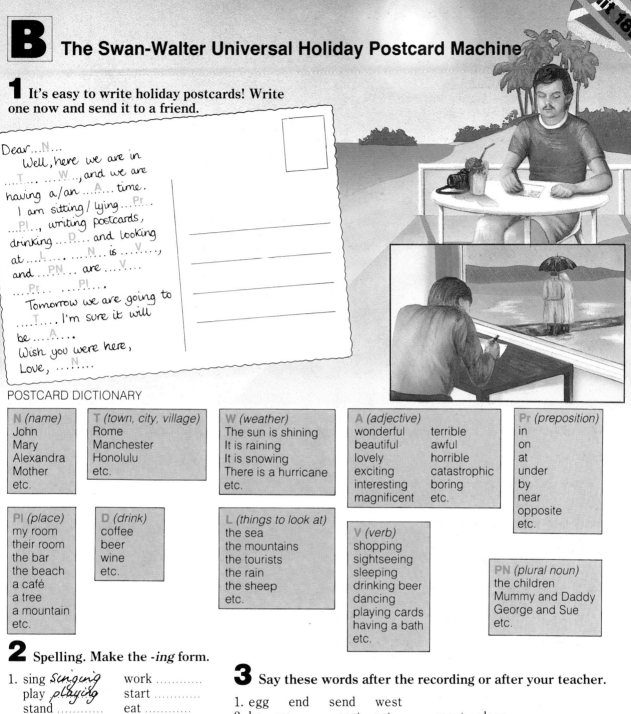

Dear ...N...

Well, here we are in ...T... ...W..., and we are having a/an ...A... time. I am sitting / lying ...Pr... ...Pl..., writing postcards, drinking ...D... and looking at ...L... ...N... is ...V..., and ...PN... are ...V... ...Pr... ...Pl...

Tomorrow we are going to ...T... I'm sure it will be ...A...

Wish you were here,

Love, ...N...

POSTCARD DICTIONARY

N (name)	T (town, city, village)	W (weather)	A (adjective)		Pr (preposition)
John	Rome	The sun is shining	wonderful	terrible	in
Mary	Manchester	It is raining	beautiful	awful	on
Alexandra	Honolulu	It is snowing	lovely	horrible	at
Mother	etc.	There is a hurricane	exciting	catastrophic	under
etc.		etc.	interesting	boring	by
			magnificent	etc.	near
					opposite
					etc.

Pl (place)	D (drink)	L (things to look at)	V (verb)
my room	coffee	the sea	shopping
their room	beer	the mountains	sightseeing
the bar	wine	the tourists	sleeping
the beach	etc.	the rain	drinking beer
a café		the sheep	dancing
a tree		etc.	playing cards
a mountain			having a bath
etc.			etc.

PN (plural noun)
the children
Mummy and Daddy
George and Sue
etc.

2 Spelling. Make the *-ing* form.

1. sing *singing*   work ....
   play *playing*   start ....
   stand ....   eat ....
   read ....   go ....

2. make *making*   dance ....
   smoke *smoking*   drive ....
   write ....   like ....

3. stop *stopping*   shop ....
   sit *sitting*   run ....
   get ....   begin ....

4. lie *lying*   die ....

3 Say these words after the recording or after your teacher.

1. egg   end   send   west
2. he   we   east   eat   meet   sleep

1 or 2? Decide how to pronounce these words and check with your teacher or the recording.

| went | meat | men | bed | be | left |
| reading | sheep | mean | me | get | speak |

Which group do these words go in?

| many | friend | head | any |

75

C Things are changing

1 What is happening to food prices in Fantasia?
Look at the graph and make sentences.

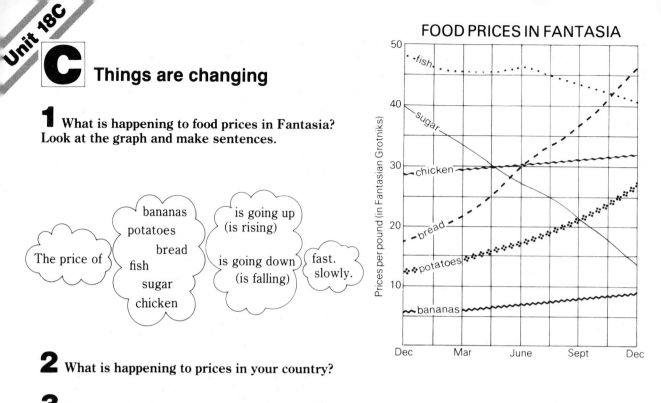

FOOD PRICES IN FANTASIA

The price of | bananas potatoes bread fish sugar chicken | is going up (is rising) is going down (is falling) | fast. slowly.

2 What is happening to prices in your country?

3 Listen to the figures and complete the table.

FANTASIA: SOME STATISTICS	100 YEARS AGO	50 YEARS AGO	NOW
Population	20m	35m	46m
Average number of children per family	4.5	3.6	2
Average July temperature	33°C	....	
Average January temperature		....	7°C
Average height (men)	....	1m67	....
Average height (women)	....	1m62	....
Length of working week	54hrs	....	....
Paid holiday	–	....	....
Average time taken for letter to travel 100km	....	2 days	....
Size of Fantasian army	500,000	....	....
Population of San Fantastico	....	....	3m
Percentage of population without homes	....	....	8%
Percentage of population unemployed	....	7%	....

4 How are things changing in Fantasia? Look at the table and make sentences.

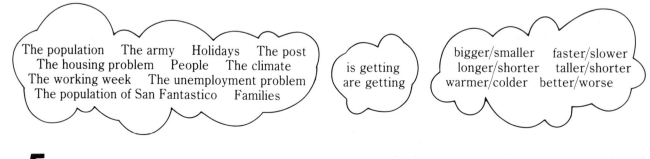

The population   The army   Holidays   The post
The housing problem   People   The climate
The working week   The unemployment problem
The population of San Fantastico   Families | is getting are getting | bigger/smaller   faster/slower longer/shorter   taller/shorter warmer/colder   better/worse

5 How are things changing in your country?

Unit 18: Lesson C

Students learn to talk about change.
Structures: more work on Present Progressive: *get* + comparative.
Words and expressions to learn: *up; down; go up; go down; fall; rise; change; get (= become); average; length; post; problem.*

Language notes

A common use of the Present Progressive is to talk about things that are changing. The verb *get* is often used in this context, generally followed by a comparative adjective.

1 Interpreting the graph

- Ask students to look at the graph.
- Not everybody finds it easy to understand information presented in this way, and some students may need help (from you or from other students) to work it out.
- When they are ready, look at one of the lines (for instance, the one for the price of potatoes), and get the students to tell you what is happening to the price – is it going up or down, fast or slowly?
- Write on the board:
  The price of potatoes is going up fast.
- Teach *rise* and *fall* as alternatives to *go up* and *go down.*
- Get students to make more sentences about the graph.
- Let them compare notes to make sure they all interpret the information correctly.

2 Extension

- It should now be easy for students to make a few examples about real prices.
- Mention the possibility of saying, for instance, *Cigarettes are going up* instead of *The price of cigarettes is going up.*

3 Listening for information 📼

- Go through the table of statistics with the students and explain any words and expressions that they don't know.
- To demonstrate the meaning of *average*, take the heights or ages of five students, add them and divide by five (do this on the board); explain that the result is the *average height* or *average age.*
- When everything is clear, play the recording and get the students to fill in the table. (If you don't want them to write in their books, get them to copy the headings on a separate piece of paper first.)
- Note that the missing information is not always given in chronological order – students have to understand what they hear in order to do the exercise properly.
- Let students compare notes when they have finished; then go over the answers with them.

Tapescript for Exercise 3

- Fifty years ago the average July temperature was thirty-four degrees Centigrade. Now it is thirty-five degrees.
- Fifty years ago, the average temperature in January was eight degrees. A hundred years ago it was nine degrees.
- The average height of Fantasian men today is 1 metre 70. A hundred years ago it was 1 metre 65.
- A hundred years ago the average height of women was 1 metre 60. Now it is 1 metre 65.
- Fifty years ago, Fantasians worked forty-nine hours a week. Now they work forty-two hours.
- Fantasians have five weeks' paid holiday a year. Fifty years ago they only had two weeks.
- It takes a letter three days to travel a hundred kilometres in Fantasia. A hundred years ago it only took one day.
- Fifty years ago there were two hundred thousand men in the Fantasian army. Today there are fifty thousand.
- Fifty years ago, the population of San Fantastico, the Fantasian capital, was four million. A hundred years ago it was one million.
- Twenty-three per cent of the population had no homes a hundred years ago. Fifty years ago, the figure was seventeen per cent.
- Unemployment today is running at seventeen per cent of the working population. This is nearly as bad as the situation a hundred years ago, when unemployment was twenty per cent.

4 How are things changing?

- Now that students have completed the table, they can say how things are changing.
- Go over the words in the exercise and explain any difficulties. Practise the pronunciation where necessary.
- Do one or two of the examples together; then ask individuals for more.
- Get students to write one or two of the sentences.

5 Extension

- Students should be able to think of examples about the real world without too much difficulty.
- You may need to help with vocabulary.

Practice Book

- Tell students which exercises you want them to do.

Unit 18: Lesson D

Students look at and contrast the 'central' meanings of the two present tenses.
Structures: Present Progressive tense; Simple Present tense.
Words and expressions to learn: spend (time); stay; wash; clean.

Language notes and possible problems

1. Meanings of the tenses Both of the 'present' tenses have several uses. Students are only concerned here with their 'central' meanings.

2. Grammatical explanations Students (and teachers) vary widely in their reactions to explicit grammatical information of the kind provided here. The point in question is a very difficult one, and knowledge of the rules is likely to act as a valuable support to students. It will not, however, stop them making mistakes – they are likely to confuse the two tenses for some time to come, and frequent revision will be necessary.

Presentation

● Give students plenty of time to read through the explanation and examples of the use of the two present tenses. Let them work at their own pace; give whatever help is needed.

1 Discrimination test

● This will show whether students have really mastered the distinction between the two present tenses.
● It is probably better to ask for written answers (at least to some of the questions) so that you can check up on everybody's understanding of the point.
● Discuss the reasons for the choice of tense in each case.

2 Listening

● Play the recording (or ask the questions), pausing for students to answer.
● Either pick out individuals to answer the questions, or tell students to write the answers.

The questions
1. What are you wearing?
2. What colours do you usually wear?
3. Are you wearing them now?
4. Who smokes in the class?
5. Who is smoking?
6. Who is sitting next to you now?
7. Does he or she usually sit there?
8. What's the weather like just now?
9. Is it raining?
10. Does it often rain?
11. What language are you speaking?
12. What languages do you speak?

3 Listening (preliminary exercise)

● Go over the list of verbs with the students. They should know most of them; explain the ones they haven't met yet.
● Tell them to copy the list if you don't want them to write in their books.
● Play the conversation through once without stopping;

then again with a few pauses so that students can circle the verbs.
● Let them compare notes and tell them the answers (*spending, staying, having, washing, doing, eating, cleaning, cooking*).

4 Listening for information

● Students can probably start Exercise 4 without hearing the conversation again.
● Let them fill in as much of the table as they can manage, and then play the recording once more.
● They will not understand everything; this does not matter.
● Let them compare notes, and discuss the answers with them.

Answers
Jane is talking to Polly.
Polly is talking to Jane.
Jane's mother is staying with Jane's sister.
Bill: we don't know what he's doing. Possibly cleaning the car or having a drink.
The baby is eating the newspaper.
Sue is having breakfast.
Frank is washing his hair.

Tapescript for Exercises 3 and 4
Hello. 656 790. Jane Parker speaking... Oh, Polly! Hello! How are you? ... Me? Oh, I'm OK. ... Yes... No. ... No, we're spending Christmas at home... No, we usually go to my mother's, but she's staying with my sister this year, so we didn't go.
... No. No, it's terrible when the kids are at home. It's murder, Polly. I mean it. They're everywhere. Sue's just got up: she's having lunch.
(SUE: No, I'm not! I'm having breakfast.)
Frank's washing his feet in the kitchen.
(FRANK: No, I'm not, Mum. I'm washing my hair!)
And the baby. God knows what the baby's doing.
(SUE: He's eating the newspaper!)
... Bill? He's out somewhere. Probably cleaning the car, or having a drink at the pub. I don't know. ... Yes. Look, I'm sorry, Poll, I must go. I'm just cooking lunch. I'll call you back, OK? Bye.

5 Summary

● Look over the summary with your students.

Practice Book

● Tell students which exercises you want them to do.

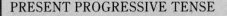

 Grammar: the two present tenses

PRESENT PROGRESSIVE TENSE	SIMPLE PRESENT TENSE
I'm working. You're working. etc. Am I working? Are you working? etc. I'm not working. You aren't working. etc.	I work. You work. He/she works. etc. Do I work? Do you work? Does he/she work? etc. I/you don't work. He/she doesn't work. etc.

We use the Present Progressive tense to talk about:
1. things that are happening now, these days.
2. things that are changing.

We use the Simple Present tense to talk about:
1. things that are always true.
2. things that happen often, usually, always, never, etc.

Examples:

'*Are you free now?*' '*Sorry, I'm studying.*'
'*Look. Helen's wearing a lovely dress.*'
'*What are you cooking?*' '*Steak.*'
'*My car isn't going very well. I must take it to the garage.*'
'*Food prices are going up.*'

Examples:

'*I always study from five to seven o'clock.*'
'*Helen often wears red.*'
'*I usually cook steak for dinner on Saturday.*'
'*It's a good car. It doesn't often break down.*'

'*Food prices go up every year.*'

1 Put in the correct verb tense.

1. 'Can you help me for a minute?' 'I'm sorry,
   ....' (I work / I'm working)
2. .... on Saturdays? (Do you work / Are you working)
3. 'Have you got a light?' 'Sorry, ...' (I don't smoke / I'm not smoking)
4. How many languages ....? (do you speak / are you speaking)
5. Why .... a sweater? It isn't cold. (do you wear / are you wearing)
6. My father .... to Ireland in August. (always goes / is always going)
7. Robert .... football most weekends. (plays / is playing)
8. 'Where's Lucy?' '............' (She shops / She's shopping)
9. 'What ....?' 'Chocolate.' (do you eat / are you eating)

2 Listen to the recording and answer the questions.

3 What are they doing? Listen to the conversation and circle any of these verbs that you hear.

sending   spending   standing   staying
playing   having   working   watching
washing   doing   reading   eating   writing
raining   cleaning   drinking   thinking
looking   cooking   going   opening

4 Who is doing what? Listen again and fill in the table.

JANE	*is talking to Polly*
POLLY	
JANE'S MOTHER	
BILL	
THE BABY	
SUE	
FRANK	

5 Look over the summary on page 149 with your teacher.

Plans

A   Who's doing what when?

1 **Read the problem and complete the solution.**

PROBLEM

Arsenal, Manchester, Liverpool and Tottenham are
   four football teams.

Each team is playing against one of the others on
   the next three Saturdays – a different one each
   time.

On Saturday the 12th, Arsenal are playing against
   Manchester.

Manchester are playing against Tottenham on the
   19th.

Who is playing against who on the 26th?

SOLUTION

Manchester .... against Arsenal on the 12th, ... they are playing .... Tottenham on the			
.... on the 26th they .... against Arsenal .... Tottenham.			
.... they are playing against .... on the 26th.			
.... are playing against .... on the 26th.			

Words to put in:

Arsenal	Liverpool	Tottenham	are playing
are not playing	against	19th	and or
so	so	so	

After you have solved the problem, you can
listen to a recording of some British people
trying to do it.

2 Can you think of some things that are
happening in this town or country during the
next week or so? (Concerts, football matches,
visits, ...)

3 What are you doing this evening? What are
you doing next weekend? What are you doing
for your next holiday?

4 Complete this dialogue and practise it in pairs

A: Are you doing anything this evening?
B: I'm not sure. Why?
A: Well, would you like to .... with me?
B: I'd love to, but I'm probably .... ing.
A: Well, how about tomorrow? Are you free?
B: ....
A: ....

5 Say these words after the recording or after
your teacher.

1. hungry   husband   industrial   up
2. blue   Tuesday   excuse   rude
3. purple   return   surname   Thursday

**1, 2 or 3? Decide how to pronounce these words
and check with your teacher or the recording.**

furniture	lunch	supermarket	supper
true	number	uncle	turn
June	curly	summer	sun

Unit 19: Lesson A

Students learn to talk about plans for the future.
Structures: Present Progressive with future reference; co-ordination with *so*; singular collective noun with plural verb; *each* + singular; *who* as object.
Words and expressions to learn: *football*; *against*; *each*; *this morning/afternoon/evening*; *so*; *I'd love to*; *How about . . . ?*; *free*.
Phonology: pronunciation of the letter *u*.

Language notes and possible problems

1. The future   This is one of the most complex areas of English grammar. Students have already met the use of *will* for predictions. Now they start learning to use present forms (Present Progressive and – in Unit 25 – *am going to*) to talk about future events which are already decided.

The Present Progressive is often used for future events which are planned for a particular time or date.

The Simple Present is not often used like this. Typical mistakes: **I see her tomorrow* or **Do you come on Friday evening?* The Simple Present is only used to talk about the future (in main clauses) in certain special cases – for example, in railway and school timetables.

2. Arsenal are playing...   Singular collective nouns (e.g. *Arsenal, team, family*) often have plural verbs in English.

3. Each   Students may find it surprising that *each* (which has a plural kind of meaning) is used with a singular verb.

4. Who is more common as an object form than *whom*.

5. Prepositions are omitted in expressions like *this afternoon* (*evening* etc.) and *next weekend* (*Monday* etc.).

6. To   Note the ellipsis in *I'd love to* (Exercise 4).

1 Logic problem

● Ask students to mask the solution.
● Explain any language difficulties.
● See if they can work out the solution by discussion.
● When they are ready, tell them to uncover the solution.
● This is a completion exercise. Ask students to do it individually, and then to compare notes in groups.
● When they have finished, they should all have found the solution (Manchester v Liverpool; Arsenal v Tottenham), and the use of *so* should be clear.
● You will probably want to comment briefly on the use of the Present Progressive to talk about the future.

Answers to Exercise 1

Manchester *are playing* against Arsenal on the 12th, *and they are playing against* Tottenham on the *19th. So* on the 26th they *are not playing* against Arsenal *or* Tottenham. *So* they are playing against *Liverpool* on the 26th. *So Arsenal* are playing against *Tottenham* on the 26th.

● Students may like to listen to British people trying to solve the problem (on the cassette).

2 Coming events

● Students will make some examples using the Present Progressive and some using other structures (e.g. *There's a Western at the Olympia cinema next week*).
● Encourage the use of the Present Progressive, but not at the price of making unnatural sentences.
● This exercise might lead to the compiling of a list of forthcoming events for the class notice-board.

3 Personalization

● Students should easily be able to make examples.
● Give more expressions of time without prepositions (*this morning/afternoon*; *next week/Monday* etc.).

4 Dialogue

● Go through the text and explain any difficulties.
● Ask for suggestions for the blanks.
● Get students to prepare complete versions in pairs and practise them (help with vocabulary).
● There is a completed version recorded.
● This can be extended to an improvisation exercise: students 'telephone' other students and invite them out.

5 Pronunciation and spelling

● The three common pronunciations of the letter *u* correspond to three different spellings:
  u alone = /ʌ/ (e.g. *up*)
  u followed by *e* = /uː/ (e.g. *excuse*, *blue*)
  ur = /ɜː/ (e.g. *Thursday*).
● When students have done the exercise and compared notes, go over the answers with them, and practise the pronunciation some more if necessary.
● Exceptions: minute (/ˈmɪnɪt/), businessman (/ˈbɪznɪsmən/).

Optional activity   Memory test

● Get two volunteers to tell the class about their plans for the next few days – what they are doing this evening, tomorrow, next weekend and so on.
● Then ask the class questions to see how much they can remember about who is doing what.

Optional activity   Holiday plans

● Write on the board: *June   July   August*
● Tell students that they are going on holiday in one of these months – they can choose, but must not tell anybody their choice.
● Write on the board: *Rome   Miami   Bangkok* (or other suitable holiday towns).
● Again, students choose one without telling anybody.
● Finally, write: *Hilton   Park   Traveller's Inn*
● Explain that the Hilton is expensive, the Park middle-priced, the Traveller's cheap and primitive. Tell students to choose one.
● Practise the following exchanges:
  'When are you going?' 'In June.'
  'Where are you going?' 'To Rome.'
  'Where are you staying?' 'At the Hilton.'
● Tell students to get up and walk round asking and answering questions until they find somebody who will be in the same hotel as them at the same time.
● (Idea by Donn Byrne. See *Let's Go Together*, in *Three Communicative Activities*, published in *Visual Aids for Classroom Interaction*, ed. Holden, MEP, 1978.)

Practice Book

● Tell students which exercises you want them to do.

Unit 19: Lesson B

Students learn ways of referring to future time; they practise reading quickly for specific information.
Structures: Present Progressive with future reference; prepositions of time.
Words and expressions to learn: *think so; ticket; get* (= 'obtain'); *cheque; traveller's cheque; forget; do the packing; I hope; excited; somebody; office.*

Language notes and possible problems
Prepositions of time   Students should learn the following facts:

1. *On* is used with the names of days of the week (e.g. *on Tuesday; on Monday morning*).
2. *At* is used in *at the weekend*, and also in *at Christmas, at Easter* etc.
3. *At* is also used (as students should already know) in *at … o'clock.*
4. *In* is used to say how close a future event is to the present – how soon it is going to happen (e.g. *in ten minutes; in six weeks*).
5. *In* is also used in the expressions *in the morning/afternoon/evening* (not exemplified in the dialogue).
6. *For* is used to say how long something lasts (e.g. *for three weeks*).
7. No preposition is used before *today, tomorrow,* (and *yesterday*); *this* and *next* (and *last*) *week/Monday/weekend* etc.
Note that American usage is slightly different in some cases (*on* is often dropped before the names of days of the week; Americans say *on the weekend*).

1 Scanning

• This exercise gives practice in the skill of reading quickly for specific information.
• It can be done as a competition if you wish.
• The correct answer is: I, C, K, L, A, H, G, D, E, B, J, F.
• With a very bright class, you may like to see whether students can get some way towards answering the question just by listening with their books closed (you will need to put the events on the board).
• After the scanning exercise, the dialogue can be used for language study and/or pronunciation practice if you wish.
• The most important thing to do is to see how prepositions of time are used – get students to look through, underlining or noting all expressions like *on Wednesday morning, at the weekend.*

2 Adverbials of future time
• This can be done either orally or in writing.
• If you do it orally, you may like to make up a few more examples so that everybody has a turn.

3 Personalization
• Again, you can make up more examples, depending on the time of year and what public events, public holidays etc. are close.

4 Test on prepositions
• This will show you whether any individuals are having difficulty in learning the correct use of the prepositions.

5 Journeys
• Get students to talk about their journeys in the Present Progressive tense (as far as possible).
• An amusing variant is to ask two students to tell the class about complicated journeys they are planning, one after the other, and then to ask the class to try to recall the details without mixing up the two separate journeys.

Practice Book
• Tell students which exercises you want them to do.
• Exercise 4 is a crossword puzzle designed to reactivate vocabulary from the earlier part of the course.

B We're leaving on Monday

(Janet and Bill are talking on Monday April 19th, at nine o'clock in the morning.)

JANET: Is everything all right?

BILL: Yes, I think so. I'm picking up the visas on Wednesday morning and the tickets in the afternoon, and I'm getting the traveller's cheques from the bank tomorrow.

JANET: Oh, good. Don't forget that the children are going to Mother on the 22nd – you're driving them.

BILL: Oh, yes. How long for?

JANET: Just for two days. Back on Friday night.

BILL: That isn't long.

JANET: Darling – you know it's John's birthday on the 24th.

BILL: So it is. We must have him home for his birthday. What are we giving him?

JANET: A bike.

BILL: Oh yes, that's right. When are you going to do the packing?

JANET: At the weekend, at the last possible moment. You're going to help, I hope.

BILL: Oh, yes. Yes, of course.

JANET: And then on Monday we're off! British Airways Flight 011 to Australia. For three months! I'm so excited!

BILL: OK. Remember Peter and Sally are coming this evening.

JANET: No, they aren't. It's tomorrow.

BILL: Well, somebody's coming this evening.

JANET: Your father. And Mary Rawson's telephoning this afternoon. She wants to ask you about insurance.

BILL: Well, I'm sorry, but I'm leaving in about two minutes. I have to be at the office in half an hour, and I won't be back before six.

JANET: All right. I'll give Mary your love.

BILL: OK. Bye, darling. Have a nice day.

JANET: You too. Bye-bye.

1 Put these events in the right order as fast as you can.

A Bill's visit to the bank
B John's birthday
C Mary Rawson's phone call
D Bill picking up the tickets
E children leaving to stay with their grandmother
F family leaving for Australia
G Bill picking up the visas
H Peter and Sally's visit
I Bill leaving for the office
J Janet packing (with Bill's help)
K Bill coming back from the office
L Bill's father's visit

2 Janet and Bill are talking at nine o'clock on Monday April 19th. They can talk about the future in two or three different ways. Example:

on the 22nd = on Thursday = in three days.

How could Bill and Janet say these differently?
on Wednesday   on the 24th   in a week
at ten o'clock   in three hours   in four days

3 How soon are the following: your birthday; Christmas; the end of your English course; the end of this lesson? (**Use** *in.*)

4 Put *at, on, in, for* or no preposition.

1. What are you doing .... the weekend?
2. I'm seeing Carlo .... Tuesday.
3. My mother's telephoning .... three o'clock.
4. 'Can I talk to you?' 'Sorry, I'm leaving .... five minutes.'
5. I think it's going to rain .... this afternoon.
6. We're going to Dakar in June .... three weeks.
7. Would you like to go out with me .... Monday evening?
8. Telephone me .... tomorrow if you have time.
9. 'I'm going to Norway .... August.' 'That's nice. How long ....?'

5 Are you going on a journey soon? If so, tell the class about it.

79

C Let's go to Scotland

1 How far do you think these places are from each other? (The distances are in the table.)

I think Oxford is .... from London.
I think Moscow is .... from Paris.
I think San Francisco is .... from Miami.
I think London is .... from Edinburgh.
I think Paris is .... from London.
I think Peking is .... from Caracas.

MILES	60	209	378	1540	2582	10350
KILOMETRES	96	336	608	2478	4155	16656

Listen to a recording of some English-speaking people trying to answer the questions.

2 Suggestions.

Listen to the conversations.
There are three answers to the first suggestion.
What are they?
What are the three answers to the second
    suggestion?

SUGGESTION   ANSWERS
Let's go to Scotland 1. ....
for our holiday.   2. ....
     3. ....

SUGGESTION   ANSWERS
Why don't we   1. ....
go to California?   2. ....
     3. ....

"Somewhere with no irregular verbs."

3 Work in groups of four. Prepare and practise conversations about holidays, films, restaurants, visits, or evening/weekend activities. One student makes a suggestion; the others answer. Examples of suggestions:

'Let's go to .... for our holiday.'
'Let's go and see (name of film).'
'Let's have lunch/dinner at (name of restaurant).'
'Let's go and see (name of friend).'
'Let's go and see a film this evening.'
'Let's go to Scotland this weekend.'

4 Listen to the recording. How many words are there? What are they? (Contractions like *don't* count as two words.)

"Artie, how would you pack if you were going to Mars?"

Unit 19: Lesson C

Students learn to make and reply to suggestions and to talk about distances.
Structures: *How far is ... from ...?; Oxford is 60 miles from London; a long way; I think + (that) clause; Let's + infinitive without to; Why don't we ...?*
Words and expressions to learn: *Let's; why; Why don't we ...?; I don't want to; suggestion; conversation; visit.*
Phonology: decoding the fast colloquial pronunciation of some common phrases.

Language notes and possible problems

1. Let's The structure with *Let's* corresponds to a first-person plural imperative verb form in many European languages.
2. Politeness Both *I (don't) want to* and *I'd like to* come in the recorded answers in Exercise 2. You may like to talk about the difference in formality.
3. Far Note that *far* is generally avoided in affirmative sentences, except after *too* and in one or two fixed expressions. We prefer to say, for instance, *It's a long way,* rather than *It's far.*

1 Talking about distances 📼 Ⓐ
* This can be done individually or in groups.
* Give students a few minutes to make their guesses and fill in the answers (in miles or kilometres, as they wish).
* Ask for their answers (beginning *I think* or *We think*).
* Note the pronunciation of *Moscow*: /ˈmɒskəʊ/ (British English); /ˈmɒskaʊ/ (American English).
* Teach the expression *a long way* (see Language notes).

Oxford–London: 60 miles/96km
Moscow–Paris: 1540 miles/2478km
San Francisco–Miami: 2582 miles/4155km
London–Edinburgh: 378 miles/608km
Paris–London 209 miles/336km
Peking–Caracas 10350 miles/16656km

* When they have finished, students may like to hear some English-speaking people trying to answer the questions. Point out that they are using miles.

2 Suggestions: presentation 📼
* Go over the instructions with the students. Make sure they understand *suggestion* and *answer*, and that they know what they have to do.
* Play each conversation several times – first straight through and then pausing if necessary after each sentence.
* Students should first try to tell you what they hear and then write it down; but don't let quick students give the answers before everybody has had a chance to try to work them out.

Tapescript for Exercise 2
'Let's go to Scotland for our holiday.'
'OK.'
'No, let's go to Ireland.'
'Why don't we go to America?'

'Why don't we go to California?'
'Yes, all right.'
'No, I don't want to.'
'I'd like to go to New York.'

3 Suggestions: practice
* Spend some time going over the instructions and examples, explaining anything that is not clear.
* Demonstrate the exercise with three good students and yourself.
* Then ask the class to do it in groups of four. If the results are good you may like to ask groups to perform their conversations for the rest of the class.

Optional activity
* With a good class, Exercise 3 can continue as an improvisation.
* Bring each group out to the front and write a word on the board:
   holiday or *film* or *restaurant* or *visit* or
   this evening/weekend
* (Alternatively, you can have the words on cards and have one of the group draw a card.)
* As soon as the group gets its word it must start talking, making and reacting to suggestions about the topic in question, while the rest of the class listen.

4 How many words? 📼
* Play each sentence separately.
* Ask students how many words they think it contains.
* Then ask them to try to write it down.
* Play the recording again two or three times if necessary.
* This exercise should be done individually, not in groups. Good students should keep their answers to themselves until weak students have had enough time to try to work out the sentences.
* It may be necessary to remind students that the pronunciations they hear in this exercise are not 'careless' or 'incorrect' – they are normal ways of saying the phrases in fast colloquial speech. This kind of practice is essential if students are to understand natural spoken English.

Tapescript and answers to Exercise 4
1. I don't know. (4)
2. Is there any bread? (4)
3. No, there isn't any. (5)
4. Excuse me. (2)
5. What's the time, do you know? (7)
6. What's her name? (4)
7. Where's the station? (4)
8. Let's go to London. (5)
9. Why don't we go to Paris? (7)
10. All right. (2)
11. I think there's some wine in the kitchen. (9)
12. How are you? (3)

Practice Book
* Tell students which exercises you want them to do.
* Exercise 3 is the first part of a guided composition exercise which will be continued in the next lesson.

80

Unit 19: Lesson D

Students practise writing and replying to informal invitations.
Structures: revision of various structures used for suggesting and requesting; preview of imperatives.
Words and expressions to learn: *have a drink; pub; idea; usual; important; catch a plane/train/etc.*

1 and 2

- Let the students spend a few minutes looking at the notes and asking questions.
- They should match up the invitations and replies. (There is no reply to Judy's note.)
- Tell them to make up a diary page (like the one in the book) for the next seven days, with space for two or three appointments each day. The names of the days should be in English.
- Now they start writing each other invitations, using words and expressions from the notes in the book.
- Their purpose is to make appointments with as many people as possible, so that they really fill up their diary page.
- They should reply to each invitation they receive.
- If you notice a student who isn't getting invitations, send him/her one yourself.
- You will probably need to deliver the students' letters to everyone.

3 Summary

- Go over the summary with the students at the end of the lesson.

Practice Book

- Tell students which exercises you want them to do.
- Exercise 3 is a guided composition exercise (based on the text in Practice Book Lesson 19C).

D Meet me at eight

Dear Carlos,
Why don't we go and see 'Rock, rock, rock of ages' tomorrow evening? Let's meet at the station at 6.55. O.K.?
Yours, Annie

Dear Sally,
Let's have a drink after the class. Shall we meet at the pub at 6.30?
Yours,
Polly

Dear Alex,
Meet me at seven o'clock at the usual place. Don't tell Carola.
Love,
Judy

Dear Susan,
Would you like to have dinner with me at the Ritz next Friday? I'll call for you in the Rolls about 7.30.
Yours,
Jonathan.

Dear Polly,
What a nice idea! See you at 6.30
Yours,
Sally

Dear Joe,
I'm afraid I'm not free today. How about tomorrow?
Janet

Dear Jonathan,
Thank you. I should be delighted to have dinner with you on Friday.
Yours,
Susan

DEAR JANE,
LET'S CATCH A PLANE TO SPAIN.
LOVE, FRED

Dear Annie,
Sorry. I can't go this evening. Perhaps another day?
Yours, Carlos

Dear Oliver,
Meet me at Joe's house. It's very important.
Yours,
Al

JANET—
LUNCH TODAY?
JOE

DEAR AL,
OK. WHERE'S JOE'S HOUSE?
OLIVER

Sorry, Fred.
I'm going with Ted.

1 Read the notes. Write similar notes to other students. Reply to the notes that you get.

2 Fill up your diary for the next week with a list of appointments.

3 Look at the summary on page 149 with your teacher.

June

1 Sun	8.00 cinema with Mario
2 Mon	
3 Tues	
4 Wed	Lunch with Barbara, 1.15
5 Thurs	Dentist 10.30
6 Fri	Dinner with George and Catherine
7 Sat	Henry's party.
8 Sun	
9 Mon	Meeting with M.C.

Getting to know you

A Is this seat free?

1 Look at the pictures. What do you think the people are saying in each picture?

2 Revision. Ask to borrow things from other students.

'Could I borrow your pen?'
'Yes, of course.'

'Can I use your dictionary for a moment?'
'Yes, here you are.'

'Can I borrow your watch?'
'Sorry, I need it.'

3 Work with another student. You are on a train, and you want to sit down, open the window, etc. Ask and answer.

ASK FOR PERMISSION	GIVE PERMISSION
Do you mind if I sit here?	Not at all.
Do you mind if I open the window?	No, please do.
	Go ahead.
Do you mind if I smoke?	
Do you mind if I look at your paper?	REFUSE PERMISSION
	I'm sorry. It's not free.
	Well, it's a bit cold.
	Well, I'd rather you didn't.
	Well, I'm reading it myself, actually.

4 Close your books, listen to the recording and answer.

a. Give permission.
b. Refuse permission.

5 Improvisation.
Work in groups of between four and six. You are sitting together on a train. Begin a conversation.
OR:
Work in pairs. You are both in a coffee-bar, a pub or a park. Begin a conversation.

6 Pronunciation. Say these words and expressions.

a. Is this seat free?
b. seat sit eat it sheep ship
c. heat need cheap
   steam steel leak
   seek peach keep
d. win spit hit pick lip

Unit 20: Lesson A

Students learn ways of politely getting into conversation with strangers.
Structures: *Do you mind if...?*; revision of *Can/Could I borrow...?*
Words and expressions to learn: *seat; mind; if; myself; for a moment; paper (= newspaper); please do; go ahead; I'd rather you didn't.*
Phonology: practice on the *sheep/ship* distinction.

Language notes and possible problems

1. Subject-matter The basic situation here (getting into conversation with strangers) will be familiar to most students. Some of them, indeed, are likely to be experts at it, and there will probably be a lot of questions about how to formulate this or that expression in English. (Encourage *How do you say...?* or *How can I say...?*) Note, however, that students from certain cultural backgrounds may find the situation unfamiliar; they may have more difficulty with this lesson, especially with Exercise 5.

2. Do you mind if ...? is likely to cause difficulty (because the answer *No* means 'Yes, you can' and *Yes* means 'No, you can't'). You can explain *mind* as 'not want' or 'not like'. *If* is previewed here, but is not studied in detail at this stage.

3. Can and could reappear here. Remind students that *could* is used when we want to be more polite.

---

1 Predicting a conversation

- Ask students to look at the pictures for a minute or two.
- Get them to suggest sentences for the six speech-balloons.
- Ask how they think the conversation continues.
- Build up the complete conversation (with alternatives) on the board.
- Play the recording, and answer any questions.
- Get students to note down the sentence *Do you mind if I sit here?*
- Ask volunteers to try to act out the recorded conversation from memory.

Tapescript for Exercise 1
'Excuse me. Is this seat free?'
'Yes, it is.'
'Do you mind if I sit here?'
'Not at all.'
'Could I borrow your newspaper?'
'Yes, of course.'

2 Borrowing (revision)

- Practise the pronunciation of the example sentences.
- Ask students to walk round (or to speak to their immediate neighbours), asking to borrow, use or look at things.

3 *Do you mind?*

- Look over the examples with the students.
- Practise the intonation with the recording.
- It is important for them to realize the meaning of *mind*, and to understand that a negative answer to *Do you mind...?* means 'It's all right'.

- They must also realize that it is common to refuse a 'Do you mind...?' request by giving some sort of reason.
- When students are ready, ask them to close their books and practise asking and answering with a partner.
- If they have difficulty, let them look back at their books and then try again.

4 Listening and answering

- Tell students to look again at the answers used for giving permission in Exercises 2 and 3.
- Get them to close their books.
- Play the recording straight through, while students answer the requests by giving permission.
- *Do you mind...?* and *Can/Could I...?* are mixed here, so students will have to pay attention to the form of the question.
- Students can answer all together or in turn, as you wish.
- If they are slow, stop the recording so as to give more time.
- When you have gone through all the requests, get students to open their books and look again at ways of refusing permission.
- Then tell them to close their books; play the requests again from the beginning while students refuse.

Tapescript for Exercise 4
Do you mind if I sit here?
Do you mind if I smoke?
Do you mind if I use your dictionary?
Do you mind if I ask you a question?
Can I look at your newspaper?
Could I open the window?
Do you mind if I make a telephone call?
Could I possibly borrow your pen?
Do you mind if I play some records?
Could I borrow your keys for a moment?

5 Improvisation

- The second alternative will work best in mixed classes; in a single-sex class the railway-carriage situation may go better.
- The conversations will probably not go on for very long; the important thing is to get them started.

6 Pronunciation

- The sentence *Is this seat free?* makes a good jumping-off point for further work on the contrast between /ɪ/ and /iː/.
- The second part of the exercise (b) can be done as an ear-training activity – see Lesson 9B Exercise 5 for suggestions.
- The third part of the exercise (c) reminds students that they can generally pronounce words written with *ea* and *ee* even if they don't know them. (They may be able to think of a few cases where these letters are pronounced differently: for example *bread, steak.*)
- The fourth part (d) does the same for words written with *i*.

Practice Book
- Tell students which exercises you want them to do.

Unit 20: Lesson B

Students learn more about how to express the idea of frequency, and practise reply questions in the context of polite conversational exchanges.
Structures: position of adverbs and adverbials of frequency; *once a week, twice a month* etc.; *every three days* etc.; 'reply questions'; *go ...-ing.*
Words and expressions to learn: *always; hardly ever; twice; three times; tonight; record; hairdresser; go to the cinema; go for a walk.*

Language notes and possible problems

1. Word order Students have already learnt that frequency adverbs tend to go before the main verb. This is not true of most adverbials (longer expressions which function as adverbs): these often go at the end of a clause. Exercise 2 practises the point.

2. Reply questions There may be some resistance to reply questions, which often seem silly to speakers of languages which do not have a similar device. Point out that *Is it?, Do you?* and so on are not real questions but simply show interest on the part of the listener.

Students who find it too difficult to produce all the different combinations of subject + auxiliary can just say *Oh, yes?* or *Really?* instead.

3. Articles Note the 'generalizing' use of the article in *the cinema/opera/hairdresser.*

4. Come and go both occur in the conversation; you may wish to explain the difference.

5. Actually is a 'false friend' – speakers of European languages may think it means 'now'.

6. A drink Note the common use of *a drink* to mean 'an alcoholic drink'. Compare *something to drink* (which might also be coffee, fruit juice etc.).

7. Every is used here with plural numerical expressions; point out that it is normally followed by a singular noun.

Presentation The illustration

● Before doing Exercise 1, let students have a good look at the illustration.
● Answer questions on the text and explain difficulties.
● Draw students' attention to the position of frequency adverbs and adverbials.
● Then tell them to close their books and see how much they can remember of the exchanges.

1 *How often?*

● Look at the possible questions and answers.
● Explain vocabulary; practise pronunciation.
● Get students to ask you as many questions as they can; try to give true answers.
● Then set up a 'chain-drill': ask one of the students a question; he/she answers it and asks another student.

2 Word order

● Ask students to write three or more sentences of each kind, so that they can get a fair amount of practice in putting the adverbs in the right place.

Optional activity Where do you stand?

● One corner of the room is 'always'; the corner diagonally opposite is 'never'. In between are 'very often', 'quite often', 'sometimes', 'occasionally', 'hardly ever'.
● Students show how often they do various things (see Exercise 1) by standing in the appropriate position.
● As you ask each question, students take up their places. Ask one or two what they are expressing by standing there (e.g. *I never have cornflakes for breakfast; I occasionally go to the cinema*).
● Students enjoy seeing who they are with at each new change of position.
● Other possible questions: ask how often they: *take a shower in the evenings, smoke cigars, drink whisky, read poetry, go jogging, fall in love.*

Optional activity Class survey

● Get each student to go round the class finding out how often everybody does one of the things mentioned in Exercise 1 (or anything else).
● Students note the answers and report.
● Example: *Six people go to the cinema once a week. Three people go twice a week. One never goes.*

3 Reply questions

● First of all, tell students to decide which is the right answer to each sentence. Help them to see why.
● Play the recording of the eight sentences with the replies, and practise the intonation.
● Play the recording of the rest of the exercise: students have to produce reply questions spontaneously.
● If they find it difficult, play the recording twice: the first time, students answer *Oh, yes?* or *Really?*, and the second time they try the forms with auxiliary verbs.

Tapescript for Exercise 3
'My brother's a doctor.' 'Is he?'
'My sister's got five children.' 'Has she?'
'Maria likes fast cars.' 'Does she?'
'It's raining again.' 'Is it?'
'I slept badly last night.' 'Did you?'
'I love skiing.' 'Do you?'
'My father can speak five languages.' 'Can he?'
'I'm tired.' 'Are you?'

'It's three o'clock.'
'I'm hungry.'
'We live in a very small house.'
'I like dancing.'
'Mary telephoned yesterday.'
'Mr and Mrs Harris are coming tomorrow.'
'I forgot to buy bread.'
'We're going on holiday next week.'
'It's snowing.'
'You're late.'
'John's here.'
'My sister works in a cinema.'

4 Personalization

● This gives a natural context for reply questions.
● To add interest, students could be asked to spend a few minutes inventing imaginary identities and personal data before beginning the exercise.

Practice Book

● Tell students which exercises you want them to do.

B | Do you often come here?

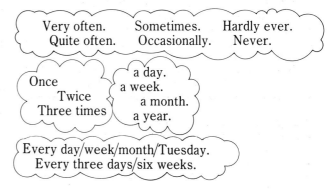

*I always come here on
Sunday mornings.*
Oh, do you? So do I...

I'm Pisces.
Are you? So am I...

I go to the cinema at least once a week...
How often do you...?
Every two or three days...

Do you like 'Top of the Pops'?
I never watch it...

My brother...
Does he?...

I've got a...
Oh, have you?...

Do you ever go to the opera? Oh, yes. I love opera.
*So do I. Actually, I've got two tickets for
'Carmen' tonight.* Oh, have you?
Would you like to go with me?
I'd love to.
Let's go and have a drink.
Why not?

1 | Ask and answer.

How often do you:

go to the hairdresser / watch TV / travel by
train / go on holiday / go for a walk / go to
the cinema / listen to records / go skiing /
write letters / drink beer / drink coffee /
eat in a restaurant / go swimming / go
dancing / play tennis / wash your hair?

Very often.   Sometimes.   Hardly ever.
   Quite often.   Occasionally.   Never.

Once   a day.
   Twice   a week.
Three times   a month.
              a year.

Every day/week/month/Tuesday.
Every three days/six weeks.

2 | Word order. Write sentences like the examples.

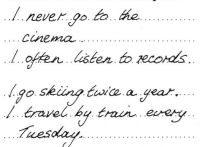

*..I. never. go. to. the............
...cinema......................
..I. often. listen. to. records..*

*..I. go. skiing. twice. a. year.....
..I. travel. by. train. every...
...Tuesday....................*

3 | Reply questions. Match sentences and answers. Practise the intonation. Then close your books and answer the recorded sentences.

My brother's a doctor.	Do you? Oh, yes?
My sister's got five children.	Is it? Really?
Maria likes fast cars.	Is he?
It's raining again.	Has she?
I slept badly last night.	Are you?
I love skiing.	Can he?
My father can speak five languages.	Does she?
I'm tired.	Did you?

4
Work in pairs. Tell your partner things about yourself, your friends and your family. Your
partner will answer '*Are you?*' '*Do you?*' etc.

C What do you think of...?

1 Read the picture story. Your teacher will help you.

2 Look at the questions in frame 3. Choose possible answers from these.

Yes, I do.	For about seven years.	Terrible!
Cheesecake.	No, I don't.	Yes, lots of times.
All my life.	Not bad.	No, I haven't. Great!
Not much.	No, never.	

3 Ask other students questions about well-known singers, writers, etc.

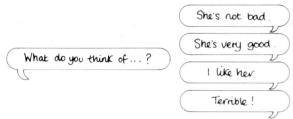

What do you think of...?

She's not bad.

She's very good.

I like her.

Terrible!

4 What are their favourite colours? Listen to the recording to find out.

red	orange	yellow	green	blue
purple	light blue	light green		

Now ask other students *What's/Who's your favourite...?*
Then copy the form and fill it in.

MY FAVOURITE FOOD ....
MY FAVOURITE COLOUR ....
MY FAVOURITE GAME/SPORT ....
MY FAVOURITE WRITER ....
MY FAVOURITE SINGER ....
MY FAVOURITE PLACE ....
MY FAVOURITE SEASON ....
MY FAVOURITE ANIMAL ....

A PINT OF BITTER AND A HALF OF LAGER PLEASE.

CHEERS!

HOW DO YOU LIKE THIS PUB?
HAVE YOU SEEN "CARMEN" BEFORE?
WHAT'S YOUR FAVOURITE FOOD?
HOW LONG HAVE YOU LIVED IN LONDON?

WHAT DO YOU THINK OF THE GOVERNMENT?
HAVE YOU EVER BEEN TO AFRICA?
DO YOU LIKE MODERN JAZZ?

HAVE ANOTHER DRINK.

NO, I MUST GO. I'M LATE. SEE YOU TOMORROW.

5 Match the sentences and the answers. (Two answers for each sentence.)

I like fish.   I'm tired.
  I've got too much work.
I can speak German.

So can I.   I haven't.   I don't.   So am I.
So have I.   I can't.   I'm not.   So do I.

6 Say things about yourself beginning:
I like ...   I'm ...   I've got ...   I can ...
The class will answer: *So do I, I don't*, etc.

7 Pronunciation. Say these words.

who   how   hundred   have   half   hair
hand   hate   house   hello

Unit 20: Lesson C

Students learn to ask for, express and react to opinions.
Structures: preview of Present Perfect tense: *What do you think of ...?*; *So do/can/am/have I*; *must + infinitive without to* (preview).
Words and expressions to learn: *favourite; pint; cheers; Have another drink; great; life; all my life; so (adverb); seen; been; ever; must.*
Phonology: initial /h/.

Language notes and possible problems

1. *So do I*, etc. Students will probably find the variety of forms complicated and confusing, but they are not in fact very difficult to learn.

2. Present Perfect This will be dealt with in the next lesson. However, make sure students realize that *How long have you lived in London?* implies that the hearer lives in London now. (Some students would expect a present tense to be used in this situation.)

3. *Ever* Perhaps the best way to explain this if you don't speak the students' language is to define it as meaning 'until now' or 'in your life'. A time-line on the board might help. It will be practised in the next lesson.

4. *Must* This verb is previewed in the expression *I must go*, but is not taught systematically here.

---

1 The picture story

- Let students read the story, asking you questions if they wish.
- You may like to play the recording and work on intonation.
- (Note that the recording only contains one of the exchanges from frame 3.)

2 Answers to questions in frame 3

- Students can answer this question by group discussion. Note that there are several possible answers in some cases.
- See if students can suggest other answers that are not on the page.

3 Personalization

- The subject matter of this exercise depends on the students' interests: they can ask about writers, singers, composers, footballers, people they know, politicians, ...
- Students may be able to suggest other answers besides the ones on the page.

4 Favourite

- Explain *favourite*.
- Get students to copy the list of colours if you do not want them writing in their books.
- Play the recording, and get students to check off the colours they hear (you may want to play the recording twice).
- This should be fairly unproblematic; the colours are: purple, green (twice), red (twice), light green and blue.
- Go back to the question on the recording. Play it and point out the pronunciation of *favourite* (in two syllables)

and the stress pattern of the sentence:

☐ ◻ ☐ ◻ ☐ ◻
What's your favourite colour?

- Get the students to practise the question.
- Ask a few students to tell you their favourite food, colour etc. Let them ask you and each other, too.
- Then get students to copy and fill in the form *without writing their names on it*. Do one yourself.
- Collect the forms and shuffle them.
- Get students to read some of them out, and see if the class can guess who wrote each one.

5 *So do I*, etc.

- Explain that *So can I* means 'I can too', *So do I* means 'I do too', and so on.
- The exercise will help students to grasp the details of the structure, if they find this difficult.
- It is probably best to ask them to write the answers, so that you can make sure everybody has understood the point.

6 Personalization

- Start by saying some things about yourself and getting the class to respond.
- Students should try to say things that the others don't already know. (There's not much point in telling people who are in the same room with you that you've got red hair, for example.)
- If you put the names of the astrological signs on the board (see page 67), students can find out who shares their sign.

7 Pronunciation

- This gives quick revision of /h/. Drop it if students don't need it.

Practice Book

- Tell students which exercises you want them to do.

Unit 20: Lesson D

Students learn to refer to periods of time extending up to the present, and to say how long they have known people, lived in places, etc.
Structures: Present Perfect tense referring to states (know, have, live, be), and to actions in the frame Have you ever...?; since and for.
Words and expressions to learn: for (time); since; already; believe; and so on; in love; I feel; learn.

Language notes and possible problems

1. The Present Perfect tense: forms Students now have to learn another verb form – the 'past participle'.

2. The Present Perfect tense: use This is not an easy tense for students. It has several meanings (continuation up to the present; current importance; completion): these ideas may not be expressed by choice of tense in the students' languages, and the use of the Present Perfect may therefore seem abstract and difficult to grasp.

Many European languages have a form which looks like the Present Perfect, but is not used in the same way – it may correspond to the English Simple Past, leading to mistakes like *I have seen the lawyer yesterday*.

Conversely, students' languages may use a present tense to talk about duration up to the present (causing mistakes like *I am here since last Tuesday*).

Students learn two uses of the Present Perfect – *I have been/known/had...* with *since* and *for*, and *Have you ever...?* Other aspects will be dealt with later in the course.

3. Since and for Students may only have one word in their language corresponding to *since* and *for* – look out for mistakes like *I have known her since three years*.

---

1 Restoring a text 📼

● Look over the two 'letter fragments' and vocabulary with the students, and answer any questions.
● The exercise can be done in groups. Note that students first have to decide which of the sets of vocabulary in Exercise 1 goes with which text.
● Only the language for the 'torn-off' right-hand part of each page is provided; the letters remain incomplete at the top and bottom.

Answers to Exercise 1 (recorded)
... the nicest *man*
I've met for years. I've only *known him* since yesterday, but I'm already *sure* it's going to be very important. *He's* tall and slim, with a beautiful *smile*, and – believe it or not, Sally – *he's* interested in the same things as *I am*: films, music, travel and so on. *He's* Pisces, and so *am I*.

... met this wonderful *girl*.
John, I really think I'm *in love*. It's funny. I've only *known her* for 24 hours, but I feel *we've known* each other all our lives. *We've got* so many interests in common: *music*, films, travel... We're both *Pisces*.

2 How long have you lived...?
● Ask students to say and write their answers.

3 Since and for
● Look at the examples with the students.
● They should see that *since* is used with a reference to the beginning of a period, while *for* introduces an expression naming the whole period.
● Get students to fill in the gaps.

4 How long have you had/been/known?
● Ask students how long they have had various possessions. Get them to ask you and each other.
● Continue with *How long have you been...?* and *How long have you known...?*
● Then explain the grammar.
● Draw a 'time-line' on the board as follows:

PAST (THEN)		PRESENT (NOW)
PAST → PRESENT		
(SINCE THEN)		
I had	I have had	I have (got)
I was	I have been	I am
I knew	I have known	I know
I saw	I have seen	I see

● Point out that regular past participles are the same as past tense forms, but that irregular participles are often different. Note the two pronunciations of *read*.

5 Have you ever read...?
● Ask a few questions yourself.
● Try to develop each exchange (for instance, you can answer the second reply, saying *Oh, I thought it was wonderful/very good/terrible/etc.*).
● Get students to ask you questions.
● Continue in groups or as a 'chain-drill'.
● Teach *I've never heard of it* if necessary.
● Note that *ever* means 'in your life': it is not appropriate when students are asking about recent films, for instance.

Optional activity
● Students can write reviews of local films, concerts etc.
● Display these on the notice-board under the heading 'Have you seen...? Have you heard...? Have you read...?'
● One-line notes will do (e.g. *Massacre of the Vampires*: Terrible – Roberto   Great! – Silvia).

6 Summary
● Show students the list of irregular verbs on the inside back cover of Student's and Teacher's Books – this contains all the irregular verbs in the book, and they can consult it for irregular past participles.
● From now on, the Practice Book exercises for each Lesson D will contain irregular verbs.

Practice Book
● Tell students which exercises you want them to do.
● Exercises 1–3 practise the forms and use of the Present Perfect tense. These are important exercises, and you may wish to go over them in class.

D I've only known her for twenty-four hours, but…

the nicest

I've met for years. I've only
since yesterday, but I'm already
it's going to be very important
tall and slim, with a beautif
and – believe it or not, Sally –
interested in the same things as
films, music, travel and so on.
Pisces, and so

met this wonderf
John, I really think I
It's funny. I've only
for 24 hours, but I feel
each other all our lives.
so many interests in common:
films, travel… We're bot

1 Can you complete the sentences in the two torn letters? These words and expressions will help.

We've got music	sure he's He's
Pisces. known her	I am: man
girl. we've known	known him am I.
in love	smile He's

2 How long have you lived in your city/town/village/etc.? Examples:

'I've lived in Cardiff since 1979.'
'I've lived in Boston for the last five years.'
'I've lived in London all my life.'

3 *Since* and *for*.

since yesterday = for 24 hours
since the 16th century = for 400 years
since last Tuesday = for ....
since last .... = for five days
since 1977 = for ....
.... = since my birthday
since nine o'clock = ...
since last July = ...
for ten years = ...

4 Ask and answer (with *since* or *for*).

'How long have you | been in this town?'
been in this class?'
been learning English?'
been married?'
etc.

'How long have you had | that watch?'
that sweater?'
that ring?'
etc.

'How long have you known | the teacher?'
your friend Alex?'
etc.

5 Ask and answer.

'Have you (ever) read…?' | 'Yes, I have.' | 'What did you think of it?' | 'Great.'
'Have you (ever) seen…?' | 'No, I haven't.' | | 'Not bad.'
'Have you (ever) been to…?' | 'Not yet.' | | 'OK.'
| | | 'I didn't like it.'
| | | etc.

6 Look at the summary on page 150 with your teacher.

Things

A Why…? Because…

1 Listen to the song; find out what the words mean.

WHY, OH WHY?

Why can't a dish break a hammer?
Tell me why, oh why?
Because a hammer's
    got a pretty hard head.
Goodbye, goodbye, goodbye.

Why can't a bird eat an elephant?
Tell me why, oh why?
Well, for one thing an
    elephant's got a very
    tough skin.
Goodbye, goodbye, goodbye.

Why, oh why, oh why, oh why
Tell me why, oh why?
Just because, because, because, because.
Goodbye, goodbye.

Now why won't you answer my question?
Tell me why, oh why?
Because to tell you the plain truth, honey,
I just don't know the answers.

Goodbye, goodbye.

(*Why, oh Why* by Woody Guthrie © copyright 1960, 1964, and 1972 Ludlow Music, Inc.)

2 Answer these questions; use *too*. You can use a dictionary.
Example:

WHY CAN'T YOU PICK UP A CAR?

BECAUSE IT'S TOO HEAVY.

1000 kg.

You can use these words in the answers:

heavy	cold	light	big	quiet	soft
hard	strong	tall	loud	dark	hot
wide	high	small			

1. Why can't a knife cut a stone?
2. Why can't you jump over a house?
3. Why can't you throw a fridge?
4. Why can't you sunbathe at the North Pole?
5. Why can't you put a car in your bath?
6. Why can't you hear your heart beating?
7. Why can't you drink boiling water?
8. Why can't you read in a forest in the middle of the night?
9. Why can't you jump across the Mississippi?
10. Why can't you eat rice before it's cooked?
11. Why can't you stand up in a car?

3 Now answer the same questions again; use *enough*.
Example:

WHY CAN'T YOU PICK UP A CAR?

BECAUSE I'M NOT STRONG ENOUGH.

4 Match the opposites.

heavy	light	wide	big	quiet	tall	hard	cold	high	loud
small	hot	light	short	quiet	low	dark	narrow	soft	noisy

5 Look round the classroom, and try to find something heavy, something light, something wide, something narrow, etc. Use the adjectives from Exercise 4.

6 Which one is different? Why?

1. a tent   the Empire State Building
   the Eiffel Tower   St Paul's Cathedral
2. Siberia   Greenland   Morocco   Alaska
3. a flower   a leaf   a gold watch   a hair
4. Russia   Wales   China   South America
5. butter   wool   a knife   a mushroom

Unit 21: Lesson A

Students learn to ask for and give reasons, and to talk about physical qualities.
Structures: *why* + negative verb; *too* + adjective; adjective + *enough*.
Words and expressions to learn: some of these (see summary): *skin*; *break*; *hard*; *soft*; *tough*; *light* (opposite of *heavy*); *wide*; *high*; *loud*; *narrow*; *low*; *because*; *knife*; *stone*; *jump*; *sunbathe*; *boil*; *rice*; *bird*.

Language notes and possible problems

Notions   Students need to learn grammar (how the nuts and bolts of the language operate) and functions (how to do things like make requests). But they also need to know how to express the most common concepts or notions in a language. In this lesson, for example, causality and physical qualities are dealt with. Lessons organized around notions will tend to teach more vocabulary than grammar; in the absence of a small number of central structures, students may feel there is no point to the lesson. It might be worth suggesting to them that skill in talking about physical qualities is just as important as skill in making requests.

For a more detailed discussion of the syllabus organization of the book, see pages VI-VII of this Teacher's Book.

1 Presentation: song

• With books closed, let the students listen to the song once and try to tell you any words they remember.
• Then play the recording again, books open.
• Let students find out what the new words mean, by using their dictionaries, asking each other, or asking you.
• Play the song again, giving them an opportunity to sing along.
• Finally, tell them to close their books and see how much they can remember.

2 Practice with *too*

• Before beginning the exercise, explain or demonstrate the meanings of the new words in the box, or let the students use their dictionaries to find them.
• Then get the students to look at the illustration and practise the sample sentences.
• Afterwards, get the students to go through the questions, answering each one with a sentence containing *too*. You may need to supply some help with the vocabulary of the questions.
• You can do this exercise in several ways:
– as a whole-class exercise;
– by getting students to prepare answers individually and then compare their answers in groups of about five;
– by getting them to prepare the answers in groups of two or three before comparing answers with the rest of the class.

3 Practice with *enough*

• Look at the illustration with the students and practise the sample question and answer.

• Point out the difference in word order between expressions with *too* and expressions with *enough*.
• Then let them answer the questions again, this time using *enough*.

4 Opposites (consolidation)

• Students will know most of the words in this exercise.
• Let them work through the exercise individually, comparing answers in small groups to see if they can help one another with any pairs they have not been able to make.
• Check their answers and give them any words they have not been able to work out.

5 Something light

• This can be done as a team game, with teams trying to build up lists with as many different adjectives as possible in, say, five minutes.
• Another approach is to play 'I spy...'. Students in turn say *I can see something light (big, hard, ...) beginning with A (or B, C etc.).*
• The rest of the class have to guess what it is.
• 'I spy' can be played in groups.

6 Odd one out

• Do the first question with the whole class: ask them which of the four is different.
• Tell them they must give a reason for their answer. They may answer, for example:
   A tent, because it's soft.; or
   The Eiffel Tower, because you can see through it.
• Strictly speaking, they should try to use the adjectives they have been studying; but other answers should not be discouraged.
• Then divide the class into groups and let each prepare answers for the other four questions.
• When they have finished, they can compare answers.

Optional activity

• Students can make up groups of words like those in Exercise 6 and give them to one another to solve.

Practice Book

• Tell students which exercises you want them to do.
• Exercise 3 is a test on the use of articles. It should help you to see if any of your students are having particular difficulty in this area; if so, you may want to give one or two remedial lessons.

Unit 21: Lesson B

Students learn more about describing objects.
Structures: preview of the Passive.
Words and expressions to learn: names of some common materials; *useful*; *liquid*; *clock*.
Phonology: linking final consonants to initial vowels.

Language notes and possible problems

1. Made of   Students have already met one or two questions ending in prepositions. This is a difficult structure for many learners of English, and there will be a detailed lesson on it later in the course. In the present lesson students are only called upon to understand, and not produce, the question.

2. Dictionary use   In the first exercise students are asked to use their dictionaries to find the English equivalents of words they know in their own languages. This is a fairly safe procedure when a good dictionary is used and words for concrete things or actions are involved. If you speak the students' language(s), you may wish to warn against the limitations of this approach. You may also want to invite the students to check their results with you if they use this approach outside class to try and learn new words.

3. Linking   Students may have a tendency to leave a gap, or insert a /h/ or a 'glottal stop' in sentences like *The fifth object is made of leather*. You will want to help them practise linking.

4. Twenty questions   This game may be a bit slow starting off as students learn the procedure and the new language. However, once they have played it a few times, it becomes a very successful group activity or team game which is particularly useful for revising and practising interrogative structures.

Optional extra materials

One object made of each of the following materials: wool, wood, glass, china, leather, metal, paper, stone, rubber, plastic.

1 Presentation

● Let students use their dictionaries to find out the names for the materials the different objects are made of. If you can bring real objects into the classroom instead of using the pictures in the book, it will make the exercise more vivid for the students.
● In a class where students speak the same first language, they can do the dictionary work in groups.
● If they work individually, let them compare answers before checking with you.
● Their answers should be in the form:
   The first object is made of wool,
and you should help them with linking.
Alternatively, if you do not wish them to use dictionaries, this can be done as a matching game; put the words on the board in this order: *stone, leather, wood, rubber, metal, wool, china, paper, glass, leather, plastic,* and let the students pool their knowledge or ask you *yes/no* questions to find the answers. (*Is the fourth object made of stone?*)

2 Freer practice

● Each of the objects in this list is made of several different materials; students should try to give all the different materials for each one.
● This could be done in small groups.

3 Listening

● Get students to copy the list of objects.
● Tell them they will hear three people speak. The speakers are numbered 1, 2 and 3; after listening to each one, students should put the number against the object they think is being described.
● There is much that they will not understand; they must listen carefully for clues to the answers.
● Play the recording through once without stopping.
● Ask students if they want it played again, and if so, play it with pauses after each speaker.
● Play a third time if necessary.
● When going over the answers with the students (1. coat 2. bicycle 3. typewriter), point out the important words, or get the students to do so.

Tapescript for Exercise 3

1. It's made of wool and some kind of synthetic fabric and plastic. It's nice and long. It was expensive when I bought it, but I've got very good use out of it – it's really warm, it fits me well and the colour suits me.
2. It's blue; it's made mostly of metal, with some rubber, plastic and glass. It's very handy – makes it easy for me to get to work. I don't use it in the winter, though – it's too cold and windy.
3. Well, it's made of metal and plastic, and it's got a *lot* of parts. Mine is about the size of two loaves of bread, but some are much bigger. It's fairly noisy. I never really learnt to use it in school, but I'm pretty fast now all the same.

4 Preparation for Twenty questions

● Explain the four terms. Help the students to see the difference between *animal* (meaning 'of animal origin') used as an adjective after the verb *to be*, and *an animal*; similarly, between *vegetable* and *a vegetable*, *mineral* and *a mineral*.
● Then let the students classify the objects. Make sure they pronounce *vegetable* /ˈvedʒtəbl/ – with three syllables and not four.

Answers

Animal: a woollen sweater, a pair of shoes; your nose.
Vegetable: a book; a tree.
Mineral: a glass, a typewriter (mostly); a cassette.
Abstract: age; an idea.

5 Twenty questions

● You may want to explain *useful*, *liquid*, and *manufactured* before you begin.
● Then get a volunteer to think of an object and ask the others to ask questions that can be answered *Yes* or *No*.
● When the class has discovered the first object, divide them into groups and let them continue playing.
● Then let them listen once or twice to the recording of a group of British people playing 'Twenty questions'. There is no task.

Practice Book

● Tell students which exercises you want them to do.

B What's a car made of?

1 Use your dictionary. Look at the pictures and find out what the different things are made of.
Example: '*The fifth object is made of leather.*'

2 What are these made of?

a clock   a car   a cinema
a sofa   a TV   a secretary's chair
Example: '*A cinema is made of metal, stone,...*'

3 Listen. Which three objects are the people talking about? Number them 1, 2, 3.

a car   an armchair   a typewriter
a bicycle   a coat   a fridge

4 Animal, vegetable, mineral or abstract?

a glass   a woollen sweater   a book
a pair of shoes   a typewriter   a tree
a cassette   an idea   age   your nose

5 Twenty questions. Think of an object.

Tell the other students whether it is animal, vegetable, mineral or abstract. They must find out what it is; they can ask twenty questions, but you can only answer '*Yes*' or '*No*'.
Possible questions:

'*Can you eat it?*'
'*Is it made of wood/metal/glass/...?*'
'*Is it useful?*'
'*Can you find it in a house/shop/car/...?*'
'*Is it liquid?*'
'*Is it hard/soft/heavy/light/...?*'
'*Have you got one of these?*'
'*Is it manufactured?*'
'*Is there one in this room?*'

Then listen to some people playing 'Twenty questions.'

C 'The best car in the world'

The first Royce car (1904)

The Silver Ghost (1906-1925)

The Silver Cloud (1959-1966)

The Silver Spirit (1981)

Henry Royce did not like his Decauville car, which ran badly and often broke down. So he decided to make a better car himself, and in 1904 he produced his first two-cylinder model. Charles Rolls, a car manufacturer, was very impressed by Royce's car, and soon Rolls and Royce went into business together. One of their first models was the Silver Ghost. In 1907, a Silver Ghost broke the world's endurance record by driving 14,371 miles (23,120km) without breaking down once. After the drive, it cost just over £2 to put the car back into perfect condition. It is not surprising that the Silver Ghost was called 'the best car in the world'. Rolls-Royce cars are famous for running quietly: an advertisement for one model said 'the loudest noise is the ticking of the clock'. The cars are made very carefully. A lot of the work is done by hand, and they take a long time to manufacture: only twelve cars leave the factory every day.

1 **What do you think these words and expressions mean?**
Look at the text, but do not use a dictionary. Choose one answer for each question.

1. *It broke down*:   a. It made a noise.
   b. Pieces fell off it.   c. It stopped working.
2. *Charles Rolls was very impressed by Royce's car*:
   a. He thought it was good.   b. He wanted it.
   c. He did not understand it.
3. *model*:   a. picture   b. small car
   c. sort of car
4. *endurance*:   a. going fast   b. going on for a long time   c. being easy to drive
5. *Rolls-Royce cars are famous*:   a. They are very good.   b. Everybody knows about them.
   c. They are very quiet.
6. *ticking*:   a. a sort of clock   b. a part of a car
   c. a sort of noise
7. *manufacture*:   a. make   b. sell   c. finish
8. *factory*:   a. town   b. place where cars are made   c. shop

2 **Choose an object from the list in the box. Ask other students these questions about it. Note their answers and report to the class.**

car	motorbike	watch	radio
cassette player		television	calculator
camera			

1. Have you got a ....?
2. How long have you had it?
3. Where was it made?
4. Where did you buy it?
5. Has it ever broken down?
6. Have you used it a lot?
7. Are you happy with it, or would you like a better one?

Unit 21: Lesson C

Students practise guessing unknown words from a reading text.
Structures: revision of Simple Past versus Present Perfect verb tenses.
Words and expressions to learn: *produce; manufacture; use* (verb); *break down; together; carefully; business; cost; perfect.*

Language notes and possible problems

1. Guessing unknown words   This lesson introduces students to a skill that can be very useful to them in a foreign language: that of guessing unknown words in a written text. Some of the students will already be proficient in this skill; but others, especially those who have not studied formally for a while or who are not in the habit of reading for their jobs, may find it less easy. Exercise 1 should help the first group of students to transfer their skills to English, and the second group will begin learning or re-learning to use available clues to deduce meaning.

2. Survey: timing   Oral reporting on the class survey in Exercise 2 will make the class last longer than 45 minutes; if time is tight, you may wish students to report in writing for homework.

1 Guessing unknown words

● Let the students do the exercise individually, asking them to try and do as many of the questions as they can by referring to the text without using a dictionary.
● Then let them compare answers in groups. You may want to put students who speak the same language in a group together, so they can discuss in their own language how they came to their conclusions – something which is too difficult for them in English as yet.
● Then check the answers with them and note which students have had particular difficulty – you may wish to give them more exercises of this type.
● If you wish, you can then let the students read the text again and ask you questions about any words they want to know.

Optional activity

● If students are interested in learning words relating to cars, a good approach is to take them out of the classroom to go and have a look at the nearest car.
● Tell them the words they want to know; when you come back to the classroom, write the words on the board.

2 Class survey

● Ask for a volunteer. Ask him/her the questions in Exercise 2, beginning with *Have you got a fridge?*.
● As the student answers, note the details on the board in this or another convenient form:
  1. Yes
  2. 2 years
  3. don't know
  4. (name or type of shop/store)
  5. Yes
  6. Yes
  7. happy

● Then get your first volunteer to ask the questions of another student, as you note the new answers on the board beside the first list. This will show students how to organize their own surveys.
● Explain any new words in the list of objects.
● Get each student to choose an object; it does not matter if more than one student chooses the same object, but you should try to get as many of the objects covered as possible.
● Let the students walk round interviewing as many people as possible.
● When they have finished, or when you think the exercise has gone on long enough, stop them and ask each student to report to the class; or ask them to write up the results for homework. You may want to give a model for their reports, e.g.

Three students have motorbikes.
Two have had their bikes for a year, and one has had her bike for two years.
All the motorbikes were made in Japan.

Practice Book

● Tell students which exercises you want them to do.
● Students are given the choice of two out of three activities in the first Practice Book exercise. This is because the first text proposed will only interest car enthusiasts.
● Make sure that the students understand that for text B they must order the *pictures*, and for text C they must order the *text*.

Unit 21: Lesson D

Students practise talking about production, imports and exports.
Structures: Passive (present and past); relative *which*; *to* and *from* contrasted.
Words and expressions to learn: *export* (noun and verb); *import* (noun and verb); *mainly*; *mostly*; *machine*; *region*; *butter*; *chocolate*; *chemical* (noun); *camera*.
Phonology: linking between adjacent vowels.

Language notes and possible problems

1. Passive Students are asked to use some passive structures in this lesson.

We have chosen to introduce the Passive soon after the Present Perfect tense in order to try and avoid:
a. students' overgeneralization of the active function of the past participle (as in the Present Perfect);
b. the assumption by speakers of certain Western European languages that *am/is/are* + past participle is a variant of the Present Perfect construction.

2. Linking When one word ends with a vowel and the next one begins with a vowel, they are usually pronounced in English as if they were one word. Some students will need to practise this point of pronunciation. There are three possible links between two vowels:
1) When the first vowel is /iː/, /i/, /eɪ/, /aɪ/ or /ɔɪ/, a very slight *y* (/j/) sound is used between the two words ('The USAʸexports').
2) When the first vowel is /uː/, /əʊ/ or /aʊ/, a slight *w* sound is used ('Mexicoʷexports').
3) When the first vowel is /ə/, we simply pass directly from this to the next vowel ('India exports'). Some British people put in an *r* ('Indiaʳexports'), especially when the *r* is written ('Madagascar exports').

3. Relative *which* is used here in non-identifying relative clauses. Note that these are more usual in writing.

1 Present Passive
● Get students to look at the illustrations. Go over the pronunciation of the words with them, and practise the sample sentence *Wine is made in Italy*.
● Divide the class into groups of four or five, to try to list as many countries as possible where each product is made. Give a time limit, perhaps seven minutes.
● Write the names of the products on the board and let the students give you the countries to put under them.
● Students should give complete sentences; groups should speak in turn, giving one country each time.
● The group that can continue giving countries when the others have stopped wins for that product.

2 Past Passive; questions
● Choose a student whom you know to have a car, ask him or her *Where was your car made?*, and let the student answer.
● Then get the students to ask you about as many of your possessions as they can think of.
● Pay attention to the stress and rhythm in their questions, and the weak forms of *was* (/wəz/) and *were* (/wə(r)/).

● Put students in pairs to ask each other questions.
● Students who finish quickly can change partners.

3 Exports
● Make sure the students understand *exports*, practise the sample sentences with them, and then put the table up on the board.
● Let students volunteer a few more entries.
● Then give your place at the board to a student, who will write up three entries before passing the place to another student.
● Continue until they have all spoken a fair amount.

4 Imports
● Make sure the students understand *import*.
● Get each student to fill in a table of what his/her country imports and from where.
● Ask a few students each to say one sentence to the class; then get the students to walk round telling each other about their countries' imports.
● Alternatively, if your students are all from the same country, you can get them to do the exercise in groups and report to the class.

5 Linking vowels
● Before getting the students to say the sentences, you may want to write one example of each type of linking on the board and show how the link is realized.
● If you speak the students' language(s), you may wish to explain that the linking consonant is the one whose sound is closest to the first vowel. (See Language notes.)

6 Reading: presentation
● Let the students read the text, using their dictionaries or asking about new words.
● If you have a map of Britain in the room, you may want to show them where the regions are; but it is not important to know exactly where each region is.
● You may want to point out the use of *which* and the new words *mainly*, *mostly* and *region*; but another approach is to continue straight to the next exercise, letting the students think about the words themselves.

7 Practice
● This exercise calls on students to use words they have seen in the previous exercise.
● Let them work individually and then compare their answers with one another before checking with you; or let them do the initial work in groups.

8 Writing
● Let students write individually to produce a text like those in Exercises 6 and 7.
● Walk around as they work to give help if needed.
● Alternatively, if time is tight, you can get them to do this exercise for homework.

9 Summary
● Go over the summary with the students.

Practice Book
● Tell students which exercises you want them to do.

D Where was your car made?

1 Where are they made?

Example: *'Wine is made in Italy, France, ...'*

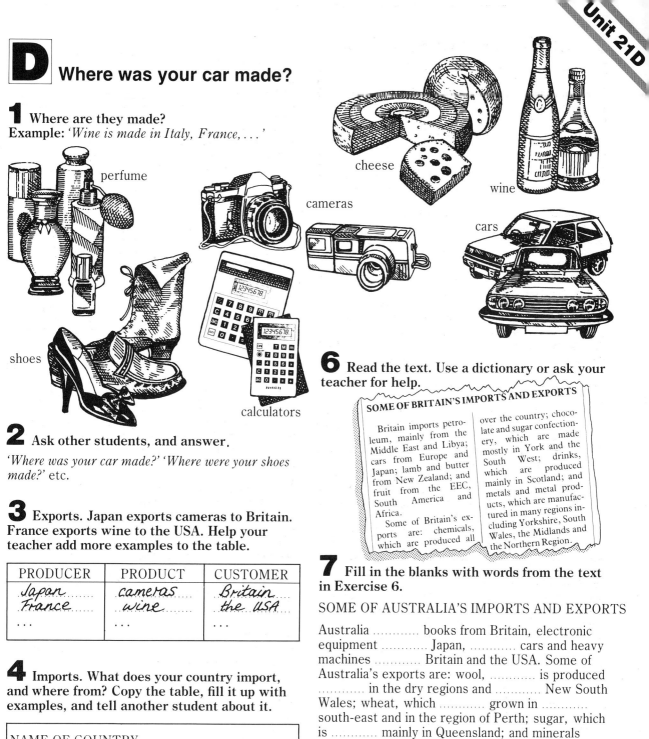

perfume

cheese

wine

cameras

cars

shoes

calculators

2 Ask other students, and answer.

'Where was your car made?' 'Where were your shoes made?' etc.

3 Exports. Japan exports cameras to Britain. France exports wine to the USA. Help your teacher add more examples to the table.

PRODUCER	PRODUCT	CUSTOMER
Japan	cameras	Britain
France	wine	the USA
...	...	...

4 Imports. What does your country import, and where from? Copy the table, fill it up with examples, and tell another student about it.

NAME OF COUNTRY	
PRODUCT	PRODUCER

5 Say these sentences.

1. Germany exports cars. Italy exports wine. The USA exports corn. Turkey imports radios.
2. Mexico exports oil. Morocco exports oranges.
3. Canada exports paper. India imports chemicals.

6 Read the text. Use a dictionary or ask your teacher for help.

SOME OF BRITAIN'S IMPORTS AND EXPORTS

Britain imports petroleum, mainly from the Middle East and Libya; cars from Europe and Japan; lamb and butter from New Zealand; and fruit from the EEC, South America and Africa.

Some of Britain's exports are: chemicals, which are produced all over the country; chocolate and sugar confectionery, which are made mostly in York and the South West; drinks, which are produced mainly in Scotland; and metals and metal products, which are manufactured in many regions including Yorkshire, South Wales, the Midlands and the Northern Region.

7 Fill in the blanks with words from the text in Exercise 6.

SOME OF AUSTRALIA'S IMPORTS AND EXPORTS

Australia .... books from Britain, electronic equipment .... Japan, ... cars and heavy machines .... Britain and the USA. Some of Australia's exports are: wool, ... is produced .... in the dry regions and .... New South Wales; wheat, which .... grown in .... south-east and in the region of Perth; sugar, which is .... mainly in Queensland; and minerals (lead, zinc, etc.), which .... imported .... by Britain and Japan.

8 Write a text about some of your country's exports and imports.

9 Read through the summary on page 152 with your teacher.

Revision and fluency practice

A Comparison

Dürer - Self-portrait

Clouet - Francois I,
King of France

1 How many differences can you find between the two pictures? Examples:

'Dürer's hair is lighter than the king's.'
'Dürer's hands are together; the king's are not.'

2 Listen, and choose the correct one.
Example:

1. 'It's smaller than a piano; it's got more strings than a violin.' **Answer:** *'Guitar.'*

1. piano   clarinet   organ   guitar   violin
2. cloud   snow   sun   ice   rain
3. dog   mouse   kangaroo   cat   elephant
4. fridge   car   cooker   typewriter   bus
5. horse   taxi   bicycle   car   bus
6. Evèrest   Mont Blanc   Eiffel Tower   tree
7. Japan   Kenya   France   Germany   Norway
8. champagne   whisky   Coca Cola   milk
9. wool   wood   iron   glass   aluminium

3 Now make your own questions about these.

1. sofa   chair   table   wardrobe   TV
2. shirt   raincoat   skirt   shoe   belt
3. India   Tibet   Bolivia   Switzerland   Canada
4. The USA   The USSR   China   Norway   Ghana
5. London   Paris   New York   Hong Kong   Cairo
6. elephant   whale   double-decker bus   bicycle   cat
7. doctor   teacher   dentist   shop assistant   footballer
8. cheese   carrot   potato   ice-cream   apple

90

Unit 22: Lesson A

Students revise the use of comparative adjectives and other 'comparison' structures.
Structures: *more . . . than; as . . . as; not as . . . as; less . . . than; (not) the same as; different from; but.*
Words and expressions to learn: none.

Optional extra materials
Pairs of similar pictures (see note in Lesson 18B, page 75).

1 Comparison of pictures
● This can be done orally or in writing.
● Before starting, remind students (or get them to remind you) of the structures listed above.
● You can turn the exercise into a memory test by giving students three minutes to look at the pictures and then telling them to close their books and write down as many differences as they can think of.

Optional activities
● This can be followed up by getting students to make a detailed comparison of two members of the class.
● Another good follow-up is to use pairs of pictures (students have to talk about them without showing them to each other, and find a specified number of differences – see Lesson 18B).
● Note, however, that this does not really practise comparative adjectives or the other structures listed above.

2 Listening: comparatives
● Go through the lists and make sure students know all the words.
● Play the definitions; students should note down the word they think is referred to.

Tapescript and answers to Exercise 2
1. It's smaller than a piano; it's got more strings than a violin. (*guitar*)
2. It's colder than rain; it's softer than ice. (*snow*)
3. It's bigger than a dog; it can jump higher than an elephant. (*kangaroo*)
4. It's bigger than a typewriter; it's colder than a cooker. (*fridge*)
5. It goes faster than a bicycle; it takes more people than a car. (*bus*)
6. It's not as high as Everest; it's higher than the Eiffel Tower. (*Mont Blanc*)
7. It's twice as big as Norway; it's hotter than Germany. (*Kenya*)
8. It's cheaper than champagne; it's darker than whisky. (*Coca Cola*)
9. It's not as heavy as iron; it's not as hard as wood. (*wool*)

3 Students' questions
● Students will need a few minutes to make up questions; they can do it individually or in groups, as you wish. Help with vocabulary.
● Make it clear that more than one question can be asked about each list.
● When they are ready, get them to ask each other their questions and try to answer.

Practice Book
● Note that there is no Practice Book work with this unit. Students should spend homework time revising what they have learnt in Units 1–21, in preparation for the test that follows Unit 22.

Unit 22: Lesson B

Students prepare and perform short dramatic sketches revising material learnt during the course. Two options are given, one more ambitious and difficult than the other.

You may need to spread the work over more than one lesson.

1 Shopping sketch

● This is the easier of the two options.

INTRODUCTORY NOTE

● Students will already have done sketches once or twice. But they will probably still need a lot of support and encouragement from you, as many of them will not be used to doing this sort of thing in the classroom. Be generous with praise for good ideas and successful performances. Try not to make anybody feel a failure: a sketch which doesn't come off may still have taught the students a lot of English.

● You may want to tape-record or video-record the students' sketches. This gives them feedback on how they sound, and provides a powerful incentive to produce work of a high standard.

PRESENTATION

● Divide the class into groups of three or four, trying to mix strong and weak students.

● Go over the instructions, giving students time to look at the illustration and decide what they are going to do. Tell them if you are going to record them.

● It might be good to work with one group in front of the class for a minute or two, demonstrating how to start:

All right. Who wants to buy something?
What do you want to buy?
Who's a shop assistant?
Who's going to speak first?
What are you going to say?

PLANNING AND WRITING SKETCHES

● Walk around while the groups are working, to help those in difficulty.

● If any group is really stuck, suggest roles and things to buy.

● They will want to look back at Unit 13 as they work.

● Discourage groups from trying to write over-complicated difficult material which only they will understand. The purpose of this exercise is to *re-use creatively what has been learnt.*

● You may like to set a time-limit (20–30 minutes) for planning, writing and practice.

● Make sure each student ends up with his/her own clear copy of the sketch, with his/her part underlined.

PRACTICE

● When groups are ready, ask them to practise their sketches a few times.

● Correct grammar and pronunciation where necessary.

● They should do this practice with appropriate actions and movements, so that when they perform their sketches for the class they will know how to position themselves.

● Groups that finish early can fill in the time with

revision work; or they can go as observers to other groups; or they can do some supplementary reading.

● Don't let late groups drag on too long; help them to find some way of finishing the sketch.

PERFORMANCE

● When groups perform their sketches, make sure that the others keep quiet and listen.

● Don't take the best group first, but start with a group that is likely to do a reasonable job.

● It's nice if the class applauds each group after its sketch.

● Students will want to read their parts from the scripts they have written, and there is nothing particularly wrong about this.

● However, if time allows you may like to ask students to learn their parts by heart – this will certainly give more natural and lively performances.

IMPROVISATION

● After the sketches have been recorded, you may like to progress to a short improvisation.

● Ask the shop assistants to position themselves round the room, with large signs saying what they are selling.

● Customers walk round and try to buy things, trying to visit all the shops.

2 General revision sketch

● This is a more elaborate exercise. It will take longer than the shop sketch, and is probably unsuitable for very weak classes. The purpose of the exercise is to give students practice in combining what they have learnt into longer communicative exchanges.

● The simplest approach is for a group to prepare a sketch that has four main sections, as follows:
– getting to know somebody (as in Lesson 17B or 20A);
– developing a conversation (as in 20B and 20C);
– an invitation (as in 19D or 20B);
– a meal at a restaurant (as in 17A).

● For this sketch, three characters are needed (the two main actors and a third person to play the waiter/barman etc.), but more can of course be added.

● Given enough time, students can work in rather larger groups and prepare sketches containing a wider variety of material, more episodes and more characters.

● It will probably be necessary to spread the preparation over parts of several lessons, so that students' scripts can be worked out in groups, corrected, copied and learnt, and so that there is adequate time for practice before students perform their sketches. (For detailed suggestions about how to organize the work, see above.)

● If there is a lot of time available (and if students are well-motivated and reasonably confident), the activity can be done as a play involving the whole class, with several scenes and as many characters as students. The more gifted and enthusiastic students will do most of the writing and planning and take the bigger parts; less confident students can be given easier writing jobs and smaller parts. This takes a lot of time and work, but it is an extremely rich and rewarding activity, which can give impressive results in terms of increased fluency, confidence and motivation.

B Sketches

1 Work in groups of three or four. Some of you are shop assistants:

and some of you want to buy things:

Prepare and practise a sketch. Use all the English you can.

2 Getting to know somebody. Work in groups. Prepare and practise a sketch with several characters, using the new language from Unit 20 and some of the other words and expressions that you have learnt. Include some of the following:

getting to know somebody	asking for things	lending and borrowing	exchanging opinions

saying how often you do things   telling the time   names   addresses   telephone numbers
spelling   telephoning   complimenting   asking the way   a meal in a restaurant   a letter   offering

C People

1 Prepare a copy of the form. Work with a student that you don't know very well. Ask him/her questions about him/herself, and fill in the answers.

Name ...Charlotte Jones...
Address ...14, The Broadway, Leek, Staffs...
Telephone number ...Leek 30497...
Age last birthday ...36...
Marital status ...divorced...
Nationality ...British...
Height ...5 ft. 8 ins...
Shoe size ...7½...
Occupation ...cabaret singer...
Place of work ...Las Vegas All-Night Diamond Disco, Le...
Starts work at ...9.00 p.m...
Finishes work at ...4.00 a.m...
Works on Saturdays? ...Yes...
Smokes? (If so, how many?) ...40 a day...
Drinks? (If so, what?) ...whisky, champagne, alka seltzer...
Favourite foods ...caviar, scrambled eggs...
Languages spoken ...—...
Likes – sport ...—...
   books ...love stories...
   music ...traditional jazz, opera...
   films ...westerns...
   other ...staying in bed...
Dislikes ...paying bills; men who can't dance...
Favourite type of girl/man ...tall, dark and rich...
Sign ...Taurus...
Appearance ...blonde, blue eyes, attractive...
Personality ...lively, but gets depressed easily...

2 Find five things that you have in common with the student you interviewed, and five differences. Say what they are. Examples:

'He drinks Coke, and so do I.'
'He is tall, and so am I.'
'He likes driving fast cars, but I don't.'
'He's got blue eyes, but I haven't.'

3 Work in pairs. One student's mother/father/grandmother/grandfather/aunt/uncle/child/friend has disappeared; the other student is a policeman or policewoman. The first student gives a detailed description of the missing person; the other asks questions.

Unit 22: Lesson C

Students revise the language needed to talk about people, their appearance and behaviour.

Optional extra materials
Copies of the form in the Student's Book with the answers removed.

1 Personal data
- This exercise revises question-structures.
- Get students to read the form and explain any difficulties.
- Ask them to construct the questions that are needed to get the information on the form: *What's your name?*, *Where do you live?* etc.
- This can be done in groups.
- When students are ready, get them to do the exercise. If you can prepare blank copies of the form, this will save a lot of time. Make sure that they ask the questions correctly (they should say, for instance, *Where do you work?* rather than *Place of work?*).
- The exercise can also be·done with fictitious personalities.

2 Things in common
- These should emerge from the form, but students may need to ask supplementary questions to make up the number.

3 Role-playing: missing person
- Divide students into members of the public and police.
- Give them a few minutes to prepare their description or questions (depending on the role).
- You will need to teach one or two expressions to introduce and close the conversation:
   (*My mother has disappeared*; *When did you last see her? We'll telephone if we have any news*).
- Make sure the main part of the conversation is devoted to a description of the person's appearance and clothes.
- Get two volunteers to start the activity off.
- After listening to them and commenting, you can get the others to work simultaneously or in pairs, as you wish.

Optional activity   'Who am I?'
- One student is a well-known living person.
- The other students have to find out who, by asking not more than twenty questions.
- The only answers allowed are *Yes* and *No*.
- Put a list of useful questions on the board:
   Are you English/American/Russian/etc.?
   Do you live in Europe/America/...?
   Are you a man/woman/child?
   Are you an entertainer/politican/artist/writer/soldier/
      businessman/sportswoman/scientist?
   Are you over 50/under 30/etc.?
   Are you married?
   Is your wife/husband well known?
   Do you travel a lot?
   Do we often see you on TV?
   Do you work in films?

Optional activity   Finding out about a third person
- Write on the board the name of somebody you know
- Tell the students this is a friend (or acquaintance) of yours.
- They have to find out as much as they possibly can by asking questions in English.
- Encourage supplementary questions about each point. For instance: 'Does he like sport?' 'Yes.' 'What sort of sport?' 'Football.' 'Does he play?' 'Yes.' 'What position?' 'Is he good?' 'How often does he play?'

Unit 22: Lesson D

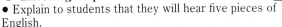

Students practise listening skills and revise the use of tenses.

1 Listening for particular information

- Explain to students that they will hear five pieces of English.
- They will not understand everything, but this is not important.
- Their task is to note (in each case) the time of departure of the person or train referred to, the destination (if known), the time of arrival (if known) and whether it is necessary to change (if known).
- Stop after each extract for students to note their answers.
- Play it a second time so that they can catch any information they missed the first time round.
- Let them compare notes before giving them the answers.

Tapescript and answers to Exercise 1

1. The next train from platform one will be the four twenty for Hereford, calling at . . .

2. 'Oh God. It's going to take all day.'
   'What time do you leave?'
   'I'm catching the ten twenty from Victoria. I don't get there until half past nine in the evening.'
   'Half past nine?'
   'Yes. I have to change at Ashton, then I have to change at Stoke, Adderbury and Caldon. Change everywhere...'

3. 'What time's the next train for London?'
   'Three fifteen. Platform six. Change at Reading.'
   'What time does it get in?'
   'Four thirty-five.'

4. A: 'Excuse me.'
   B: 'Yes?'
   A: 'Is this the Birmingham train?'
   B: 'Birmingham? Oh, no, dear. This is the 6.16 for Manchester.'
   A: 'Manchester? But I don't want to go to Manchester.'
   C: 'What's wrong with Manchester?'
   A: 'Nothing. But I want to go to Birmingham. What time do we arrive?'
   B: 'Ten to ten.'
   C: 'No, ten past ten.'
   CHORUS OF VOICES: 'Ten to ten.'
   A: 'Oh, no!'

5. 'I always take the 10.27, myself.'
   'Do you, dear?'
   'Yes. You get a nice cup of tea on the 10.27.'
   'D'you have to change?'
   'Oh, no. It's direct. I don't like changing.'
   'No, neither do I.'
   'I remember once, I was with Aunty Mary. It was during the war. We were living in Ashford...'

	DEPARTURE TIME	DESTINATION	ARRIVAL TIME	CHANGE?
1	4.20	Hereford	?	–
2	10.20	?	9.30 (p.m.)	yes
3	3.15	London	4.35	yes
4	6.16	Manchester	9.50	?
5	10.27	?	?	no

2 Sounds

- Play the recording through once so that students can start thinking about it.
- Then play it again, stopping after each sound so that students can write the answer.
- In each case they should write a Present Progressive sentence (as in the example).

The sounds are:
1. Somebody is walking.
2. A man is having a bath.
3. A woman is singing.
4. Some people are drinking.
5. Some cats are fighting.
6. It's raining.
7. Children are playing.
8. Somebody is typing.
9. Somebody is eating.

3-5 Grammar revision

- Students should do at least some of the sentences in writing, so that you can see which people are having difficulty.

Summary
- There is no summary for this unit.

NOW DO REVISION TEST TWO. (See page 167 and the Test Book.)

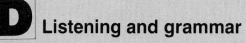

D Listening and grammar

1 Listen to the recording and fill in the table.

	DEPARTURE TIME	DESTINATION	ARRIVAL TIME	CHANGE?
1				
2				
3				
4				
5				

Place names: Hereford Victoria   Ashton   Stoke Adderbury   Caldon London   Reading Birmingham   Manchester Ashford

2 Listen to the sounds. What is happening? Example:

1. Somebody is walking.

3 Complete the sentences.

1. Look! It .... (rains / is raining)
2. It always .... on Sundays. (rains / is raining)
3. 'What ....?' 'I'm looking at the weather forecast.' (do you do / are you doing)
4. '............ oysters?' 'Yes, I love them.' (Do you like / Are you liking)
5. 'Have you got a cigarette?' 'Sorry, I ....' (don't smoke / am not smoking)
6. 'What time ....?' 'At seven o'clock, usually.' (do you get up / are you getting up)
7. 'Can you come and see me tomorrow?' 'Sorry. ....' (I work / I'm working)
8. I .... on Saturdays. (usually work / am usually working)
9. 'Is John here?' 'No, ... football.' (he plays / he's playing)

4 Put in the right tense: Simple Past, Present Perfect or Present.

1. 'I .... John yesterday.' (saw / have seen)
2. 'Did you? I .... him for weeks.' (didn't see / haven't seen)
3. How long .... living here? (are you / have you been)
4. I .... Mary since 1980. (know / have known)
5. I think I .... her very well. (know / have known)
6. .... to India? (Have you ever been / Did you ever go)
7. .... his latest book? (Have you read / Did you read)
8. How long .... that watch? (have you had / did you have / do you have)

5 Put in *since*, *for* or *ago*.

1. We've lived in London .... eight years.
2. I've only known her .... yesterday.
3. My grandmother died three years ....
4. I've been working .... four o'clock this morning.
5. She's been a teacher .... eighteen years.
6. It's been raining .... three days.
7. I first went to Africa about seven years ....
8. Mary phoned a few minutes ....
9. I haven't seen her .... weeks.

93

Instructions

A How to do it

1 Here is some advice about running. Some of it is good, and some is not. Which sentences give you good advice?

RUNNING①– DOs and DON'Ts

Wear good running shoes.
Run early in the morning – it's better.
Wear comfortable clothing②
Always warm up③ before you run.
Always run with somebody – never run alone.
Rest every ten minutes or so.
Walk for a few minutes after you finish.

Don't run if you feel tired.
Never drink water while you are running.
Don't run until two hours after eating.
Don't run if you have got a cold④
Don't run fast downhill⑤
Don't run if you are over 50.
Don't run on roads in fog⑥

When you have finished the exercise, listen to some British people trying to do it.

2 Work in groups. Think of some advice (good or bad) for one of the following.

– a tourist in your country
– somebody who is learning to drive
– somebody who is learning your language
– somebody who is learning English
– somebody who wants to get rich
– somebody who wants more friends

Make a list of three (or more) DOs and three (or more) DON'Ts.

3 Listen, and try to draw the picture.

4 Work in groups.
One student draws a simple picture, but does not show it to the others.
He or she gives the others instructions, and they try to draw the same picture.

5 Say these words after the recording or your teacher.

1. fog   hot   long   doctor   dollar   office
2. comfortable   front   another   brother

Find some more words that go in group 1. Can you find any more that go in group 2?

Unit 23: Lesson A

Students practise giving instructions and advice.
Structures: imperative and negative imperative;
position of *always* and *never* in imperatives; simple
if-clauses.
Words and expressions to learn: *advice; early;
before; alone; rest; a cold; picture; after (conj.)*.
Phonology: Letter *o* pronounced /ɒ/ and /ʌ/
(revision).

Language notes and possible problems

1. Word order *Always* and *never* come before imperatives.
2. Advice Students may tend to use *advice* as a countable noun: look out for *an advice* and *advices*.
3. Drawing Exercises 3 and 4 require students to draw
pictures. This may strike panic into the hearts of students
(and teachers) who can't draw, but in fact only simple pin-
man drawings are required, and almost everybody should
be able to produce something.

1 Advice about running

● Make sure students understand the task: they are
supposed to decide which pieces of advice are good and
which are not.
● Go through the text, explaining any difficulties and
teaching the pronunciation of the new words. Point out
that the numbered words in the text are illustrated by
the pictures on the right. Note *comfortable* (three
syllables: /ˈkʌmftəbl/).
● Students will probably start classifying the advice into
good and bad as you go through the text.
● Don't give your own opinion at this stage.
● Ask students to discuss the question in groups, and to
produce a group decision (if possible).
● After they have got into their stride, you may like to
tell them that four of the DOs and four of the DON'Ts
are good advice.

Answers to Exercise 1

Good advice: Wear good running shoes.
Wear comfortable clothing.
Always warm up before you run.
Walk for a few minutes after you finish.
Don't run if you feel tired.
Don't run until two hours after eating.
Don't run if you have got a cold.
Don't run on roads in fog.
Misleading: Never drink water while you are running.
The other pieces of advice are of no value.

● Once the students have checked their answers with
you, get them to listen once or twice to some British
people doing the same exercise. (There is no task.)

2 Giving advice

● Students can either take this seriously (giving good
advice), or choose a more entertaining treatment by
deliberately thinking up misleading advice.
● Help with vocabulary, but discourage students from
using too many words that have not already been learnt.
● When groups are ready, let each one read out its
advice.

3 Listening to instructions

● Make sure students have a blank piece of paper and a
pen or pencil ready.
● Remind them what *draw* means.
● Play the recording once through without stopping.
● Play it again, stopping at the pauses to give students
time to draw.
● Draw the table and chairs yourself, very simply, so
that students can see it is unnecessary to be good at
drawing to do the exercise.
● Play the recording a third time, giving students a
chance to make any changes they wish.
● Let them compare drawings and check their results.

Tapescript for Exercise 3

Draw a table and two chairs in a room.
Don't draw a window. Draw a cat under one of the chairs.
Draw a spoon on the table, and a cup to the right of the spoon.
Draw some men or women in the room; don't draw any
    children.
Draw one other thing in the room, but don't put it on the table.

4 Giving instructions

● Get each student to draw another picture, making
sure they do not show their pictures to one another.
● Explain that they are to work in groups, each partner
giving the others precise instructions so that the
original drawing is reproduced.

5 Revision of pronunciation

● This gives students another chance to practise the
normal pronunciation of 'short' *o* (/ɒ/), and to note the
words where *o* is pronounced /ʌ/.
● Other words in group 2 (/ʌ/): *mother, one, once, some,
love, money, come, colour, son*.

Practice Book

● Tell students which exercises you want them to do.

Unit 23: Lesson B

Students learn a number of common phrases used for advising and directing people.
Structures: imperative and negative imperative.
Words and expressions to learn: *be; wait; Look out!; Don't worry; Follow me; Be careful; Hurry; Take your time.*

Practice Book
● Tell students which exercises you want them to do.

1 Matching expressions and pictures
● Let students try this by themselves, using dictionaries or consulting each other to find out the meanings of the expressions.
● Help them out if they get stuck.
● When they are ready and have compared notes, go over the answers with them. Practise saying the expressions. *Look out!* and *Be careful* are similar. However, *Look out!* (which draws somebody's attention to a danger he/she is unaware of) is more appropriate to picture 1, and *Be careful* (which simply advises caution) is more appropriate to picture 7.

2 Mini-sketches
● The instruction asks students to illustrate one or more of the expressions in a brief sketch.
● However, confident and ambitious students ought to be able to get several of the expressions in.
● Don't let the exercise go on too long; elaborate sketches which take a long time to write are not required.
● As a follow-up, you can ask groups to mime a situation involving one of the expressions. The class has to guess which it is.
● If video is available, you might record the sketches.

3 Listening for specific points
● You will probably need to play the conversation at least twice for students to pick out some of the imperatives and negative imperatives.
● After the second time, ask them how many they have noticed, and see whether they can remember some of them. (The answer is six imperatives and four negative imperatives.)

Tapescript for Exercise 3
Sit down, children. Time for your story. Are you all sitting comfortably? Good. Then I'll begin. Once upon a time, long long ago, there was a beautiful girl who lived with her mother and father in a small village. She – don't do that, George – she worked very hard on her father's farm looking after the cows – George, stop that! Mary, sit down at once – looking after the cows and the horses and the sheep. No, Sally, you are not a sweet little baby baa-lamb. You are a nice sensible little girl who is listening to a story. Every day – Bill, take that out of your mouth – she got up very early and milked the cows – don't make that stupid noise, Alice, please. Then she cleaned the house, and fed the animals, and made breakfast – Don't do that, George – breakfast for her mother and father.
   One day, while she was cleaning the kitchen, she looked out of the window, and she saw – what do you think she saw, children? No, George, not Superman. No, Sylvia, not Mickey Mouse. Now don't be stupid, children. Think. What do you think she saw? James Bond, Louisa? Really! Sit down, please, Mary. And you, Celia. George...
(Inspired by a sketch by Joyce Grenfell.)

B | Be careful!

1 Put the following expressions into the pictures.

Please hurry!   Take your time.   Don't worry.   Look.   Come in.   Wait here, please.
Be careful.   Follow me, please.   Look out!

2 Work in groups. Prepare and practise a very short sketch using one or more of the expressions from Exercise 1.

3 Listen to the recording.
Write ✓ every time you hear an imperative (like *Walk*, *Come in*, *Be careful*), and ✗ every time you hear a negative imperative (like *Don't run*, *Don't worry*).
Listen again, and then try to remember some of the imperatives and negative imperatives.

95

C On and off

1 Look at the picture. Where are things? Where should they be? Example:

'There's a chair on the piano. It should be on the floor.'

Useful words:	on	in	under	by

2 Some friends are going to help you to put things in the right places.
What will you say to them? Example:

'Could you take the chair off the piano and put it by the window?'

Useful words:	take	put	off	out of	in(to)

3 Listen to the song and try to put in the missing words. Your teacher will help you with vocabulary.

'I dropped my ....'
'Pick .... up, pick .... up
and put .... away in .... closet.'

'I dropped my ....'
'Pick .... up, pick .... up
and throw .... away .... basket.'

'I dropped my ....'
'Pick .... up, pick .... up
and wash .... clean in the ....'

'I dropped my dolly.'
'Pick .... up, pick .... up
and .... back in .... cradle.'

'I dropped my toys.'
'Pick .... up, pick .... up
and put .... back in .... places.'

(*Pick it up* by Woody Guthrie; © copyright 1954
Folkways Music Publishers, Inc.)

Unit 23: Lesson C

Students learn more about the expression of position, direction and change of position.
Structures: prepositions of place and movement (revision and extension); *should* + infinitive (introduction); verbs with adverb particles (*pick up, put away* etc.).
Words and expressions to learn: *floor; drop; pick up; throw; away; put away; into; off; should.*

Language notes and possible problems

1. *In* and *into* Note that *in* is often used to refer to movement after certain verbs such as *put, throw* – we tend to say *Put it in the kitchen* rather than *Put it into the kitchen*, for example.
2. Phrasal verbs (verbs with adverb particles such as *away, back, up*) are previewed here, but are not studied systematically in this book. You may wish to comment on the word order with object pronouns (*pick it up*, not **pick up it*).
3. *Put on*, *take off* While teaching the use of *put* and *take*, you may want to mention the use of *put on* and *take off* when talking about clothing.
4. *Out of* While practising *out of*, remind students that we talk about looking *out of* a window.
5. *Should* is introduced here (with a sense of 'desirability' rather than 'obligation'). Students should note that it is used with a 'bare infinitive' (like *would* and *can*), and there is no *-s* on the third person.

1 Where are things?
● Give students a few minutes to look at the picture.
● Write on the board:
   What's the thing on the fridge?
● Get them to find out the names of the things in the picture in this way, identifying things by position.
● Let them ask similar questions about things in the classroom.
● Then get them to make sentences about where things are and where they should be (as in the example).
● If they close their books, this becomes a memory test.

2 Putting the room straight
● Do this orally, with students suggesting sentences.
● Follow it up by asking them to write one or two of the sentences.

Optional activity   Changing places
● Tell people to get up and go and sit somewhere else in the classroom.
● Write on the board:
   X was sitting by...
                between...
                in front of...
                behind...
                on the left of...
                on the right of...
● Get students to try to remember where everybody was sitting.

Optional activity   Moving things round
● Half the class goes out of the room, while the others rearrange as many things as possible.
● The people who went out come back, observe the room, and then work with partners, saying where things should be.
● The aim is for the 'observers' to find all the changes that have been made.
● When they have found everything they can, they take turns telling the others to put things back in their places.
● Take the opportunity to teach *put...back*.

3 Children's song
● This exercise helps students to perceive unstressed words. Explain *drop, closet, throw, basket, dolly, cradle* and *toys*.
● Play the recording two or three times and see if students can identify most of the missing words.

Answers: *shoe, it, it, it, the*
           gum, it, it, it, in the
           apple, it, it, it, water
           her, her, put her, her
           them, them, them, their

Optional activity   Remembering actions
● Tell the class to watch exactly what you do.
● Go round the room moving things in various ways: take things off other things and put them in new places; take something out of your pocket/bag and put it somewhere else; pick things up, put them down, drop things, throw them away.
● Do about ten actions altogether.
● Then ask students to remember exactly what you did.
● Help them to structure their answers with *first, then, after that*, etc.

Practice Book
● Tell students which exercises you want them to do.

Unit 23: Lesson D

Students learn to interpret summary written instructions, and to explain how to carry out a series of operations. The context is cooking.

Structures: Imperatives; *you* with Simple Present in spoken instructions; the special grammar of written instructions.

Words and expressions to learn: some of these (see summary): *lemon; pepper; salt; juice; fresh; fork; tablespoon; saucepan; frying pan; fry; bowl; oil; cloth; slice; mix; pour; most of.*

Language notes and possible problems

Grammar of instructions The Imperative is used for instructions which are likely to be carried out immediately on being heard or read. (Note that in this context it is perfectly polite.) When we are simply describing how to do something (for somebody who is not about to do it immediately) we tend to use the Simple Present with the subject *you*, especially in spoken English. The two forms will be contrasted here.

In written instructions (including recipes), articles and object pronouns are often left out. Example: *Wash (the) mushrooms and pat (them) dry.* Note also the omission of *of* after quantities (*4 tablespoons olive oil*).

1 Reading and matching

● Students do not need to understand every word.
● They should use their dictionaries just enough to enable them to match up the instructions and the pictures.
● Point out that one instruction has two pictures.

Answers: 1. C, F 2. B 3. A 4. D 5. E

2 How to do it

● Get the students to listen to the recording while they follow the recipe in their books.
● Ask if they can remember any sentences from the recording.
● Write correct sentences on the board as students say them.
● Ask if they notice any grammatical differences from the written recipe.
● They should pick out the fact that the Simple Present is used (because the speaker is telling somebody *how to* do something, not telling her *to* do it); and that some words are missed out in the written recipe.
● See if students can tell you what kinds of words are missed out.

Tapescript for Exercise 2

'This is delicious! Could you tell me how to make it?'
'Of course. You take half a pound of very fresh white mushrooms, a tablespoon of lemon juice, pepper and salt, a few chives or a little parsley, and 4 tablespoons of olive oil. First you wash the mushrooms and pat them dry – don't peel them. You cut off most of the stalk and slice the rest thinly, and put them into a salad bowl. Then you mix the oil with the lemon juice, the salt and the pepper, and you beat well. You pour about two thirds of this dressing over the mushrooms and stir gently; then you put the mushrooms aside for an hour. You add the rest of the dressing and put it all aside again until most of the dressing is absorbed – that usually takes about half an hour. Meanwhile, you chop your chives or parsley. When the dressing is absorbed, you sprinkle the chives or parsley over the salad and serve it.'

3 Guided writing and speaking

● Students will need to ask you for help with vocabulary.
● Give them a time limit for writing the recipe – perhaps fifteen minutes.
● Then get two volunteers to tell each other how to make whatever dish they have written about (using the Simple Present and putting in all the necessary words which were left out in the written version).
● If students say they don't know how to cook anything, suggest that they write instructions for cooking a tin of soup or boiling an egg.

4 Summary

● Go over the summary with the students.

Practice Book
● Tell students which exercises you want them to do.

 **Recipes**

Mushroom Salad

Ingredients
½lb white mushrooms, very fresh
1 tablespoon lemon juice
Pepper, salt
A few chives or a little parsley
4 tablespoons olive oil

Utensils
Bowl   Fork
Clean cloth   Knife

Time
10 mins to prepare,
1½ hrs to stand.

1. Wash mushrooms and pat dry. (Do not peel.) Cut off most of stalk. Slice the rest thinly and put in salad bowl.
2. Mix oil with lemon juice, salt and pepper, and beat well.
3. Pour about ⅔ of this dressing over mushrooms, stir gently and put aside for an hour.
4. Add rest of dressing and put aside again until most of dressing is absorbed, about ½ hour.
5. Meanwhile, chop chives or parsley. Sprinkle this over salad, and serve.

(from *The Beginner's Cookery Book* by Betty Falk)

1 Match each picture to one of the numbered instructions in the recipe. Use one number twice.

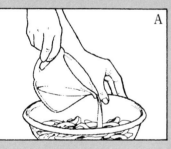
A

B

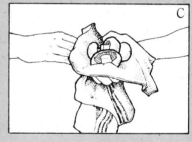
C

D

E

F

2 Listen to someone telling you how to make a mushroom salad. The grammar of the spoken recipe is different from that of the written recipe. In what ways?

3 Write a recipe (begin *Ingredients......*).
Then give instructions to another student.
(Begin '*You take…*') Here are some words you can use:
saucepan, frying-pan, casserole, oven, fry, boil, melt.

4 Look at the summary on page 153 with your teacher.

Getting around

A A room for two nights

1 Study and practise the dialogue.

RECEPTIONIST: Can I help you?
TRAVELLER: Yes, I'd like a room, please.
RECEPTIONIST: Single or double?
TRAVELLER: Single, please.
RECEPTIONIST: For one night?
TRAVELLER: No, two nights.
RECEPTIONIST: With bath or with shower?
TRAVELLER: With bath, please. How much is the room?
RECEPTIONIST: £23 a night, including breakfast.
TRAVELLER: Can I pay by credit card?
RECEPTIONIST: Yes, of course. Could you register, please?
TRAVELLER: Pardon?
RECEPTIONIST: Could you fill in the form, please?
TRAVELLER: Oh, yes.
RECEPTIONIST: Your room number is 403. Have a good stay.
TRAVELLER: Thank you.

2 Think of other expressions that can be useful in a hotel. Ask your teacher how to say them.

3 Work with a partner. Make up a new traveller–receptionist conversation, with as many changes as possible. Your teacher will help you.

Hilton International London

Hotel Features:

- Address: 22 Park Lane, London W1A 2HH, England
- Telephone: 01-493-8000 Telex: 24873 Cable: HILTELS–London
- Located in the heart of Mayfair, overlooking Hyde Park Minutes from the elegant shopping and theatre districts
- 40 minutes from Heathrow Airport, 45 minutes from London–Gatwick Airport, 5 minutes from Victoria Station
- 509 comfortable guest rooms featuring:
  individual climate control
  direct-dial telephone
  electronic locks for maximum security
  radio and taped music
  self service mini-bar
  television with in-house films
- 104 one- two- and three bedroom suites
- 5 restaurants, cocktail lounge, bar and discotheque
- 24-hour room service
- Same day laundry/valet service at no extra charge (Monday-Friday)
- Meeting facilities for up to 1000 persons
- 24-hour telex, cable, interpreter, secretarial service, typewriters, mail and postage facilities
- Pocket bleepers available for individual guest paging
- Worldwide courier service for documents guaranteeing one to three day delivery
- Teleplan – guarantees reasonable surcharges on international telephone calls
- Currency exchange at daily bank rates plus a modest handling charge of approximately 1% to cover only direct expenses
- Guest shops including beauty and barber, fashion, florist, drugstore, newsstand, speciality shops and transportation desk
- Indoor parking for 350 cars
- Hilton International Family Plan: there is no room charge for one or more children, regardless of age, when sharing the same room(s) with their parent(s) Maximum occupancy per room 3 persons

In England, there are two other fine Hilton International hotels – Hilton International Kensington on Holland Park Avenue near London's West End, and Hilton International Stratford-upon-Avon, 5 minutes from the Royal Shakespeare Theatre. And look for the new Gatwick Hilton International.

For reservations call your travel agent, any Hilton hotel or Hilton Reservation Service

4 Answer the questions. Time-limit: five minutes.

1. What street is the Hilton Hotel in?
2. How many cars can be parked in the Hilton garage?
3. How far is the Hilton from Victoria Station?
4. How many other Hilton hotels are there in London?
5. How much do guests at the Hilton pay for children if they sleep in the same room as their parents?

Unit 24: Lesson A

Students learn to get along in basic hotel situations.
Structures: *a = per* (e.g. £23 a night).
Words and expressions to learn: *by credit card; by cheque; in cash; shower; including; double room; pay; fill in; form.*

1 Presentation dialogue

- Get the students to leave their books closed.
- Ask for two volunteers, or pick out two students who are fairly confident.
- Bring them to the front of the class; tell them that one is a hotel receptionist and the other is a traveller who wants a room. Put the receptionist behind a desk.
- Get them to talk through the situation; don't correct them, but make a note of what they say.
- (They will, of course, make mistakes and use inappropriate expressions; this does not matter at this stage provided they manage to communicate effectively.)
- When they have finished, ask the class for suggestions for improvements; make your own corrections (as supportively as possible), and tell them the normal ways of expressing the various ideas that arise in this situation.
- Now play the dialogue once or twice. Students will be interested to hear the similarities and differences between this conversation and the one they made up.
- Ask the class to try to recall some of what they heard.
- Then let them open their books and look through the dialogue.
- You may wish to remind students that *I'd like* is the contraction of *I would like*; to draw their attention to the use of *a* in *£23 a night*; to point out how we say room numbers (*four oh three*, not *four hundred and three*); and to teach the expressions *by cheque* and *in cash*.
- Work on the pronunciation, paying attention to rhythm and intonation; get students to practise the dialogue in pairs.

2 Extension
- Give students a chance to find out how to say other things that are appropriate to this situation.
- They should ask questions beginning *How do you say...?* or *Can I say...?*. Let them use their own language (if you speak it); mime and drawings are other possible approaches.

3 Practice
- Ask the students to work in pairs making up new receptionist/traveller conversations.
- They should make as many changes as possible to the original dialogue, asking you for words and expressions as necessary.
- Walk around as they work to give any help that is needed.
- When they are ready, listen to their dialogues.
- If time allows, you may want to have some of them performed for the rest of the class.

Optional activity Improvisation
- If there is plenty of time, you may like to finish the oral work with an improvisation exercise.
- Put a third of the class behind desks to play the part of hotel receptionists; divide the others into pairs and give them roles: married couple, mother and daughter, father and son, etc.
- Tell the receptionists to decide whether they are working for cheap, middle-priced or expensive hotels, and to fix their prices.
- Tell the couples to decide what they want: cheap or expensive, how many nights, etc.
- Then send the travellers round to try to find a hotel that suits them.
- With a good class, you can make the situation more complicated by telling the people in each couple to disagree (for example, one is tired and wants to find somewhere fast; the other is fussy and wants to shop around for the perfect hotel).

4 Scanning for information
- This exercise can be done in class or at home depending on the time available.
- Tell students to find the answers to the questions in the brochure.
- Emphasize that it is not necessary to read and understand the entire brochure; students should scan the text quickly to find the information they need.

Answers: 1. Park Lane   2. 350   3. Five minutes   4. One   5. Nothing

Practice Book
- Tell students which exercises you want them to do.

Unit 24: Lesson B

Students learn to speak about public transport systems.
Structures: introduction to: *have to*, infinitive of purpose, preposition + *-ing* form.
Words and expressions to learn: *on the way*; *line*; *stop* (noun); *get to*.
Phonology: devoicing of /v/ in *have to* (/'hæftə/).

Language notes

1. Have to The structure is introduced here in the affirmative form only. Note that *have got to* is also possible, but this form of the structure is more common when referring to immediate obligation (e.g. *I've got to go now*). There is more work on *have to* in Unit 32.

If students ask about the difference between *must* and *have to*, tell them that they mean the same. (The slight difference of usage will be dealt with later in the course.)
2. Without -ing You may wish to explain that the *-ing* form is used after all prepositions.

1 Presentation: true or false?

● Give students a minute or two to look at the London tube map – enough to see what it is.
● Make sure they realize how the different lines are shown, and that they remember what 'change' means in this context.
● Explain or demonstrate *on the way from . . . to . . .*
● You can treat the exercise as a competition – see who can be first to answer the twelve questions correctly.
● Warn students not to go *too* fast – some of the questions are deliberately confusing.
● When most students have finished, let them compare notes and then give them the answers:

Answers: 1. True 2. True (by the Circle Line) 3. False 4. False 5. False 6. True 7. False 8. True 9. True 10. False (west, not east) 11. True if you take the most direct route. 12. True

● Then go over the sentences, answering questions and giving explanations where necessary.
● Draw students' attention to the word *without*, and to the fact that it is followed by an *-ing* form (like all prepositions).
● Point out, too, the use of *have to* to express obligation, and get students to practise saying *You have to change twice*, making sure they say /'hæftə/).
● Make sure students notice the abbreviations *St* and *Rd*.

2 Practice

● Ask students to make up at least one 'true or false' statement using *without*, and one using *have to* (taking their facts from the underground map).
● When they are ready, ask them to make their statements (either to the whole class or in groups) and tell the others to decide whether the statements are true or not.

3 Further practice

● Get the students to read the facts about the San Fantastico underground, and try to draw a map of the system.
● Let them work individually and then compare answers with one another.
● There is more than one possible map: let students who think they have valid variants come to the board and draw them for the other students to check against the sentences in the book. One possibility:

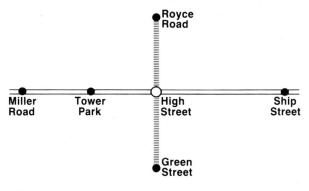

4 Personalization

● Get students to do one of the two options, as a class or in groups.
● Encourage them to use words and expressions from the lesson.

Practice Book

● Tell students which exercises you want them to do.

B   You have to change twice

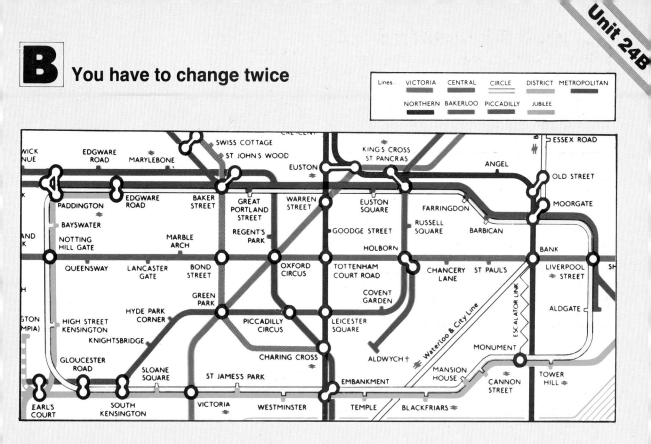

Lines...	VICTORIA	CENTRAL	CIRCLE	DISTRICT	METROPOLITAN
	NORTHERN	BAKERLOO	PICCADILLY	JUBILEE	

1 The London Underground. True or False?

1. Baker St is on the way from Paddington to Euston Square.
2. You can get from Victoria to Baker St without changing.
3. To get from Oxford Circus to Paddington, you have to change twice.
4. Piccadilly Circus is on the way from South Kensington to Bond St.
5. You can get from Bond St to Leicester Square without changing.
6. If you go from Edgware Rd to Hyde Park Corner by the shortest way, you have to change twice.
7. You can go there by a longer way without changing.
8. Notting Hill Gate is on the same line as Holborn.
9. You can't get from Covent Garden to Victoria without changing.
10. If you travel east from Temple on the Circle Line, you can change to the Bakerloo Line at the first stop.
11. If you go from Notting Hill Gate to Green Park, you have to change at the fourth stop.
12. Knightsbridge is not on the way from Paddington to Oxford Circus.

2 Make up your own true or false sentences about the London Underground, and test other students with them.

3 San Fantastico, the capital of Fantasia, has got a new underground system, with two lines and six stops. Read the sentences and draw a map of the SF Underground.

1. Miller Rd and High St are on the same line.
2. To get from Tower Park to Royce Rd you have to change at the first stop.
3. Tower Park is on the way from Miller Rd to Ship St.
4. If you travel east from High St, Ship St is the first stop.
5. High St is on the same line as Green St.
6. You can go from Royce Rd to Green St without changing.

4 Do number 1 or number 2.

1. If all the students in the class are from the same place, make up true or false sentences about the transport system in your own city/country.

2. If the students in the class are from different places, tell the other students two things about the transport system in your city/country.

C Flight 3 to Hong Kong

1 Which picture?

1. Your passport and boarding card, please, sir.
2. British Airways Flight 3 to Hong Kong boarding now at Gate 11.
3. British Airways announce the arrival of Flight 623 from Geneva.
4. I'd like to change my reservation, please.
5. Have you any hand baggage, madam?

2 What do these mean? Make sure you know. Then find each one in the timetable.

British Airways flight number 3   arrival time   Wednesday   departure time   Monday
Boeing 747 Jumbo Jet plane   stopping at   Sunday   minutes   minimum

LONDON – HONG KONG 747

DEPART London, Heathrow Airport, Terminal 3 (Minimum check-in time 60 mins; BA First & Club class 45 mins)
ARRIVE Hong Kong, Kai Tak Airport

Frequency	Aircraft		Via	Transfer Times	Flight	Air-craft	Class & Catering
	Dep	Arr					
Mo	1025	0835†	Abu Dhabi		BA3	747	PCM ✕
Tu	1700	1535†	Bombay		BA3	747	PCM ✕
We	1025	1035†	Rome, Bahrain		BA3	747	PCM ✕
Th	1700	1535†	Bombay		BA3	747	PCM ✕
Fr	1025	0835†	Abu Dhabi		BA3	747	PCM ✕
Sa	1700	1645†	Rome, Calcutta		BA3	747	PCM ✕
Su	1700	1520†	Bahrain		BA3	747	PCM ✕
† – Next day							

3 Answer the questions by looking at the timetable, and make new questions to ask other students.

1. What time does the Hong Kong flight leave London on Tuesdays?
2. What is the flight number?
3. How often does the flight go via Abu Dhabi?
4. What time do flights via Bombay arrive in Hong Kong?
5. On what days can you go from London to Hong Kong via Rome?
6. Where does the flight stop on Wednesdays?
7. By what time must you check in for the Wednesday flight?

4 Listen to the announcements and complete the sentences.

1. Passengers for Birmingham on Flight BD .... – this flight is now boarding at gate number ....
2. British Midland passengers to East Midlands on .... BD .... – this flight is now boarding at ....
3. Would Mr Mattox travelling to .... please contact the British Airways .... office opposite island J on the .... floor?
4. Would Mr Rowley from .... please .... British Midland .... ?

5 Listen to the recording. How many words are there in each sentence? What are they? (Contractions like *don't*, *I've* count as two words.)

Unit 24: Lesson C

Students learn some of the language associated with air travel.
Structures: no new structures.
Words and expressions to learn: *boarding pass; gate; flight; arrival; departure; reservation; hand baggage; timetable; air; airport; airline; by air; check in.*

Language notes and possible problems
Vocabulary load Students are asked to use a large number of new words and expressions in this lesson, especially in Exercises 2 and 3. We have tried to restrict this to the minimum necessary for coping in an airport situation.

1 Presentation: matching

● This is best done as a listening exercise, although it can be made a reading activity if you prefer.
● For listening work: ask students to cover the whole of the page except the pictures at the top.
● Play the recording one or more times, getting the students to write the number of the sentence and the letter of the picture they think it goes with.
● Let the students compare notes before checking the answers with you.
● Then go over the sentences with the students, answering questions and giving explanations where necessary.
● The students will probably want to ask you for other words and expressions connected with air travel (e.g. *delay, land, take off, customs, visa*).
● Encourage them to use appropriate structures when asking their questions (*How do you say . . . ?, Can I say . . . ?, What's . . . in English?* and so on).
● If you wish, this can become an 'autonomous learning' session, with the students consulting their dictionaries and each other as well as you.

2 Introduction to timetables
● This sensitization exercise will introduce students to the conventions of air timetables, in preparation for the more difficult practice activity in Exercise 3.
● Let students work on their own, consulting you or their dictionaries if they are unsure of any meanings, and trying to match each item in the list to something on the timetable.
● Then get them to compare answers in groups before checking with you.

3 Practice
● Let students prepare answers to the seven questions in groups of three or four.
● Then ask the questions and let volunteers respond orally.
● Then get each student to write one other question, using the information on the timetable.
● Students should ask their questions, addressing them to the class or to a group of about five other students.

● Groups who finish quickly can split up and go to other groups.

Answers: 1. 1700   2. BA3   3. Twice a week.   4. 1535
5. Wednesday and Saturday   6. Rome and Bahrain   7. 925

4 Listening
● Tell students that they are going to hear some airport announcements, and that they will need to concentrate to pick out the information that they need, just as in real life.
● Play the recording twice or more until students are satisfied that they have understood.
● Then check the answers with them.

Tapescript for Exercise 4
1. Passengers for Birmingham on Flight BD776 – this flight is now boarding at gate number 2. BD776 to Birmingham boarding now at gate number 2.
2. British Midland passengers to East Midlands on flight BD224 – this flight is now boarding at gate number 9. BD224 to East Midlands boarding now at gate number 9.
3. Would Mr Mattox travelling to Milan please contact the British Airways ticket office opposite island J on the first floor. Mr Mattox travelling to Milan to please contact the British Airways ticket office opposite island J on the first floor.
4. Would Mr Rowley from Birmingham please contact British Midland check-in. Mr Rowley from Birmingham to please contact British Midland check-in.

5 How many words?
● Play each sentence two or three times. Let students compare notes before giving them the answers.

Tapescript
1. He's a pilot. (4)
2. Is there a post office near here? (7)
3. What are you talking about? (5)
4. What's your phone number? (5)
5. First on the right, second on the left. (8)
6. I think it's raining again. (6)
7. Have you ever been to Moscow? (6)
8. Can I have a look at your dictionary? (8)

Practice Book
● Tell students which exercises you want them to do.

Unit 24: Lesson D

Students increase their familiarity with prepositions of place and direction.
Structures: no new structures.
Words and expressions to learn: *side; over; along; crossroads; bridge; river; on to.*

Language notes and possible problems

Treasure hunt Most of this lesson is taken up by a 'treasure hunt'. The clues are arranged so that it is difficult to find the right place without following them in order, as students will realize if they try to take short cuts. Note that there are various false clues – for instance, there are five number 5s. If students follow the correct route they will only come to true clues.

Two clues that students must be careful about are numbers 7 and 9. Reading clue 14 gets students to the number 7 near B; but turning around and reading clue 14 again gets them to the 13 near the railway bridge. The words are the same, but because they are coming to 14 from a different direction, 'right' and 'left' do not get them to the same places both times. There is a similar situation with clue 9.

1 Treasure hunt

- Explain or demonstrate the words *side, over, bridge, river, crossroads, on to, along.*
- Explain to students what treasure is, and what they have to do to find this treasure.
- Tell them that they can only find it if they read each clue carefully and do exactly what it says.
- You may want to do the first couple of clues with them before letting them work by themselves.
- Tell them to be especially careful with clues 7 and 9.
- Walk round as they are working to help with any problems that come up.
- When students have finished, get them to compare answers with one another before checking with you.
- The treasure is buried at D. The correct route goes via the following sequence of clues: 6, 14, 7, 14, 13, 9, 3, 4, 12, 1, 11, 8, 15, 2, 10, 5, D.
- You may like to offer a small prize to the winner.

2 Reinforcement: writing

- Get students to write down the route they took to find the treasure.
- They can do this individually, or in groups with a secretary noting down the sentences (in which case they should write *We* instead of *I*).
- Check the sentences by getting students to come up to the board in turn to write one sentence each.

Optional activity

- Get students to explain (for instance, as they would to a motorist) how to get to various places in the town where they are studying.

3 Summary

- Go through the summary with the students, answering any questions that come up.

Practice Book

- Tell students which exercises you want them to do.

Answers to Practice Book Exercise 1
1. understand
2. narrow (not a comparative)
3. factory (nothing to do with air travel)
4. interesting (not a physical characteristic)
5. grapes (edible, not manufactured)
6. radio
7. been (past participle)
8. door (nothing to do with travel)
9. region (nothing to do with hotels)

D Walk along the river bank…

1 Treasure hunt. The treasure is buried under one of the trees, at A, B, C, D, E, F, G or H. Follow the clues and find it. Start by reading clue number 6.

1. Go to the nearest railway station. Go into the station.
2. Keep straight on until you see the next clue.
3. Climb up on to the railway line.
4. Turn left and walk along the railway line until you see the next clue.
5. Turn right. Go to the nearest crossroads and turn right. The treasure is under the second tree on the right.
6. Go straight on over the bridge to the crossroads.
7. Walk back and read the last clue again.
8. Go into the nearest field. The next clue is under the first tree on the right.

9. This clue says the same as number 13.
10. Walk along the river bank to the next bridge.
11. Get on the next train; get off at the other station.
12. There's a train coming. Turn to your left and get off the railway line.
13. Go under the bridge. The next clue is just on the other side.
14. Turn left and go to the second tree on the right.
15. Go straight out of the field and take the shortest way to the river by road. The next clue is at the crossroads.
16. You're lost.

2 Describe the route you took to the treasure.

I went straight over the bridge to the crossroads; then I turned left and went to the second tree on the right; ....

3 Look at the summary on page 153 with your teacher.

101

Knowing about the future

A This is going to be my room

1 What are your plans for this evening? Are you going to do any of these things?

write letters	see a film
play cards	see friends
watch TV	wash your hair
listen to music	study

Examples:

'I'm going to write letters.'
'I'm not going to watch TV.'

2 This is going to be your house. It isn't finished yet. Look at the plan and decide what the various rooms are going to be and how you are going to furnish them. Include some or all of the following: kitchen, bathroom(s), toilet(s), bedrooms, living room, dining room, study, playroom, and any other rooms that you want. If you haven't got enough rooms, put on another floor.

When you have finished, work with another student and tell him/her what the rooms are going to be. Example:

'This is going to be the kitchen.'

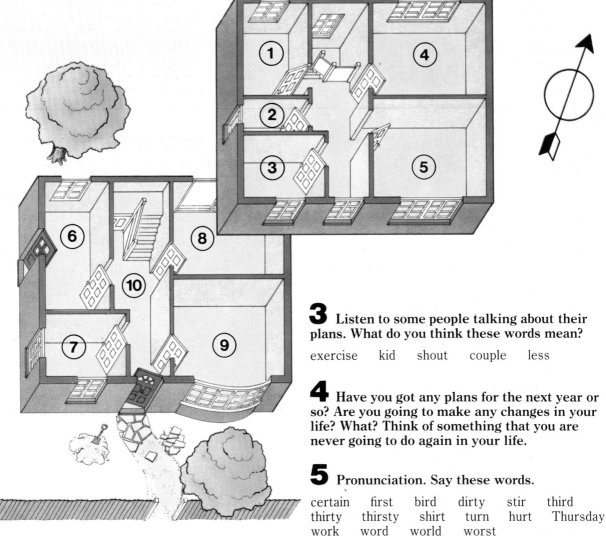

3 Listen to some people talking about their plans. What do you think these words mean?

exercise   kid   shout   couple   less

4 Have you got any plans for the next year or so? Are you going to make any changes in your life? What? Think of something that you are never going to do again in your life.

5 Pronunciation. Say these words.

certain	first	bird	dirty	stir	third
thirty	thirsty	shirt	turn	hurt	Thursday
work	word	world	worst		
learn	heard	early	year		

Unit 25: Lesson A

Students learn more about the expression of the future. They talk about future events which are resolved or planned, or for which there is present evidence.
Structures: *going to.*
Words and expressions to learn: *plan; study* (verb); *play cards; not yet.*
Phonology: spellings of /ɜː/; pronunciation of *going to.*

Language notes and possible problems

Going to   Students have already learnt to use the Present Progressive when talking about future plans (Unit 19). The Present Progressive is used particularly to talk about future actions or events which have been planned to take place at a particular time or date, and the tense is often used with adverbs or adverbials of future time. (This may be necessary to show that the meaning is future and not present.)

Going to has a rather wider use than the Present Progressive. It is more often used to talk about plans and resolutions with no fixed date; and it can be used to talk about other kinds of future event besides those that are planned (see next lesson).

It is probably better if students simply pick up the use of the structure through practice at this stage, leaving a study of the rules until later.

1 Plans for this evening

● Write on the board:
   I'm writing letters this evening.
   I'm going to write letters this evening.
● Explain that *going to* is another way of talking about plans for the future.
● Talk about what you are going to do this evening.
● Get students to tell you their plans, and some of the things that they are not going to do (see exercise examples).
● Note that *going to go* is unusual; we are more likely to say, for example; *I'm going to the cinema* than *I'm going to go to the cinema.*
● Work on the stress and pronunciation of students' sentences. *Going to* is pronounced with a 'weak' *to* (/tə/) except before a vowel. In fast speech it often sounds like 'gointa' or 'gonna'.

2 Rooms

● You may want to set a time limit: some students could happily spend hours planning a house for themselves.
● Help with vocabulary.
● When they are ready, get two volunteers to start telling each other about their houses.
● Make sure they use *going to* appropriately.
● Then tell the other students to start doing the same. Walk round and monitor; help where necessary.

3 Listening: guessing unknown words

● Students will hear four people talking about their New Year's resolutions.
● The task is to guess the meanings of five of the words

that are used.
● If it is easy you may want to begin by introducing the topic of New Year's resolutions.
● Then get each student to copy the five words on a piece of paper and tell them they are to decide what each word means by listening to the recording.
● Play the recording twice or more while students listen.
● If the students all speak the same language, or if they can form language groups, you may wish them to compare answers before checking with you.
● They can communicate their answers by paraphrase or mime, or by translation in a monolingual class.

Tapescript for Exercise 3
'I'm going to get more exercise, run more often, write more letters, and teach my kid to read.' 'And that's January!' (laughter)

'I'm going to try very hard not to shout at Sarah, 'cause I hate her shouting back. That's my eldest kid, three and a half, and I kill her for shouting, and I obviously shout at her, and she says why do I shout at her, so, fair enough.'

'I'm just going to try and get to know my family a bit better. I think over the last couple of years I've tended to sort of forget about them, and I've got to rediscover my family.'

'I'm going to eat less, drink less, run more, get on top of my work, and I'm going to see much more of all my children.' 'You've got quite a task, haven't you?' 'Yes, you have.' 'How many children do you have?' 'How many have you got altogether?' 'Uh, I've got four.'

4 Long-term plans and resolutions

● Get students to volunteer information.
● Where possible, ask follow-up questions so as to develop the exercise into a mini-conversation.

5 Spellings of /ɜː/

● Students have already learnt to pronounce /ɜː/ for *er, ir* and *ur*, in separate lessons.
● This exercise pulls together what they have learnt and adds some new points.
● Say or play the words and let students imitate.
● If they want a standard British accent, they should avoid pronouncing an *r* after the vowel.
● Note that the words in the last two groups are exceptions. The combination *or* is not normally pronounced /ɜː/; this only happens after *w*. And *ear* is more often pronounced /ɪə/ (as in *beard*).
● Note that *year* has two pronunciations: /jɪə(r)/ and /jɜː(r)/.

Practice Book
● Tell students which exercises you want them to do.

Unit 25: Lesson B

Students learn to make predictions in English.
Structures: *going to.*
Words and expressions to learn: *win; have a baby; crash; organize; country; hard work; fit; join; cost; inclusive; details.*

Language notes and possible problems

Going to is not only used to talk about people's plans and resolutions. It can also be used to make predictions about what is going to happen. This is especially the case when there is 'present evidence' for the future event – when it is obviously on the way, or starting to happen. (In cases where we are predicting without obvious present evidence, we generally use *will*.)

Optional extra materials

Pictures to illustrate things that are going to happen (see Exercise 1).
Flashcards for mime (Exercise 3).

1 Pictures

● Each picture shows a situation in which it would be natural to talk about the future with *going to.*
● Let students look at the pictures and decide (individually or in groups) what is going to happen.
● Tell them to write their answers – they will need to ask you for vocabulary.
● When they have compared notes, go over the answers with them.
● Additional pictures taken from magazines, showing things that are going to happen, would be a great help.

2 Guided composition

● Go over the advertisement with the students, explaining difficulties.
● Then give them 15–20 minutes to compose one or more similar advertisements in groups, using the framework provided but choosing a different situation.
● When they are ready, get a spokesman for each group to read out what they have written.
● The class could vote for the holiday they would most like to go on.

3 Mime

● Get one or two volunteers to mime first (take part yourself if you like).
● Then give students a couple of minutes to think, before you go round the class getting them to do their mimes.
● Encourage everybody to participate, but don't force a student who is really shy.
● It may help things along if you give students cards with the names of actions to mime.
● Possibilities: preparing to eat, drink, shave, wash, go to bed, watch TV, play chess, play the guitar/violin, write, read, cook something, go out with a boyfriend/girlfriend, drive; being about to sneeze, faint, be sick, wake up, go to sleep.

Optional activity

● If your students are interested in economics, politics etc., ask them what they think is going to happen in the world in the next few years.
● Put some key words on the board first of all: inflation, unemployment, government, prices, war.
● Help them to formulate what they want to say, and encourage agreement and disagreement from other students.
● Note, however, that this is a difficult exercise, and might be heavy going with a not very fluent class.

Practice Book

● Tell students which exercises you want them to do.

B It's going to rain

1 Look at the pictures. What is going to happen? (If you don't know the words, use your dictionary or ask your teacher.)

2 Read the advertisement. Then make up advertisements yourselves (working in groups) to get people to join your holiday trip.

HOLIDAY IN SCOTLAND
We are organizing a holiday walking tour in the North of Scotland.
We are going to cover 150 miles of mountainous country in ten days.
It's going to be hard work.
It's going to be tough.
You're going to be wet, cold and tired a lot of the time.
But it's going to be fun!
If you are young and fit, and if you like beautiful places – why not join us? Cost £38 inclusive.
For more details, write Box 1346, *Edinburgh Times.*

We are organizing a trip to
....
We are going to ....
....
It's going to be ....
....
It's going to be ....
....
And/But it's going to be ..
....
If you are ....
....,
...., and
....,
why not join us?
Cost: £............ inclusive.

3 Mime a person who is going to do something. The other students will try to say what you are going to do.

You're going to swim.

C Why? To...

1 You go to a university to study.
Why do you go to these places?

2 Can you make five more sentences like these?

'People don't go to Nigeria to ski.'
'People don't go to Iceland to drink wine.'

3 Why are you learning English?

4 Mr Andrews is an English tourist who is travelling to Eastern Europe tomorrow. Just now he's having breakfast at home. After breakfast, he's going out to do a lot of things. (For example, he's going to Harrods to buy a suitcase.) Look at the pictures, and then write a paragraph to say where he's going and why. Connect your sentences with *First of all, then, and then, after that, next, tomorrow.*

Where? **Why?**

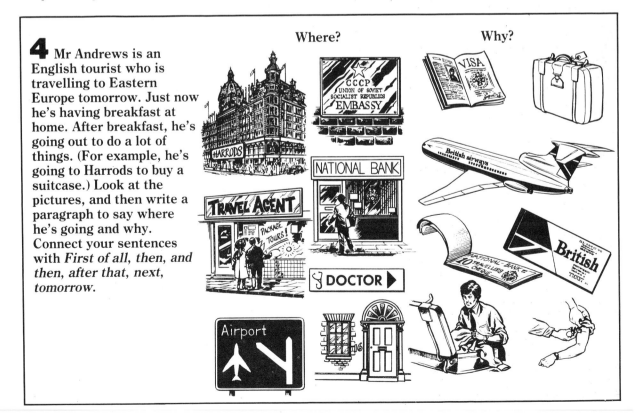

Unit 25: Lesson C

Students learn to talk about purposes; they practise using connectors in paragraph-writing.
Structures: infinitive of purpose; paragraph-structuring adverbials.
Words and expressions to learn: *library; butcher's; embassy; travel agent; information; visa; suitcase; aeroplane; air ticket; first of all.*

Language notes and possible problems
1. Infinitive of purpose In other languages it may not be possible to express purpose with a simple infinitive. Look out for mistakes like *for go*, *for going* or *for to go* instead of *to go*.
2. Connectors The use of structuring words (to link sentences into paragraphs and show the structure of discourse) may be difficult for some students to get used to, because prose is not organized in the same way in all languages.
3. *Library* Teach the difference between *library* and *bookshop* if necessary; *library* is a false friend in some European languages.
4. *Butcher's* Explain the reason for the possessive *'s*, and mention other examples.

1 Places and purposes
● Look at the first sentence. Explain that we can use the *to*-infinitive to answer the question *Why?*
● Get students to say or write answers to the questions.
● You may like to take the opportunity to mention the names of other kinds of shop.

2 Negatives
● It should be easy to think of examples.
● Students who are studying in Britain may be able to think of a large number of things to say about the country. (They will need to say *come* instead of *go*).
● The verb *find* may be useful: e.g. *You don't go to Alaska to find sunshine.*

3 Personalization
● Ask one or two good students first.
● See if they can express their reasons for learning English with a *to*-infinitive.
● Then ask the rest to try.
● It will not always be easy (within the limitations of the vocabulary they know), and you may want to teach expressions such as *for interest, for pleasure* where necessary.
● In some cases, it will be easier for students to express what they want to say by using *because*.

4 Paragraph writing
● First of all, get students to link the 'where' pictures and the 'why' pictures.
● Supply words where they are needed; practise pronunciation.
● Then tell students to try to make sentences about where Mr Andrews is going.
● Put the sentences on the board.

● Get students to link the sentences into a paragraph (they can decide themselves what order the actions will be done in).
● Obviously this exercise is not going to produce an elegant piece of writing, but it will help to sensitize students to the way in which written language can be structured by adverbs expressing time and sequence.
● This is particularly important for students who speak non-European languages, in which writing may be structured in very different ways.
● A possible paragraph is as follows:

First of all, Mr Andrews is going to the embassy to get a visa. Then he is going to the bank, to pick up his traveller's cheques, and to the travel agent to buy an air ticket. Next, he is going to the doctor to get a vaccination. After that he is going to Harrods to buy a suitcase, and then he is going home to pack. Tomorrow he is going to the airport to catch his plane.

Practice Book
● Tell students which exercises you want them to do.

104

Unit 25: Lesson D

Students look at the use of infinitives and *-ing* forms.

Structures: infinitive without *to*; infinitive with *to*; *-ing* form.

Words and expressions to learn: none.

Language notes and possible problems

Students have already met infinitives and *-ing* forms in a number of expressions, and they are probably beginning to wonder about the differences between them. The purpose of this lesson is to give some simple guidelines.

Many languages have just one form corresponding to the three English forms. So, for instance, in *I can **dance**, I want **to dance*** and *I like **dancing***, students may find to their surprise that one word in their own language is translated in three different ways. Unfortunately there is no simple rule which is valid in all cases, and this point of grammar causes recurrent problems.

In this lesson students are given simple rules which should help them to classify and understand the structures they have learnt so far.

Note that the rules for the use of *-ing* after *like*, *love* and *hate* are less valid for American English, where these verbs are often followed by the infinitive with *to*.

Presentation

• There are various possible ways to approach a lesson like this.

• One way is to get the students to work out the grammar for themselves (with their books closed), with your help.

• Draw a table on the board like this:

	go swim speak
	to go to swim to speak
	going swimming speaking

• Then give the class some sentence beginnings (such as *I can*; *I'd like*; *I love*), and ask which row they belong in.

• Students should be able to suggest other expressions to put in the three rows.

• When they have found a number of examples, they should be able to see some regularities.

• At this point, ask them to open their books and study the rules and examples.

1 and 2 Infinitive with and without *to*; *-ing* form

• These are tests which will help you and your students see whether they have mastered the rules.

3 I know an old lady...

• Students may already have read the words of this in

Practice Book Lesson 25C (page 98).

• If not, go through the words explaining any difficulties.

• Then tell students to close their books.

• Play the song, stopping after the first two lines of each verse (except the first) to see if the students can remember why the old lady swallowed the animal in question.

• Finally, see if the students are interested in singing the song (either with the recording or by themselves).

4 Summary

• Look over the summary with the students.

Practice Book

• Tell students which exercises you want them to do.

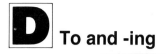

D To and -ing

INFINITIVE WITHOUT TO (Examples: go, speak)

Used after 'auxiliary verbs':

can	*I can speak German.*
could	*Could you speak more slowly?*
will	*It will rain tomorrow.*
should	*You should be at home.*
do	*Does he smoke?*
	Don't stop.
let's	*Let's have a drink.*

INFINITIVE WITH TO (Examples: to go, to speak)

Used in many kinds of sentence. After:

something	*Would you like something to eat?*
nothing	*There's nothing to do.*
anything	*Have you got anything to drink?*
I'm sorry	*I'm sorry to trouble you.*

Also used after many verbs:

would like	*Would you like to dance?*
would love	*I'd love to speak German.*
hope	*I hope to see you soon.*
want	*I don't want to go home.*
have	*You have to change at the next station.*

And used to say why we do things:

'Why did you come here?' 'To see you.'

-ING FORM (Examples: going, speaking)

Used in many kinds of sentence. After some verbs:

like	*I like speaking French.*
love	*I love going to the theatre.*
hate	*I hate waiting for people.*

And after all prepositions:

after	*After seeing the doctor I felt better.*
before	*Before going to bed I usually read the paper.*
for	*Thank you for inviting me.*
at	*She's good at swimming.*
without	*Can you get there without changing?*

And in the Present Progressive tense:

'What are you doing?' 'I'm writing letters.'

---

1 Put in the infinitive with or without *to*.

1. Can you .... ? (swim)
2. Have you got anything .... ? (read)
3. Could I .... to Lucy? (speak)
4. I don't .... (understand)
5. I'd like .... you again. (see)
6. I hope .... to America in May. (go)
7. It takes a long time .... English. (learn)
8. Let's .... (dance)
9. Why don't we .... a drink? (have)

2 Put in the infinitive or the *-ing* form.

1. Would you like .... ? (dance)
2. Do you like .... ? (dance)
3. Can you .... chess? (play)
4. Thank you for .... me. (help)
5. I'm very bad at .... (ski)
6. You can't live without .... (eat)
7. How do you .... 'please'? (pronounce)
8. Could you .... me the time? (tell)
9. I love .... (cook)
10. My husband can't .... (cook)

3 Listen to the song. When the recording stops, say what is coming next.

4 Look at the summary on page 154 with your teacher.

105

Feelings

A I feel ill

1. I've got a cold.

2. I've got toothache.

3. I've got a temperature.

4. I've got flu.

5. I've got a headache.

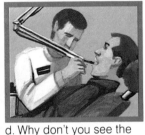
6. My leg hurts.

a. Why don't you go home and lie down?

b. Why don't you take an aspirin?

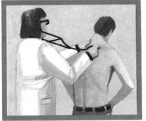
c. Why don't you see the doctor?

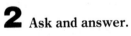
d. Why don't you see the dentist?

1 Match the letters and the numbers. You can use a dictionary.

2 Ask and answer.

'How do you feel?'
'I'm very hungry, and my arm hurts a bit.'

3 Listen to the dialogue. Then change some of the words and practise it with a partner. Your teacher will help you.

WOMAN: Good morning, Mr Culham. How are you?
MAN: I feel ill.
WOMAN: I *am* sorry. What's the matter?
MAN: My eyes hurt, and I've got a bad headache.
WOMAN: Well, why don't you take an aspirin?
MAN: That's a good idea.

4 At the doctor's. Write the other half of this dialogue. Work in groups if you can. Your teacher will help you.

DOCTOR: Good morning. What's the problem?
YOU: Well, ...
DOCTOR: I see. Does it / Do they hurt very badly?
YOU: ....
DOCTOR: How long have you had this?
YOU: ....
DOCTOR: Yes, right. I'd like to examine you, then. Mmm... Mmm...
YOU: ....?
DOCTOR: No, it doesn't look too bad. Here's a prescription for some medicine. Phone me if you're not better by the day after tomorrow.
YOU: ....
DOCTOR: Goodbye.
YOU: ....

5 Ask your teacher how to say three other words you can use at the doctor's.

Unit 26: Lesson A

Students learn to ask and talk about common physical problems and to express sympathy, as well as practising making suggestions.
Structures: no new structures.
Words and expressions to learn: *flu*; *headache*; *toothache*; *aspirin*; *medicine*; *hurt* (intransitive verb); *ill*; *What's the matter?*; *a temperature*; *lie down*; *take medicine*; *feel*.

Language notes and possible problems

1. Ache/hurt Although we can say *backache, stomach-ache, earache* in English, it is equally correct to say *My back/stomach/ear hurts*. In the interests of simplicity, we have chosen to teach only *toothache* and *a headache* (these ideas cannot be expressed in another way), and to use the verb *hurt* with the other parts of the body.

2. Countable and uncountable nouns Note that *headache* and *temperature* are countable, while *tooth-ache* and *flu* are uncountable (and therefore not used with the article *a*). Students may find this confusing.

3. Pronunciation Make sure students note the pronunciation of *aspirin* (/ˈæsprɪn/) and *medicine* (/ˈmedsən/) – each word has two syllables, not three; and of *tempera-ture* (/ˈtemprɪtʃə/), which has only three syllables.

1 Presentation: matching

- Divide the class into groups, so students can pool the English they have learnt outside your class.
- Let the students look at the illustrations for a moment, and make sure they understand that they are to match the physical problems shown at the top of the page with the solutions underneath.
- Tell them they can use their dictionaries.
- Of course, the students can differ on what solution to propose for each problem; there are at least two 'correct' answers in each case.
- Go over the pronunciation of the sentences with the students and answer any questions they may have. Point out the absence of an article in *I've got toothache* and *I've got flu*.

2 Personalization

- Ask one student, *How do you feel?*; you will probably get the answer *Fine*.
- Then get him or her to ask you the same question and respond with a couple of problems, e.g. *I'm thirsty, and I've got a bit of a headache*.
- Get the students to walk round asking and telling one another how they feel (or get each student to talk to as many others as possible without moving from his or her seat).
- If the students' culture makes it difficult for them to talk about these things, you may wish them to assume English-speaking identities.

3 Dialogue construction

- Ask the students to close their books, and write the first line of the dialogue on the board.
- Under it write *Man:*, and get students to suggest things for the man to say.

- Accept any suggestions that would be logical answers to the woman's question (*Fine, thanks, and you?*; *I'm not very well today*, etc.). Write the suggestions up.
- Then play or read out the first two lines of the dialogue, and get the students to repeat what the man actually says, paying attention to the intonation pattern.
- Point out any of the students' suggestions which mean the same thing as the man's answer.
- Erase the suggestions and write *I feel ill.* on the second line.
- Continue in the same way for the succeeding sentences in the dialogue.
- Make sure the students give you several sentences with *hurt/hurts*, so that they become aware of the coverage of this verb.
- When the entire dialogue has been put on the board, play it through without stopping.
- Divide the class into pairs and ask them to make new dialogues by changing some of the words. When a pair has finished they should change partners and make another dialogue.
- You may like to tape/video-record their dialogues.

4 Extension

- Divide the class into groups of three or four and let them try to invent the other half of the dialogue.
- Make sure they understand that there is no one 'correct' answer.
- Move around helping with problems and checking that sentences are correct.
- You may wish one or more groups to perform their dialogues for the class.

Optional activity

- When students have produced a corrected version of the 'half dialogue' in Exercise 3, they can practise it with the recording. This contains the doctor's part, with pauses left for the patient's part.
- This can be done in the language lab or listening centre with individual recordings, or in the classroom with the class cassette.
- The object of the exercise is for the students to say their sentences, to their own satisfaction, in the allotted time.

5 Vocabulary extension

- There are several ways to organize this exercise.
- You can simply get students to ask you questions as they think of them.
- You can get them to write you notes asking how to say things.
- They can make a list of the things they want to know, and walk round the classroom seeing if they can find out from another student before checking with you.
- Make sure they use the forms they have learnt (*How do you say... in English?*, etc.) to ask their questions.

Practice Book

- Tell students which exercises you want them to do.
- Exercise 4 is a scanning reading activity; make sure the students realize that it is not necessary to understand every word in the text in order to do the exercise (though interested students can look up more words if they wish).

Unit 26: Lesson B

> **Students learn** simple ways of expressing emotions like pleasure and anger, and practise responding to expressions of negative emotion.
> **Structures:** it + Simple Present + *me* (e.g. *It depresses me*); *It makes me* + adjective; *I think it's . . .*
> **Words and expressions to learn:** *frighten; depress; disgust; dinner; angry; That's very nice of you.*

Language notes and possible problems

1. Expressing opinions This lesson is deliberately slightly over-ambitious; we feel it is important for the students to begin trying to talk about their opinions on serious and important things, even though their linguistic ability may be markedly inadequate to express their thoughts. If you think that your students will be daunted or frustrated by this, you may wish to skip this lesson.

2. -ing and -ed In this lesson students learn the participles *depressing* and *depressed*. They have already come across other participles used as adjectives. You may wish to explain that we use the *-ed* form (*interested, bored, excited*, etc.) to say how we feel about something or someone and the *-ing* form (*interesting, boring, exciting*) to talk about the person or thing that makes us feel that way. There is an exercise in the Practice Book which practises these forms.

Optional extra equipment Tape or cassette recorder with microphone and blank tape, or video.

---

1 Presentation

- Use the sketches of facial expressions or your own presentation device to teach the new vocabulary students will be using in this exercise.
- Go over the seven sentences with the students.
- Then choose one of the pictures at the top of the page, preferably one that will evoke varying responses from different members of the class, and ask a few students, *How do you feel about this picture?*.
- Get the class to practise the question, and then get them to ask one another about the pictures at the top of the page.
- This can be done as a walk-round, or each student can ask as many people as possible without moving from his or her seat.

2 Practice

- This gives students a chance to talk about things they feel strongly about, if they wish to do so.
- Get them to choose four other subjects and write about their feelings towards them. Point out the box containing words they already know, and which they can use in this exercise.
- Encourage them to use their dictionaries if they wish; walk round the classroom while they are writing to help with any problems.
- Some of them may wish to read out one or more sentences to a group or to the class.

3 Survey

- Get each student to choose one thing to survey the rest of the class about. Remind them that they must keep notes of the answers they get.
- Help them report the results to the class (e.g. *Seven people think Formula 1 racing is wonderful; it makes one person angry...*)

4 Dialogue completion and listening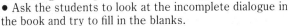

- Ask the students to look at the incomplete dialogue in the book and try to fill in the blanks.
- They can do this in small groups if you wish.
- Remind them that a blank can contain one or more words.
- When the groups have reached some sort of consensus, play the recording one or more times so that they can check the answers.
- Help them practise the sentences *What's the matter?* and *That's very nice of you.*

Tapescript for Exercise 4

TOM: Hello, Jill. How are you?
JILL: I'm depressed.
TOM: I *am* sorry. What's the matter?
JILL: My boyfriend isn't here. He's in America.
TOM: Oh dear! Well, would you like to have dinner with us tonight?
JILL: That's very nice of you, Tom. Yes, I would.
TOM: See you at seven o'clock, then. Bye.
JILL: Bye.

5 Inventing conversations

- Put the students in pairs or threes.
- Each group should write its own conversation, using words from the lesson, in which one person has a problem and the other or others are sympathetic.
- If you can record or videotape the students' conversations, it will give them an incentive to practise the conversations once they have written them.
- In this case, walk round while the students are working to give any help that is needed, and let each group tell you when they are ready to record.
- Alternatively, you may wish the students to improvise their conversations without writing, and move to a new group when they have finished one conversation.
- If you take this second option, it is a good idea to put the important vocabulary from the lesson on the board for easy reference.

Practice Book

- Tell students which exercises you want them to do.

107

B It frightens me

1 Choose one of the pictures above. Ask other students: *'How do you feel about this picture?'*
Examples of answers:

'It frightens   'It depresses   'It makes me   'I think it's   'I think it's   'I think it's   'I don't like it
me.'   me.'   angry.'   lovely.'   interesting.'   disgusting.'   much.'

2 Think of four other things and write about your feelings towards them. You can use words from Exercise 1 or from the box. Examples:

Unemployment worries me.
I think cigarettes are disgusting.

worries bores	happy unhappy	funny pretty stupid nice	wonderful beautiful exciting

3 Survey. Ask other students about one of the things you wrote about. Report the results to the class.

4 Put a word or words in each blank. Then listen and practise.

TOM: ...., Jill. How ....?
JILL: .... depressed.
TOM: I .... What's the matter?
JILL: .... boyfriend isn't here. .... America.
TOM: Oh dear! Well, ... you .... to .... dinner with us tonight?
JILL: That's .... nice of you, Tom. ...., I ....
TOM: See you .... seven o'clock, then. ....
JILL: ....

5 Work with a partner. Make and practise a new conversation using words from the lesson.

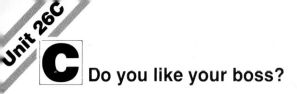

C Do you like your boss?

WE ASKED THREE PEOPLE:

Celia

I really like my boss. She's a lovely person, very easy to work for, very fair. She always asks what I think before she changes anything. If there's a problem, we solve it together. She never gets angry. I trust her, and she trusts me. It's a pleasure to work for her.

George

I get on all right with my .... He .... worry about .... details of .... work; he's .... fair, and .... gives me a lot .... freedom. .... like that. It .... me a bit angry when he .... me more work .... I can .... I don't .... he understands that parts .... my job .... very difficult. But on the whole, I don't .... we .... on too badly.

Lesley

I .... job, ... can't stand
.... difficult
....;
.... talk
.... really listen. And he's not
.... : *he* can make mistakes, and that's all right; but
.... angry. It
when .... he ....
really .... *me* angry when he changes his mind about
.... again and again. I can't leave
.... right now, ... really fed up.

1 Read Celia's text; put one word in each blank in George's text; put one or more words in each blank in Lesley's text. You can use a dictionary.

2 Think of one person you know (boss/ sister/uncle etc.). Write four sentences about how you get on with that person. Try to use words from the texts.

3 Work in groups. Each person reads the sentences from Exercise 2 and the others ask questions. Some words you can use in your questions:

| easy/difficult to talk to | angry | problems |
| trust | freedom | listen | mistakes |

4 Copy this list. Then listen, and mark off each expression when you hear it.

in a pub   he's smashing   sense of humour
easy to get on with   very fair   when I first came
everything that I needed to know
wasn't unfair   I made mistakes   very good to me

How does the person feel about her boss – more like Celia, more like George or more like Lesley?

Unit 26: Lesson C

Students begin learning to express their feelings about people they know.
Structures: adjective + *to*-infinitive (+ preposition) (e.g. *easy to do*, *easy to talk to*); *get* + adjective (e.g. *get angry*).
Words and expressions to learn: *solve; trust; get on with; can't stand; change one's mind; pleasure; freedom; mistake; on the whole; fed up; fair.*

Language notes and possible problems

1. Talking about relationships   Some students may be hesitant about discussing any of their relationships in class, even professional or casual ones. For these students you may want to suggest that in Exercises 2 and 3 they have the option of imagining they live or work with a famous person (film star, politician, singer, etc.).

2. *Get angry*   Students have already encountered *get* with comparative adjectives; you may wish to point out that it can also be used, as here, with most of the adjectives (or -*ed* words used as adjectives) that describe how people feel, e.g. *depressed, excited, worried*.

3. *Get on (with)*   Make sure students notice when *with* is used and when it is not.

1 Presentation: text completion

● There is more than one way of dealing with the new vocabulary in this lesson: you can present the new items before the students look at the texts; you can let them use their dictionaries while working on the texts; or you can get them to ask you questions as they come up.
● If students all speak the same language, you may wish them to do Exercise 1 in small groups.
● Make sure students understand that each blank in George's text requires one word only, while the blanks in Lesley's text are each for one or more words.
● Here are two sample completed texts; some variation is obviously possible.

Completed texts for Exercise 1

I get on all right with my *boss*. He *doesn't* worry about *the* details of *my* work; he's *very* fair, and *he* gives me a lot *of* freedom. *I* like that. It *makes* me a bit angry when he *gives* me more work *than* I can *do*. I don't *think* he understands that parts *of* my job *are* very difficult. But on the whole, I don't *think* we *get* on too badly.

I *like my* job, *but I* can't stand *my boss*. He's *very* difficult *to* talk *to*; he *doesn't* really listen. And he's not *very fair*; *he* can make mistakes, and that's all right; but when *I make a mistake*, he *gets* angry. It really *makes me* angry when he changes his mind about *things* again and again. I can't leave *my job* right now, *but I'm* really fed up.
(**Note:** For some blanks other words or phrases may be correct.)

● When you have finished checking the answers, ask the students if there are any words they would like help in pronouncing.
● Tell them that you will let *them* decide when they have pronounced a word satisfactorily; say the word, let them say it, and say it again; continue until they are satisfied, and try to avoid letting them know what you think of their pronunciation.

2 Practice

● Get the students each to write four sentences about how they get on with someone they know (or an imaginary person – see Language Note 1).
● Walk round the room while the students are working to help with any problems.
● Write four sentences yourself to use in the next exercise.

3 Further practice

● Read your four sentences from the previous exercise to the class.
● Get them to look at the words in Exercise 3 and ask you further questions about the relationship you have described.
● Try to be perfectly honest; it will be more interesting for the students, and will encourage them to do the same.
● Help out with any pronunciation or grammar problems that occur as they question you.
● Then divide the class into groups of four or five and let them read their sentences to one another and ask questions.
● Walk around as the groups are working to give any help that is needed, but try not to correct mistakes that do not impede communication. You can always note down prevalent mistakes for work in a later lesson.

4 Listening for information   🔊 Ⓐ

● Teach the students the meanings of *smashing* (in the sense of *great!*), *sense of humour*, and *unfair*.
● Then get them to copy the list of expressions down on a piece of paper.
● Play the recording, more than once if necessary, getting the students to tick off the expressions as they hear them.
● All the expressions are in the text, but you need not tell the students so before beginning.
● When they have finished, ask them how the person in the recording feels about her boss – more like Celia, more like George, or more like Lesley.

Tapescript for Exercise 4

Um, I work part-time in a pub, and my boss is obviously a landlord. Um, he's...smashing. He's got a great sense of humour, um, very easy to get on with, um, and is very fair. Um, he's ... basically taught me the trade, because I was new when he, when I first came and he'd only just come to that pub as well, and he taught me, you know, everything that I needed to know, and wasn't, wasn't unfair when I made mistakes, and was very good to me, and uh, smashing guy.

Practice Book

● Tell students which exercises you want them to do.

Unit 26: Lesson D

Students practise talking about relationships.
Structures: no new structures.
Words and expressions to learn: *appreciate*;
share; *married*; *couple*.
Phonology: spelling rules for 'long' and 'short'
vowels.

Language notes and possible problems

'Long' and 'short' vowels The exact rules governing
the pronunciation of vowels are rather complicated, but
there is enough regularity to make it worth students' learning a simplified rule of thumb.

Help them to see that the words ending in *-e* in the four
lists are all short words constructed in the same way: they
end with one vowel + one consonant + *-e*. In words of
this kind, the vowel 'says its name': *a* is generally pronounced /eɪ/, *i* is /aɪ/, *o* is /əʊ/, and *u* is /juː/ or (less often)
/uː/. In short words without *-e* at the end, *a* is usually /æ/, *i*
is /ɪ/, *o* is /ɒ/ and *u* is /ʌ/. (In longer words the situation is
more complicated, partly because of the effect of stress.)

1 Long-term relationships

- Students get a bit more practice in talking about
relationships.
- Divide the class into groups of three or four.
- Explain that each group must decide which people are
being talked about in text 1 and which are being talked
about in text 2.
- You will want to explain or demonstrate the meanings
of *marriage*, *appreciate* and *share*, or let the students use
their dictionaries to look them up.
- Walk around while the students are working to give
any help that is needed.
- Do not let the groups talk to one another: it will be
more enjoyable if you save the results until the end of
the exercise.
- When each group has come to its decision, tell the
students to write a few (two to four) sentences about
the couple that is left over.
- When all the groups have finished writing, get them to
give their answers and read their texts.
- (The couples are: *Text 1*: E and F; *Text 2*: A and C.)

2 -e and pronunciation 📼

- Get students to look at the first list, and see if they
can work out for themselves, without your help, how *a*
is pronounced in the first and second rows.
- When they are able to see the rule, ask them in turn
to try to say the words in the list entitled 'NOW
PRONOUNCE'.
- Then, ask them if they can think of any other words
that fit into these patterns.
- Go on to do the same with the other three sections.
- Finally, draw their attention to the exceptions.
- Tell them that there are more exceptions, but that
enough words follow the rule for it to be useful.
- Some students will probably ask what the new words
mean. You can explain that they are not important
words (except for pronunciation practice), and that they
can look them up in their dictionaries if they really want
to know the meanings.

3 Summary

- Go over the summary with your students, answering
any questions that come up.

Practice Book
- Tell students which exercises you want them to do.

D Love at first sight

1 Which people do you think go with text 1? Which people do you think go with text 2? Write a text for the third couple.

A B C

D E F

1. We've been married for 15 years. We met on holiday in the mountains, and it was love at first sight. We've had a few problems over the years, but we're still happy to be together. We do nearly everything together.

2. We both had terrible first marriages. It made us appreciate each other much more. We've been together for four years now. We don't spend all our time together, but we're happy to share a lot of things.

2 How does -e change the pronunciation?

WITHOUT -e:	fat	cat	am	plan	hat	NOW PRONOUNCE: man same take that
WITH -e:	gate	late	name	plane	hate	make bad lemonade bale safe tap tape
WITHOUT -e:	sit	in	begin	if	swim	NOW PRONOUNCE: fit inside still mile hid
WITH -e:	invite	fine	wine	wife	time	ride tide like pipe strip
WITHOUT -e:	stop	top	not	hot	clock	NOW PRONOUNCE: job stone rose God
WITH -e:	hope	home	note	nose	smoke	joke dome bone on spot coke
WITHOUT -e:	bus	run	pub	sun	just	NOW PRONOUNCE: much fuse cube cub
WITH -e:	excuse	June	tube	rude	use	fuss tune gun fun duke luck
EXCEPTIONS:	some	come	one	have	give	live love

3 Look at the summary on page 155 with your teacher.

Movement and action

A How to get from A to B

1 Travelling. You can often say the same thing in two different ways. Try to complete the table.

ride	= go on horseback
....	= go on foot
drive	= go ....
fly	= ....
cycle	= ....

Other expressions:
hitchhike   go by boat   go by bus
go by train   go by motorbike

2 A man makes a journey across Britain. He uses several different forms of transport. Listen, and say how he is travelling.

3 This is the story of the man's journey. Fill in the missing words.

boat	broke	down	drove	fast	flew
hitchhiking		motorbike	one day		packed
rode	so	so	so	train	walked
when	who	worse			

Paul Lewis lives in the south of England; he has a brother John, ... lives on Barra, a small island near the west coast of Scotland. .... a friend of John's telephoned to say John was very ill, and he wanted Paul with him. Paul .... as .... as he could, caught the next .... to Heathrow Airport, and .... to Glasgow. There he hired a car and .... off to catch the .... for Barra. Unfortunately the car .... three miles from the ferry. Paul tried ...., but he couldn't get a lift, ... he .... to the ferry. .... he landed on Barra the island's one taxi was not there, ... he borrowed a horse and .... to John's house. John was much ...., ... Paul took his brother's .... and went to call the doctor.

4 Talk about a journey that you have made.
Example: *'When I was 16 I cycled from Munich to Cologne.'*

Unit 27: Lesson A

Students learn to talk about various ways of travelling.
Structures: no new structures.
Words and expressions to learn: *ride; fly; hitch-hike; boat; taxi; bus; motorbike; by plane; by boat; journey; one day.*

Language notes and possible problems
Learning vocabulary   This is another 'notional' lesson, in which students learn the vocabulary needed to express concepts relating to travel. The lesson does not contain any structural points or 'functional' work, and it may be necessary to say a word of explanation to students who feel that they are not learning anything useful because they are not 'ticking off' items on a structural or functional syllabus.

Optional extra materials
Cards with situations for optional mime activity.

Presentation
• Use the picture to elicit vocabulary. See if students can tell you some of the nouns and verbs illustrated. Write them on the board.

1 Alternative expressions
• This can be done orally. Students will probably remember the expression *by car*; they may not know *by plane*, or *by bicycle/bike*.
• Explain *hitchhike* (which does not have an associated *go by . . .* expression); point out that the other four expressions under the table do not have exact single-word equivalents.

2 Listening
• Students will hear various sound effects from which they will be able to tell how the man is travelling at each point.
• Stop the recording after each sound effect.
• Students should then say or write *He is driving, He is going by boat,* or whatever.
• It's better to do the exercise with books closed. (Exercise 3 gives a clue to the correct sequence of actions, and could distract students.)

Answers: 1. He's going by train.   2. He's flying.
3. He's driving.   4. He's hitchhiking.   5. He's walking.
6. He's going by boat.   7. He's riding.   8. He's going by motorbike.

3 Text completion
• Before starting, go over the words in the box with the students and make sure they know them all.
• Let them work individually and then compare notes.
• You may like to give the text for dictation either at the end of the lesson or on another occasion – this will help to reinforce the learning.

Answers to Exercise 3
Paul Lewis lives in the south of England; he has a brother John, *who* lives on Barra, a small island near the west coast of Scotland. *One day,* a friend of John's telephoned to say John was very ill, and he wanted Paul with him. Paul *packed* as *fast* as he could, caught the next *train* to Heathrow Airport, and *flew* to Glasgow. There he hired a car and *drove* off to catch the *boat* for Barra. Unfortunately the car *broke down* three miles from the ferry. Paul tried *hitchhiking,* but he couldn't get a lift, so he *walked* to the ferry. *When* he landed on Barra the island's one taxi was not there, *so* he borrowed a horse and *rode* to John's house. John was much *worse,* so Paul took his brother's *motorbike* and went to call the doctor.

4 Personalization
• Get students to say at least two sentences about a journey they have made.
• Make sure they use the Simple Past tense, as in the example.

Optional activity   Mime
• This is a useful way of practising the difference between *at/in* and *to* (which is a problem for some students).
• Write the following situations on the board:

going to a wedding	at a wedding
going to an English lesson	at an English lesson
going to church	in church
going home after a party	at home
going to a football match	at a football match
going to a funeral	at a funeral
going to the moon	on the moon
going to hospital	in hospital
going to a restaurant	in a restaurant

• Write each situation on a separate card or piece of paper. Keep the *to*-cards and the *at/in*-cards separate.
• Put students in groups of four or so.
• Get each group to draw one *to*-card and one *at/in*-card.
• They have to mime the situation on their two cards. The others try to guess which of the expressions they have on their card.

Practice Book
• Tell students which exercises you want them to do.

Unit 27: Lesson B

Students learn to talk about speed.
Structures: superlatives; ... *kilometres an hour*.
Words and expressions to learn: *lightning*; *like lightning*; *race*; *speed*; *guess*; *record*; *second*; *breathe*.
Phonology: decoding fast speech.

Language note
Speeds are given here in *kilometres an hour*, abbreviated as *kph*. An alternative abbreviation is *km/h*. You may prefer to use *miles an hour (mph)* with students in Britain.

1 Matching
● Don't spend too much time on this – it is simply an introduction to the next exercise, and can be done by class discussion.
● Students should learn *race* and *lightning*; they don't need to learn the other words unless they are particularly interested.

2 Relative speeds
● Discuss with the class which is the next fastest and the slowest.
● Then ask them to continue the discussion in groups.
● They will need to use comparatives (*faster/slower than*), the structure *next fastest*, and expressions of agreement/disagreement. Put these on the board.

The correct order is:
lightning, a racing pigeon, a cheetah, a racehorse, a rhinoceros, a salmon, a sprinter, a wasp, a snail, a glacier.

3 Guessing speeds
● Ask students to write one or two sentences.
● Then do the whole exercise by class discussion.
● Note that *mmph* = 'millimetres per hour'.

Answers
A racing pigeon flies at up to 176kph (110mph).
A cheetah runs at up to 100kph (63mph).
A racehorse gallops at up to 68kph (43mph).
A rhinoceros runs at up to 56kph (35mph).
A salmon swims at up to 36.8kph (23mph).
A sprinter runs at up to 36kph (22.5mph) over 100 metres.
A wasp flies at up to 19.2kph (12mph).
A snail crawls at up to 50 metres per hour.
Most glaciers move at a few millimetres per hour.

4 Personalization
● It might be interesting to find out one or two facts by experiment.
● For instance, ask students to take their pulse rate, and tell you how many beats a minute they have measured (*My pulse rate is ... beats a minute*). Do the same with breathing (how many breaths a minute?) See what the effect is on the pulse and breathing rate of jumping up and down for a minute, or smoking a cigarette.
● Reading speed in English can be measured by giving students a text from an earlier lesson. Ask them to read, without skipping, for 60 seconds, and then count the words they have read.

5 Listening for information
● Tell students that they will hear a good deal of information. Their job is to pick out just the facts that they need in order to fill in the table.
● Before starting, make sure they understand expressions like 'thirty-six point three' (36.3). Note that in some languages a comma is used where English uses a decimal point.
● You will probably want to play the recording two or three times before letting students compare notes and going over the answers with them.
● They must not worry about the fact that they do not understand everything. Discourage them from asking detailed questions about the whole of the recording – this is not a very profitable activity.
Tapescript for Exercise 5: see page 181

Answers to Exercise 5

EVENT	TIME	SPEED
Men's 100m	*10.00secs*	*36kph*
Women's marathon	*2hrs 38mins 3secs*	*16kph*
Women's 100m swimming (freestyle)	*51.4secs*	*7kph*
Downhill Alpine skiing	*74.6secs*	*96.3kph*

6 Listening to fast speech
● You will probably need to play each sentence two or three times.
● The first time, ask students to note what they think the second word is.
● Then play the sentence again and see if students can write all the words.
● Play it once more if necessary, discuss the answer and go on to the next sentence.
● Finally, get students to say the sentences – more slowly and clearly than on the recording, but with the same rhythm.

Tapescript for Exercise 6
1. What are you doing?
2. What's she eating?
3. Where are they going?
4. What did she say?
5. How do you know?
6. Why are you drinking my tea?
7. When do you want to come?
8. What time are you going to work tomorrow?
9. Who did you see yesterday?
10. What are you doing this evening?

Practice Book
● Tell students which exercises you want them to do.

B Like lightning

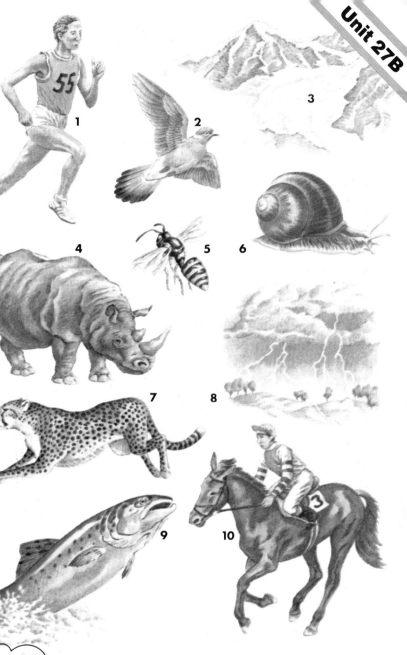

1 Match the words and the pictures.

a cheetah   a glacier
lightning   a racehorse
a racing pigeon   a rhinoceros
a salmon   a sprinter
a wasp   a snail

2 Lightning is the fastest of the things in the pictures. Which do you think is the next fastest? Which do you think is the slowest? Put them in order of speed.

3 Match the nouns and verbs, and guess the speeds. Example:

Lightning travels at 140,000 kilometres a second.

A cheetah   A glacier
Lightning   A racehorse
A rhinoceros
A salmon   A racing pigeon
A wasp   A sprinter
A snail

flies   gallops   runs
moves   crawls
swims   travels

at

50 metres per hour.   176kph.
36kph.   19kph.   56kph.
3mm per hour.   100kph.
36kph.   68kph.   140,000kps.

4 How fast do you think you walk, run, cycle, drive, read, breathe, . . . ?

5 Listening for information. Copy the table. Listen to today's results from the Fantasian National Games, and note the times and speeds.

EVENT	TIME	SPEED
Men's 100m		
Women's marathon		
Women's 100m swimming (freestyle)		
Downhill Alpine skiing		

6 Listening to fast speech. What is the second word in each sentence? (Contractions like *what's* count as two words.)

111

C If you press button A,...

1 *Get* has several different meanings. Put these sentences in groups, according to the meaning of *get*.

What time do you usually get up?
It's getting late.
My English is getting better.
Where can I get some cigarettes?
John got into his car and drove away.

It takes me an hour to get to work.
I get a letter from my mother every week.
The housing problem is getting worse.
If you go to the shops, can you get me some bread, please?
You've got beautiful eyes.

2 How does the machine work?

If you

press push
pull
turn

button
lever
handle

A B
 D F
C E

you get

a cup of coffee.
a packet of cigarettes.
a flower.
music. a surprise.
an electric shock.

3 Where did you get...? Ask and answer.
Examples:

'Where did you get your shoes?' 'In Tokyo.'
'Where did you get your dictionary?' 'At the University Bookshop.'
'Where did you get that watch?' 'From my father.'

4 Put in *on, off, into, out of, up.*

1. What time did you get .... this morning?
2. She got .... her car and drove away.
3. I got .... my car and walked up to the front door.
4. 'Why are you late?' 'I got .... the wrong bus.'
5. We have to get .... at the next stop.

5 Put in suitable adjectives.

1. If you don't eat, you get ....
2. If you eat too much, you get ....
3. If you don't drink, you get ....
4. If you drink too much alcohol, you get ....
5. If you run a long way, you get ....
6. If you go out in the rain without an umbrella, you get ....
7. If you go out in the snow without a coat, you get ....
8. In the evening, when the sun goes down, it gets ....
9. We are all getting ....

Unit 27: Lesson C

Students learn to distinguish the different meanings of *get*.
Structures: *get* + direct object; *get* + adverb particle or preposition; *get* + adjective; simple structures with *if*.
Words and expressions to learn: *press; pull; push; turn; button; handle; packet; flower; electric; get on; get off; get into; get out of; thin.*

Language notes and possible problems

1. Get   Students have met three main uses of *get*:

A. *Get* + direct object (e.g. *Where can I get some cigarettes?*). The meaning here is *obtain, receive, fetch, buy* or something similar, depending on the context.

B. *Get* + adverb particle or preposition (e.g. *I get up at six*; *He got off the bus at the next stop*). In this case, the meaning generally involves some kind of movement – the exact meaning depends on the particular expression.

C. *Get* + adjective (e.g. *I'm getting old*; *My English is getting better*). Here *get* means *become*, and is used to refer to changes.

Note also the use of *got* (with no separate meaning) as part of the verb *have*, especially in spoken English (e.g. *I've got two children*).

2. Get and go   Students may confuse these two verbs from time to time. This is partly because of the second meaning of *get* mentioned above, which is quite close to that of *go* (compare *I go to work every day*; *I get to work at eight o'clock*). It is also unfortunate that *got* looks more like the past of *go* than *went* does.

1 Deducing the rules

● Explain what you want students to do (starting the exercise on the board if necessary).
● Give them five or ten minutes to do the exercise and compare notes.
● They will probably not manage to sort out the sentences into exactly the right categories, but they will get some way towards understanding the point.
● Go over the answers. Note that in some cases students' answers may be quite valid even if they are different from those given below (for instance, they may put *get some cigarettes* and *get a letter* into different groups because *get* means *buy* in one case and *receive* in the other).
● Show how the meaning depends on the structure.

Answers to Exercise 1
Get + *direct object* (= 'receive', 'obtain')
Where can I get some cigarettes?
I get a letter from my mother every week.
If you go to the shops, can you get me some bread, please?

Get + *adverb particle/preposition* (= 'move')
What time do you usually get up?
John got into his car...
It takes me an hour to get to work.

Get + *adjective* (= 'become')
It's getting late.
My English is getting better.
The housing problem is getting worse.

Have got
You've got beautiful eyes.

2 *Get* + direct object (the machine)

● Look at the balloons and explain the new vocabulary (or see if students can tell you what the words mean).
● Ask volunteers to make sentences about the machine.
● When all the controls have been discussed, consolidate by asking everybody to write two sentences.
● Look around the classroom with the students. How many buttons, levers and handles can they find?
● Go out and look at a car if possible – find some more buttons, levers and handles.

Optional activity

● Ask students to work in groups of three or four and design new machines, with instructions beginning *If you pull/push/etc...*
● When they are ready, they explain to other groups, or to the whole class, how their machines work.

3 *Get* + direct object (possessions)

● Get students to ask each other about their possessions.
● If you wish, the exercise can be extended in several directions:
1. Revise *How long have you had it?*
2. Teach the names of more kinds of shop.
3. Teach the names of some more possessions.

4 *Get* + adverb particle/preposition

● Note the difference between *get in(to)/out (of)* (used with cars, vans, lorries etc.), and *get on/off* (used mainly with public transport – buses, trains etc.).

5 *Get* + adjective

● This is a straightforward revision exercise, which gives further incidental practice in simple *if*-structures.

Practice Book

● Tell students which exercises you want them to do.

Unit 27: Lesson D

Students learn to say more about the ways in which things are done.

Structures: formation, use and position of adverbs of manner; distinction between adjectives and adverbs.

Words and expressions to learn: *sleepy; sleepily; happily; kindly; angrily; loudly; quietly; coldly; shyly; noisily; badly; nicely; comfortably.*

Language notes and possible problems

Adverbs Not all languages distinguish 'adverbs' and 'adjectives' as separate grammatical categories. And in some European languages, adverbs of manner often have the same form as the corresponding adjectives. So many students have difficulty in using adverbs correctly in English, or in distinguishing them from adjectives.

In this lesson, students concentrate on adverbs of manner. Most of the ones practised end in *-ly*. Note, however, that *fast* is both adjective and adverb, and one or two words ending in *-ly* (e.g. *lovely*, *friendly*) are adjectives. *Loud* can often be used as an adverb, but *loudly* is used in this lesson to avoid confusion.

Position and spelling of adverbs can cause problems. For rules, see below in the notes on the exercises.

Optional extra materials

Verb and adverb cue-cards (Exercise 4).

1 Listening and matching

- Run over the list of adverbs with the students and make sure of meaning and pronunciation. (The ending *-ily* is usually pronounced /əli/).
- Tell the students to write the numbers 1–5.
- Play the first sentence. Ask students to write down an adverb that describes how it is spoken.
- Note that they are not asked to *understand* the sentence, only to interpret the tone of the voice.
- When students have agreed on the adverb, play the other sentences, with pauses for writing.
- Play the sentences a second time.
- Let students compare notes; go over the answers.

Tapescript and answers to Exercise 1
1. If you touch my records again there's going to be trouble. *(angrily)*
2. Good morning. Are there any letters for me? *(sleepily)*
3. I'm sorry. I can't help you. *(coldly)*
4. What a lovely surprise! Flowers – that *is* nice. *(happily)*
5. All right, Mary, just wait there for a minute and I'll see what I can do for you. *(kindly)*

2 Extension

- This exercise is similar to Exercise 1, except that students have to supply the adverbs themselves.
- The words required (*fast, slowly, loudly, quietly, unhappily*) are already known, or correspond to adjectives which are already known.
- Again, students do not need to understand everything they hear.

Tapescript and answers to Exercise 2
1. The trouble with this government is that they think they know what's happening. *(fast)*

2. 'Can you understand what I'm saying?' 'Please speak more slowly.' *(slowly)*
3. Can you hear me all right? *(loudly)*
4. There's no need to shout. I'm not deaf. *(quietly)*
5. Oh, dear. It's terrible. He doesn't love me any more. *(unhappily)*

3 Practice

- Write the complete list of adverbs from Exercises 1 and 2 on the board.
- Practise the pronunciation.
- Ask students to try saying *Hello* in all ten ways.
- Give them a minute or two to work in pairs preparing a short conversation (one sentence each is enough).
- Listen to the conversations; see if the class can identify the adverbs.

4 Miming

- If you wish, you can prepare cue-cards and ask students to take a verb-card and an adverb-card to see what they have to do.
- They should be told to reject absurd combinations (e.g. sleep kindly) and take new cards.
- The exercise can also be done in groups.

5 Adjective or adverb?

- It should be clear to students from the previous exercises that adverbs are used after most verbs, to say how things are done. They already know how adjectives are used, so this exercise should present little difficulty.
- Sentence 6 contains an example of a different structure: the use of an adverb to emphasize an adjective. You may wish to comment on this.
- The last two sentences illustrate the relationship between the adjective *good* and the adverb *well*, and show how adjectives and adverbs go in different positions.

6 Position of adverbs

- This exercise discourages the common mistake of putting an adverb between the verb and the direct object (e.g. *I like very much skiing*; *She speaks very well English*).
- More than one answer is sometimes possible, but it's best just to teach students to put the adverb after the object at this stage.
- Ask students how well they speak English (and other languages if appropriate) to get one or two personal examples.

7 Spelling

- Help students to work out the rules for the formation of adverbs in *-ly*. They are:
1. Add *-ly* to the adjective.
2. Don't drop *-e* (*extremely*, not *extremly*).
3. Change *y* to *i* (*happily*). Exception: *shyly*.
4. If the adjective ends in *-ble* the adverb ends in *-bly* (*comfortably*).

8 Summary

- Go over the summary with the students.

Practice Book

- Tell students which exercises you want them to do.

D Please speak more slowly

1 How are the people speaking? Listen to the recording, and choose one adverb for each sentence.

coldly	
sleepily	kindly
happily	angrily

2 Now listen to the next five sentences, and find more adverbs to say how the people are speaking.

3 Now practise speaking in all ten ways. Then work with a partner and make up a short conversation. Speak coldly, or angrily, or fast, . . . ; the other students must say how you are speaking.

4 Choose a verb and an adverb, and demonstrate or mime the action (for example: *walk happily; drink slowly*). The other students must say what you are doing, and how you are doing it.

> write   eat   drink   walk
> sing   speak   run   drive
> fly   sleep   cook   dance
> swim   smoke   type   wash
> play (the guitar/piano/etc.)

> fast   slowly   loudly   quietly
> happily   unhappily   angrily
> sleepily   coldly   kindly
> shyly   noisily   badly

> You're walking happily.

5 Adjective or adverb?

1. I'm very .... with you. (angry/angrily)
2. She spoke to me .... (angry/angrily)
3. I don't think your mother drives very .... (good/well)
4. You've got a .... face. (nice/nicely)
5. I play the guitar very .... (bad/badly)
6. It's .... cold. (terrible/terribly)
7. Your father's got a very .... voice. (loud/loudly)
8. Why are you looking at me ....? (cold/coldly)
9. You speak very .... English. (good/well)
10. You speak English very .... (good/well)

6 Put the adverb in the right place.

1. He read the letter without speaking. (slowly)
   He read the letter slowly without speaking.
2. She speaks French. (badly)
3. I like dancing. (very much)
4. Please write your name. (clearly)
5. You should eat your food. (slowly)
6. She read his letter. (carefully)
7. I said 'Hello' and walked away. (coldly)

7 Spelling. Look carefully at these adverbs.

| badly | quietly | nicely | completely |
| angrily | happily | carefully | comfortably |

Now make adverbs from these adjectives.

| warm | great | extreme | sincere |
| hungry | lazy | real | terrible |

8 Look at the summary on page 155 with your teacher.

Parts

GCE: General Certificate of Education.
There are two parts:
O Level (Ordinary Level), taken at age 16.
A Level (Advanced Level), taken at age 18.

A Education

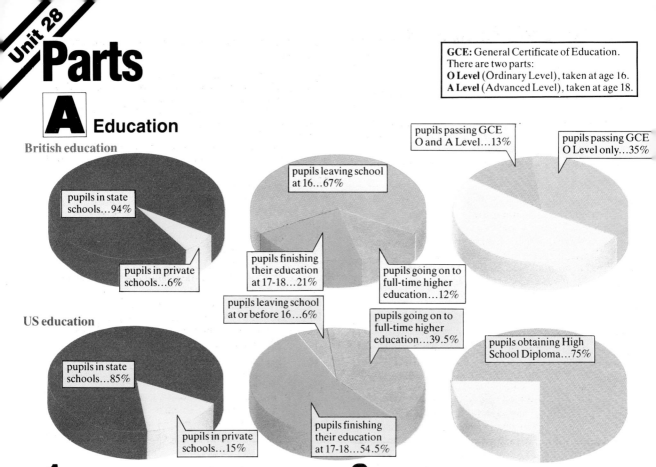

British education

pupils in state schools...94%

pupils in private schools...6%

pupils leaving school at 16...67%

pupils passing GCE O and A Level...13%

pupils passing GCE O Level only...35%

pupils finishing their education at 17-18...21%

pupils going on to full-time higher education...12%

pupils leaving school at or before 16...6%

pupils going on to full-time higher education...39.5%

US education

pupils in state schools...85%

pupils in private schools...15%

pupils finishing their education at 17-18...54.5%

pupils obtaining High School Diploma...75%

1 Look at the statistics. Then complete the following sentences with some of these words and expressions.

very few	not many	some	two thirds
three quarters	nearly all	more	
far more	nearly	less than	

1. .... British pupils go to private schools.
2. .... British pupils go to state schools.
3. .... American than British pupils go to private schools.
4. About .... of British pupils leave school at 16.
5. .... American pupils leave school at 16.
6. .... 40% of American pupils go on to full-time higher education.
7. .... 15% of British pupils go on to full-time higher education.
8. .... of American pupils obtain the High School Diploma.
9. .... British pupils pass GCE A Level.
10. .... American than British pupils go on to full-time higher education.

2 Listen to the six recorded sentences and say whether they are true or false.

3 Say something about the educational system in your country. Is it different from the British and American systems?

4 Now listen to some sentences about you and the other students.
If you think they are true, write 'true'; if not, write 'false'.
If you are not sure, write 'probably' or 'probably not'.
If you have no idea, write 'don't know'.
Examples:

1. 'You all speak some English.' *True*

2. 'Most of you smoke.' *False*

3. 'Nearly all of you are over 18.' *Don't know.*

5 Ask questions to find out the truth about the statements in Exercise 4.
Tell the other students what you have found out, or make a statistical diagram and show it to the other students.

Unit 28: Lesson A

Students learn some facts about the British and American education systems, while revising ways of expressing quantity.
Structures: quantifying expressions; construction of fractions.
Words and expressions to learn: *far more; most; less; nearly; two thirds; three quarters; private school; state school; at 16; true; country.*

Presentation

- You will want to spend some time allowing the students to look at the statistics.
- Give whatever explanations are necessary.
- Students may like to have some more information about British and American examinations.

1. British examinations (England and Wales)

A (Advanced) Level This exam is usually taken at about age 18. Pupils do one or more subjects – usually three. (There is a wide range of choice.) To get into a university it is generally necessary to have two A Levels (with reasonable grades) and five O Levels. The figure given here for pupils 'passing' is for those who have two or more subjects at A level.

O (Ordinary) Level This exam is usually taken at about age 16. There is a wide range of choice, and pupils do not have to take a fixed number of subjects. In order to have a useful qualification, it is usually considered necessary to have five or more subjects at O Level, preferably including English language. The figure given here for pupils 'passing' is for those who pass in any subject at all. About 12% of pupils leave school with five or more O Levels.

CSE (Certificate of Secondary Education)
This is a lower-level examination which can be taken at around the age of 16. The highest grade in CSE is regarded as equivalent to a GCE pass. About 15% of British pupils leave school with no passes in any of these examinations.

2. The American High School Diploma
This is given to pupils who complete their course with satisfactory *credits* (marks given for attendance) and *grades* (marks given for quality of work). Most pupils study 4–5 subjects, including a major and a minor speciality. There is a very wide range of choice.

It is more difficult to get into a university in Britain than in the United States. This is because there are fewer university places in Britain.

1 Quantifiers and fractions

- Look through the list of quantifying expressions. Students already know most of them.
- Show them how to make fractions in English.
- The exercise can be done orally in groups, or as a whole-class exercise with students discussing which is the best answer.

2 Listening comprehension

- Tell students to write the numbers 1–6.
- Play the sentences (or read them at normal speed) more than once if necessary, pausing after each sentence for students to write *true* or *false*.

- Let students compare notes, and go over the answers with them.

Tapescript and answers to Exercise 2
1. Nearly half of American pupils go to private schools. (False)
2. Most British pupils stay at school until 18. (False)
3. Most American pupils stay at school until 17 or 18. (True)
4. Over a third of American pupils go on to full-time higher education. (True)
5. More British pupils pass O Level than A Level. (True)
6. Very few American pupils get the High School Diploma. (False)

3 Personalization

- Obviously students will not be able to say a great deal about their country's educational system with their limited English.
- However, they will be able to use the language they have learnt to say something, and most students ought to be able to manage two or three sentences.
- Encourage them to use the quantifying expressions from Exercise 1.
- In multinational groups, students will probably be anxious to tell each other about what happens in their countries. In single-nationality groups, there is less motivation for talking about the educational system (since nobody will learn anything new from the discussion), and the exercise may not last so long.

4 Listening: statements about the students

- Tell students to write the numbers 1–15.
- They will hear some statements about themselves.
- They should write *true, false, probably, probably not* or *don't know.*

Tapescript for Exercise 4
1. You all speak some English.
2. Most of you smoke.
3. Nearly all of you are over eighteen.
4. Some of you are beautiful.
5. More than half of you believe in a god.
6. Three quarters of you like dogs.
7. About a third of you drink too much.
8. Very few of you are wearing jeans.
9. Most of you wear glasses.
10. All of you can understand this sentence.
11. Two thirds of you live in flats.
12. Most of you have one or more brothers and sisters.
13. Nearly all of you watch TV every day.
14. 50% of you are women.
15. None of you can speak Russian.

5 Survey

- Ask students to work out three questions each, to find out the truth about three of the points raised in Exercise 4. (You may need to play the recording again to remind students what the statements were.)
- Let them do a walk-round, asking everybody their questions (e.g. *Do you believe in a god? Do you live in a flat?*)
- When students have obtained all the information they need they should write appropriate sentences (e.g. *Nearly everybody believes in a god* or *A third of the students live in flats*).
- Get them to read out their sentences.

Practice Book

- Tell students which exercises you want them to do.

Unit 28: Lesson B

Students learn to talk about some basic shapes, about the parts of things, and about position.
Structures: *at the top*, *bottom* etc.
Words and expressions to learn: *top*; *bottom*; *front*; *back*; *corner*; *middle*; *circle*; *cross*; *triangle*; *square*; *inside*; *outside*; *map*.

Language notes and possible problems

Prepositions   Later on, students will have to learn the difference between *at the bottom* and *on the bottom*, *at the top of* and *on top of*, etc. For the moment, just teach the expressions with *at*; leave the others unless you actually need to bring them in to correct a mistake.

1 Mystery pictures

● Let students do the exercise in groups. See if any group can identify all the pictures.
● Supply vocabulary if needed.

The objects are:
1. the front of an aeroplane
2. the bottom of a car
3. the back of a TV
4. the side of a calculator
5. the top of an umbrella
6. the corner of a chess board

2 *At the top* etc.

● Practise the pronunciation of the expressions.
● Note the weak pronunciation of *at* (/ət/).
● Note also the vowel in *front* (/frʌnt/).
● Do the exercise orally, but ask students to write one or two of the sentences.
● When they have finished, students may be able to think up some examples of their own (e.g. the buttons on a coat; the teacher in a classroom; the ice cubes in a fridge; the engine in an old-style Volkswagen).

3 Guided writing/speaking

● Look at the first text with the students.
● Practise the pronunciation of the new words.
● Get them to write or say the second description.
● Go on to try the third description.

4 Listening

● Tell students to listen to the description and to try to draw what they hear.
● Say the description or play the recording (with pauses).

Tapescript
There's a big circle.
Inside the circle there are four small circles: one at the top, one at the bottom, one on the left and one on the right.
There's a cross in the middle of the big circle, and a small square outside on the right.

5 Students' pictures

● Students have probably got tired of squares and triangles by this time.
● Tell them to draw simple pictures of anything they like and describe them to the others in their groups, using *at the top*, *at the side* etc.
● The others (who are not allowed to look at the pictures) try to draw them.
● When they have finished they compare their versions with the original.

Practice Book

● Tell students which exercises you want them to do.

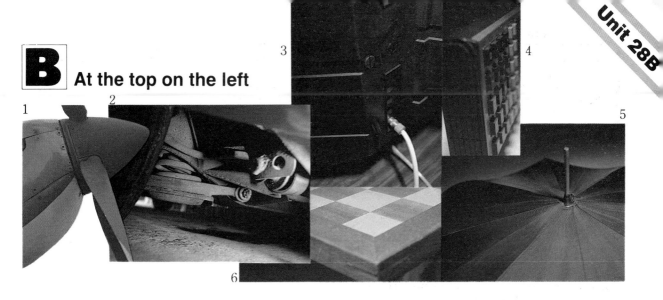

B At the top on the left

1   2   3   4   5   6

1 What can you see in the pictures? Write sentences.

Picture 1 is
Picture 2 is
Picture 3 is
Picture 4 is
Picture 5 is
Picture 6 is

the top of ....
the side of ....
the front of ....
the back of ....
the bottom of ....
the corner of ....

2 Use *at the top/bottom/front/back/side(s)* in your answers to these questions.

1. Where is 6 on a clock face? Where is 12?
2. Where are the doors of a car? Of a house?
3. Where is north on a map? Where is south?
4. Where is the engine of a train?
5. Where does a bus driver sit?
6. Where is the garage of a house, usually?
7. Where are your ears?
8. Where is the index in a book?
9. Where are the stars on an American flag?

3 Read the description of the first picture; complete the description of the second picture; and write the third description yourself.

There's a big circle. Inside the circle at the top there's a small triangle. On the right at the side there are two small circles. On the left at the side there's a dot, and there's another dot at the bottom. In the middle there's a small square.

There's a big ....
.... the triangle at the
.... there's a ....
.... On the .... at the
.... there are three
............; .... the
.... the ....
there are four .... Outside
the triangle on the ....
....
circle, and there's a small
.... near the bottom
left-hand ....

4 Listen to the recording and draw the picture.

5 Draw a picture. Describe it to another student and see if he/she can draw it.

C The beginning of the end

1 At the beginning; in the middle; at the end.

A is at the beginning of the alphabet; M is in the middle of the
alphabet; W is near the end of the alphabet. Where is C?
Where is K? Where is Z?

Where is Unit 1 in this course? Unit 16? Unit 27? Unit 32?

When is June? June 15th? Three a.m.? Three p.m.? Monday?

When do people usually have soup?

When do you buy a train ticket?

When do you clap in a theatre?

When do the lights go out in a cinema?

When is a person's funeral?

2 Listen to the sounds and answer the questions.

1. When was the music loud? When was it quiet? When did somebody say 'Hello'?
2. Describe what you heard.
3. When did the telephone ring? When did somebody say 'Hello'? What else did you hear? When?
4. When did you hear the baby? When did somebody say 'Hello'? When did somebody say 'Goodbye'?
5. When did you hear the wind? the motorbike? the water? the door? What did you hear in the middle?
   Did the train come before or after the clock?
6. Describe what you heard. About how long did it last?

3 Pronunciation. How many words? Listen to each sentence, and write the number of words you hear.

4 Where does the stress come in these words? Where does the sound /ə/ come?

machine   about   usually
mother   photograph   alphabet
pronunciation   China   Japan
remember   cinema   America

'In the beginning was the Word.'   The Bible

'In my beginning is my end.'   T.S. Eliot

'This is the beginning of the end.'   Talleyrand, 1812

'This is not the end. It is not even the
beginning of the end. But it is, perhaps,
the end of the beginning.'   Churchill, 1942

'Where shall I begin, please,
Your Majesty?' he asked.
'Begin at the beginning,' the
King said, gravely, 'and go on
till you come to the end.
Then stop.'   Carroll, *Alice in Wonderland*

'I like a film to have a beginning, a middle and an end, but not necessarily in that order.'

Jean-Luc Godard

Unit 28: Lesson C

Students learn to talk about the structuring of time sequences.
Structures: prepositions *in*, *at* referring to time-divisions.
Words and expressions to learn: *beginning*; *at the beginning*; *end*; *at the end*; *soup*; *theatre*; *go out* (lights); *what else?*; *ring* (verb).
Phonology: identifying unstressed words; word-stress and /ə/; /ɪ/.

Language notes and possible problems

1. Prepositions *At the beginning/end* and *in the middle* are taught here. Other prepositions are possible in all three cases (with slight differences of meaning); students will learn these later.

2. Pronunciation It may be worth paying attention to the pronunciation of /ɪ/ in *in the middle* and *beginning* (/bɪ'gɪnɪŋ/).
Note the linking in *the end* (almost with a *y* between the two words).

Optional extra material
Divided sentences (see Optional activity).

1 *At the beginning* etc.
● This can be done orally; you will need to explain one or two words.
● You may like to take the opportunity to revise the alphabet, days of the week and months.
● Teach *in the first half* and *in the second half* (e.g. *H is in the first half of the alphabet*).

2 Sound sequences
● This can give very rich and varied language practice, depending on the class's precise needs.
● Apart from using *at the beginning* etc., students can say that one sound was *before* or *after* another; they can express degrees of certainty (*I think*, *I'm sure* etc.); they can say that a sound *got louder*, that it lasted *for* such-and-such a time, and so on.
● See how much you can elicit while working on each sequence.
● Further practice based on sound sequences is provided by *Sounds Interesting* and *Sounds Intriguing*, by Alan Maley and Alan Duff (Cambridge University Press).

3 Perceiving unstressed syllables
● Play each sentence, and ask students to write down the number of words they hear.
● Ask for their answers.
● If there is disagreement, play it again.
● When most students have heard exactly what is there, get them to say the sentence and then go on to the next one.

Tapescript for Exercise 3
What did you say?
What can I give you?
Where did you get your sweater?
When are you going to America?

What was the answer to your question?
How did you get here?
Who did you talk to on the phone?
Who was the girl I saw you with yesterday?
There was a dog in the kitchen.

4 Stress and /ə/
● Students should already have learnt that /ə/ only comes in unstressed syllables.
● Ask them to decide where the stresses are.
● Then play the recording, or say the words, and let students change their answers if they wish.
● Ask where /ə/ comes and discuss the answers.

The pronunciations:
/mə'ʃi:n/
/ə'baʊt/
/'ju:ʒəli/
/'mʌðə(r)/
/'fəʊtəgrɑ:f/
/'ælfəbet/
/prənʌnsi'eɪʃən/
/'tʃaɪnə/
/dʒə'pæn/
/rɪ'membə(r)/
/'sɪnəmə/
/ə'merɪkə/

Optional activity Sentence beginnings and ends
● Copy out the following sentence beginnings and ends.
● Give one to each student.
● Tell students to walk round saying their fragments to everybody, trying to find their 'other half'.

Would you like
something to drink?
I've known Mary
for eight years.
I was thirsty
so I had a beer.
I can do anything
better than you.
Why don't we
go and see a film?
I live in
a small flat near the station.
What time
are you getting up tomorrow?
I always come here
on Sunday mornings.
I had a wonderful time
when I was on holiday.

Note that there is sometimes more than one possibility.

The quotations
● These are included merely for interest. There is no task associated with them.

Practice Book
● Tell students which exercises you want them to do.

116

Unit 28: Lesson D

Students begin to learn ways of structuring narrative; they learn more things to say about daily routines.
Structures: organization of narrative paragraphs; use of structuring adverbs and conjunctions.
Words and expressions to learn: *shave; wash; get dressed; brush* (hair, teeth); *zoo; policeman; put on; take off.*

Optional extra materials
Copy of penguin story (Exercise 4) cut up into separate strips.

1 Picture sequence
• This is best done by students working in small groups.
• Encourage students to use the expressions in the exercise instruction (*comes first, is next*, etc.).
• Put these on the board, along with:

I'm sure	*I'm fairly sure*	
I think	*I don't think*	
Perhaps	*probably*	*certainly*
I agree/don't agree	*You're right/wrong*	

• A correct sequence is E, C, F, H, B, A, D, I, G. (But variations are acceptable in the middle.)

2 Structuring words and expressions
• Get students to do this individually.
• Then let them compare notes, and go over possible answers.
• *After that, then* and *next* are virtually interchangeable in this text. Students should use each of them once, but it doesn't matter very much what order they put them in.
• Take the opportunity to see whether students want to learn other vocabulary in the area of 'daily routines'.
• Teach *put on* and *take off* (clothes).

3 Watching a series of actions
• You may already have done this exercise (see Teacher's Book Lesson 23C, page 96, Optional activity).
• This time it is used as the input for a structured writing exercise.
• Tell the class to watch exactly what you do.
• Do a series of simple actions which the students can describe with the words and expressions they already know.
• For example: walk to the door; sit down; stand up again; pick up somebody's pen; give it to another student; jump up and down; sing a few notes; push a table...
• Try to include a few unusual actions (like standing on a chair, or putting your bag on your head) if you feel able to; this will encourage the students to be inventive when their turn comes.
• When you have finished, ask them to recall what you did, as far as possible in the correct order. (Make sure you can remember yourself!)

• When they have done this orally, tell them to write about what you did, using the words and expressions they have already practised (first, then, next, etc.).
• Go round helping and making corrections where necessary.
• Finally, get the students to try the exercise in groups (orally only), with each one in turn doing a series of actions for the others to remember.

Alternatives to Exercise 3
1. Instead of watching a series of actions, students close their eyes and *listen* to what happens; they then say what they heard.
2. If the classroom is over a busy street (or if there are plenty of noises to be heard around the place), get students to listen in complete silence for a couple of minutes, and then to see and/or write what they heard.

4 Mixed-up story
• Before the lesson, prepare a copy of the story cut into separate strips. (Be careful to copy punctuation and capitalization exactly.)
• Give out papers, one to each student.
• Tell them to learn their sections by heart.
• Explain any difficulties; help with pronunciation if necessary.
• Get students to say their sections and work out the correct order. (17, 4, 13, 16, 9, 2, 8, 14, 12, 6, 1, 15, 10, 5, 3, 7, 11.)
• If possible, they should do this without your help (for instance, sitting in a circle, with one of them perhaps acting as secretary and noting down the order as they discover it; they can change places so as to sit in the same order as the sections).
• Finally, get the class to tell the story in the right order without stopping.

5 Summary
• Go over the summary with the students.

Practice Book
• Tell students which exercises you want them to do.

D What happened next?

1 Here is a story called *The Medical Book*.
Put the pictures in the right order.
Which picture comes first?
Which one is next?
Which one comes after that?...
Which one is last?

2 Read the text, and put in the following words and expressions.

next	first	after that	then	finally

GETTING UP
.... I get out of bed, go to the toilet, and wash and shave. .... I get dressed and brush my hair. .... I go downstairs and pick up the post and the newspaper. .... I have a long slow breakfast while I read my letters and the paper. .... I brush my teeth, put on my coat and leave for work.

3 Watch the actions, and then write down what happened. Try to use some of these words and expressions.

first	then	next	after that	finally

4 Put the parts of the story in order.

1. 'Didn't I tell you
2. 'Take it to the zoo,'
3. said the man,
4. a man was walking in the park
5. 'I did,'
6. He still had the penguin.
7. 'and he liked it very much.'
8. answered the policeman.
9. and asked what to do.
10. he asked.
11. 'Now I'm taking him to the cinema.'
12. the policeman saw the man again.
13. when he met a penguin.
14. Next day
15. to take that penguin to the zoo?'
16. So he took it to a policeman
17. One day

5 Look at the summary on page 156 with your teacher.

117

Predictions

A Are you sure you'll be all right?

1 Study and practise the dialogue.

A: I'm going to hitchhike round the world.
B: Oh, that's very dangerous.
A: No, it isn't. I'll be all right.
B: Where will you sleep?
A: Oh, I don't know. In youth hostels. Cheap hotels.
B: You'll get lost.
A: No, I won't.
B: You won't get lifts.
A: Yes, I will.
B: What will you do for money?
A: I'll take money with me.
B: You haven't got enough.
A: I'll find jobs.
B: Well, ... are you sure you'll be all right?
A: Of course I'll be all right.

2 Complete these dialogues.

A: I'm .... be a racing driver.
B: Oh, that's ....
A: No, it ....
B: You'll crash. .... get killed.
A: No, ...
B: You .... find a job.
A: Yes, ... I'm a good driver.
B: Are you sure ....?
A: Of course ....

◇

A: .... a doctor.
B: .... have to study for seven years.
A: Yes, I know. I don't mind.
B: .... finish.
A: Yes, I ....
B: .... have a really hard life.
A: Yes, but it'............ interesting.
B: .... have to work very long hours.
A: I know. But I'............ enjoy it.
B: OK. If that's what you want.
A: It is.

3 Write and pronounce the contractions.

I will *I'll*
you will
he will
she will
it will
we will
they will
I will not *I won't*
you will not
it will not

4 Work with another student. Make up a short conversation beginning:

A: *'I'm going to get married.'*
or A: *'I'm going to work in a circus.'*
or A: *'I'm going to be a teacher.'*
or A: *'I'm going to ski down Everest.'*
or A: *'I'm going to be a pilot.'*

5 Listen. Which sentence do you hear?

1. I stop work at six.
   I'll stop work at six.
2. You know the answer.
   You'll know the answer.
3. I have coffee for breakfast.
   I'll have coffee for breakfast.
4. You have to change at Coventry.
   You'll have to change at Coventry.
5. I drive carefully.
   I'll drive carefully.
6. I know you like my brother.
   I know you'll like my brother.

6 Where will you be this time tomorrow? What will you be doing? Example:

'I'll be at home. I'll be watching TV.'

118

Unit 29: Lesson A

Students practise predicting, warning, and raising and countering objections.
Structures: *will* + infinitive without *to* (affirmative and negative full and contracted forms; short answers); *get lost/killed/married*.
Words and expressions to learn: *round* (preposition); *dangerous*; *youth hostel*; *get lost*; *get married*; *pilot*; *won't*; *enjoy*.
Phonology: pronunciation of *w*; *'ll*; *won't*.

Language notes and possible problems

1. Will and shall *Will* is taught here as a future auxiliary for all persons. (*Shall* is common instead of *will* in the first person, but *will* is equally correct in most contexts in modern English.) In Unit 31, students will learn to use *shall* to make offers.

2. Will, going to and Present Progressive The differences between these three ways of talking about the future are complicated and difficult to analyse. Students should probably just practise each one in context, for the moment, without paying too much attention to theoretical rules about the use of each form. Some basic guidelines for reference:

a. The Present Progressive and *going to* are both used to talk about plans. For the difference, see notes to Lesson 25A.

b. *Going to* and *will* are both used to predict the future.
Going to is preferred when we talk about an event that is already starting to happen, or on the way, so that we can see it coming (see notes to Lesson 25B). Sentences with *going to* almost have a present meaning (for instance, *She's going to have a baby* means *She's pregnant*).
Will is used for more 'open' predictions, when something is not already determined but we still feel that it is likely or certain to happen.
Compare:
– *Look out! We're going to crash!*
– *Don't drive so fast. You'll crash.*

3. Get Students meet some examples of the use of *get* as a kind of passive auxiliary (*get lost*, *get killed*, *get married*).

4. Pronunciation Most students will find the 'dark *l*' in *'ll* difficult to pronounce correctly (which does not matter very much), and difficult to hear (which does matter). To pronounce a good dark *l*, students should begin by saying /ʊ/ (e.g. the *oo* in *good*), and then make an *l* while continuing the vowel. Exercise 5 will help with perception; it may be a good idea to do it more than once, at intervals of a few weeks.

You may also want to pay special attention in this unit to the pronunciation of *w* (for students who find it difficult) and /əʊ/ (as in *won't*). Students should make a clear distinction between *won't* and *want*.

1 Dialogue 🔊

● This can be presented with books closed. Play the recording once, and ask students how much they have understood. See if they can remember some words and expressions.

● Ask what they think is the relationship between the speakers.
● Play the recording again. See if students can help you to build up the dialogue on the board from memory.
● Open books. Go through the dialogue explaining difficult points.
● Practise the pronunciation.
● Get students to practise the dialogue in pairs.

2 Dialogue completion

● Students can do this individually or by group discussion, as you like.
● Explain that all the expressions needed come in the dialogue in Exercise 1.

3 Contractions 🔊

● Students should pronounce the contraction *'ll* as a separate syllable – almost '*ull*'.
● Use the recording as a model if necessary.

4 New dialogues

● Students should build up their conversations by taking elements from the dialogues they have just studied. The conversations should be short.
● They will probably need to ask you for a few words and expressions.
● When ready, students should practise their conversations until they can say them from memory. Pay attention to pronunciation.
● You may like to ask the class to listen to selected conversations.

5 Ear-training 🔊

● Play each sentence and ask students to write the key words (e.g. *I stop* or *I'll stop*).
● Play through the exercise more than once if they are having difficulty.
● Let them compare notes before giving them the answers.

Tapescript
1. I stop work at six.
2. You'll know the answer.
3. I'll have coffee for breakfast.
4. You'll have to change at Coventry.
5. I drive carefully.
6. I know you'll like my brother.

6 Personalization

● Give students a minute or two to work out their answers.
● Try to get sentences from everybody. You may have to help with vocabulary.

Practice Book
● Tell students which exercises you want them to do.

Unit 29: Lesson B

Students practise predicting.
Structures: use of *will* to predict.
Words and expressions to learn: *dead; heart; word; lover; in prison; dream; fall in love; pass; famous.*

Language notes and possible problems

1. Tenses   Students are asked (Exercise 3) to predict what will happen in the third act, using *will*. This would be a natural verb-form to use if one was in the theatre waiting for the third act to begin, for instance. Note, however, that it would be normal to use present tenses to continue the written synopsis.

2. Vocabulary   In order not to slow down students' reading of the text to the point where they lose interest, essential new vocabulary is taken out and taught in advance (Exercise 1).

3. *Married to*   Note the preposition.

---

1 Pre-teaching vocabulary
• Either go through the list (asking students if anybody knows the meanings of the words), or let students work through them with dictionaries.

2 Reading and remembering
• Give students ten minutes or so to read through the text and ask questions.
• Then tell them to close their books and see how much they can remember.
• You may like to prompt their memories by asking a few questions. For example:

Act 1 How old is Anna?
     Where does she work?
     What's her lover's name?
     Why is he in prison?
     Does she like her job?
     Why not?
     What happens when the Grand Duke sees her?
     What does he tell her when she goes to the
       palace?
     Does she agree?
     What does she say to Boris?
     What does Boris do?
Act 2 Who does Anna meet in Paris?
     What is he doing now?
     Who does he love?
     Do you think Anna loves him?
     Who is Yvette?
     What does Boris say he will do?
     Who does he say Anna is?
     What does Yvette think?

3 Prediction
• Start by asking students to suggest what they think will happen.
• Then get them to form groups.
• Ask each group to imagine that they are in the theatre at the end of the second act, and to talk about what they think will happen.

• They should use *will* and *won't* in their discussion.
• When they are ready, get a spokesperson from each group to tell the others what they think will happen.

4 What will the next word be?
• Play each sentence, and stop the recording at the break.
• Ask students to say or write what they think will come next.
• If you want to get examples of *will*, tell students to say or write *I think the next word will be . . .*
• When they have decided, start the recording again and they will hear the rest of the sentence.

Tapescript for Exercise 4
1. 'What's the time?' 'Three // o'clock.'
2. Europe Asia Africa America // Australia.
3. 'Can I speak to Alan?' 'Speaking. Who's // that?'
4. 'Excuse me. Can you lend me £5?' 'I'm sorry, I'm afraid I // can't.'
5. One, four, seven, ten, thirteen, sixteen, // nineteen.
6. Darling, I love // you.
7. The car's top speed is ninety-five miles an // hour.
8. 'How long are you going to stay in England this time?' 'Oh, about five // weeks.'
9. To be or not to be, that is the // question.

Practice Book
• Tell students which exercises you want them to do.

B   What will happen next?

1 Find out what these words mean. Ask your teacher or use a dictionary.

dead	prison	revolution
employer	royal	
procession	Duke	palace
mistress	famous	
successful	heart	
refuse(*verb*)	cousin	

2 Read the 'opera synopsis'. Then close your book and see how much you can remember.

3 You are at a performance of the opera *Death in Paris*. It is the interval between the second and third acts. What do you think will happen in the third act?

4 Listening. Listen to the recording. When each sentence stops, say what you think the next word will be. Example:

1. 'What's the time?' 'Three...' *'I think the next word will be 'o'clock'.'*

DEATH IN PARIS

An Opera in Three Acts
by
Zoltan Grmljavina

SYNOPSIS

ACT ONE

Anna, a beautiful 18-year-old girl, works in a shop in the old town of Goroda, in Central Moldenia. Her parents are dead; her lover, Boris, is in prison for revolutionary activities; her employer is very unkind to her. She dreams of a happier life. One day a royal procession passes in the street. The Grand Duke sees Anna and falls in love with her. He sends for her; when she goes to the palace he tells her that she must become his mistress. If not, Boris will die. Anna agrees. Boris is released from prison; in a letter Anna tells him that she can never see him again. Boris leaves Moldenia.

ACT TWO

Three years have passed. Anna and the Duke are in Paris. The Duke is dying – he has only six months to live – but the doctors have not told him. Only Anna knows the truth. One day, Anna is walking in the Tuileries when a man stops her. It is Boris. He tells her that he is now a famous artist, rich and successful. He is married to a Frenchwoman, Yvette; but in his heart he still loves Anna. 'Come away with me', he says. Anna refuses, and Boris says that he will do something terrible. At this moment, Yvette joins them. Boris tells Yvette that Anna is his cousin from Moldenia, but Yvette does not believe him.

ACT THREE

Anna and

C What do the stars say?

AQUARIUS (Jan 21–Feb 18) An old friend will come back into your life, bringing new problems. Don't make any quick decisions.

PISCES (Feb 19–Mar 20) In three days you will receive an exciting offer. But your family will make difficulties.

ARIES (Mar 21–Apr 20) Money will come to you at the end of the week. Be careful – it could go away again very fast!

TAURUS (Apr 21–May 21) You will have trouble with a child. Try to be patient. You will have a small accident on Sunday – nothing serious.

GEMINI (May 22–June 21) This will be a good time for love, but there will be a serious misunderstanding with somebody close to you. Try to tell the truth.

CANCER (June 22–July 22) You will meet somebody who could change your life. Don't be too cautious – the opportunity won't come again.

LEO (July 23–Aug 23) Something very strange will happen next Thursday. Try to laugh about it.

VIRGO (Aug 24–Sept 23) This will be a terrible week. The weekend will be the worst time. Stay in bed on Sunday. Don't open the door. Don't answer the phone.

LIBRA (Sept 24–Oct 23) There will be bad news the day after tomorrow; but the bad news will turn to good.

SCORPIO (Oct 24–Nov 22) You will make an unexpected journey, and you will find something very good at the end of it.

SAGITTARIUS (Nov 23–Dec 21) You will have trouble with a person who loves you; and you will have help from a person who doesn't.

CAPRICORN (Dec 22–Jan 20) A letter will bring a very great surprise, and some unhappiness, but a good friend will make things better.

1 Read your horoscope with a dictionary. Memorize it – and see if it comes true.

2 Work with some more people who have the same sign as you, if possible.
Write a new horoscope for your sign, and for another one.

3 Make some predictions about football matches. Examples:

'*Arsenal will beat Liverpool 3 – 1 next Saturday.*'

Or make predictions about some other sport. Or about the 'top twenty' records. Example:

'"*Baby come here*" *will be number one.*'
'"*Get out of my heart*" *will go up three places.*'

Remember your predictions and see if they come true.

4 How old will you be in the year 2000? What do you think you will be like? What about other people in the class? Write a few sentences about the future of yourself and some of the other students.

Students continue to practise predicting.
Structures: *will.*
Words and expressions to learn: vocabulary chosen by students.

expressions they think it is most useful for them to learn.

Practice Book
- Tell students which exercises you want them to do.

Optional extra materials
Set of horoscopes from a current newspaper or magazine, if available. (Copy for each student.)

1 Reading your horoscope
- Give students a few minutes to read their own horoscopes. If they are interested, let them read some of the others too.
- Tell them to memorize their prediction.
- In the next lesson, ask if any of the predicted things happened.
- If it's possible to get an English-language newspaper or magazine with a horoscope in, this can be used instead (or as well). But note that the language may be difficult.

2 Writing horoscopes
- If this can be done in groups of people who share the same sign it gives a nice focus to the exercise.
- Each group can write a splendid horoscope for its own sign and a terrible horoscope for one of the other groups.
- Lone students can join one of the groups, or work individually, as they wish.
- When the horoscopes are ready, get students to read them out.

3 Predicting results
- How you do this depends on the students' knowledge and shared interests.
- Possible subjects are sport, pop music, politics, the stock exchange, the weather.
- Get one of the students to act as 'class secretary' and note down what everybody has said.
- Check in a week's time (or whenever) to see who was right.

4 The year 2000
- Do the exercise orally until students are beginning to dry up.
- Then get them to write some sentences; this will give them more time to think and to express more difficult ideas.
- Provide vocabulary as necessary.

Optional activity
- There is usually somebody in the class who enjoys fortune-telling of one kind or another (for example, by reading people's palms or turning up cards).
- If so, ask them if they would prepare something for one of the next lessons with your help (unless they feel able to improvise in English).

Vocabulary learning
- Tell students to choose themselves which words and

> **Students use** discussion to solve a simple problem.
> **Structures:** no new structures.
> **Words and expressions to learn:** *rope; tin; tinned; tin-opener; bottle; blanket; tent; gas; sunglasses; matches; death; toothbrush; tractor; compass; rifle; backpack.*
> Note: This exercise is adapted from *Discussions that Work*, by Penny Ur, Cambridge University Press, 1981.

1 Survival exercise

PRESENTATION

• Ask the students to work in groups, trying to match the words in the list with the numbered pictures.
• Go through the list with them, making sure they understand all the words, and can pronounce them.
• Ask how much weight they think one person can carry on a 100-mile march in the Arctic. (20kg is a heavy load for an average person in easy walking conditions.)
• Ask how long they think the march will take. (Remember that storms can cause delays.)

STAGE 1

• Tell students to draw up their lists individually.
• Point out that they can split some of the items (they don't have to take all the blankets, or all the food, for example).

STAGE 2

• When this has been done, students move into groups.
• Their task now is to draw up a group list (still trying to solve the problem of what one person can carry).
• They must go on discussing until they reach agreement and produce their group list.

STAGE 3

• A spokesperson from each group reads out the list to the others.

2 Summary

• Go over the summary with the students.

Practice Book

• Tell students which exercises you want them to do.

Answers to Practice Book Exercise 1: 1. half
2. picture 3. top 4. go to bed 5. by air
6. lightning (not alive) or snail (slow) 7. very old
8. sit down (intransitive) 9. Wednesday

D A matter of life and death

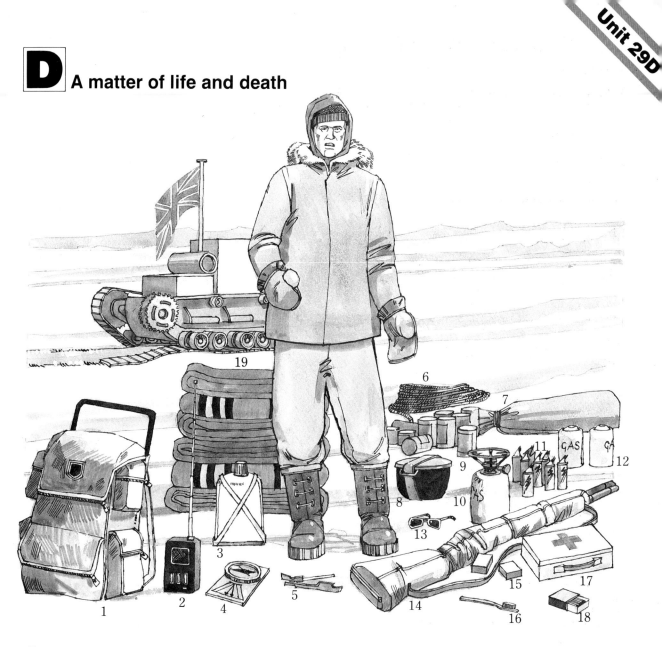

1 You are at the North Pole. Your tractor and radio transmitter have broken down and you cannot repair them. You have to walk 100 miles (160 km) to the nearest camp. You have enough warm clothing and boots; you also have the following things on the tractor, but you can't carry them all. What will you take? Choose carefully – it's a matter of life and death.

matches (20g)
saucepan (500g)
large water bottle (empty 300g, full 2.5kg)
tent (4kg)
tin-opener (80g)
first aid kit (500g)
backpack (1.5kg)
sunglasses (40g)
gas cartridges (300g each)

ten blankets (1.5kg each)
gas cooker (1.2kg)
toothbrush (10g)
20m of rope (3kg)
compass (50g)
small radio receiver (1.2kg)
rifle and ammunition (6.9kg)
30kg of tinned food
ten signal flares (1.5kg)

2 Look at the summary on page 157 with your teacher.

Useful; useless

A All you need is love

1 Who needs what? Make some sentences.

People   Men
Women   Babies
Fish   Cars
Animals   Gardens

need
don't need

people.   men.
women.   babies.   fish.
bicycles.   cars.   milk.
love.   freedom.   water.
petrol.   oil.   sleep.
politicians.   books.
clothes.

2 What do people need in life? Make a list of ten things. You can use your dictionary. What do *you* need now?

3 How important are these things to you? Very important? Quite important? Not very important?
Which is the most important? Which is the least important? List them in order of importance, and compare lists with three other students.

a car	children	TV	interesting work
money	love	freedom	nice clothes
music	friends	books	time to be alone

4 We asked some people to name two things each that were very important to them. Which ten different things do you think they named?

family	home	life	freedom	car
friends	friendship	music	happiness	
money	rugby boots	work	health	

Now listen, and see if you were right. Try to note how many times each thing is named as important.

5 Listen to the short extracts from songs, and try to write the words.

"He's got toothache, a sprained ankle, a bad back, gout, influenza, a broken arm and an ulcer and he's just hoping someone will ring him up and ask him how he is."

KenPyne

Unit 30: Lesson A

Students learn elementary ways of talking about need and importance.
Structures: no new structures.
Words and expressions to learn: *garden; petrol; oil; happiness; friendship; health; least.*

Possible problem

Authentic listening   There are two activities proposed in the listening section of Exercise 4: one is to recognize whether a thing is named, and the other is to count the number of times it is named. The second task may be too difficult for some students, as the speech is fast in the recording, and strict turn-taking is not observed. You may want to skip this part or make it optional.

1 *Need*

• Go over the new vocabulary with the students.
• Point out that *fish* is a plural without *s* in this case, and tell or remind students of the difference between *petrol* and *oil*.
• Then ask each of them to write three sentences with the words in the exercise.
• Walk around while they are working to give any help that is needed and to check the sentences.
• Continue the exercise orally for a few minutes, with students reading out their sentences or making up new ones.

2 Vocabulary extension

• This is a chance for students to choose words to learn.
• Give them a few minutes to list the things that people need, looking up necessary words in their dictionaries.
• Walk round checking that they are in fact finding the correct words and using their dictionaries intelligently.
• If time allows, you may want to do the Optional activity now; or you may want to ask students to read out their lists, to the class or to a smaller group.
• Then ask students why they need English, and help them to express their answers correctly.
• Finish by talking about what you yourself need now (e.g. a new coat, a rest, a drink), and getting the students to do the same.

Optional activity   Listening

• Collect the students' lists (make sure their names are on them).
• Number the lists 1, 2, 3 etc., and read them to the class, getting them to write down the number and whose list they think it is for each one.
• Check to see how many right answers there were.

3 Importance

• Run over the list of items, making sure that students understand all the words.
• Ask what they feel about the importance of one or two of the items (e.g. a car, music), and then give them some time to work individually on the exercise.
• Demonstrate on the board how they are to work: first make three columns headed *Very important*, *Quite important* and *Not very important*.
• They should put each of the items into one column.

• They should then try to arrange the items in order of importance from most to least.
• When they are ready, ask them to compare their lists with those of three other students sitting close to them.
• Ask everybody to say which item is the most important for them and which is the least important. (Make sure they use the expressions *most important* and *least important* in their answers.)
• It is a good idea for you to do the exercise as well – students will be interested in your values.

4 Listening for specific information

• Go over the list of words, explaining any new ones.
• Explain that they are going to hear people talking about things that are important to them.
• Tell them they will only hear ten of the thirteen things on the list; ask them to decide in small groups which ones they hear.
• Then play the recording once or twice so they can check which things actually are mentioned.
• (If you do not want them writing in their books, it is best they copy the list before beginning so they can just put a mark by an item when it is mentioned.)
• If you do not think it is too difficult for your students, ask them to listen again and mark how many times each item is named as important. (But note that this is a very demanding exercise.)

Answers

family 6, home 1, life 1, freedom 0, car 3, friends 2, friendship 1, music 0, happiness 2, money 0, rugby boots 1, work 1, health 2.

Tapescript for Exercise 4: see page 181

5 Intensive listening

• The recording is of a series of fragments from Beatles songs.
• Play each fragment – several times if necessary – and get students to try to write down the words.
• The last three fragments are more difficult, and can be left out if you prefer.

The words are:

1. All you need is love (x3); love, love is all you need. (from *All you need is love*)
2. Do you need anybody?... I need somebody to love... I just need someone to love. (from *A little help from my friends*)
3. If you need somebody to love. (from *Any time at all*)
4. Just to dance with you is everything I need. (from *I'm happy just to dance with you.*)
5. Help! I need somebody... You know I need someone... (from *Help*)
6. When I was younger, so much younger than today, I never needed anybody's help in any way. (from *Help*)
7. I need to make you see what you mean to me. (from *Michelle*)
8. Will you still need me, will you still feed me, when I'm sixty-four? (from *When I'm sixty-four*)

Practice Book

• Tell students which exercises you want them to do.

Ending the lesson

• As the lesson breaks up, you may want to take the opportunity to use *need* in a natural context by remarking *I need a drink/a rest/my lunch*, or something of the kind.

Unit 30: Lesson B

Students learn some ways of talking about the uses and usefulness of things, and contrast necessity and usefulness.
Structures: *x uses y to do z (with); x does z with y.*
Words and expressions to learn: *useless; necessary;* names of some subjects of study and professions.

Language notes and possible problems
These notes deal with the structures in Exercise 4.
1. Infinitive The infinitive in sentences like *Farmers use tractors to plough fields with* is similar to the infinitive of purpose students have already met in Lesson 25C.
2. Prepositions at the ends of clauses This common English structure is difficult for some learners. It has come up casually before, but is practised systematically in this lesson.
3. With You may wish to point out to students that *with* is used to denote the instrument used to do something. (The other prepositions should not cause problems.)

1 Presentation and practice
● Explain the meanings of *useful, useless* and *necessary.*
● Then divide the class into pairs and get them to classify the list of school subjects into those they think necessary, useful and useless for a good education.
● You may have to help with the meanings of some of the words.
● There are no right answers, of course; you may wish to tabulate the results on the board when the pairs have finished working, as the students will probably be interested in how the others chose.

2 Further practice
● Explain any new words in the table that are likely to give trouble.
● Divide the class into groups of three or four.
● Explain that each group must choose four of the listed professions.
● If you do not want the students to write in their books, get them to copy the appropriate parts of the table onto another sheet of paper.
● They can add one more subject if they wish; in a monolingual class this might be the mother tongue.
● When the groups have finished deciding which subjects are necessary, useful and useless for the professions they have chosen, get them to report to the class.
● Encourage them to use complete sentences, e.g. *If you want to be a banker, mathematics is necessary; English and...*
● If there is time, and some of the groups disagree with each other, you may want them to explain their answers: *Latin is necessary if you want to be a doctor, because you have to ...*

3 Which subjects?
● This is a continuation of the last exercise.
● Students should go back into the same groups, and decide on five subjects for each of the people.

● They should be prepared to explain their choices.
● One person from each group should then visit the other groups, explaining their choices, and discussing them.

4 *use* and *with*
● Students should do these in writing, individually.
● Point out the use of the infinitive, the phrase-final prepositions, and the use of *with*.
● Note that some of the sentences have singular subjects and some have plural subjects.
● When students have finished writing, let them compare answers with each other before checking them with you.
● See if they can make up any sentences on the same patterns.

Practice Book
● Tell students which exercises you want them to do.

B Is it useful?

1 Work in pairs. Which of these subjects are necessary for a good education? Which are useful? Which are useless? Make three lists to read to the class.

reading	spelling	mathematics	history
geography	sports	physical sciences	
literature	biology	religious education	
English	typing	cookery	

2 Work in groups. Choose four jobs and decide which school subjects are ✓✓ necessary ✓ useful ✗ useless for each one.

	Architect	Banker	Doctor	Engineer	Farmer	Journalist	Photographer	Secretary	Businessman or Businesswoman
Mathematics									
English									
Geography									
Latin									
History									
Typing									
Biology									
Art									
Physics									
Chemistry									

3 These people are beginning their last two years of school. They can each take five of the subjects from Exercise 2. Which five subjects should each one take? Why?

1. Pat wants to be a doctor. She enjoys languages.
2. John would like to be an architect. He does well in sciences, but they are not his favourite subjects.
3. Judy will own and manage the family farm when she is older. She likes to travel.
4. Tom plans to be a journalist. He would like to write about international politics.

4 Complete the sentences.

1. A photographer uses a camera to take pictures with.
2. A journalist uses a tape recorder to record interviews with.
3. ....
4. An architect .... drafting table .... draw plans on.
5. .... in.
6. .... tractors .... plough fields ....
7. ....
8. .... a barn .... keep cows ....

1. A photographer takes pictures with a camera.
2. ....
3. Farmers milk cows with milking machines.
4. ....
5. .... secretary takes notes in shorthand.
6. ....
7. Nurses take temperatures .... thermometers.
8. ....

shorthand

thermometer

tape recorder

tractor

field

barn

C It's useless (part one)

ASSISTANT: Good afternoon, madam. Can I help you?
CUSTOMER: Yes, I'd like to see the manager, please.
ASSISTANT: Furniture, madam? Second floor.
CUSTOMER: No, the *manager*. *Ma-na-ger*.
ASSISTANT: Oh, I *am* sorry. I thought you said furniture.
CUSTOMER: That's all right. But can I see the manager, please?
ASSISTANT: Well, I'm afraid he's *very* busy just now. Have you an appointment?
CUSTOMER: No, I haven't. I want to make a complaint.
ASSISTANT: A complaint. Oh, I see. Well, I'll just see if he's free.

1 Listen to the conversation. Then decide whether these sentences are true or false.

1. The conversation happens in the afternoon.
2. The customer wants to buy furniture.
3. She is on the second floor.
4. The assistant doesn't understand what she wants.
5. The woman hasn't got an appointment.
6. The manager is not free.
7. The woman wants to complain about something.

2 Study the conversation, and practise it in pairs.

3 Work with a partner, and make up a short conversation which includes a misunderstanding and an apology. You can use one of these sentences if you like.

I thought you said Thursday.
I thought you said goodbye.
I thought you said five pence.
I thought you said five o'clock.
I thought you said steak.
I thought you were talking to me.

4 Stress. List each of these words under one of the stress patterns. Then pronounce them.

happiness	furniture	animal
bicycle	afternoon	literature
mathematics	appointment	

□ □ □	□ □ □	□ □ □
manager	*engineer*	*already*

Unit 30: Lesson C

Students learn ways of making and accepting emphatic apologies and correcting misunderstandings.
Structures: no new structures.
Words and expressions to learn: *customer; complaint; appointment; busy; That's all right; I thought you said* . . .
Phonology: use of stress for emphasis and contrast.

Language notes and possible problems

1. Stress for emphasis   Students' own languages may not use stress for emphasis as English does (for example, in the sentence in the dialogue *He's **very** busy just now*). You may need to reassure students that they will not seem overly dramatic if they emphasize in this way.
2. Stress for contrast   Students learn to correct misunderstandings by stressing the right word or expression. Again, this may not come easily to some nationalities.
3. Emphatic apologies; accepting   An emphatic apology can be expressed by saying *I **am** sorry* (instead of *I'm sorry*), and accepted by saying *That's all right.*
4. Got   Note the omission of *got* in *Have you an appointment?* (formal style)

1 Listening

- Get the students to look at the illustration, masking the rest of the page.
- Elicit information about the situation, i.e. where the people are, if she is buying something from him, does she look happy, etc.
- Then get the students to close their books.
- Write the sentences on the board, and answer any questions about the vocabulary in them.
- Teach the word *complaint.*
- Play the dialogue once and let the class try to answer the questions; then play it once or twice more and give them a chance to improve their performance.
- Let students compare notes on the answers, and then tell them which sentences are true and which are false.
- In a very weak class, you may like to let them look at the text after they have made a first attempt to understand the recording and answer the questions. They can then treat the exercise as a reading comprehension test.

2 Practice

- Ask if anyone can remember the first line of the dialogue. Write the students' best approximation on the board.
- Then see if they can give you the second line, and so on to the end.
- Play the recording once more so they can check their version and correct any mistakes.
- Let them look through the text and ask questions.
- Give any explanations you consider necessary.
- You may like to mention the verb *to complain.*
- Then play the recording again and get students to imitate the pronunciation.

- Concentrate particularly on the use of stress to make a contrast or to emphasize the meaning of a word (in italics in the text).
- When students have a good grasp of the pronunciation, ask them to practise in pairs, changing over after a time so that each of them does both parts.
- If a man student is playing the part of the customer, the assistant should of course call him 'sir'.

3 Misunderstanding and apologies

- Ask students to make up very short exchanges.
- Each exchange must contain one of the sentences given, an apology and an acceptance.
- As an example of what is wanted, you could give them something like this:

    A: I'm thirsty.
    B: No, it's Friday.
    A: No, *thirsty.* I'd like a drink.
    B: Oh, I *am* sorry. I thought you said Thursday.
    A: That's all right.

4 Stress patterns

- This exercise revises some three-syllable words already learnt, including two (*literature* and *mathematics*) whose pronunciation can give rise to difficulty because of the spelling.
- Ask students to draw the three stress patterns on a piece of paper.
- Show how the three sample words follow the patterns they are written under.
- Then get students to work individually classifying the other words. (Do not play the recording yet.)
- Let them compare answers with one another before checking with you:

☐ ☐ ☐	☐ ☐ ☐	☐ ☐ ☐
manager	engineer	already
happiness	afternoon	mathematics
bicycle		appointment
furniture		
animal		
literature		

- Then get them to pronounce the words, using the recording if you wish. Take special care that they pronounce *literature* (/ˈlɪtrɪtʃə/) and *mathematics* (/mæθˈmætɪks/) as three-syllable words.

Practice Book

- Tell students which exercises you want them to do.
- Exercise 4 is an important free writing exercise, which involves revision of a large number of points from the course. You may wish to prepare it (or get the students to do it) in class.

Unit 30: Lesson D

Students learn some of the language of complaints and apologies and continue working on sentence stress.
Structures: words having various grammatical functions.
Words and expressions to learn: *order; switch on; switch off; secondly; thirdly; strange; (It doesn't) work; go (bzzz); I **do** apologize; replace; refund; instead; prefer.*
Phonology: stress for emphasis and contrast.

Language notes and possible problems
1. Sketch Exercise 7 can take up to two hours of extra class time. If time is very tight, you may wish to skip it; but it will be very rewarding if you can find the time for it.
2. Do *I **do** apologize* occurs in the dialogue. You will want to point out to students that *do*, *does* and *did* can be used for emphasis in appropriate cases, and are stressed.
3. Am A similar case occurs with *I really **am** very sorry*. The normally unstressed auxiliary is stressed, and put in an unusual place, after *really*.
4. Grammatical terminology If students are not familiar with grammatical terminology, they may find the explanation in Exercise 4 difficult, and need a bit more help with Exercises 4 and 5.
5. Nouns as pre-modifiers Nouns can be used a little like adjectives in English: so the cover you put on a typewriter is a *typewriter cover*. But you may want to point out that these are not really adjectives: they can only appear before a noun (so **The shop was shoe* makes no sense); and they cannot be compared or modified (you cannot say **a more kitchen window* or **a very bicycle wheel*).

When plural nouns are used like adjectives, they are usually singular in form; you will want to point this out.

1 Listening
• Get students to listen to the dialogue, books closed. (You may prefer weak students to follow the text in their books as they listen.)
• When they have heard it once or twice, ask them to recall any words or phrases that they can remember – the order doesn't matter.
• Ask them to open their books and read the text.
• Give whatever explanations are needed (encourage students to say *What does . . . mean?*).
• Note the emphatic uses of *do* and *am*.

2 Practice
• You will probably want just to use selections of the dialogue for practice in pairs, unless you have a good deal of time and very highly motivated students.
• Make sure, however, that students practise the examples of emphatic stress (It only arrived *yesterday*; *Mrs Paula Jones*; *39*; I really *am* very sorry; I *do* apologize.

3 Contrastive stress
• This exercise shows students how a change in stress can alter the meaning of a sentence.
• Go slowly over the examples, making sure that

students can hear the difference in stress and understand what it implies.
• Get them to imitate the two example sentences (saying the stressed words on a higher pitch); this will help them to hear the difference.
• Play the rest of the sentences.
• Discuss the answer to each one before going on.
• They are stressed as follows:

   3. You *work* in London, don't you? (Possible answer: No, I live there – I work outside London.)
   4. Is that *Mary's* father? (No, it's Ann's father.)
   5. . . . a new *red* Lancia? (No, a white one.)
   6. Do you need *English*. . . ? (No, French.)
   7. a) Would you like *me* to telephone. . . ? (No, not you.)
      b) Would you like me to *telephone*. . . ? (No, write.)
      c) . . . Peter *and* Anne? (No, just Peter.)

4 Words with various grammatical functions: presentation
• You may need to give a few more examples for students not familiar with grammatical terminology.
• Let the students work in small groups to try to find the common words in the text that have more than one possible grammatical function: *dry* (adjective and verb); *trouble* (noun and verb); *address* (used both as noun and verb in the text); *work* (noun and verb).
• Do not bother with *switch* or *refund* unless they ask you about them.

5 Practice
• Get students to work individually, comparing their answers among themselves before checking with you.

Answers
answer (verb, noun); orange (noun, adjective); phone (v, n); clean (v, a); bath (v, n); change (v, n); warm (v, a).

6 Nouns used as adjectives
• Go over the instructions with the students, pointing out that it is *a shoe shop* and not **a shoes shop*.
• Then go down the list, explaining any words that you need to and letting the students volunteer the answers.
• Be careful that no plural forms creep in.

7 Sketch
• Let the students prepare their sketches in groups of two to four (customer, manager, and optionally assistant and customer's wife/husband/friend etc.).
• The subject should be a complaint about faulty goods; leave students free to decide on the details.
• Tell them they can look back over the last few lessons, and try to use plenty of language from them.
• Ask them not to 'invent' the English for too many things they don't know.
• For detailed suggestions on how to organize sketches, see Lesson 11D, page 49.

8 Summary
• Go over the summary with your students, answering any questions that come up.

Practice Book
• Tell students which exercises you want them to do.

D It's useless (part two)

MANAGER: Good afternoon, madam. I understand you have a complaint.
CUSTOMER: Yes, I've got a problem with this hair-drier.
MANAGER: I'm sorry to hear that. What's the trouble?
CUSTOMER: Well, first of all, I ordered it two months ago and it only arrived yesterday.
MANAGER: Oh dear. That's very strange.
CUSTOMER: Well, it's probably because you addressed it to Mr Paul Jones at 29 Cannon Street. I'm *Mrs Paula* Jones, and my address is *39* Cannon Street.
MANAGER: Well, I'm really sorry about that, madam. We do...
CUSTOMER: And secondly, I'm afraid it's useless. It doesn't work.
MANAGER: Doesn't work?
CUSTOMER: No. It doesn't work. It doesn't dry my hair. When I switch it on, it just goes 'bzzzzz', but it doesn't get hot at all.
MANAGER: Well, I really am very sorry about this, madam. I do apologize. We'll be happy to replace the drier for you. Or we'll give you a refund instead, if you prefer.
CUSTOMER: And thirdly,...

1 Listen to the conversation. Find out what the new words and expressions mean.

2 Practise the conversation with a partner.

3 Stress. Listen carefully to these questions, and then write answers to them (beginning *No, ...*). When you have done that, practise saying the questions and answers.

1. You've got *two* sisters, haven't you?
   No, just one.
2. You've got two *sisters*, haven't you?
   No, two brothers.
3. You work in London, don't you?
4. Is that Mary's father?
5. Did you say you had a new red Lancia?
6. Do you need English for your work?

Now listen to this question. You will hear it three times, with three different stresses. Can you write suitable answers (a different answer each time)?

7. Would you like me to telephone Peter and Anne?

4 Many words in English can be used in different ways. For example, *rain* can be used as a noun (*Look at the rain!*), or as a verb (*It will rain tomorrow*); and *open* can be used as a verb (*Is it OK if I open the window?*) or an adjective (*the open door*). Can you find any words in the conversation that can be used in different ways like this? Can you think of any other words?

5 Which of these words can be used in more than one way?

arrive	answer	orange	music	phone
cold	pub	hear	clean	bath	change	warm

6 A *shop* that sells *shoes* is a *shoe shop* (not a shoes shop). How can you say:

a *lamp* in the *street*   a *shop* that sells *books*
the *door* of a *garage*   a *window* in a *kitchen*
a *wheel* of a *bicycle*   a *horse* that runs in *races*
a *bottle* for *beer*   a *boy* who brings *newspapers*
a *race* for *horses*   a *finger* you put a *ring* on

7 Prepare and practise a sketch about a complaint.

8 Look at the summary on page 158 with your teacher.

125

Self and others

A Do it yourself

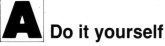

falling in love
with each other
xx

1 Work with two other people. Tell them to do things, like this:

Look at   Sing to
Touch   Talk about
Talk to
Shake hands with

yourselves.

each other.

a woman looking at herself in a mirror

a man looking at himself in a mirror

2 You can look at yourself, or you can look at somebody else.
You can talk to yourself or to somebody else.
Can you do all these things to somebody else *and* to yourself?

hurt   visit   fall in love with   photograph
marry   employ   teach   wash
think about   telephone

3 Draw small pictures for these situations.

He's looking at her.
She's looking at herself.
They're looking at each other.
He's not looking at her, he's looking at somebody
    else.

4 Alan bought six things yesterday – three for himself and three for somebody else. Which were which, do you think?

a bunch of roses   a bottle of perfume
a train ticket   a stamp
a cigar   a birthday card

5 Do you do these things yourself, or does somebody else do them for you? Examples:

1. *'I do the ironing myself.'*
2. *'Somebody else does the decorating.'*

1. ironing   2. decorating   3. cooking   4. washing

5. cleaning   6. washing-up   7. shopping

Now listen to an English person answering the same questions.

6 Do you prefer to do these things by yourself or with somebody else?

listen to music   go to the cinema
go shopping   go on holiday
have lunch   go for a walk

126

Unit 31: Lesson A

Students learn to express the ideas of reciprocal and reflexive action, and to contrast self and others.
Structures: reflexive/emphatic pronouns; *each other*; *somebody else*; *do the ironing/shopping* etc.
Words and expressions to learn: *shake hands with*; *about (= on the subject of)*; *myself, yourself* etc.; *hurt* (transitive); *visit* (verb); *teach*; *the ironing / cleaning / washing / washing-up / shopping; else*.

Language notes and possible problems

1. Reflexive/emphatic pronouns Both meanings of *myself, yourself* etc. are taught here: the 'reflexive' meaning in Exercises 1–4 and the 'emphatic' meaning ('I and nobody else') in Exercises 5 and 6.

Note that the forms are irregular: first and second person forms begin with a possessive, third person forms with an object pronoun.

2. Each other In some languages the same pronouns are used to talk about both reflexive and reciprocal actions. This may lead some students to make mistakes like **They've known themselves for about two years*.

3. Reflexives and passives In some languages, too, reflexive pronouns are used where we would use passives (leading to mistakes like **Address writes itself with two d's* or **Steak tartare eats itself cold*).

4. Reflexive pronouns and object pronouns These can have the same form in some languages (leading to mistakes like **I often talk to me when I'm alone*).

5. Omission of pronouns Note that reflexive pronouns are dropped in a few expressions referring to actions that people generally do to themselves rather than other people. The commonest are *wash* and *dress*.

6. Each other and one another Most people make no distinction between these in modern English.

Presentation

- Let students look at the pictures for a minute or two.
- Ask who the woman and man are looking at in the first picture – see if anybody can produce *They are looking at each other*, and write this on the board.
- Ask about the second and third pictures, and see if anybody knows *themselves*.
- Write on the board: *They are looking at themselves*.
- When you are sure students understand the difference, write up the full list of reflexive/emphatic pronouns:

myself	*himself*	*ourselves*
yourself	*herself*	*yourselves*
	itself	*themselves*

- Practise the pronunciation (make sure students stress the second syllable).

1 *Yourselves/each other*

- Go over the words in the exercise instruction; make sure everybody is clear about the meaning and pronunciation.
- Get two students to come out in front of the class and give them instructions as shown (e.g. *Look at yourselves; Talk to each other*).

- Then get the class to continue the exercise in groups.
- Finish by asking students to think of other things which people can do to each other. (For instance: *like, love, hate, kiss, write to, think about*.)

2 *Somebody else*

- Explain if necessary that *somebody else* means *another person*.
- Go over the vocabulary and make sure students understand all the words.
- Discuss the first example; write on the board:
  You can hurt somebody else, or you can hurt yourself.
- Discuss the second example; write on the board:
  You can visit somebody else, but you can't visit yourself.
- Ask students to write sentences for some or all of the other examples.

3 Drawing pictures

- Most students ought to be able to do 'pin-men' pictures to illustrate their understanding of the situations.
- When they have finished, get them to compare notes, and ask volunteers to reproduce their pictures on the board.

4 Presents

- Various answers are possible, of course.
- Most people will probably decide that Alan bought the roses, perfume and birthday card for somebody else. Students who disagree should try to do so in English.

5 Who does the housework?

- This exercise introduces the use of *myself* as subject complement.
- Run over the vocabulary; note the pronunciation of *ironing* (/ˈaɪənɪŋ/).
- You may like to start the exercise by giving students your own answers to the questions.
- Ask students to write at least some of the examples.
- When the students have finished doing the exercise, let them listen to an English person doing it.
- You may want them to write down a table first, and tick off for each job whether the person does it himself or has someone else do it, or does it with someone|else.
- You can extend the exercise in two ways:
1. Ask students to talk about other people (e.g. *My father does his ironing himself, but my mother does all the cooking*).
2. Introduce the names of some more everyday jobs: car repairs; mending (of clothes), etc., and talk about who does them.

Tapescript for Exercise 5: see page 182

6 By oneself

- Students will probably want to say that 'it depends'. Help them to explain when they prefer to do things by themselves, and when they prefer company.
- They will no doubt be able to suggest other things that they like to do by themselves, or that it is more fun to do with somebody else.

Practice Book

- Tell students which exercises you want them to do.

Unit 31: Lesson B

Students learn to make offers, and to accept and reject them politely.

Structures: *Shall I...?*; use of *I'll* when making decisions and offers; *would* in *I'd love*, *I'd prefer* and *Would you like?*; *to* as a pro-verb in *I'd love to*; *just* with Present Perfect.

Words and expressions to learn: *shall*; *carry*; *just* (= a moment ago); *just now* (= at the moment); *toast*; *put on* (TV); *keep on* (clothes); *have a look*; *have a rest*; *wash your hands* (= go to the toilet).

Phonology: strong and weak pronunciations of *shall*; decoding unstressed words in fast colloquial speech.

Language notes and possible problems

1. Shall In modern English, *shall* is not very common except in the first person. Its main functions are as an alternative to *will*, and as a special auxiliary verb for making offers and suggestions (practised here).

2. I'll... Note the use of *'ll* to announce decisions and firm offers (*I'll go, shall I?*; *I'll keep it on*).

3. I'd Make sure students realize that *I'd* (in *I'd love to*, *I'd prefer to*) is a contraction of *I would*. Conditionals will be studied in detail later in the course.

---

1 Shall I?

• Give students a minute or two to decide which sentence goes with which picture.

• Let them compare notes and then go over the answers with them.

• Explain any difficulties.

• Note the weak pronunciation (/ʃəl/) in the first four sentences. In the last two, the pronunciation is strong (/ʃæl/): there is no other verb after *shall*, so it carries the stress.

Picture 1: *Shall I open it for you?*
Picture 2: *Shall I get it for you?*
Picture 3: *I'll answer it, shall I?*
    or: *Shall I get it for you?*
Picture 4: *Shall I carry something for you?*
Picture 5: *Shall I have a look?*
Picture 6: *I'll go, shall I?*
    or: *I'll answer it, shall I?*

2 Accepting and rejecting offers

• This is a prediction exercise. Tell students that they will hear all the complete sentences on the recording, but that they must try to guess what they are going to hear first of all.

• Take each section separately, and get students to write or say what they think is the complete form of each sentence.

• Then play the recording and practise the pronunciation. Explain any difficulties. (Note that *toast* is uncountable.)

• In many cases, of course, there are several possible answers – if students guess something different from the recorded sentence they are not necessarily wrong.

Tapescript for Exercise 2: see page 182

3 Practice

• Go over the questions with students, explaining any difficulties.

• Ask them to decide how they would answer each offer (they can accept it or reject it, as they wish). Check their answers.

• They should use expressions from Exercise 2 for most or all of their answers.

• Mention that the last offer (*Would you like to wash your hands?*) often means *Would you like to go to the toilet?*

• When students are ready, ask them to close their books and play the recording, or say the sentences at normal speed.

• Let students answer in chorus; stop the recording and pick out individuals to repeat their answers.

• You may like to go through the exercise several times until students are fluent.

4 Mime

• Tell students to prepare and write down a short conversation, working in pairs (one sentence each will do).

• Each conversation should contain an offer and an acceptance or rejection.

• When they are ready, each pair should come to the front and act out their conversation silently, trying to show by mime what the situation is.

• The class must try to guess the exact words that were written down.

5 How many words?

• It is probably best to play the recording right through once before starting work.

• Then take each sentence separately.

• Play it two or three times; get students to say how many words they hear and to try to write the first three.

• When they have worked out as much as they can, give them the answer and play the sentence again.

• Note that the pronunciation in this exercise is *very* fast and casual.

Tapescript for Exercise 5
What would you like to drink?
Shall I open the door?
Would you like to dance?
Can I take your coat?
Can I help you?
Can I give you a drink?
That's very kind of you.
I'd love to.
Would you like something to eat?
That would be nice.

Practice Book

• Tell students which exercises you want them to do.

127

B ## Shall I open it for you?

1 Put the sentences in the right pictures.

Shall I open it for you?	Shall I get it for you?
Shall I carry something for you?	I'll go, shall I?
Shall I have a look?	I'll answer it, shall I?

2 What do you think the answers will be?
Can you complete the sentences?

1. 'Can I take your coat?'
   'Oh, thank you. Here ....'
   'No, thanks. I'll keep .... on. I'm ....'

2. 'Shall I make you a cup of tea?'
   'Thank you very much. I'd love ....'
   'Not just now, thanks. I'm not ....'
   'I'd prefer coffee, if you've ....'

3. 'Would you like some toast?'
   'No, nothing ...., thanks.'
   'Yes, ... love .... Thank you.'
   'No, I've just ...., thanks.'

4. 'Would you like to go and see a film this evening?'
   'That would be very ....'
   'I'd love .... time?'
   'Not this evening, ... Perhaps .... time?'

5. 'Would you like to dance?'
   'Thanks. .... love ....'
   'Not .... now, thanks. I'm a bit ....'

6. 'Shall I help you to carry that?'
   'That's .... kind of you. Thank you.'
   'No, thanks. I can do it ....'

3 Prepare your answers to the following questions.
Then close your book, listen to the recording and answer.

Can I take your coat?
Shall I make you a cup of tea?
Would you like some toast?
Would you like to go and see a film this evening?
Shall I put the TV on?
Would you like a drink?

Would you like to have a rest?
Would you like to see my family photos?
Shall I telephone the station for you?
Would you like to wash your hands?

4 Prepare a conversation with another student (an offer and an answer). Act the conversation *without speaking*. The other students will try to decide what the words are.

5 Listen to the sentences. How many words do you hear? Write the first three words in each sentence. (Contractions like *that's* or *I'd* count as two words.)

C Whose is that?

1 Match the pictures and the sentences.

> Mine, mine, all mine!   Is this yours?   It's his.
> Our baby's prettier than theirs.   Whose is that?
> My feet are smaller than hers.   At last! It's ours!

2 *His, hers* or *not sure*?

3 Exchange possessions with other students.
Then ask '*Whose is this?*'
See if everybody can remember.

4 Put in *my, mine, your, yours, his, her, hers, our, ours, their* or *theirs*.

1. 'Excuse me, that's .... coat.'
2. 'Oh, is it? I'm sorry – I thought it was ....'
3. We've got the same kind of house as Mr and Mrs Martin, but .... is a bit bigger than ours.
4. Could we have .... bill, please?
5. 'Is that Jane's cat?' 'No, this one's white. .... is black.'
6. 'Have you seen .... new motorbike?' 'Oh, it isn't .... He's just borrowed it.'
7. 'When's .... birthday?' 'December 15th.' 'Really? Mine's the day before ....'
8. Mary and .... boyfriend are taking .... holiday in June – the same time as we're taking .... Why don't we all go together?

5 Listen to the conversations and fill in the table.

	George	Keith	Pat	Edna	Jane
The car belongs to					
The new trousers belong to					
The glasses belong to					
The dictionary belongs to					
The plate belongs to					
The history book belongs to					

Unit 31: Lesson C

Students learn new ways of expressing the idea of possession.
Structures: possessive pronouns *mine, yours* etc.; *whose* (pronoun use); *belong to*; revision of possessive *'s*.
Words and expressions to learn: *mine; yours; his; hers; ours; theirs; whose* (interrogative pronoun); *belong to; plate*.

Language note
Whose can be used as a pronoun (*Whose is that? Whose is this pen?*) or as a determiner (*Whose pen is this?*). The first use is taught here, but you may like to mention the other.

Optional extra materials
Little objects (toys or whatever) to give out as 'presents' – see Exercise 3: Alternative.

1 Presentation
● Give students a minute or two to look at the pictures and match the sentences.
● They should write each sentence against the number of the appropriate picture.
● Let them compare notes and check the answers.
● Practise the pronunciation of the pronouns.
● Write on the board:
   It's my money. It's mine.
   Is this your ear-ring? Is this yours?
   It's his coat. It's his.
   My feet are smaller than her feet. My feet are smaller than hers.
   At last! It's our house! At last! It's ours!
   Our baby's prettier than their baby. Our baby's prettier than theirs.
● This should make clear the difference in use between the *my*-series (determiners) and the *mine*-series (pronouns).

2 His or hers?
● Ask students to look at each picture and decide whether the thing belongs to a man or a woman.
● Get them to write *his* or *hers* against the number of the picture in each case.
● If they think it could belong to either a man or a woman, they should write *not sure*.
● There will probably be disagreement about some of the items, especially if students come from cultures with different attitudes to sex-roles.

3 Whose is this?
● Tell all the students to pick up one of their possessions and hold it up for half a minute (all at the same time).
● The possession should be something fairly distinctive – not a ballpoint pen that looks the same as everybody else's.
● During the half minute, students should look around and try to memorize the owners of the various objects.
● Then get students to exchange possessions (or collect them up yourself and redistribute them).
● Each student in turn holds up his/her new object and says *Whose is this?*
● The others should reply with a possessive (e.g. *It's Mario's* or *It's his*).
● When they have correctly identified the owner, he or she says *Yes, it's mine* and takes it back.

Alternative approach to Exercise 3
● If your students don't mind slightly childish activities, take into the classroom a set of little 'presents' (toys etc.), and give them out.
● When students have all got a present, get them to hold them up and try to memorize what everybody has got.
● Then proceed as in Exercise 3.

Optional activity   Recognition by touch
● Bring a student out to the front of the class.
● Borrow his/her watch (or keys or glasses), and borrow some things of the same kind from the class.
● Get the victim to stand with his/her back to the class.
● Put the objects one at a time into his or her hands (which must be behind his/her back), and see if your victim can identify his/her own property.
● The victim should say for each object *This one isn't mine/These aren't mine* or *This one's mine/These are mine*. (Put these sentences on the board.)

Optional activity   Stealing students' possessions
● As you walk round the class, try to 'steal' things from students' desks.
● As soon as somebody notices you doing this, teach *Hey, that's mine!* and get the whole class to practise it.
● Go on doing this through the lesson.

4 *My* and *mine*, etc.
● This can be done orally or in writing, as you prefer.

5 Listening for information
● Make sure students know all the words in the table. Explain *belong to*.
● The conversations are not difficult. Play each one through and stop for students to write their answers.
● Play through the recording a second time if necessary.
● Let students compare notes; check the answers with them.

Tapescript for Exercise 5: see page 182

Answer to Exercise 5
The car belongs to Jane, the trousers to Pat, the glasses to George, the dictionary to Edna, the plate to Jane and the book to Keith.

Practice Book
● Tell students which exercises you want them to do.

Unit 31: Lesson D

Students practise eliciting and analysing information.

Structures: Simple Present interrogative; *somebody, anybody* etc.; *something, anything* etc.; *somewhere, anywhere* etc.

Words and expressions to learn: *shut; get away from; argument; awake; mirror; anybody; anywhere; nowhere.*

Language notes and possible problems

***Somebody, something, somewhere,* etc.** Students have already met most of the words in this series. Exercise 3 pulls them together. Students should realize that the difference between *somebody* and *anybody* is the same as the difference between *some* and *any* (which may need revising).

Some students may have met *someone, anyone* etc.: these mean exactly the same as the compounds with *-body.*

Note that in American English *someplace* is common as a variant of *somewhere.*

1 Survey

- Run through the questions with the students.
- Make sure they understand all of them and know how to express their answers.
- Divide up the questions so that each student has a different one to ask. (In a small class, give each student more than one question.)
- In a relaxed and broad-minded class, you may be able to add some more indiscreet questions if you wish (e.g. *Do you often fall in love? Do you pick your nose when nobody's looking?*).
- Let the students ask you their questions before they start, so as to check their pronunciation.
- Then continue with the walk-round and survey as in the exercise instructions.

2 *Somebody, something, somewhere* etc.

- Before starting, make sure students remember the difference between *some* and *any*.
- Do the first few examples orally, making sure all the students understand the reasons for the answers.
- Then get them to write down the answers to the others.
- Let them compare notes, and go over the answers.

3 Which word is different?

- Students can do this by group discussion, or try it individually before comparing notes.
- You will need to help them to find some of the 'superordinate' words.

Answers
1. *bread* is different (the others are all *drinks*) 2. *dancing* (*housework*) 3. *big* (*colours*) 4. *green* (*hair colours*) 5. *water* (*food*) 6. *sheep* (*vehicles; means of transport*) 7. *Mars* (*star signs*) 8. *Christmas* (*months*) 9. *TV* (*things you can read*); *a letter* (*not public*) 10. *friend* (*relations*)

4 Authentic listening

- Students listen to a three-year-old doing a 'Which word is different?' exercise.
- The first time you play the recording, ask the students to listen only for which word the child chooses in each case.
- Then play the recording again, pausing after each answer, to give students time to write down the reason the child gives.
- You will probably have to pause after each of the three reasons in question 6.
- Play the recording another time if students seem to need it.

Answers
1. Book – because it's something to read in.
2. Fish – because it lives underwater.
3. Banana – because I can't eat it.
4. Cup – because you drink out of it.
5. Chair – because it's something to sit on.
6. Tree, grass, flower (and 'tree') – because sometimes you can climb on a tree; and you can smell the flowers sometimes; and you can walk on grass.
7. Sing – because it's something that you enjoy.
8. None of them are different; they're just all people.
9. Watch – because the others are a bit like watch, but not the same looking, not the same things doing.
(You might want to point out to your students that the grammar in the last answer is not standard.)

5 Summary

- Go over the summary with the students.
- This may be a good moment to advise them to start revision for the final test which comes after Unit 32.

Practice Book

- Tell students which exercises you want them to do.

D Do you ever talk to yourself?

1 Survey of people's personal habits.
a. Make sure you know how to answer all the following questions in English.
b. Choose one of the questions (a different one from the other students), and go round the class asking the others your question.
c. Work out a statistic. Examples:

'Seventy-five per cent of the students in this class eat between meals.'
'Three students out of eight talk to themselves.'

1. Do you lie in bed after waking up?
2. Do you like people to talk to you before breakfast?
3. What do you have for breakfast?
4. Do you get dressed before or after breakfast?
5. What do you wear in bed?
6. Do you eat between meals?
7. Do you ever shut yourself in the bathroom to get away from people?
8. Do you ever talk to yourself?
9. Do you daydream at work?
10. Do you have arguments with other people in your head?
11. Are you more awake in the morning or the evening?
12. Do you sing in the bath?
13. Do you wash your clothes yourself, or does somebody else wash them for you?
14. Do you often cook for yourself?
15. Do you like shopping?
16. Do you do your ironing yourself, or does somebody else do it for you?
17. Do you eat in bed?
18. Do you like looking in a mirror?

2 Put in one of these words.

somebody	anybody	everybody	nobody
something	anything	everything	nothing
somewhere	anywhere	everywhere	nowhere

1. .... can speak all the languages in the world.
2. I think there's .... at the door.
3. 'Where are my keys?' 'I've seen them ...., but I can't remember where.'
4. Have you got .... to eat?
5. Does .... know where I put my glasses?
6. You can find Coca Cola ....
7. I need .... to read – have you got a paper?
8. I'm bored – there's .... to do.
9. .... needs love.
10. My wife and I always tell each other ....
11. 'Come and see a film with us.' 'I don't want to go ....'
12. 'Where can I find a good job with plenty of money and no work?' '...........'

3 Vocabulary revision. Which word is different?
Can you find a word that names all the others? Example:

sofa   chair   table   wall   bed
'Wall is different. The others are all furniture.'

1. tea   coffee   bread   milk
2. cooking   cleaning   ironing   dancing
3. green   big   blue   red
4. fair   blond   red   green   grey   dark
5. water   meat   bread   fish
6. car   sheep   train   bicycle
7. Aries   Taurus   Mars   Gemini
8. July   Christmas   March   January
9. book   letter   TV   newspaper
10. uncle   friend   sister   mother

4 Now listen to a little boy doing the same kind of exercise. Which word does he choose each time, and what is his reason?

1. horse   dog   book   cat
2. fish   lamb   beef   pork
3. apple   orange   pear   banana
4. knife   fork   cup   spoon
5. run   walk   chair   jump
6. TV   grass   flower   tree
7. shout   cry   laugh   sing
8. Mummy   Daddy   Mark   Granny
9. watch   calculator   shirt   camera

5 Look at the summary on page 159 with your teacher.

Revision and fluency practice

A You have to throw a six

1 Put the beginnings and ends together.

SOME OF THE RULES OF SNAKES AND LADDERS

In order to move,	you have to throw a dice.
Before starting,	you have to go down it.
If you come to a snake,	you have to go back four squares.
If you come to a ladder,	you have to throw a six.
If you throw a six,	you have to go up it.
If you land on an occupied square,	you have to miss a turn.
If you throw three sixes one after another,	you can have another throw.

2 Match the games and the rules.

You have to hit a ball over a net.
You have to kick a ball into a net.
You have to hit a ball into a small hole.
You have to capture a king.
You have to hit a ball and run.
You have to hit a ball into a net with a
stick.

hockey
chess
football
golf
tennis
baseball

3

In Britain: nobody has to do military service;
you don't have to carry an identity card; you have
to drive on the left; you don't have to pay to go into
a museum; you have to be over 18 to drink alcohol
in a pub or bar; you have to pay for your drink
before you drink it.
What is the situation in your country?

4 What do these people have to do?

A person who wants to travel by air.
A secretary.
Somebody who wants to cook a steak.
A person who wants to get into a university in
your country.
A person who wants a driving licence.

5 Work in pairs. One of you chooses a job from this list (without telling his/her partner).

architect	lorry driver	coal miner	doctor
electrician	photographer	businessman	
secretary	pilot	teacher	shop assistant

The other asks the following questions, and then tries to guess his/her partner's job.

Do you have to get up early?
Do you have to get your hands dirty?
Do you have to travel?
Do you have to think a lot?
Do you have to study for a long time to learn the job?
Do you have to work long hours?
Do you have to handle money?
Do you have to work with people a lot?
Do you have to write letters?
Do you have to use machines?

Unit 32: Lesson A

> **Students revise** the use of *have to* talk about obligation.

Language notes
Have to You may need to remind students that *have to*, unlike *have got*, is often used as an ordinary 'lexical' verb (questions and negatives constructed with *do*).

For a note on the difference between *have to* and *have got to*, see page 99.

Note the pronunciation of *have to* (/'hæftə/).

Optional extra materials
A snakes and ladders board would, of course, make a nice visual aid for Exercise 1. You could even spend a few minutes playing the game, if time is not short.

1 Snakes and ladders
• Explain to students that the complete board has 100 squares, that you move by throwing a dice (draw a dice on the board), and that the first person to get to the top is the winner.
• Don't tell students any more than this: they can work out the rest of the rules by doing the exercise.
• Help with vocabulary or let students use dictionaries.
• When they are ready, let them compare notes and then give them the answers.

Answers
In order to move, you have to throw a dice.
Before starting, you have to throw a six.
If you come to a snake, you have to go down it.
If you come to a ladder, you have to go up it.
If you throw a six, you can have another throw.
If you land on an occupied square, you have to go back four
    squares.
If you throw three sixes one after another, you have to miss a
    turn.

2 Games and rules
• See if students can do this without asking questions about vocabulary or using dictionaries – if they are familiar with most of the games they ought to be able to solve the problem by making intelligent guesses.

Optional activity
• Follow up by asking volunteers to explain the rules of other games.

3 Rules and regulations
• Go through the text with the students explaining difficulties.
• Then ask them to write a few sentences saying what the equivalent situation in their country is.
• You may also like to ask them to comment on the British laws (teach *I think it's a good thing; I think it's a bad thing.*)
• This might lead to a small-scale discussion.

4 Requirements
• Ask students to work in groups of three or four.
• Each group should choose two of the situations and try to draw up a complete list of the requirements for each one.
• When they are ready, get a spokesperson for each group to read the group's list to the class.

5 Professions
• This exercise gives students a chance to practise question-forms, and affirmative and negative short answers (*Yes, I do*; *No, I don't*).
• Demonstrate yourself first of all (choose a profession and get the students to ask you the questions).
• Then let them continue in groups.

Practice Book
• There is no Practice Book work in Unit 32. Students should use homework time to prepare for the test that follows the unit.

Unit 32: Lesson B

> **Students do** a variety of revision activities involving the idea of correctness.

1 Picture mistakes
● Ask students to write their answers to some of the problems; others can be done by discussion.
● You may like to write some useful sentence-patterns on the board before starting:
The ... should(n't) be ...
The ... should(n't) have ...
The ... has(n't) got ...
The ... is in the wrong place.
● Students have met *should* briefly, but you may need to remind them of its meaning and use.

2 The gorilla story
● The best approach is for students to have the parts of the story on separate pieces of paper, and to work with their books closed.
● Before the lesson, copy out the sections of the story on separate pieces of paper (don't bother to write the numbers). Be very careful to get punctuation and capitalization right.
● If you have too many students, split some of the sections; if you have too few students, miss out the sections that don't belong (4, 9, 17) and/or run some of the sections together, or give some students two sections.
● Tell students to close their books and give out the papers. Tell students to memorize their sections.
● Walk round explaining any difficulties and helping with pronunciation.
● Get students to sit in a circle, if possible, and say their sections in turn.
● Ask them to decide which section begins the story. (The indefinite article in section 7 gives a clue.)
● Then see if students can work out which is the next section. The person with this section should go and sit next to the one with the beginning.
● Students should continue in the same way until they have worked out the whole story.
● It may be useful for them to appoint a 'secretary' to help coordinate what they are doing.
● Finally, they should recite the story from beginning to end; check that they've got it right.
● If it is not convenient to do the exercise in this way, it can be done with books open, working directly from the text, preferably in small groups.
● During the exercise, encourage students to use *at the beginning, first, next, in the middle, before, after,* etc.

The correct sequence is: 7, 19, 2, 16, 6, 3, 18, 10, 5, 14, 8, 12, 1, 11, 15, 13.

3 Listening and correcting
● Each sentence in this exercise is accompanied by some words or a sound effect on the recording.
● What the students hear will contradict what they read in some way; their job is to change the words in the sentences so that they are correct.
● A good way to do the exercise is in two stages: play the recording right through once while students simply underline or circle what is wrong; then play it again sentence by sentence while they make their corrections.
● In most cases the right answer can be expressed in more than one way.

Tapescript for Exercise 3
1. Man saying very slowly 'Hello, Ann, I'm home'.
2. Woman saying very unhappily 'Look – a terrible thing has happened.'
3. Sound of a car running very badly.
4. Noise of taps running; taps being turned off; person getting into bath and shouting with pain.
5. Woman saying 'Peter! How are you?' in a very seductive voice.
6. Sound of somebody knocking at door. Enraged scream of 'Go away!'
7. Sound of heavy rain, wind etc.
8. Man singing very badly.
9. Noise of man falling down stairs.

4 Revision of verbal grammar
● This should preferably be done as an individual exercise (followed by discussion of the points) so that you can see if any students are having difficulty with specific items.
● Note that two answers are possible for question 5: *I don't like shopping* or *I don't like to shop.* The first structure is more common in British English.

5 Revision of interrogatives
● Here, students have to choose the correct auxiliary verb and get the word order right.
● The exercise is a little more difficult; it is a good test of students' mastery of the verbal grammar they have studied so far.

131

B Get it right

1 What's wrong with the pictures? Examples:

'*The elephant's ears should be bigger.*'
'*The elephant's ears are too small.*'

2 Put the parts of the story in the right order. Three of the parts don't belong in the story.

1. 'Excuse me,
2. and ordered a whisky.
3. and then he thought
4. so he stood up
5. The gorilla gave him the money
6. but he gave him the whisky,
7. A gorilla went into a pub,
8. There was silence for a few minutes,
9. 'Is it raining?'
10. so he asked him for £5.
11. but you don't often see a gorilla in a pub.'
12. and then the barman said
13. 'with whisky at £5 a glass.'
14. and started drinking.
15. 'It's not surprising,' said the gorilla
16. The barman was rather surprised,
17. on the other side of the room
18. 'Gorillas probably don't understand much about money,'
19. walked up to the bar,

3 In these sentences, some of the words are wrong. Listen to the recording and correct them.

1. 'Hello, Mary, I'm home,' said John, speaking rather fast.
2. 'John!' she said happily. 'Listen – a wonderful thing has happened.'
3. 'How's the car running?' 'Very well.'
4. 'Is your bath OK?' 'Just fine.'
5. 'Peter – how are you?' she said coldly.
6. Sally knocked at the door. 'Come in!' said a friendly voice.
7. It's a fine day. The sun's shining.
8. Little birds are singing.
9. Robert walked quietly up the stairs.

4 Put the correct verb form into the sentences.

1. I .... 800km yesterday. (drive)
2. We .... our cousins from Scotland last weekend. (see)
3. 'How was the party?' 'Very nice. George .... too much.' (drink)
4. That child .... too much TV. (watch)
5. I don't like .... (shop)
6. 'Would you like a cigarette?' 'No, thanks. ....'
   (I don't smoke / I'm not smoking)
7. What .... tomorrow? (do you do / are you doing)
8. 'Shall we go out?' 'No, ...' (it rains / it's raining)
9. I .... Mary for about six years. (know)
10. .... you ever .... Japanese food? (eat)

5 Make questions.

1. where | your wife | work?
2. your children | live | with you?
3. you ever | been | to Africa?
4. Mary and Peter | going to | get married?
5. What | your father | do | when he stops work next year?
6. why | you | come home so late last night?

131

C Listening and cartoons

1 Listen to the song, and try to write down the words.

2 Listen to the story, and imagine or mime the actions.

3 Say what you think of the cartoons. Examples:

'I think number one's funny. I don't like number two.'
'I don't understand number three. I like number four best.'

"Bills, bills, bills..."

1

2

MY SON IS INNOCENT

3

ACKEN.

" I'M SURE YOU AND MOTHER WILL LIKE EACH OTHER."

4

'Well, If I Called the Wrong Number, Why Did You Answer the Phone?'

5

Unit 32: Lesson C

Students practise listening skills and discuss their reactions to a group of cartoons.

1 Song (*Hello Goodbye*)

● The words are extremely easy – there is not one word that students have not met.
● Play the recording right through twice first of all. Ask students what they have understood.
● Play it again with pauses; let them write down what they hear.
● Let them compare notes, and then tell them the words.

Text of the song for Exercise 1

You say yes, I say no,
You say stop and I say go go go.

Oh no
You say goodbye and I say hello,
Hello, hello.
I don't know why you say goodbye,
I say hello, hello, hello.
I don't know why you say goodbye,
I say hello.

I say high, you say low,
You say why and I say I don't know, oh no.
You say goodbye, and I say hello.
Hello, hello.
I don't know why you say goodbye.
I say hello.

Hello, hello.
I don't know why you say goodbye,
I say hello. Hello.

2 Miming to a story

●This exercise is most interesting if you have a reasonably large room or a hall with space for the whole class to move around. Failing this, you can have the whole mime done by three or four volunteers in front of the class.
● First of all, explain to the people who are going to mime that they will hear a story in the present tense, beginning *You are walking*..., and that it is their job to do or mime the actions that they hear.
● The exercise is unlikely to work with adolescents or shy students. As an alternative, you can ask them to listen and imagine the story, telling you afterwards how much they understood.
● If you want a more structured task, ask people to listen twice and note down all the *changes* they notice in the story. (For instance, you are walking and then you stop; you feel tired, but after standing in the sea you feel better.)

Text of the story for Exercise 2

You are walking along a beach, by the sea. It's a hot day. The sun is burning down on your head. You're hot and tired. You're walking slowly... more and more slowly... you stop. You sit down on the sand. You look at the sea. You pick up some small stones from the beach, and you throw them into the sea. One... two... three... four... five... You stand up slowly, and you take off your shoes. You walk forward, and stand with your feet in the water. That feels good. It's very good; very, very good.

Suddenly you see something in the water. A long way away. You look very hard, but you can't see just what it is. It comes nearer, nearer. It's a person. A man. He walks towards you out of the sea. An old man, with white hair, and a beautiful face. He stops. There he is, standing in front of you. He smiles at you – a wonderful warm smile. You smile back at him. You close your eyes for a moment. You open them again: he's gone. He isn't there any more. Where is he? You look round – you look everywhere. Nothing to be seen. Was it a dream?

You start walking again. Now the sun has gone. It's cold. Very, very cold. You walk faster, to get warm. Faster and faster. There are stones under your feet – hard, sharp stones. Your feet hurt. You feel unhappy. Suddenly you see a small house in front of you. You walk up to the door. You open the door and walk in. There he is, smiling at you – the old man. You close the door and walk towards him.

You wake up.

3 Reactions to cartoons

● This can begin as a relatively structured exercise, with students expressing their reactions as in the examples.
● As they continue talking, it may develop into a small-scale discussion as students exchange views.
● Attitudes to humour vary widely from one culture to another; some students may have difficulty seeing why a particular cartoon is supposed to be funny.

Unit 32: Lesson D

Students prepare and perform sketches, in which they use some of the language they have learnt during the course.

They should be fairly used to this kind of activity by now, and it is probably unnecessary to give detailed instructions.

See instructions for Lesson 22B for notes on procedure if required.

The sketch is likely to take some time to prepare and rehearse, particularly if students learn their parts by heart (which is preferable). However, the results are likely to justify the time spent.

Some students may be baffled by the range of choice given; help them make up their minds if necessary.

It might be pleasant to invite students or teachers from other classes to see the students perform, if this is feasible.

You may also wish to tape- or video-record the sketches.

NOW DO REVISION TEST THREE. (See page 172 and the Test Book.)

D A visitor

Prepare and practise a sketch with two or three other students. In your sketch, you must have:

A VISITOR

This can be a person, an animal, a thing... You decide.

A PROBLEM

For example:

Somebody is feeling ill.
There isn't enough money.
Somebody or something is lost.
Somebody can't understand.
Somebody is unhappy.
Something is broken.
Something doesn't work.

ROLES

Decide who you are.

What are your names?
What are your jobs?
What kind of personalities do you have?

'LANGUAGE FUNCTIONS'

Use English to do some of these things:

buy
sell
ask for information
explain
complain
invite
greet
suggest
order
offer
describe
compliment
compare
give instructions
express feelings
predict
borrow
lend
get to know somebody
give opinions
thank
apologize

A PLACE

Where are you? Perhaps:

at an airport
on a plane
on a ship
on a train
in a hotel
in a restaurant
in a shop
at a station
in a park
in the street
at home
in a pub
at the doctor's
at the North Pole
in the Sahara Desert
on the moon

Unit 1

Grammar and structures

Be: singular

I am /aɪ æm/	I'm /aɪm/	am I...? /æm aɪ/
you are /ju: ɑ:(r)/	you're /jɔ:(r)/	are you...? /ɑ: ju:/
he is /hi: ɪz/	he's /hi:z/	is he...? /ɪz hi:/
she is /ʃi: ɪz/	she's /ʃi:z/	is she...? /ɪz ʃi:/
it is /ɪt ɪz/	it's /ɪts/	is it...? /ɪz ɪt/
my name is /maɪ neɪm ɪz/	my name's /maɪ neɪmz/	is your name...? /ɪz jɔ: neɪm/

I am not /aɪ æm nɒt/	I'm not /aɪm nɒt/
you are not /ju: ɑ: nɒt/	you aren't /ju: ɑ:nt/
he is not /hi: ɪz nɒt/	he isn't /hi: ɪznt/
she is not /ʃi: ɪz nɒt/	she isn't /ʃi: ɪznt/
it is not /ɪt ɪz nɒt/	it isn't /ɪt ɪznt/
my name is not /maɪ neɪm ɪz nɒt/	my name isn't /maɪ neɪm ɪznt/

'Is your/his/her name Mark Perkins?'
'Yes, it is.' ~~(Yes, it's.)~~ 'No, it isn't.'

'Are you Fred Andrews?'
'Yes, I am.' ~~(Yes, I'm.)~~

Possessives

What is / What's	your / his / her	name?

My / Your / His / Her	name is / name's	John. / Catherine. / Mary Lake. / Harry Brown.

From

'Where are you from?' 'I'm from Canada.'

Where is / Where's	he / she	from?

He / She	's / is	from Scotland.

I speak a little English.

Here's my bus.

Words and expressions to learn

Nouns person, place or thing
name /neɪm/
first name /'fɜ:st neɪm/
surname /'sɜ:neɪm/
Britain /'brɪtn/
England /'ɪŋglənd/
Scotland /'skɒtlənd/
the United States /ðə ju:'naɪtɪd 'steɪts/

Pronouns
my /maɪ/
your /jɔ:(r)/
his /hɪz/
her /hə(r), hɜ:(r)/
I /aɪ/
you /jʊ, ju:/
he /hi, hi:/
she /ʃi, ʃi:/
it /ɪt/

Verbs action
am /əm, æm/
are /ə(r), ɑ:(r)/
is /ɪz/
speak /spi:k/

Adjectives describes
British /'brɪtɪʃ/
English /'ɪŋglɪʃ/
Scottish /'skɒtɪʃ/
American /ə'merɪkən/

Question-words
what /wɒt/
where /weə(r)/
how /haʊ/

Numbers
1 one /wʌn/
2 two /tu:/
3 three /θri:/
4 four /fɔ:(r)/
5 five /faɪv/
6 six /sɪks/
7 seven /'sevən/
8 eight /eɪt/
9 nine /naɪn/
10 ten /ten/
11 eleven /ɪ'levən/
12 twelve /twelv/
13 thirteen /θɜ:'ti:n/
14 fourteen /fɔ:'ti:n/
15 fifteen /fɪf'ti:n/
16 sixteen /sɪks'ti:n/
17 seventeen /sevən'ti:n/
18 eighteen /eɪ'ti:n/
19 nineteen /naɪn'ti:n/
20 twenty /'twenti/

Other words and expressions

and /ənd, ænd/
from /frəm, frɒm/
not /nɒt/
here /hɪə(r)/
a little /ə 'lɪtl/
Hello. /hə'ləʊ/
Hi. /haɪ/

How are you? /haʊ 'ɑ: jʊ/
Fine, thanks. /'faɪn 'θæŋks/
How do you do? /'haʊ djə 'du:/
Goodbye. /gʊd'baɪ/
Bye. /baɪ/
See you. /'si: jʊ/
Thank you. /'θæŋkju/

Yes. /jes/
No. /nəʊ/
I don't know. /aɪ dəʊnt 'nəʊ/
Excuse me. /ɪks'kju:z mi/
(I'm) sorry. /(aɪm) 'sɒri/
That's right. /'ðæts 'raɪt/
Oh. /əʊ/

Unit 2

Grammar and structures

Asking and answering

What do you do?

I'm a	doctor.
	dentist.
	teacher.
	student.
	housewife.

I'm an	artist.
	engineer.
	electrician.

(I'm doctor.)

'How old are you?' 'I'm thirty-six.'

Words and expressions to learn

Nouns

Learn three or more of these:
teacher /'ti:tʃə(r)/
artist /'ɑ:tɪst/
shop assistant /'ʃɒp ə'sɪstənt/
secretary /'sekrətri/
doctor /'dɒktə(r)/
dentist /'dentɪst/
student /'stju:dnt/
engineer /endʒə'nɪə(r)/
electrician /ɪlek'trɪʃən/
housewife /'haʊswaɪf/

morning /'mɔ:nɪŋ/
afternoon /ɑ:ftə'nu:n/
evening /'i:vnɪŋ/
night /naɪt/
nationality /næʃə'næləti/

Adjectives

married /'mærɪd/
single /'sɪŋgl/
divorced /dɪ'vɔ:st/
different /'dɪfrənt/
good /gʊd/
old /əʊld/

Numbers

30 thirty /'θɜ:ti/
31 thirty-one /θɜ:ti'wʌn/
40 forty /'fɔ:ti/
50 fifty /'fɪfti/
60 sixty /'sɪksti/
70 seventy /'sevənti/
80 eighty /'eɪti/
90 ninety /'naɪnti/
100 a hundred /ə 'hʌndrəd/

Other words and expressions

or /ɔ:(r)/
well /wel/
Good morning (afternoon etc.).
I'm very well, thank you.
not bad /nɒt 'bæd/
How old are you? /haʊ 'əʊld ɑ: jʊ/
How do you spell ...?
/'haʊ dju 'spel/
write /raɪt/
a, an /ə, ən/
do /də, du:/
Mr /'mɪstə(r)/
Mrs /'mɪsɪz/
Ms /mɪz/or/məz/
Miss /mɪs/

Unit 3

Grammar and structures

Be: plural

we are /wi: ə(r), wi: ɑ:(r)/	we're /wɪə(r)/
you are /ju: ə(r), ju: ɑ:(r)/	you're /jɔ:(r)/
they are /ðeɪ ə(r), ðeɪ ɑ:(r)/	they're /ðeə(r)/

are we...? /ɑ: wi:/
are you...? /ɑ: ju:/
are they...? /ɑ: ðeɪ/

we are not /wi: ə nɒt/	we aren't /wi: ɑ:nt/
you are not /ju: ə nɒt/	you aren't /ju: ɑ:nt/
they are not /ðeɪ ə nɒt/	they aren't /ðeɪ ɑ:nt/

Have got

I have got (I've got) two brothers.
Bruce and Sally have got one daughter. They've got one
   daughter.
'Have you got any children?' 'Yes, I have.' (Yes, I've.)
   'No, I haven't.'

Noun plurals

Singular	Plural
parent	parents
boy	boys
family	families
boss	bosses
wife	wives
child	children

Possessive: 's

John's father. (father's John the John's father)
Joyce's (/'dʒɔɪsɪz/) mother.

Personal pronouns and possessives

dai meishi

Singular	Plural	
I	we	
you	you	
he		*personal pronouns*
she	they	
it		
my	our	
your	your	
his		*possessives*
her	their	
its		

Time

What time is it?	It's ten past seven.
	It's a quarter past seven.
	It's half past seven.
	It's ten to eight.
	It's eight o'clock.

'Who is John's wife?' 'Mary is.' (Mary's.)

John is tall. John and Mary are tall. (talls)

Words and expressions to learn

Nouns

child /tʃaɪld/
   (*plural* children /'tʃɪldrən/)
boy /bɔɪ/
girl /gɜ:l/
family /'fæməli/
   (*plural* families /'fæməlɪz/)
friend /frend/
boyfriend /'bɔɪfrend/
girlfriend /'gɜ:lfrend/
boss /bɒs/ (*plural* bosses/'bɒsɪz/)
question /'kwestʃən/
age /eɪdʒ/
time /taɪm/

Learn seven or more of these:	
wife /waɪf/ (*plural* wives /waɪvz/)	nephew /'nevju:/
husband /'hʌzbənd/	niece /ni:s/
brother /'brʌðə(r)/	aunt /ɑ:nt/
sister /'sɪstə(r)/	uncle /'ʌŋkl/
son /sʌn/	cousin /'kʌzən/
daughter /'dɔ:tə(r)/	parent /'peərənt/
mother /'mʌðə(r)/	
father /'fɑ:ðə(r)/	
grandmother /'grændmʌðə(r)/	
grandfather /'grændfɑ:ðə(r)/	
grandson /'grændsʌn/	
granddaughter /'grænddɔ:tə(r)/	

Pronouns

we /wiː/
they /ðeɪ/

Possessives

our /aʊə(r)/
their /ðeə(r)/

Adjectives

> **Learn five or more of these:**
> tall /tɔːl/
> fair /feə(r)/
> dark /dɑːk/
> pretty /'prɪti/
> short /ʃɔːt/
> good-looking /gʊd'lʊkɪŋ/
> strong /strɒŋ/
> young /jʌŋ/
> intelligent /ɪn'telɪdʒənt/
> fat /fæt/
> slim /slɪm/

Other words and expressions

have (got) /həv, hæv (gɒt)/
who /huː/
very /'veri/
fairly /'feəli/
not very /'nɒt veri/
sit down /sɪt 'daʊn/
please /pliːz/
of course /əv 'kɔːs/
aren't you? /'ɑːnt jʊ/
Pardon? /'pɑːdn/
too /tuː/
but /bət, bʌt/
a moment /ə 'məʊmənt/
half /hɑːf/
a quarter /ə 'kwɔːtə(r)/
past /pɑːst/
to /tuː/
o'clock /ə'klɒk/
What time is it? /wɒt 'taɪm ɪz ɪt/
What does . . . mean? /'wɒt dəz . . . 'miːn/

Unit 4

Grammar and structures

Newcastle is **a** large town in **the** north of England.

a small town (a town small)

on the beach   **in** Paris   **at** the Kremlin

That's in Brazil, **isn't it**?

Words and expressions to learn

Nouns

the north /ðə 'nɔːθ/
the south /ðə 'saʊθ/
the east /ði 'iːst/
the west /ðə 'west/
the north-east
the north-west
town /taʊn/
village /'vɪlɪdʒ/
city /'sɪti/ (*plural* cities /'sɪtɪz/)
coast /kəʊst/
capital /'kæpɪtl/
tourist /'tʊərɪst/
centre /'sentə(r)/
mountain /'maʊntɪn/
beach /biːtʃ/
population /pɒpjʊ'leɪʃn/
place /pleɪs/

Adjectives

large /lɑːdʒ/
small /smɔːl/
industrial /ɪn'dʌstrɪəl/
nice /naɪs/
exciting /ɪk'saɪtɪŋ/
noisy /'nɔɪzi/
quiet /'kwaɪət/

Prepositions

in /ɪn/
on /ɒn/
at /ət, æt/
near /nɪə(r)/
of /əv, ɒv/

Numbers

101 a hundred and one
132 a hundred and thirty-two
300 three hundred (three hundreds)
1,000 a thousand /'θaʊznd/
1,400 one thousand four hundred
1,000,000 a million /'mɪljən/

Other words and expressions

the /ðə, ði/
about /ə'baʊt/
that /ðæt/
I think /aɪ 'θɪŋk/
Where in . . . ? /'weər ɪn/

Grammar and structures

There is / There are

There is a big kitchen in the flat.
(/ðərɪzə.../)
There's a small bathroom.
(/ðəzə.../)
There are two bedrooms.
(/ðərə.../)
Is there a...? (/'ɪz ðərə.../)
Are there...? (/'ɑː ðə.../)
There is not... (/ðərɪznɒt/)
There isn't... (/ðər'ɪznt/)
There are not... (/ðərənɒt/)
There aren't... (/ðər'ɑːnt/)
Yes, there is. (Yes, there's.)
   No, there isn't.
Yes, there are. No, there aren't.

Simple Present tense

I live	I work
you live	you work
he/she live**s**	he/she work**s**
we live	we work
you live	you work
they live	they work

Prepositions of place

in Birmingham   **in** Queen Street
   in a flat
at 17 Queen Street, Birmingham
on the fourth floor

Telephones

Can I take a message?
Could I speak to Sally?
'Who's that?' 'This is John.'
Could you tell Mary that Bill called?

Noun plurals

	Singular	Plural
Regular:	flat	flats
	room	rooms
	family	families
	address	addresses
Irregular:	man	men
	woman	women
	child	children
	person	people
	wife	wives

Words and expressions to learn

Nouns

house /haʊs/
   (*plural* houses /'haʊzɪz/)
room /ruːm/
flat /flæt/
floor /flɔː(r)/
ground floor /graʊnd flɔː(r)/
first floor /fɜːst flɔː(r)/
street /striːt/
road /rəʊd/
address /ə'dres/
telephone /'telɪfəʊn/
phone /fəʊn/
number /'nʌmbə(r)/
(tele)phone number
food /fuːd/
man /mæn/ (*plural* men /men/)
woman /'wʊmən/
   (*plural* women /'wɪmɪn/)
person /'pɜːsən/
   (*plural* people /'piːpl/)

> **Learn four or more of these:**
> bedroom /'bedruːm/
> kitchen /'kɪtʃɪn/
> bathroom /'bɑːθruːm/
> toilet /'tɔɪlɪt/
> living room /'lɪvɪŋ ruːm/
> window /'wɪndəʊ/
> door /dɔː(r)/
> stairs /steəz/
> wall /wɔːl/
> garage /'gærɑːʒ/

> **Learn four or more of these:**
> furniture /'fɜːnɪtʃə(r)/
> chair /tʃeə(r)/
> bed /bed/
> cooker /'kʊkə(r)/
> sofa /'səʊfə/
> fridge /frɪdʒ/
> armchair /'ɑːmtʃeə(r)/
> television /telɪ'vɪʒn/
> TV /tiː'viː/
> cupboard /'kʌbəd/
> bath /bɑːθ/
> wardrobe /'wɔːdrəʊb/
> table /'teɪbl/

Verbs

live /lɪv/
work /wɜːk/
can /kən, kæn/
could /kʊd/

Adjectives

big /bɪg/
clean /kliːn/
next /nekst/

Numbers

1st first /fɜːst/
2nd second /'sekənd/
3rd third /θɜːd/
4th fourth /fɔːθ/
5th fifth /fɪfθ/
6th sixth /sɪksθ/
7th seventh /'sevənθ/
8th eighth /eɪtθ/
9th ninth /naɪnθ/

Other words and expressions

this /ðɪs/
well /wel/
Love /lʌv/
speaking /'spiːkɪŋ/
wrong number /rɒŋ 'nʌmbə(r)/
one moment /wʌn 'məʊmənt/
Can I take a message?
   /'kæn aɪ 'teɪk ə 'mesɪdʒ/
You're welcome. /jɔː 'welkəm/
double /'dʌbl/

Unit 6

Grammar and structures
Simple Present tense

I start you start he/she/it start**s** we start they start	do I start? do you start? do**es** he/she/it start? do we start? do they start?	I do not (don't) start you do not (don't) start he/she/it do**es** not (doesn't) start we do not (don't) start they do not (don't) start

Spelling: he start**s** he stop**s** he work**s** he like**s** he love**s**
he finish**es** he watch**es** he go**es** he do**es** he stud**ies**
Pronunciation: -(e)s = /z/: loves   goes   sells   repairs
-(e)s = /s/: works   gets   likes
-es = /ɪz/: finishes   watches
do /duː, də/   does /dʌz, dəz/   don't /dəʊnt/   doesn't /'dʌznt/
'He works on Saturdays.' 'Does he work on Saturdays?' ~~(Do he works? Does he works?)~~
'Yes, he does.' 'No, he doesn't.'
'Do you work on Saturdays?' ~~(Work you?)~~ 'Yes, I do. I work on Saturday mornings.'

'Do you like dogs?' ~~(Do you like the dogs?)~~ 'Yes, I do.' ~~(Yes, I like.)~~ 'No, I don't.'
Everybody likes children. ~~(Everybody like . . .)~~ Nobody likes Harry. ~~(Nobody like . . .)~~

Likes and dislikes
I like my work. I like it. I like skiing (dancing, watching football). I like it.
I like dogs. I like them.
George likes Mary, but Mary doesn't like him.
'Do you like Ann?' 'Yes, I like her very much.'
I like skiing very much. ~~(I like very much skiing.)~~ I quite like tennis. I neither like nor dislike football. I don't like
rugby very much at all. Do you? I like skiing best.

Have
I have breakfast at eight o'clock.

I have you have he/she has	we have you have they have

Adding *-ing*
cook – cooking   watch – watching
work – working   read – reading

dance – dancing ~~(danceing)~~
write – writing ~~(writeing)~~

shop – shopping ~~(shoping)~~
travel – travelling ~~(traveling)~~

'**How** do you get to work?' '**By** car/train/bus/bicycle.' '**On** foot.'
'(At) **what time** do you get up?' '**At** six o'clock.'

Words and expressions to learn
The days of the week
Monday /'mʌndi/
Tuesday /'tjuːzdi/
Wednesday /'wenzdi/
Thursday /'θɜːzdi/
Friday /'fraɪdi/
Saturday /'sætədi/
Sunday /'sʌndi/

Nouns

Learn six or more of these:
breakfast /'brekfəst/
lunch /lʌntʃ/
supper /'sʌpə(r)/
book /bʊk/
tea /ti:/
coffee /'kɒfi/
shop /ʃɒp/
music /'mju:zɪk/
maths /mæθs/
dog /dɒg/
whisky /'wɪski/
letter /'letə(r)/
the sea /ðə 'si:/
cat /kæt/
clothes /kləʊðz/
job /dʒɒb/
work /wɜ:k/
tennis /'tenɪs/
newspaper
  /'nju:speɪpə(r)/
language /'læŋgwɪdʒ/
beer /bɪə(r)/
wine /waɪn/
garage /'gærɑ:ʒ/

Verbs

Learn fifteen or more of these:
like /laɪk/
dislike /dɪs'laɪk/
love /lʌv/
hate /heɪt/
watch /wɒtʃ/
cook /kʊk/
dance /dɑ:ns/
go /gəʊ/
start /stɑ:t/
open /'əʊpn/
have (lunch etc.) /hæv/
  (he/she has /hæz/)
stop /stɒp/
drink /drɪŋk/
play /pleɪ/
get up /get 'ʌp/
read /ri:d/
do /du:/
shop /ʃɒp/
travel /'trævl/
sell /sel/

Other words and expressions

Learn nine or more of these:
only /'əʊnli/
not much /nɒt 'mʌtʃ/
not . . . at all /nɒt . . . ə'tɔ:l/
him /hɪm/
her /hə(r), hɜ:(r)/
it /ɪt/
them /ðəm, ðem/
after /ɑ:ftə(r)/
(At) what time . . . ?
  /(ət) wɒt 'taɪm/
What sort of . . . ? /wɒt 'sɔ:t əv/
from . . . until /frəm . . . ən'tɪl/
nobody /'nəʊbədi/
everybody /'evribɒdi/
quite /kwaɪt/
neither . . . nor
  /'naɪðə(r) . . . nɔ:(r)/
it depends /ɪt dɪ'pendz/
by bus /baɪ 'bʌs/
by car /baɪ 'kɑ:(r)/
at the weekend /ət ðə wi:'kend/
interested in /'ɪntrəstɪd ɪn/
on holiday /ɒn 'hɒlədi/
watch TV /wɒtʃ ti:'vi:/
both /bəʊθ/

Unit 7

Grammar and structures

Uncountable and countable nouns

U	C
water	a car
(a water)	two cars
(two waters)	(a cars)
bread	a litre
(a bread)	two litres
(two breads)	(a litres)

Your hair is too long. (Your hairs are . . .)

Quantifiers

U	C (plural)
how much water?	how many cars?
too much water	too many cars
not much water	not many cars
some water	some cars
any water	any cars
a lot of water	a lot of cars
enough water	enough cars

a litre **of** water (a glass of water) a kilo **of** bananas
half a litre   half a kilo of bananas
[amount]

Some and *any*

YES	?	NO
There is some water.	Is there any water?	There isn't any water.
There are some cows.	Are there any cows?	There aren't any cows.

140

Articles

In general.

Food costs a lot of money. (The food ...)
Oranges are £1.40 a kilo. (The oranges ...)

(a particular/certain one)

Furniture is expensive. (The furniture ... Furniture are ...)

Was and were

Single.   *Plural*

I was	we were
you were	you were
he/she/it was	they were

I was in Patterson's yesterday.
Bananas were £2.25 a kilo.

Words and expressions to learn

Nouns

gram /græm/
kilo(gram) /'ki:ləʊ/
litre /'li:tə(r)/
money /'mʌni/
price /praɪs/
pound /paʊnd/
penny /'peni/ (*plural* pence)
memory /'meməri/
tree /tri:/
grass /grɑ:s/
toothpaste /'tu:θpeɪst/
shaving cream /'ʃeɪvɪŋkri:m/
perfume /'pɜ:fju:m/
light /laɪt/
hair /heə(r)/ (hairs)

Learn three or more of these:

tomato /tə'mɑ:təʊ/ (*plural* tomatoes)
egg /eg/
water /'wɔ:tə(r)/
steak /steɪk/
potato /pə'teɪtəʊ/ (*plural* potatoes)
cheese /tʃi:z/
bread /bred/
orange /'ɒrɪndʒ/
milk /mɪlk/
banana /bə'nɑ:nə/

Learn two or more of these:

cow /kaʊ/
pig /pɪg/
chicken /'tʃɪkɪn/
sheep /ʃi:p/ (*plural* sheep)
horse /hɔ:s/
duck /dʌk/

Other words and expressions

terrible /'terəbl/
yesterday /'jestədi/
I know /aɪ 'nəʊ/
Do you know? /dʒʊ 'nəʊ/
I don't remember.
    /aɪ dəʊnt rɪ'membə(r)/
I don't understand.
    /aɪ dəʊnt ʌndə'stænd/
much /mʌtʃ/
many /'meni/
how much /'haʊ 'mʌtʃ/
how many /'haʊ 'meni/
too much /'tu: 'mʌtʃ/
too many /'tu: 'meni/
a lot of /ə 'lɒt əv/
enough /ɪ'nʌf/
some /səm, sʌm/
any /eni/
listen (to) /lɪsn (tə, tu:)/
try /traɪ/

Unit 8

Grammar and structures

Prepositions

at a restaurant   **at** the cinema
at the swimming pool   **at** the disco
at school (at the school)   **at** home (at the home)

by the stairs   **on** the right   **on** the left

near the police station   **for** three hundred yards

opposite the bank   **in** bed (in the bed)

I **am** cold. (I have cold.)   I'**m** hungry.
Are you thirsty?

When Fred **is** hungry he **goes** to a restaurant.
When Lucy **is** thirsty she **has** a drink of water.

He **has** a drink. He **has** a bath. She **has** a wash.

Words and expressions to learn

Nouns

the right /ðə 'raɪt/
the left /ðə 'left/
school /sku:l/
home /həʊm/
yard /jɑ:d/

Learn seven or more of these:

phone box /'fəʊn bɒks/
supermarket /'su:pəmɑ:kɪt/
bank /bæŋk/
post office /'pəʊst ɒfɪs/
police (plural) /pə'li:s/
police station /pə'li:s steɪʃn/
car park /'kɑ: pɑ:k/
bus stop /'bʌs stɒp/
station /'steɪʃn/
swimming pool /'swɪmɪŋ pu:l/
disco /'dɪskəʊ/
cinema /'sɪnəmə/
the doctor's /ðə 'dɒktəz/
the dentist's /ðə 'dentɪsts/

➡

Adjectives

Learn five or more of these:
hungry /'hʌŋgri/
thirsty /'θɜːsti/
cold /kəʊld/
hot /hɒt/
nearest /'nɪərɪst/
happy /'hæpi/
unhappy /ʌn'hæpi/
bored /bɔːd/
tired /'taɪəd/
wet /wet/
dirty /'dɜːti/

Other words and expressions

there /ðeə(r)/
over there /əʊvə 'ðeə(r)/
then /ðen/
straight on /streɪt 'ɒn/
for three hundred yards
  /fə 'θriː 'hʌndrəd 'jɑːdz/
upstairs /ʌp'steəz/
downstairs /daʊn'steəz/
near /nɪə(r)/

next to /'nekst tə/
opposite /'ɒpəzɪt/
How far? /haʊ 'fɑː(r)/
Thank you anyway.
  /θæŋk ju: 'eniweɪ/
Not at all. /nɒt ət 'ɔːl/
at home /ət 'həʊm/
at school /ət 'skuːl/
take /teɪk/

Unit 9

Grammar and structures

Complex sentences with conjunctions

These people live in the Amazon Basin, where it is very hot.

I'm sure (that) horses eat grass.
I think (that) penguins live in the Arctic.
I don't think (that) cats eat grass.
(I think that cats don't eat grass.)

Word order: position of adverbs

It **often** rains here.
  (It rains often here.)
It **never** snows in the Congo.
Cows **certainly** eat grass.

It is **often** cold. (It often is cold.)
I am **often** tired.
She is **certainly** right.

Perhaps gorillas eat insects.
Perhaps you are right.

Will

It often **rains.** It **will rain** tomorrow.
It **is** cold. It **will be** cold tomorrow.
There **is** fog. There **will be** fog tomorrow.

Words and expressions to learn

Nouns
day /deɪ/
week /wiːk/
year /jɪə(r)/
spring /sprɪŋ/
summer /'sʌmə(r)/
autumn /'ɔːtəm/
winter /'wɪntə(r)/
wood /wʊd/
the rest /ðə 'rest/

Learn three or more of these:
weather /'weðə(r)/
rain /reɪn/
sun /sʌn/
sky /skaɪ/
fog /fɒg/
temperature /'temprətʃə(r)/
wind /wɪnd/
cloud /klaʊd/

Learn two or more of these:
fish /fɪʃ/   insect /'ɪnsekt/
meat /miːt/   vegetable
fruit /fruːt/   /'vedʒtəbl/

Learn two or more of these:
animal /'ænɪml/
gorilla /gə'rɪlə/
camel /'kæml/
parrot /'pærət/
snake /sneɪk/
polar bear /pəʊlə 'beə(r)/
tiger /'taɪgə(r)/
penguin /'peŋgwɪn/
elephant /'elɪfənt/

Verbs
sleep /sliːp/   rain /reɪn/
make /meɪk/   snow /snəʊ/
made of /'meɪd əv/   wear /weə(r)/

Adjectives

Learn two or more of these:
dry /draɪ/   windy /'wɪndi/
cool /kuːl/   foggy /'fɒgi/
sunny /'sʌni/   difficult
warm /wɔːm/   /'dɪfɪkʊlt/
cloudy /'klaʊdi/

Frequency adverbs

never /'nevə(r)/
occasionally /ə'keɪʒnəli/
once every . . . years
  /'wʌns 'evri . . . 'jɪəz/
sometimes /'sʌmtaɪmz/
quite often /'kwaɪt 'ɒfn/
often /'ɒfn/
usually /'juːʒəli/

Other words and expressions

that (conjunction) /ðət/
few /fjuː/
between /bɪ'twiːn/
once /wʌns/
tomorrow /tə'mɒrəʊ/
perhaps /pə'hæps/
certainly /'sɜːtənli/
I'm sure /aɪm 'ʃɔː(r)/
on foot /ɒn 'fʊt/
every /'evri/

142

Unit 10

Grammar and structures

Have got

I have got		I've got
you have got		you've got
he/she/it has got		he's/she's/it's got
we have got		we've got
you have got		you've got
they have got		they've got

have I got?
have you got?
has he/she/it got?
have we got?
have you got?
have they got?

I have not got		I haven't got
you have not got		you haven't got
he/she/it has not got		he/she/it hasn't got
we have not got		we haven't got
you have not got		you haven't got
they have not got		they haven't got

'Have you got any brothers or sisters?'
'Yes, I have.' ~~(Yes, I've.)~~ 'No, I haven't.'

Adjectives

long red hair ~~(red long hair) (hair long red)~~
short grey hair ~~(short and grey hair)~~
a short red dress
but: a red **and** white dress

His hair **is** grey. ~~(His hair are grey.)~~
His jeans **are** light blue. ~~(His jeans is . . .)~~

Both and all

We are $\begin{vmatrix} both \\ all \end{vmatrix}$ fair.   We have $\begin{vmatrix} both \\ all \end{vmatrix}$ got fair hair.

We $\begin{vmatrix} both \\ all \end{vmatrix}$ live in London.

Compliments

What **a** pretty dress!   What nice shoes!
That's a nice jacket. **Those** are nice trousers.

What's **this** called in English? What are **these**?

How do you say *boucles d'oreille* in English?

What colour **are** her eyes?
Pat **is** wearing blue jeans.

Words and expressions to learn

Nouns

photograph (photo) /'fəʊtəgrɑ:f ('fəʊtəʊ)/
colour /'kʌlə(r)/

Learn five or more of these:	
eye /aɪ/	hand /hænd/
nose /nəʊz/	foot /fʊt/ (*plural* feet /fi:t/)
ear /ɪə(r)/	head /hed/
mouth /maʊθ/	finger /'fɪŋgə(r)/
face /feɪs/	beard /bɪəd/
arm /ɑ:m/	moustache /mə'stɑ:ʃ/
leg /leg/	tooth /tu:θ/ (*plural* teeth /ti:θ/)

Learn five or more of these:	
sweater /'swetə(r)/	blouse /blaʊz/
jacket /'dʒækɪt/	tights /taɪts/
trousers /'traʊzəz/	bra /brɑ:/
jeans /dʒi:nz/	pants /pænts/
boots /bu:ts/	shirt /ʃɜ:t/
shoes /ʃu:z/	raincoat /'reɪnkəʊt/
socks /sɒks/	coat /kəʊt/
skirt /skɜ:t/	glasses /'glɑ:sɪz/
dress /dres/	

Verbs

touch /tʌtʃ/
arrive at /ə'raɪv ət/
meet /mi:t/
say /seɪ/

Adjectives

Learn ten or more of these:	
long /lɒŋ/	orange /'ɒrɪndʒ/
short /ʃɔ:t/	yellow /'jeləʊ/
lovely /'lʌvli/	purple /'pɜ:pl/
beautiful /'bju:tɪfl/	pink /pɪŋk/
blue /blu:/	black /blæk/
brown /braʊn/	white /waɪt/
red /red/	light /laɪt/
green /gri:n/	dark /dɑ:k/
grey /greɪ/	

Other words and expressions

with /wɪð/	lots of /'lɒts əv/
these /ði:z/	like /laɪk/
those /ðəʊz/	look like /'lʊk laɪk/
all /ɔ:l/	personality /pɜ:sə'næləti/
except /ɪk'sept/	Dear /dɪə(r)/
more /mɔ:(r)/	Yours sincerely /jɔ:z sɪn'sɪəli/
a.m. /eɪ 'em/	the others /ðɪ:'ʌðəz/
p.m. /pi: 'em/	me /mi:/

Unit 12

Grammar and structures

Simple Past tense

I started you started he/she/it started we started they started	did I start? did you start? did he/she/it start? did we start? did they start?	I did not (didn't) start you did not (didn't) start he/she/it did not (didn't) start we did not (didn't) start they did not (didn't) start

Spelling: work**ed**   listen**ed**   cook**ed**
   live**d**   love**d**   hate**d**
   stop**ped**   shop**ped**   trave**lled**
   marr**ied**   stud**ied**

Pronunciation: -*(e)d* = /d/: died played opened lived remembered
   -*(e)d* = /t/: worked liked stopped danced watched
   -*(e)d* = /ɪd/: started hated depended wanted assisted

Was and *were*

I was you were he/she/it was we were they were	was I? were you? was he/she/it? were we? were they?	I was not (wasn't) you were not (weren't) he/she/it was not (wasn't) we were not (weren't) they were not (weren't)

Pro-verbs

I didn't **like** dancing when I was a boy, but now I **do**.
I **played** chess when I was a child, but now I **don't**.

Who: subject and object

Who wrote to Mary? (Who did write to Mary?)
Who did Mary write to?

Irregular verbs: Simple Past tense forms

Infinitive	*Simple Past*	*Infinitive*	*Simple Past*	*Infinitive*	*Simple Past*
be /biː/	was, were /wəz, wɒz; wə(r), wɜː(r)/	have /həv, hæv/	had /həd, hæd/	speak /spiːk/	spoke /spəʊk/
		hear /hɪə(r)/	heard /hɜːd/	spell /spel/	spelt /spelt/
		know /nəʊ/	knew /njuː/	take /teɪk/	took /tʊk/
become /bɪˈkʌm/	became /bɪˈkeɪm/	leave /liːv/	left /left/	tell /tel/	told /təʊld/
can /kən, kæn/	could /kʊd/	make /meɪk/	made /meɪd/	think /θɪŋk/	thought /θɔːt/
come /kʌm/	came /keɪm/	mean /miːn/	meant /ment/	understand	understood
do /duː/	did /dɪd/	meet /miːt/	met /met/	/ʌndəˈstænd/	/ʌndəˈstʊd/
drink /drɪŋk/	drank /dræŋk/	read /riːd/	read /red/	wear /weə(r)/	wore /wɔː(r)/
find /faɪnd/	found /faʊnd/	say /seɪ/	said /sed/	write /raɪt/	wrote /rəʊt/
get /get/	got /gɒt/	sell /sel/	sold /səʊld/		
go /gəʊ/	went /went/	sleep /sliːp/	slept /slept/		

Words and expressions to learn

Nouns

clerk /klɑːk/
manager /ˈmænɪdʒə(r)/
bus driver /ˈbʌsdraɪvə(r)/
education /edʒəˈkeɪʃn/
passport /ˈpɑːspɔːt/
paper /ˈpeɪpə(r)/
calculator /ˈkælkjəleɪtə(r)/
pocket /ˈpɒkɪt/
midnight /ˈmɪdnaɪt/

Verbs

was born, were born /wəz ˈbɔːn, wə ˈbɔːn/
die /daɪ/
marry /ˈmæri/
leave /liːv/ (*past:* left /left/)
become /bɪˈkʌm/ (*past:* became /bɪˈkeɪm/)
tell /tel/ (*past:* told /təʊld/)
come /kʌm/ (*past:* came /keɪm/)
want /wɒnt/
ask /ɑːsk/
kiss /kɪs/
find /faɪnd/ (*past:* found /faʊnd/)
hear /hɪə(r)/ (*past:* heard /hɜːd/)
answer /ˈɑːnsə(r)/

Adjectives

retired /rɪ'taɪəd/
unemployed /ˌʌnɪm'plɔɪd/
late /leɪt/

Other words and expressions

last night /lɑ:st 'naɪt/
till /tɪl/
a bit /ə 'bɪt/
through /θru:/

when /wen/
actually /'æktʃəli/
again /ə'gen/

Unit 13

Grammar and structures

This, that, these, those, one(s)

Could I see **that** watch, please?
This one?

	that one.
No,	the big **one**.
	the **one** behind the ring.

Could you show me **those** glasses?
These?

	those.
No,	the red **ones**.
	the **ones** by the teapot.

Words and expressions to learn

Nouns

Learn seven or more of these:
thing /θɪŋ/
ring /rɪŋ/
spoon /spu:n/
glass /glɑ:s/
watch /wɒtʃ/
box /bɒks/
size /saɪz/
single /'sɪŋgl/
return /rɪ'tɜ:n/
platform /'plætfɔ:m/
train /treɪn/
meal /mi:l/
cigarette /sɪgə'ret/
hotel /həʊ'tel/

Verbs

buy /baɪ/ (*past:* bought /bɔ:t/)
take /teɪk/ (*past:* took /tʊk/)
help /help/
look /lʊk/
look for /'lʊk fə(r), 'lʊk fɔ:(r)/
suit /su:t/
fit /fɪt/
try ... on /traɪ ... 'ɒn/
change /tʃeɪndʒ/
see /si:/ (*past:* saw /sɔ:/)
show /ʃəʊ/
would /wʊd/

Adjectives

larger /'lɑ:dʒə(r)/
next /nekst/
direct /dɪ'rekt/
expensive /ɪks'pensɪv/

Other words and expressions

one(s) /wʌn(z)/
Here you are. /'hɪə ju 'ɑ:/
of course /əv 'kɔ:s/
in front of /ɪn 'frʌnt əv/
behind /bɪ'haɪnd/
other /'ʌðə(r)/
another /ə'nʌðə(r)/ (an other)
really /'rɪəli/
anything /'eniθɪŋ/
I'm afraid... /aɪm ə'freɪd/
just /dʒʌst/
which /wɪtʃ/
Please speak more slowly.
    /pli:z 'spi:k mɔ: 'sləʊli/
How do you pronounce...?
    /'haʊ də ju: prə'naʊns/
Is this correct...? /ɪz 'ðɪs kə'rekt/
without /wɪ'ðaʊt/
OK /əʊ 'keɪ/

Unit 14

Grammar and structures

Can

I can you can he/she/it can we can they can	can I? can you? can he/she/it? can we? can they? (do you can?)	I cannot (can't) you cannot (can't) he/she/it cannot (can't) we cannot (can't) they cannot (can't)

Pronunciation: /kn/: I can swim.
    /kn/ or /kæn/:
        Can you play tennis?
    /kæn/: Yes, I can.
    /kɑ:nt/:
        No, I can't. I can't play tennis.

145

Adjectives

Comparatives and superlatives:
old / older / oldest; cheap / cheaper / cheapest
fat / fatter / fattest
happy / happier / happiest
fine / finer / finest
interesting / **more** interesting / **most** interesting
good / **better** / **best**
bad / **worse** / **worst**

I'm taller **than** (/ðən/) my brother.
I'm **much** taller **than** my mother.
I'm **a bit** taller **than** my sister.
I'm **the** tallest person **in** my family.

Comparing

I can cook **better** / run faster / sing higher **than** my brother.
I can ski **better** now **than** I could when I was younger.

I was **good** at maths / swimming when I was younger, but I'm not now.

Peking is **the same as** Beijing.
A typist is **not the same as** a typewriter.
A café is **different from** (/frəm/) a pub.

I'm **as** (/əz/) strong **as** (/əz/) my husband.
A Rolls-Royce is **not as** noisy **as** a Volkswagen.

Words and expressions to learn

Nouns
chess /tʃes/
typewriter /ˈtaɪpraɪtə(r)/
typist /ˈtaɪpɪst/

Verbs
run /rʌn/ (*past:* ran /ræn/)
ski /skiː/
sing /sɪŋ/ (*past:* sang /sæŋ/)
go without sleep
type /taɪp/
drive /draɪv/ (*past:* drove /drəʊv/)
draw /drɔː/ (*past:* drew /druː/)
swim /swɪm/ (*past:* swam /swæm/)
count /kaʊnt/

Adjectives
better /ˈbetə(r)/ best /best/
fast /fɑːst/
cheap /tʃiːp/
easy /ˈiːzi/
bad /bæd/ worse /wɜːs/
  worst /wɜːst/
comfortable /ˈkʌmftəbl/
economical /ekəˈnɒmɪkl/
rich /rɪtʃ/
funny /ˈfʌni/
interesting /ˈɪntrəstɪŋ/
handsome /ˈhænsəm/
heavy /ˈhevi/

Adverbs
better /ˈbetə(r)/
fast /fɑːst/
faster /ˈfɑːstə(r)/
cheaper /ˈtʃiːpə(r)/
now /naʊ/
well /wel/

Other words and expressions
the same /ðə ˈseɪm/
as /əz, æz/
than /ðən, ðæn/

Unit 15

Grammar and structures

Ago
'How long ago (/ˈhaʊ ˈlɒŋ əˈgəʊ/) did the last dinosaurs die?'
  'About 70 million years ago.' (/ˈjɪəzəˈgəʊ/)
Julius Caesar invaded Britain about 2,000 years ago.
'How long ago was Galileo born?' 'About 400 years ago.'

ten years ago	a year ago	two months ago
a week ago	two days ago	a minute ago

Time sequences
On the night of . . . , . . .
As soon as . . . , . . .
Then . . .
After . . . , . . .
And then . . .
Finally, . . .

Words and expressions to learn

Nouns

Africa /ˈæfrɪkə/
Asia /ˈeɪʃə/
Europe /ˈjʊərəp/

Australia /ɒˈstreɪljə/
America /əˈmerɪkə/
part /pɑːt/

university /juːnɪˈvɜːsɪti/
plane /pleɪn/
republic /rɪˈpʌblɪk/

world /wɜːld/
radio /ˈreɪdɪəʊ/
novel /ˈnɒvl/

146

Verbs

begin /bɪˈgɪn/ (*past:* began /bɪˈgæn/)
move /muːv/
separate /ˈsepəreɪt/
finish /ˈfɪnɪʃ/
lose /luːz/ (*past:* lost /lɒst/)
laugh /lɑːf/
take (a person to a place) /teɪk/
decide /dɪˈsaɪd/
disagree /dɪsəˈgriː/
discover /dɪsˈkʌvə(r)/
walk /wɔːk/
break (into) /breɪk (ˈɪntə)/ (*past:* broke /brəʊk/)
wake (up) /ˈweɪk (ˈʌp)/ (*past:* woke /ˈwəʊk/)
kill /kɪl/
build /bɪld/ (*past:* built /bɪlt/)

Other words and expressions

ago /əˈgəʊ/
still /stɪl/
across /əˈkrɒs/
finally /ˈfaɪnəli/
as soon as /əz ˈsuːn əz/
on the night of /ɒn ðəˌnaɪt əv/
some of /ˈsʌm əv/
slow /sləʊ/
a long time /ə ˈlɒŋ taɪm/
last /lɑːst/
back /bæk/

Unit 16

Grammar and structures

Ages, heights, weights

Our house **is** four hundred years old.
The baby **is** six months old.
John **is** thirty-two (years old).
~~(John is thirty-two years.)~~

I **am** six feet tall.
My mother **is** five feet six (inches tall).
5ft 6ins.
I **weigh** 180 pounds (lbs).

Be like / look like

'What **is** your sister **like**?' 'She's very shy.
   She likes cycling and modern dance.'
'What **does** your sister **look like**?' 'She's
   tall and dark. She's quite pretty.'

He **looks** bad-tempered.
He **looks like** a scientist.

Dates

Jan 14, 1978. January the fourteenth,
   nineteen seventy-eight.

My birthday is on January the fourteenth.

A and any

I haven't got **any** money.
I haven't got **any** cigarettes.
I haven't got **a** car.
~~(I haven't got any car.)~~

Words and expressions to learn

Nouns

building /ˈbɪldɪŋ/
foot /fʊt/ (*plural* feet /fiːt/)
inch /ɪntʃ/
pound /paʊnd/
height /haɪt/
weight /weɪt/
month /mʌnθ/
birthday /ˈbɜːθdeɪ/
date /deɪt/
bicycle /ˈbaɪsɪkl/
guitar /gɪˈtɑː(r)/
businessman /ˈbɪznɪsmən/
scientist /ˈsaɪəntɪst/
politician /pɒlɪˈtɪʃn/

Adjectives

> **Learn five or more of these:**
> new /njuː/
> kind /kaɪnd/
> shy /ʃaɪ/
> sensitive /ˈsensətɪv/
> self-confident /selfˈkɒnfɪdənt/
> stupid /ˈstjuːpɪd/
> bad-tempered /bæd ˈtempəd/
> calm /kɑːm/
> friendly /ˈfrendli/
> nervy /ˈnɜːvi/

The months

January /ˈdʒænjəri/
February /ˈfebrəri/
March /mɑːtʃ/
April /ˈeɪprʊl/
May /meɪ/
June /dʒuːn/
July /dʒuːˈlaɪ/
August /ˈɔːgəst/
September /sepˈtembə(r)/
October /ɒkˈtəʊbə(r)/
November /nəʊˈvembə(r)/
December /dɪˈsembə(r)/

Numbers

10th tenth /tenθ/
11th eleventh /ɪˈlevənθ/
12th twelfth /twelfθ/
13th thirteenth /θɜːˈtiːnθ/
20th twentieth /ˈtwentɪəθ/
21st twenty-first /twentiˈfɜːst/
22nd twenty-second
   /twentiˈsekənd/
25th twenty-fifth /twentiˈfɪfθ/
30th thirtieth /ˈθɜːtɪəθ/
40th fortieth /ˈfɔːtɪəθ/
50th fiftieth /ˈfɪftɪəθ/
100th hundredth /ˈhʌndrədθ/

Other words and expressions

weigh /weɪ/
today /təˈdeɪ/
I don't agree. /aɪ dəʊnt əˈgriː/
Happy birthday. /hæpi ˈbɜːθdeɪ/

Unit 17

Grammar and structures

Requests and answers

I'll have a rump steak.   I'll start with soup.

Could you	bring me the bill?	Yes, of course.
	give us some more coffee?	I'm sorry, I need it/them.
	show me some sweaters?	I'm afraid I can't.
	lend me a pen?	I haven't got one.
	lend me your keys?	I haven't got any.

Could you possibly lend me...?
Can I talk to you for a minute? (Can I talk you...?)

Quantities

a little water (a little of water) (a few water)
a few biscuits (a few of biscuits)
no more roast beef (no more of roast beef)
a piece of bread
a cup of coffee

Would you like **something** to eat?
I don't want **anything** to eat, thank you.
nothing to drink

Personal pronouns and possessives

SUBJECT	OBJECT	POSSESSIVE
I	me	my
you	you	your
he	him	his
she	her	her
it	it	its
we	us	our
you	you	your
they	them	their

(For examples, see Lesson 17D.)

Words and expressions to learn

Nouns

bill /bɪl/
hour /'aʊə(r)/
half an hour
   /hɑːf ən 'aʊə(r)/
minute /'mɪnɪt/
surprise /sə'praɪz/
piece /piːs/
cup /kʌp/
restaurant
   /'restrənt/

Learn two or more of these:
beef /biːf/   apple /'æpl/
chicken /'tʃɪkɪn/   biscuit
salad /'sæləd/   /'bɪskɪt/
steak /steɪk/
mushroom /'mʌʃruːm/
sugar /'ʃʊgə(r)/

Learn two or more of these:
dictionary /'dɪkʃənri/
lighter /'laɪtə(r)/
key /kiː/
umbrella /ʌm'brelə/
pen /pen/
pencil /'pensl/

Verbs

bring /brɪŋ/
   (past: brought /brɔːt/)
give /gɪv/ (past: gave /geɪv/)
lend /lend/ (past: lent /lent/)
borrow /'bɒrəʊ/
need /niːd/
talk /tɔːk/
smoke /sməʊk/
eat /iːt/ (past: ate /et/)
I'll (I will) /aɪl (aɪ 'wɪl)/

Adjectives

polite /pə'laɪt/
rude /ruːd/
all right /ɔːl 'raɪt/
not too bad /nɒt tuː 'bæd/

Other words and expressions

something /'sʌmθɪŋ/
everything /'evrɪθɪŋ/
nothing /'nʌθɪŋ/
us /əs, ʌs/
for /fə(r), fɔː(r)/
Come in. /kʌm 'ɪn/
a few /ə 'fjuː/
Is service included? /ɪz 'sɜːvɪs ɪn'kluːdɪd/
Sorry to trouble you. /'sɒri tə 'trʌbl juː/
Have you got a light? /'hæv juː 'gɒt ə 'laɪt/
Just a minute. /'dʒʌst ə 'mɪnɪt/
Help yourself to... /'help jɔː'self tə/
I don't smoke. /aɪ 'dəʊnt 'sməʊk/

Unit 18

Grammar and structures

Present Progressive tense

I am (I'm) going you are (you're) going he/she/it is ('s) going we are (we're) going they are (they're) going

am I going? are you going? is he/she/it going? are we going? are they going?

I am (I'm) not going you are not (aren't) going he/she/it is not (isn't) going we are not (aren't) going they are not (aren't) going

I'm working very hard just now. ~~(I work . . .)~~   **I work** on Saturdays. ~~(I'm working . . .)~~

The price of oil **is going** up. '**Is** your English **getting** better?' 'Yes, it is.' ~~(Yes, it's.)~~
What**'s** the woman in blue **talking** about? What**'s happening**?

Spelling

start start**ing**   look look**ing**   **make** mak**ing**   stop stop**ping**   lie ly**ing**
speak speak**ing**   play play**ing**   write writ**ing**   sit sit**ting**   die dy**ing**
lend lend**ing**

Words and expressions to learn

Nouns

postcard /'pəʊstkɑ:d/
bar /bɑ:(r)/
café /'kæfeɪ/
post /pəʊst/
problem /'prɒbləm/
length /leŋkθ/

Verbs

stand /stænd/ (*past:* stood /stʊd/)
sit /sɪt/ (*past:* sat /sæt/)
lie /laɪ/ (*past:* lay /leɪ/)
fight /faɪt/ (*past:* fought /fɔ:t/)
happen /'hæpn/

send /send/ (*past:* sent /sent/)
look at /'lʊk ət/
have a bath /'hæv ə 'bɑ:θ/
go up /gəʊ 'ʌp/
go down /gəʊ 'daʊn/
fall /fɔ:l/ (*past:* fell /fel/)
rise /raɪz/ (*past:* rose /rəʊz/)
change /tʃeɪndʒ/
get /get/ (*past:* got /gɒt/)
spend /spend/ (*past:* spent /spent/)
stay /steɪ/
wash /wɒʃ/
clean /kli:n/

Adjectives

wonderful /'wʌndəfl/
boring /'bɔ:rɪŋ/
average /'ævərɪdʒ/

Other words and expressions

out of /'aʊt əv/
on the phone /ɒn ðə 'fəʊn/
probably /'prɒbəbli/
up /ʌp/
down /daʊn/
under /'ʌndə(r)/

Unit 19

Grammar and structures

Future

I'm playing football next weekend.
What **are you doing** this evening?

Prepositions of time

on Tuesday   **on** Tuesday morning   **on** my birthday
at the weekend   **at** Christmas   **at** ten o'clock
in the morning   **in** the afternoon   **in** the evening
My train leaves **in** half an hour.

No prepositions with: today, tomorrow, yesterday,
this, next, last.

She's leaving **tomorrow**. I'm seeing him **next** Tuesday.

Suggestions

Let's go to Spain. **Let's have** a party.
Why don't we go to Spain? **Why don't we have** a party?

Distances

How far **is** Oxford from London?
Oxford **is** 60 miles from London.

So

Manchester are not playing Liverpool or Tottenham.
So Manchester are playing Arsenal.

I'm tired, **so** I'm going to bed.
She felt hungry, **so** she cooked herself an omelette.   ➡

149

Words and expressions to learn

Nouns

football /'fʊtbɔːl/
ticket /'tɪkɪt/
traveller's cheque /'trævləz 'tʃek/
office /'ɒfɪs/
suggestion /sə'dʒestʃən/
conversation /kɒnvə'seɪʃn/
visit /'vɪzɪt/
pub /pʌb/
idea /aɪ'dɪə/
cheque /tʃek/

Verbs

get (= 'obtain') /get/
forget /fə'get/ (*past:* forgot /fə'gɒt/)

Adjectives

excited /ɪk'saɪtɪd/
usual /'juːʒʊəl/
impatient /ɪm'peɪʃənt/
free /friː/

Other words and expressions

each /iːtʃ/
somebody /'sʌmbədi/
against /ə'genst/
so /səʊ/
Let's /lets/
why /waɪ/
Why don't we...?
I don't want to.
this morning
this afternoon
this evening
I'd love to.
How about...?
I think so.
do the packing /duː ðə 'pækɪŋ/
I hope /aɪ 'həʊp/
catch a plane, train etc. /kætʃ ə 'pleɪn/
have a drink /'hæv ə 'drɪŋk/
a long way /ə lɒŋ 'weɪ/

Unit 20

Grammar and structures

Present Perfect tense: forms

I have (I've)	been
you have (you've)	lived
he/she/it has ('s)	known
etc.	had
	etc.

have I	been?
etc.	lived?
	known?
	had?
	etc.

I have not (haven't)	been
etc.	lived
	known
	had
	etc.

Present Perfect tense: use

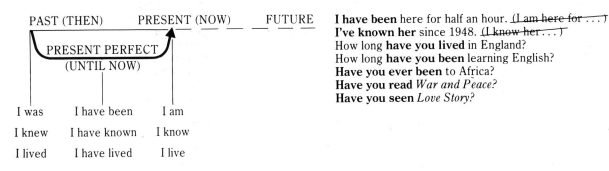

PAST (THEN)　　　PRESENT (NOW)　　　FUTURE

PRESENT PERFECT
(UNTIL NOW)

I was	I have been	I am
I knew	I have known	I know
I lived	I have lived	I live

I have been here for half an hour. (I am here for . . .)
I've known her since 1948. (I know her . . .)
How long **have you lived** in England?
How long **have you been** learning English?
Have you ever been to Africa?
Have you read *War and Peace?*
Have you seen *Love Story?*

Infinitives, past tenses and past participles

Infinitive
Would you like **to live** in Scotland?
I want **to go** home.
Let's **have** a party.
Does your mother **know** Alice and John?

Past tenses
We **lived** in Ireland when I was a child.
I **went** to bed at twelve.
We **had** a great party on Saturday.
I **knew** him at university.

Past participles
I've never **lived** in a flat.
Have you **been** to Africa?
I've always **had** lots of friends.
I've **known** her for twelve years.

INFINITIVE	PAST TENSE	PAST PARTICIPLE
Regular verbs		
live	lived	lived
work	worked	worked
stay	stayed	stayed
borrow	borrowed	borrowed
Irregular verbs		
be	was, were	been
go	went	gone, been
have	had	had
know	knew	known
see	saw	seen
hear	heard	heard
read (/riːd/)	read (/red/)	read (/red/)
write	wrote	written

Since and *for*

I've known him **since** he was a baby.
I've known him **since** 1948.
I've known him **for** nearly 40 years.
I've known him **for** a long time.

Word order

I **never** eat fish.
I **hardly ever** go to restaurants.
I **sometimes** eat beef.
I **very often** eat lamb.
I **always** drink wine.

I go to London **every Wednesday**.
I go on holiday **twice a year**.
I go to the hairdresser **every two weeks**.

Reply questions

'I'm tired'. **'Are you?'**
'It's late.' **'Is it?'**
'I love skiing.' **'Do you?'**
'I can't understand her.' **'Can't you?'**
'She's got a new boyfriend.' **'Has she?'**

So am I, etc.

'I'm tired.' **'So am I.'**
'I've got a cold.' **'So have I.'**
'I can speak Italian.' **'So can I.'**
'I like her very much.' **'So do I.'**

Requests and answers

'Do you mind if I open a window?' 'Not at all. Please do.'

'Do you mind if I smoke?' 'I'd rather you didn't.'

Words and expressions to learn

Nouns

seat /siːt/
paper (= 'newspaper') /ˈpeɪpə(r)/
record /ˈrekɔːd/
hairdresser /ˈheədresə(r)/
walk /wɔːk/
pint /paɪnt/
life /laɪf/ (*plural* lives /laɪvz/)

Verbs

mind /maɪnd/
believe /bɪˈliːv/
learn /lɜːn/ (learnt /lɜːnt/, learnt /lɜːnt/)
must /məst, mʌst/

Adverbs

always /ˈɔːlwɪz/
hardly ever /ˈhaːdli ˈevə(r)/
ever /ˈevə(r)/
twice /twaɪs/
three times /ˈθriː ˈtaɪmz/
already /ɔːlˈredi/
so /səʊ/
tonight /təˈnaɪt/

Other words and expressions

if /ɪf/
Please do.
go ahead /gəʊ əˈhed/
favourite /ˈfeɪvrɪt/
great /greɪt/
for (time) /fə(r), fɔː(r)/
for a moment /fər ə ˈməʊmənt/
since /sɪns/
go to the cinema
go for a walk
cheers /tʃɪəz/
Have another drink.
all my life
and so on
in love
I feel /aɪ ˈfiːl/
myself /maɪˈself/
I'd rather /aɪd ˈraːðə(r)/

Unit 21

Grammar and structures

Passives

Cheese Wine Perfume	is	made produced	in	Italy. France.

Cameras Cars Calculators	are	made produced manufactured	in	the USA. Japan.

Where **are** Volvos **manufactured**? Where **is** Coca Cola **made**?

Where **were** your	shoes glasses	**made**?	Where **was** your	car camera	**made**?

Reasons

Why can't you throw a fridge?
Because it's **too** heavy.
Because I'm **not** strong **enough**. (~~...enough strong.~~)

Words and expressions to learn

Nouns

Learn fifteen or more of these:
wool /wʊl/
china /ˈtʃaɪnə/
leather /ˈleðə(r)/
metal /ˈmetl/
stone /stəʊn/
rubber /ˈrʌbə(r)/
plastic /ˈplæstɪk/
chocolate /ˈtʃɒklət/
rice /raɪs/
butter /ˈbʌtə(r)/
skin /skɪn/
business /ˈbɪznɪs/
chemical /ˈkemɪkl/
clock /klɒk/
camera /ˈkæmrə/
knife /naɪf/
   (*plural* knives /naɪvz/)
bird /bɜːd/
import /ˈɪmpɔːt/
export /ˈekspɔːt/
machine /məˈʃiːn/
region /ˈriːdʒən/

Verbs

Learn six or more of these:
break /breɪk/ (broke /brəʊk/,
   broken /ˈbrəʊkn/)
break down /breɪk ˈdaʊn/
use /juːz/
export /ɪksˈpɔːt/
import /ɪmˈpɔːt/
cost /kɒst/ (cost, cost)
produce /prəˈdjuːs/
manufacture /mænjʊˈfæktʃə(r)/
boil /bɔɪl/
jump /dʒʌmp/
sunbathe /ˈsʌnbeɪð/

Adjectives

Learn six or more of these:
hard /hɑːd/
tough /tʌf/
light /laɪt/
wide /waɪd/
high /haɪ/
loud /laʊd/
narrow /ˈnærəʊ/
low /ləʊ/
useful /ˈjuːsfl/
liquid /ˈlɪkwɪd/
perfect /ˈpɜːfɪkt/

Other words and expressions

Learn four or more of these:
because /bɪˈkɒz/
together /təˈgeðə(r)/
too /tuː/
carefully /ˈkeəfli/
mainly /ˈmeɪnli/
mostly /ˈməʊstli/

THERE IS NO SUMMARY FOR UNIT 22.

Grammar and structures

Imperatives
Wear comfortable clothing.
Always **warm up**.
Never **run** in fog.
Don't run after a meal.

Don't run if you have a cold.

Prepositions of position and movement
Position: on, in, under, by
Movement: on, on to, in, into, under, by, off, out of

Instructions
Written instructions: Wash mushrooms and pat dry.
Spoken instructions: **You** wash **the** mushrooms and pat **them** dry.

It's on the chair. It **should be** on the table.

Words and expressions to learn

Nouns
advice /əd'vaɪs/ (uncountable)
a cold /ə 'kəʊld/
picture /'pɪktʃə(r)/
floor /flɔː(r)/

Learn six or more of these:
lemon /'lemən/
pepper /'pepə(r)/
salt /sɔːlt/
juice /dʒuːs/
fork /fɔːk/
tablespoon /'teɪblspuːn/
bowl /bəʊl/
oil /ɔɪl/
cloth /klɒθ/
frying pan /'fraɪɪŋ 'pæn/
saucepan /'sɔːspən/

Verbs
hurry /'hʌri/ (hurried, hurried)
worry /'wʌri/ (worried, worried)
wait /weɪt/
follow /'fɒləʊ/
drop /drɒp/ (dropped, dropped)
pick up /pɪk 'ʌp/
throw /θrəʊ/ (threw /θruː/, thrown /θrəʊn/)
throw away /θrəʊ ə'weɪ/
put away /pʊt ə'weɪ/
rest /rest/
should /ʃʊd/

Learn one or more of these:
fry /fraɪ/
slice /slaɪs/
mix /mɪks/
pour /pɔː(r)/

Other words and expressions
before /bɪ'fɔː(r)/
into /'ɪntə/
off /ɒf/
fresh /freʃ/
alone /ə'ləʊn/
most of /'məʊst əv/
early /'ɜːli/
away /ə'weɪ/
after (conjunction) /'ɑːftə(r)/
Look out. /lʊk 'aʊt/
Be careful. /bi: 'keəfl/
take (your) time /'teɪk (jə) 'taɪm/

Grammar and structures

a dollar		night
57 pence	**a**	kilo
an apple		day

To get from Oxford Circus to Paddington, you **have to** change twice.

You can get from Bond Street to Leicester Square **without changing**.

153

Words and expressions to learn

Nouns

credit card /'kredɪt kɑ:d/
cash /kæʃ/
shower /ʃaʊə(r)/
form /fɔ:m/
stop /stɒp/
line /laɪn/
way /weɪ/
boarding pass /'bɔ:dɪŋ pɑ:s/
gate /geɪt/
flight /flaɪt/
arrival /ə'raɪvl/
departure /dɪ'pɑ:tʃə/
reservation /rezə'veɪʃn/
hand baggage /'hænd 'bægɪdʒ/
timetable /'taɪmteɪbl/
air /eə(r)/
airport /'eəpɔ:t/

airline /'eəlaɪn/
side /saɪd/
crossroads /'krɒsrəʊdz/
bridge /brɪdʒ/
river /'rɪvə(r)/

Verbs

get to /'get tə, 'get tu:/
pay /peɪ/ (paid /peɪd/, paid /peɪd/)
check in /tʃek 'ɪn/
fill in /fɪl 'ɪn/
have to /'hæftə, 'hæftu:/

Other words and expressions

including /ɪŋ'klu:dɪŋ/
over /'əʊvə(r)/
along /ə'lɒŋ/
on to /'ɒntə, 'ɒntʊ/
by credit card
by cheque
in cash
on the way
by air
double room /'dʌbl 'ru:m/

Unit 25

Grammar and structures

Going to

I'm **going to write** letters this evening.
This is **going to be** my room.
She's **going to have** a baby.
What are all your friends **going to do** when they leave school?

'Why did you come here?' '**To see** you.' (~~For to see you.~~)

Infinitives and *-ing* forms

Infinitive without to: I can **swim**.
Infinitive with to: Would you like **to dance**?
-ing form: Do you like **dancing**?
(For details, see Lesson 25D.)

Words and expressions to learn

Nouns

plan /plæn/
country /'kʌntri/
cost /kɒst/
details /'di:teɪlz/
library /'laɪbri/
butcher's /'bʊtʃəz/
embassy /'embəsi/
travel agent /'trævl 'eɪdʒənt/
information /ɪnfə'meɪʃn/
visa /'vi:zə/
suitcase /'su:tkeɪs/
aeroplane /'eərəpleɪn/
air ticket /'eə tɪkɪt/
baby /'beɪbi/

Verbs

study /'stʌdi/
win /wɪn/ (won /wʌn/, won /wʌn/)
crash /kræʃ/
organize /'ɔ:gənaɪz/
join /dʒɔɪn/

Other words and expressions

fit /fɪt/
inclusive /ɪŋ'klu:sɪv/
hard work /'hɑ:d 'wɜ:k/
have a baby /'hæv ə 'beɪbi/
first of all /'fɜ:st əv 'ɔ:l/
not yet /nɒt 'jet/
play cards /pleɪ 'kɑ:dz/

Unit 26

Grammar and structures

Feelings

| It | depresses frightens | me. | | It makes me | angry. happy. unhappy. | | He gets | angry worried bored | when he goes there. |

-ed and -ing

Does this **interest** you? It **interests** me. I'm **interested** in it. It's **interesting**. (I'm interesting in it.)
Does John **bore** you? He **bores** me. I'm **bored**. He's **boring**. (I'm boring by him.)

| easy nice difficult | to | talk **to** work **with** see   etc. |

Words and expressions to learn

Nouns

flu /fluː/ (uncountable)
a temperature /ə 'temprɪtʃə(r)/
   (countable)
headache /'hedeɪk/ (countable)
toothache /'tuːθeɪk/ (uncountable)
aspirin /'æsprɪn/
medicine /'medsən/
matter /'mætə(r)/
dinner /'dɪnə(r)/
pleasure /'pleʒə(r)/
freedom /'friːdəm/
mistake /mɪs'teɪk/
marriage /'mærɪdʒ/
couple /'kʌpl/

Verbs

feel /fiːl/ (felt /felt/, felt /felt/)
hurt /hɜːt/ (hurt /hɜːt/, hurt /hɜːt/)
frighten /'fraɪtn/
depress /dɪ'pres/
disgust /dɪs'gʌst/
solve /sɒlv/
trust /trʌst/
get on (with) /get 'ɒn (wɪð)/
can't stand /kɑːnt 'stænd/
appreciate /ə'priːʃieɪt/
share /ʃeə(r)/
lie down /laɪ 'daʊn/
   (lay /leɪ/, lain /leɪn/)

Adjectives

ill /ɪl/
angry /'æŋgri/
fed up /'fed 'ʌp/
fair /feə(r)/

Other words and expressions

That's very nice of you.
on the whole /ɒn ðə 'həʊl/
take medicine /'teɪk 'medsən/
What's the matter?
change (my) mind
   /'tʃeɪndʒ (maɪ) 'maɪnd/

Unit 27

Grammar and structures

Get

Get + **noun** = *receive, obtain, fetch etc.*
   get a letter   get a drink

Get + **adverb particle/preposition** = *move*
   get up   get into a car

Get + **adjective** = *become*
   It's getting cold.

Have got

   I've got two brothers.

Adverbs of manner

She speaks English **well**. (She speaks well English.)
I like skiing **very much**. (I like very much skiing.)

slow – slow**ly**
careful – careful**ly**
nice – nice**ly**

happy – happ**ily**
comfortable – comforta**bly**

➡

Words and expressions to learn

Nouns
boat /bəʊt/
motorbike /'məʊtəbaɪk/
taxi /'tæksi/
bus /bʌs/
journey /'dʒɜːni/
lightning /'laɪtnɪŋ/
race /reɪs/
speed /spiːd/
record /'rekɔːd/
button /'bʌtn/
handle /'hændl/
packet /'pækɪt/
flower /'flaʊə(r)/
second /'sekənd/

Verbs
ride /raɪd/ (rode /rəʊd/,
ridden /'rɪdn/)
fly /flaɪ/ (flew /fluː/, flown /fləʊn/)
hitchhike /'hɪtʃhaɪk/
guess /ges/
press /pres/
pull /pʊl/
push /pʊʃ/
turn /tɜːn/
get on /get 'ɒn/
get off /get 'ɒf/
get in(to) /get 'ɪn(tə)/
get out (of) /get 'aʊt (əv)/
breathe /briːð/

Adjectives
electric /ɪ'lektrɪk/
sleepy /'sliːpi/
thin /θɪn/

Adverbs
sleepily /'sliːpəli/
happily /'hæpəli/
kindly /'kaɪndli/
angrily /'æŋgrəli/
loudly /'laʊdli/
quietly /'kwaɪətli/
coldly /'kəʊldli/
shyly /'ʃaɪli/
noisily /'nɔɪzəli/
badly /'bædli/
nicely /'naɪsli/
comfortably /'kʌmftəbli/

Other words and expressions
by plane /baɪ 'pleɪn/
by boat /baɪ 'bəʊt/
one day /wʌn 'deɪ/
like lightning /laɪk 'laɪtnɪŋ/

Unit 28

Grammar and structures

Quantifiers
Very few pupils go to private schools.
Not many pupils...
Some pupils...
Two thirds of American pupils...
Three quarters of...
Most pupils...
Nearly all pupils...
More British pupils... than American pupils...
Far more pupils...
75% of American pupils...
Less than 5% of British pupils...

Fractions
⅔ two thirds
¾ three quarters
⅞ seven eighths
³⁄₂₀ three twentieths

Prepositions
at the top   **at** the bottom
at the beginning   **at** the end
in the middle
at 16 (years old)

Structuring paragraphs
First... Next... Then... After that... Finally...

Words and expressions to learn

Nouns
private school /'praɪvɪt 'skuːl/
state school /'steɪt 'skuːl/
country /'kʌntri/
top /tɒp/
bottom /'bɒtəm/
front /frʌnt/
back /bæk/
corner /'kɔːnə(r)/
middle /'mɪdl/
circle /'sɜːkl/

cross /krɒs/
square /skweə(r)/
triangle /'traɪæŋgl/
beginning /bɪ'gɪnɪŋ/
end /end/
soup /suːp/
theatre /'θɪətə(r)/
zoo /zuː/
policeman /pə'liːsmən/
map /mæp/

Verbs

shave /ʃeɪv/
wash /wɒʃ/
get dressed /get 'drest/
put on (clothes) /pʊt 'ɒn/
take off (clothes) /teɪk 'ɒf/
brush (teeth, hair) /brʌʃ/
go out (lights etc.) /gəʊ 'aʊt/
ring (phone) /rɪŋ/ (rang/ræŋ/, rung/rʌŋ/)

Other words and expressions

far more /'fɑ: 'mɔ:(r)/
most /məʊst/
less /les/
nearly /'nɪəli/
true /tru:/
inside /in'saɪd/
outside /aʊt'saɪd/
What else? /wɒt 'els/

Unit 29

Grammar and structures

Future: *will*

I will start		I'll start
you will start		you'll start
he/she/it will start		he'll/she'll/it'll start
we will start		we'll start
they will start		they'll start

will I start?	I will not start	I won't start
will you start?	you will not start	you won't start
etc.	etc.	etc.

I'll take money with me.
You'll get lost. No, I **won't**.
You **won't** get lifts. Yes, I **will**.

Get

You'll **get** lost. You'll **get** killed.
I'm going to **get** married.

Words and expressions to learn

Nouns

Learn six or more of these:
word /wɜ:d/
death /deθ/
heart /hɑ:t/
lover /'lʌvə(r)/
youth hostel /'ju:θ hɒstl/
prison /'prɪzn/
pilot /'paɪlət/
decision /dɪ'sɪʒən/
trouble /'trʌbl/
accident /'æksɪdənt/
opportunity /ɒpə'tju:nəti/
news /nju:z/
star /stɑ:(r)/
misunderstanding
   /mɪsʌndə'stændɪŋ/

Learn six or more of these:
tractor /'træktə(r)/
rope /rəʊp/
bottle /'bɒtl/
blanket /'blæŋkɪt/
tent /tent/
gas /gæs/
sunglasses /'sʌnglɑ:sɪz/
matches /'mætʃɪz/
tin /tɪn/
tin-opener /'tɪn'əʊpnə(r)/
toothbrush /'tu:θbrʌʃ/
rifle /'raɪfl/
compass /'kʌmpəs/
backpack /'bækpæk/

Verbs

get lost /get 'lɒst/
get married /get 'mærɪd/
enjoy /ɪn'dʒɔɪ/
won't /wəʊnt/
dream /dri:m/
pass /pɑ:s/
fall in love /fɔ:l ɪn 'lʌv/

Adjectives

dangerous /'deɪndʒərəs/
dead /ded/
tinned /tɪnd/
famous /'feɪməs/

Preposition

round /raʊnd/

Grammar and structures

Use

A farmer uses a barn to keep cows in.   A farmer keeps cows in a barn.
Nurses use thermometers to take temperatures with.   Nurses take temperatures with thermometers.
You use a wallet to keep money in.   You keep money in a wallet.
You use a key to open a door with.   You open a door with a key.

Stress

'You've got *two* sisters, haven't you?' 'No, just one.'
'You've got two *sisters*, haven't you?' 'No, two brothers.'

Words having different functions

Verb	*Noun*	*Adjective*
1. **Phone** me at 7.00.	1. a blue **phone**	1. –
2. Could you **bath** the baby?	2. He's having a **bath**.	2. –
3. **Open** your mouth and say 'Ah'.	3. –	3. The door was partly **open**.
4. It doesn't **dry** my hair.	4. –	4. It was a very **dry** day.
5. –	5. Have an **orange**.	5. an **orange** car

Nouns used a little like adjectives

a **box** with a **phone** in it = a **phone box**
a **shop** that sells **books** = a **book shop** (a books shop)
a **wheel** of a **bicycle** = a **bicycle wheel**
a **race** for **horses** = a **horse race**

Words and expressions to learn

Nouns

garden /'gɑ:dn/
petrol /'petrʊl/
oil /ɔɪl/
complaint /kəm'pleɪnt/
appointment /ə'pɔɪntmənt/
customer /'kʌstəmə(r)/

Learn six or more of these:
mathematics /mæθ'mætɪks/
history /'hɪstəri/
geography /dʒɪ'ɒgrəfi/
spelling /'spelɪŋ/
literature /'lɪtrətʃə(r)/
science /'saɪəns/
biology /baɪ'ɒlədʒi/
religion /rɪ'lɪdʒən/
cookery /'kʊkəri/
art /ɑ:t/
physics /'fɪzɪks/
chemistry /'kemɪstri/
banker /'bæŋkə(r)/
farmer /'fɑ:mə(r)/
journalist /'dʒɜ:nəlɪst/
happiness /'hæpɪnəs/
friendship /'frendʃɪp/
health /helθ/
refund /'ri:fʌnd/

Verbs

order /'ɔ:də(r)/
switch on /swɪtʃ 'ɒn/
switch off /swɪtʃ 'ɒf/
(It doesn't) work
go (bzzz)
apologize /ə'pɒlədʒaɪz/
replace /rɪ'pleɪs/
prefer /prɪ'fɜ:(r)/

Adjectives

useless /'ju:sləs/
necessary /'nesəsri/
busy /'bɪzi/
strange /streɪndʒ/

Other words and expressions

least /li:st/
That's all right.
I thought you said...
secondly /'sekəndli/
thirdly /'θɜ:dli/
I *do* apologize. /aɪ 'du: ə'pɒlədʒaɪz/
instead /ɪn'sted/

Unit 31

Grammar and structures

Reflexive pronouns

myself /maɪ'self/
yourself /jɔː'self/
himself /hɪm'self/
herself /hə'self/
itself /ɪt'self/
ourselves /aʊə'selvz/
yourselves /jɔː'selvz/
themselves /ðəm'selvz/

Stop looking at **yourself** in the mirror.
'Can I help you?' 'I'll do it **myself**, thanks.'
I like going for walks **by myself**.

Possessive pronouns

mine /maɪn/
yours /jɔːz/
his /hɪz/
hers /hɜːz/
ours /aʊəz/
theirs /ðeəz/

That's not **yours** – it's **mine**.
Our baby's prettier than **theirs**.

Whose is that?

Indefinite pronouns

somebody	anybody	everybody	nobody
something	anything	everything	nothing
somewhere	anywhere	everywhere	nowhere

There's **somebody** at the door.
Would you like **anything** to drink?
You can find Coca Cola **everywhere**.
'What are you doing?' '**Nothing**.'

Shall

Shall I carry something for you?
I'll open the door, **shall** I?

Would

Would you like something to drink?
I'd like some tea.
I'd prefer coffee.
'**Would** you like to dance?' 'I'd love to.'

Else

Do you do the ironing yourself, or does **somebody**
  else do it for you?
'Would you like **something else**?' 'No, **nothing**
  else, thank you.'

Other structures

They talk to **each other** in English.
They've known **each other** for years.

do the ironing   do the cleaning   do the shopping

I've **just** had breakfast.

'Shall I take your coat?' 'No thanks, **I'll keep it on**.'

That's very kind of you.

That car belongs to my boss.

Words and expressions to learn

Nouns

the ironing /ði 'aɪənɪŋ/
the cleaning /ðə 'kliːnɪŋ/
the washing /ðə 'wɒʃɪŋ/
the washing-up /ðə wɒʃɪŋ 'ʌp/
the shopping /ðə 'ʃɒpɪŋ/
toast /təʊst/
plate /pleɪt/
argument /'ɑːgjʊmənt/
mirror /'mɪrə(r)/

Verbs

hurt /hɜːt/ (hurt /hɜːt/, hurt /hɜːt/)
visit /'vɪzɪt/
teach /tiːtʃ/ (taught /tɔːt/, taught /tɔːt/)
shall /ʃəl, ʃæl/
carry /'kæri/
put on (TV) /pʊt 'ɒn/
keep on (clothes) /kiːp 'ɒn/ (kept /kept/, kept /kept/)
belong (to) /bɪ'lɒŋ tə/
shut /ʃʌt/ (shut /ʃʌt/, shut /ʃʌt/)

Other words and expressions

about /ə'baʊt/
else /els/
just /dʒʌst/
just now /dʒʌst 'naʊ/
whose /huːz/
awake /ə'weɪk/
anybody /'enibɒdi/
anywhere /'eniweə(r)/
nowhere /'nəʊweə(r)/
shake hands with /ʃeɪk 'hændz wɪð/
get away from /get ə'weɪ frəm/
have a look /hæv ə 'lʊk/
have a rest /hæv ə 'rest/
wash (your) hands /'wɒʃ (jɔː) 'hændz/

THERE IS NO SUMMARY FOR UNIT 32.

Appendix: Teaching the articles

Introduction

If your students speak a Western European language such as German, Norwegian, Spanish or Greek, they will probably not have too much trouble with the English article system. These languages also contain definite and indefinite articles which (with a few exceptions) are used in similar ways to their English equivalents *a/an* and *the*.

In most other languages, however, there is nothing which corresponds at all closely to the English articles. Speakers of Russian, Japanese, Turkish or Chinese, for example, usually find it difficult to use articles correctly. They will tend to miss them out, to put them in where they are not required, or to confuse one article with another.

Unfortunately, it is not at all easy to teach correct article usage, especially to elementary students. This is for two reasons. First of all, the concepts which the articles express are relatively abstract: students will find them difficult to grasp and will not see why they have to be put into words. And secondly, a good deal of article usage is idiomatic – the rules have large numbers of exceptions, and these take a long time to get used to.

It is therefore important not to be perfectionist about articles. (Many foreigners communicate quite successfully in English without using them at all.) Although correctness is obviously desirable, students are certain to make mistakes, and these should be regarded with reasonable tolerance. The majority of article mistakes are unlikely to affect comprehensibility seriously.

However, you will probably want to do some additional work on this topic if your students are finding it difficult. The purpose of this appendix is to provide simple explanations, and a few basic supplementary exercises which can be copied and used in class. If possible, the explanations should be given to the students in their mother tongue. It will probably be necessary to make up additional exercises of your own to provide extra practice.

The explanations and exercises are arranged in order of difficulty, and follow roughly the order in which the points occur during the course. It is probably best to space them out over a long period.

A The use of *a/an*

Explanation

A noun such as *house, town, doctor, girl, name* symbolizes a whole class of things. When we want to talk about just one member of this class, we generally put *a/an* in front of the noun. (The original meaning of *a/an* was 'one'.)

*She lives in **a** nice big house.*
***A** girl telephoned this morning.*
*There's **a** big fridge in our kitchen.*

A/an is common in definitions and descriptions (when we say what class somebody or something belongs to).

*He's **a** doctor.*
*She's **a** beautiful woman.*

1 Say whether each of these towns is on a river.

Examples: Stoke is on a river.
Sheffield is not on a river.

2 Make sentences about the people.
Use the words in the box.
Example: Alice is a doctor.

doctor	photographer	artist	pilot
driver	housewife	teacher	dancer
athlete	footballer	secretary	waiter

Alice   George   Paul   Judy

Maurice   Pat   Deborah   Joe

Mary   Barbara   Colin   Andrew

B When *a/an* is not used

Explanation

Students need to learn that *a/an* is not used with plural nouns. (It means 'one'.)
*My parents are doctors. (Not * . . . a doctors.)*
You may also have to point out that *a/an* cannot be used with adjectives when these are not followed by nouns. Compare:
*She's **a** pretty girl. She's pretty.*
*(Not *She's a pretty.)*

3 Put in *a/an* or nothing.

1. She's ...*a*...... pretty girl.
2. They are ...⌐...... pretty girls.
3. They are ...⌐...... pretty.
4. My father is .... doctor.
5. My parents are .... doctors.
6. There's .... post office near our house.
7. There are .... two cars in the garage.
8. You're .... very nice.
9. Wantage is .... small town near Oxford.
10. My house is .... very small.
11. 'My name is Schmidt.' 'That's .... German name, isn't it?'
12. Anna and Carola are .... housewives.
13. Their husbands work in .... offices.

C The use of *the*

Explanation

The meaning of *the* is something like 'that/those particular one(s) that you know about'. (*The* was originally the same word as *that*.) It is used with both singular and plural nouns.
Common uses of *the* are:
1. To refer to people and things that have already been mentioned.
   *She's got two children: a boy and a girl. **The** boy's fourteen and **the** girl's eight.*
2. To refer to people and things as we are identifying them.
   *Who's **the** girl in **the** car over there with John?*
3. To refer to people and things that are unique in the situation (so that the hearer can be in no doubt as to which one is meant).
   *Could you close **the** door?*
   *'Where's Ann?' 'In **the** kitchen.'*

4 Put in expressions from the box.

the bathroom	the first floor	the man
the newspaper	the potatoes	the red dress
the woman	the women	the window

1. 'Is that your wife?' 'No, my wife's .... in ....'
2. 'Where's ....?' 'On ....'
3. I work with a man and two women. .... is quite nice, but .... are not very friendly.
4. Could you shut ...., please?
5. What's in ....?
6. Could you pass ...., please?

D When *the* is not used (1)

Explanation

Students must learn that *the* is not used together with other 'determiners' (demonstratives and possessives; *some*, *any*, *which* and some other words).
*This is my uncle. (Not * . . . the my uncle.)*
*That's John's car. (Not * . . . the John's car.)*
*I like this house. (Not * . . . the this house.)*
They must also realize that *the* is not generally used with proper names – the names of people and places. (There are some exceptions.)
*Mary lives in Birmingham. (Not *The Mary . . .)*
*England is a part of Britain. (Not *The England . . .)*

5 Put in *the* or nothing.

1. ...⌐...... Mary is ...⌐...... Peter's sister.
2. Could you shut ...*the*... door?
3. 'Which is .... your car?' '........... blue one in front of .... house.'
4. Can you show me .... that book, please?
5. .... my aunt Susan lives in .... Canada.
6. 'Who is .... that woman?' 'It's .... Harry's mother.'
7. .... my husband is .... man in .... blue coat.

E The difference between *a/an* and *the*

Explanation

Some students confuse the two articles, and it may be useful to focus on the difference.
Very simply:
– *a/an* just means 'one of a class'.
– *the* refers to a particular identified ('labelled') member of a class: it means 'that one/those ones that we know about'.
Compare *a* and *the* in this sentence:
*I live in **a** small flat on **the** third floor of **an** old house.*

The speaker says *a small flat*, because this flat is not completely identified – there may be two or three on the third floor. *The* is used in *the third floor*, because the floor is completely identified – there is only one third floor in the speaker's house, and so we know exactly which floor is meant. The speaker says *an old house*, because he is not telling us (and we do not already know) exactly which house – it could be one of millions.

6 Put in *a/an* or *the*.

1. My brother is .... engineer.
2. I live in .... small flat.
3. Glasgow is .... industrial town in Scotland.
4. Could you open .... door, please?
5. What's .... name of .... woman in .... red dress?
6. I study English in .... language school.
7. .... school where I study is called 'The Universal Oxford and Cambridge Language Academy'.
8. I'd like .... drink of water, please.
9. There's some ice in .... fridge.

F When *the* is not used (2)

Explanation

In English, *the* is not normally used with nouns which have a 'general' sense. If we want to talk about books, life, people or anything else in general, we normally say 'books', 'life' or 'people', not 'the books' etc. (In this respect, English is different from most Western European languages, which tend to use the definite article in generalizations.)

Compare:

Life *is hard.* (life in general)
the life *of Beethoven* (a particular life)

Cheese *is getting very expensive.*
'Where's **the cheese***?' 'I ate it.'*

7 Put in *the* or nothing.

1. .... books are expensive.
2. Who are .... people you were talking to?
3. I forgot to buy .... eggs that you asked for.
4. I don't like .... whisky.
5. .... water turns into .... ice at 0°C.
6. Could you take .... books off the table, please?
7. .... light travels at 300,000 km a second.
8. Could you put .... light on?

G Countable and uncountable nouns

Explanation

When students are familiar with the difference between countable and uncountable nouns, they are ready to learn two more rules about articles.

1. *A/an* cannot normally be used with an uncountable noun.
2. A singular countable noun must normally have an article (or other 'determiner') with it. (There are some common exceptions in prepositional phrases like *in bed*, *on holiday*.)

8 Can you put *a/an* with these nouns or not?

book *Yes*......   water ..*No*....   table ....
cheese ....   wool ....   work ....
address ....   electricity ....

9 Can you use these nouns without an article?

book ..*No*......   men ..*Yes*...   child ....
children ....   petrol ....   car ....
soap ....   pen ....   hair ....

Revision Tests

The tests on the following pages, which are also available separately in Test Books for students, have three main purposes:

1. To show you and the students whether there are any points that have not been properly learnt, for whatever reason.
2. To identify any students who are having serious difficulty with the course.
3. To motivate the students to look back over the work they have done and do some serious revision, before they move on to the next phase of the course.

It is not intended that students should 'pass' or 'fail' the tests, and it is not particularly useful to give 'marks', though students ought to be told whether their performance is satisfactory. In principle, most students ought to get most answers right; if this does not happen, efficient learning is not taking place (because of poor motivation, too rapid a pace, absenteeism, failure to do follow-up work outside class, or for some other reason). Of course, nobody can be expected to retain all the material that has been presented, but a student who finds the whole of a test too difficult may have considerable difficulty coping with the next part of the course, particularly if the main weakness is in the area of vocabulary learning.

The tests which follow Units 11 and 22 cover most of the grammar that comes in the previous 11 units, and a fair sample of the vocabulary and usage. There are also pronunciation, spelling and listening components. These tests should each take something between ninety minutes and two hours, depending on the class.

The end-of-book test is very complete, covering a wide selection of the work that has been done since the beginning of the course. It will take quite a long time (perhaps three or four hours) for students to work their way through it, and you may wish to divide it into parts and spread it over several lessons. If time is too short, it may be necessary to cut out some of the sections, but it is advisable to do the whole test if at all possible, as it gives very important feedback to both teacher and students.

Revision Test One

Grammar

1. .... your parents English?
2. No, ... aren't.
3. My sister .... got a very nice boyfriend.
4. ....'s your name?
5. Excuse me. ....'s the station?
6. **Put the words in order:**
   brother got blue has your eyes ?

   ....
7. 'Are you Greek?' 'Yes, I ....'
8. 'Have you got any children?' 'No, I
   ....'
9. *She's* hungry. (*She is* or *she has*?) ....
10. *She's* got brown eyes. (*She is* or *she has*?)

    ....
11. I live .... 17 Hazel Avenue, Dundee.
12. I live .... Dundee.
13. I live .... the fourth floor.
14. I usually get up .... six o'clock.
15. Have you got .... beer? (*some* or *any*?)
16. No, but I've got .... wine. (*some* or *any*?)
17. There .... some eggs in the fridge.
18. .... pretty dress!
19. .... nice ear-rings!
20. How .... students are there in your class?
21. What colour .... your eyes?
22. .... you cold?
23. John's British, but .... wife is French.
24. Marianne and .... husband live in France.
25. **Give the plurals:** cat ...*cats*....

    man ....   woman ....
    child ....   foot ....
    boss ....   eye ....
    boy ....   secretary ....

---

1. *Are*
2. *they*
3. *has*

4. *What*
5. *Where*

6. *Has your brother got blue eyes?*
7. *am*

8. *haven't*
9. *She is*

10. *She has*

11. *at*
12. *in*
13. *on*
14. *at*
15. *any*

16. *some*

17. *are*
18. *What a*
19. *What*
20. *many*

21. *are*
22. *Are*
23. *his*

24. *her*

25. *men   women*

    children   feet

    bosses   eyes

    boys   secretaries

26. **Make questions.**

Where | you | live?

Where do you live? ....

What time | you | usually | get up?

....   *26. What time do you usually get up?*

you | like | Beethoven?

....   *Do you like Beethoven?*

Where | your mother | work?

....   *Where does your mother work?*

27. **Complete the sentences.**

My father .... to work by bus.   *27. goes*
(go)

Both my parents .... on   *work*
Saturdays. (work)

Vocabulary

1 **Put some more words in each of these lists.**   *(various possible answers)*

1. father, brother, ...

....

....

2. artist, doctor, ...

....

....

3. France, England, ...

....

....

4. French, English, ...

....

....

5. tall, nice, ...

....

....

6. red, green, ...

....

....

7. trousers, dress, ...

....

....

....

8. chair, ...

9. living room, ...

....

10. village, ...

....

11. beer, potatoes, ...

....

....

12. eye, foot, ...

....

....

13. fog, ...

14. hungry, tired, ...

....

15. station, bank, ...

....

....

2 Write the days of the week.

Monday, ...

....

....

....

3 Write these numbers in words.

234 .... *two hundred and thirty-four*

....

6798 .... *six thousand, seven hundred and ninety-eight*

....

14 .... *fourteen*

1,000,000 .... *a million/one million*

40 .... *forty*

Language use

1. 'Are you ....?' 'No, I'm single.'   *1. married*
2. '................?' 'Fine, thanks.'   *2. How are you?*
3. 'How do you do?' '................?'   *3. How do you do?*
4. 'Thank you very much.' '................'   *4. Not at all.*
5. 'Hello, 61482.' 'Hello, ... speak to   *5. can I or could I*
   Mary?' 'Speaking. Who's ....?'   *that*

➡

165

6. 'Excuse me. Where's the nearest post office?'   6. *(various possible answers)*

'
....

....

.... ,'

Pronunciation

Underline the stressed syllables.

London   Japanese   children   potatoes   *Japanese   children   potatoes*

village   assistant   thousand   understand   *village   assistant   thousand   understand*

Listening

1 **Listen to the conversation and draw circles round the words you hear.**

Phone number: 67482   (64482)   61483   *64482*

Caller's name: Mary   Helen   Sally   *Helen*

Caller asks for: Mary   Helen   Sally   *Sally*

Film is at: 7.15   7.45   7.00   *7.45*

Name of film: 'Gone with the Wind'   *'Ben Hur'*

'Ben Hur'   'King Kong'

Cinema is in: Oxford   Cambridge   London   *London*

Meet at: station   cinema   pub   *station*

2 **Listen to the two conversations and answer the questions.**

A. What colour are the woman's ear-rings?

....   *blue*

What colour are her eyes? ....   *blue*

Is her hair short or long? ....   *short*

B. How many bedrooms are there? ....   *two*

Is the kitchen big or small? ....   *small*

Is there a garage? ....   *yes*

Is there a toilet downstairs? ....   *yes*

How much is the rent? *£350*
                                                       (a month)

Tapescript for listening test

1. MARY: Hello, 64482.
   HELEN: Hello, Mary. Can I speak to Sally?
   MARY: Hi, Helen. Just a moment.
   SALLY: Hello, Helen. How are you?
   HELEN: Hi, Sally. Do you want to go and see 'Ben Hur' in London tonight?
   SALLY: Yes, OK. Which cinema is it on at?
   HELEN: The Paramount, in Oxford Street.
   SALLY: What time?
   HELEN: Quarter to eight.
   SALLY: OK. Let's meet at the station at 7.15.
   HELEN: Right. Bye.
   SALLY: See you. Bye.

2. **A**
   MAN: I do like your ear-rings.
   WOMAN: Oh, thank you.
   MAN: They're such a lovely blue. Turquoise, aren't they?
   WOMAN: Yes.
   MAN: The same colour as your eyes. Really pretty. Your hair's nice, too.
   WOMAN: Oh, do you think so?
   MAN: Yes, I like it short. It suits you...

   B
   'Well, this is the flat. There are two bedrooms, both with double beds, and a spare room upstairs. Then downstairs there's a living room, a study and a kitchen. I'm afraid the kitchen's rather small, but it's fully equipped. Two toilets: one in the bathroom and a separate one downstairs. And there's a double garage. I expect you'd like to know the rent. It's £350 a month.'
   'My God!'

Revision Test Two

Grammar

1 Give the past.

play *played*   become *became*

leave	....	eat	....
drink	....	know	....
go	....	get	....
tell	....	come	....
hear	....	wake	....
say	....	write	....
see	....	buy	....
take	....	make	....
stand	....	give	....
cost	....	sleep	....
begin	....	drive	....

left   ate
drank   knew
went   got
told   came
heard   woke
said   wrote
saw   bought
took   made
stood   gave
cost   slept
began   drove

2 Make these verbs negative.

I had *I didn't have*

I sent	....	*I didn't send*
I brought	....	*I didn't bring*
I found	....	*I didn't find*
I could	....	*I couldn't*
I sang	....	*I didn't sing*
I lost	....	*I didn't lose*
I built	....	*I didn't build*
I sat	....	*I didn't sit*
I lay	....	*I didn't lie*
I was	....	*I wasn't*

(Uncontracted forms are also possible, of course.)

3 Fill in the blanks.

I *was* ... you .... he/she ....   *were   was*

we .... they ....   *were   were*

4 Put in the correct forms.

1. .... John tomorrow? (Are you seeing / Do you see)

   1. Are you seeing

2. How often .... to the hairdresser? (are you going / do you go)

   2. do you go

167

3. What ....? (are you
   eating / do you eat)

   3. *are you eating*

4. 'Have you got a cigarette?' 'Sorry, I

   ....' ('m not
   smoking / don't smoke)

   4. *don't smoke*

5 Give the answers. Begin with *So.*
1. 'I'm a student.' '*So am I.*............'
2. 'I like beer.' '............................'

   2. *So do I.*

3. 'I can swim.' '............................'

   3. *So can I.*

4. 'I've got four brothers.' '............................'

   4. *So have I.*

5. 'I'd like a cup of tea.' '............................'

   5. *So would I.*

6 Put in the correct forms.
1. How long have you .... John? (know)

   1. *known*

2. Have you ever .... *Hamlet*? (see)

   2. *seen*

3. Have you ever .... *Love Story*? (read)

   3. *read*

4. How long have you .... married? (be)

   4. *been*

5. How long have you .... that old car? (have)

   5. *had*

7 Fill in the blanks.

I *me*	he	we		*him*	*us*
you	she	you	*you*	*her*	*you*
	it	they		*it*	*them*

8 Put in *this, that, these* or *those.*
1. 'Could I speak to Joseph?' 'Yes, who's ....?'

   1. *that*

2. 'Which ones do you want?' '............ blue ones
   over there.'

   2. *Those*

3. Look at .... new car in front of Ann's
   house.

   3. *that*

4. Are you free .... evening?

   4. *this*

9 Give the comparative and superlative.
old *older* *oldest*

young ....

   younger, youngest

big ....

   bigger, biggest

important ....

   more important,
   most important

interesting ....

   more interesting,
   most interesting

fat	....	*fatter, fattest*
happy	....	*happier, happiest*
late	....	*later, latest*
good	....	*better, best*

10 *It* or *there*?

1. .... will be rain at the weekend.

2. .... will be warm tonight and tomorrow.

3. .... will be sunny in some parts of the country.

4. .... isn't any more milk in the fridge.

1. There

2. It

3. It

4. There

11 Put the words in the right order.

1. pen could me a lend you ?

....

2. please bring the us you bill could ?

....

1. Could you lend me a pen?

2. Could you bring us the bill please? / Could you please bring us the bill? / Please could you bring us the bill?

12 Put in *of* if necessary.

1. Would you like a piece .... bread?

2. I've got a lot .... American friends.

3. How many .... brothers and sisters have you got?

4. There are a few .... bananas in the kitchen.

1. of

2. of

3. –

4. –

13 *As* or *than*?

1. I'm older .... you.

2. Her eyes are the same colour .... mine.

3. She's not as tall .... I am.

4. I can do anything better .... you.

1. than

2. as

3. as

4. than

Vocabulary and language use

1 Put more words in each of these lists.

1. elephant, tiger, ...

....

....

2. table tennis, chess, ...

....

3. guitar, ...

(various possible answers)

4. wood, glass, ...

....

5. heavy, hard, ...

....

....

6. shy, nervy, ...

2 Put in suitable words.

1. Is this seat ....?

2. 'Who is your .... painter?' 'Picasso.'

3. Karl Marx was .... in 1818.

4. I'm very good at ...., but I'm bad at

....

5. 'What would you like?' 'I'll .... roast beef.'

6. Would you like something to ....?

7. I first met Annie seven years ....

8. I'm much .... than my mother.

9. Could you ....

.... water?

10. 'Could you lend me £5?' 'I'm .... I can't.'

11. Is service .... ?

12. 'Can I help you?' '................ .... looking.'

13. What size .... ?

14. Those shoes are nice. Can I try ....

.... ?

1. free

2. favourite

3. born

4. (various possible answers)

5. have

6. eat, drink, read...

7. ago

8. (various possibilities – comparative adjective required)

9. pass me the / give me some

10. afraid

11. included

12. I'm just / We're just

13. are you

14. them on

3 Give suitable answers to these sentences.

1. I'm Pisces. *So am I.*

2. John's got a new car. ....

3. My sister works in New York. ....

4. Would you like to come to a party? ....

5. Let's go and have a drink. ....

6. Have another drink. ....

7. Do you mind if I smoke? ....

8. Why can't a mouse eat an elephant?

....

9. What's an aeroplane made of?

....

Various answers possible; probable ones are:

2. Has he?

3. Does she?

4. I'd love to. / Yes, please.

5. All right.

6. Yes, please. / No thanks.

7. Not at all. / I'd rather you didn't.

8. Because an elephant's too big.

9. Metal, plastic, rubber, glass...

Pronunciation and spelling

1 Underline the stressed syllables.

holiday postcard birthday afraid

another hairdresser newspaper suggestion

conversation somebody morning afternoon

postcard *birthday* *afraid*

another *hairdresser* *newspaper* *suggestion*

conversation *somebody* *morning* *afternoon*

2 Give the *-ing* form.

work *working* stand .... like ....

stop .... speak .... play ....

lie .... sit .... make ....

standing liking

stopping speaking playing

lying sitting making

Listening

Listen, and answer these questions about the speaker.

1. How old is she? ....

2. Where was she born? ....

3. What is her best friend's name? ....

4. What happened when she was seven?

....

5. When did she begin to like school?

....

6. How old are her sister and brothers?

....

7. Where is her sister working now? ....

8. Does she see her little brother very often? ....

1. eighteen

2. Oxford

3. Dan

4. Her parents divorced.

5. about three years ago

6. 20, 14 and 3½

7. in a pub

8. no

The students will not understand everything, but the information they must listen for is fairly clear. Suggested procedure: play the recording once through; play it again, pausing at the places marked // for the students to write their answers; then play it through once again.

Tapescript
'I'm 18 years old. // I was born in Oxford, // um, I had quite a nice early childhood, I think, um, I grew up with a guy called Dan, who I'm still friends with, he's my best friend. // Um, my parents divorced when I was seven. // Um, I didn't like school much un-, up until about three years ago. // I've got, um, an older sister twenty, // and a younger brother of fourteen, // another brother of three and a half, um, oogh!' //
'How well do you get on with them?'
'I don't get on *too* well with my sister, but I get on pretty well with my younger brother. Um, my sister, she's working in a pub at the moment, // so I don't see *that* much of her, so I suppose we get on better. (laughter) Um, hmm, (sigh), my brother I get on pretty well with, and my little brother I don't see that often.'

171

Revision Test Three

Grammar

1 Give the past and the past participle.

go *went* *gone*

see ....   *saw, seen*

meet ....   *met, met*

eat ....   *ate, eaten*

drink ....   *drank, drunk*

have ....   *had, had*

hear ....   *heard, heard*

know ....   *knew, known*

write ....   *wrote, written*

read ....   *read, read*

make ....   *made, made*

fall ....   *fell, fallen*

2 Give the part of the verb that follows he/she.

like *likes*

think .... watch ....   *thinks   watches*

can .... could .... go ....   *can   could   goes*

am .... went .... will ....   *is   went   will*

do .... fell ....   *does   fell*

3 Put in *have, to have, having, has, had, be, to be, being* or *been*.

1. Could I .... a drink of water, please?   *1. have*

2. Have you ever .... to Moscow?   *2. been*

3. I would like .... a better job.   *3. to have*

4. Where will you .... this time tomorrow?   *4. be*

5. How long .... you .... married?   *5. have, been*

6. Can I ring you back? I'm .... breakfast just now.   *6. having*

7. I think Andrew .... got a new girlfriend.   *7. has*

8. I'd like .... taller.   *8. to be*

9. How long .... you .... this job?   *9. have, had*

4 Put in the correct form.

1. What .... this evening?
   (arc you doing / do you do)

2. How often .... to London?
   (are you going / do you go)

3. 'Have you got a cigarette?' 'Sorry,
   ....' (I'm not smoking /
   I don't smoke)

4. 'Where .... ?' 'To the post
   office.' (are you going / do you go)

5. .... everything all right? (Is / Are)

6. Your hair .... too long. (is / are)

7. Most people .... too hard. (work / works)

8. I went to America .... English.
   (to learn / for learning)

9. How .... money have you got?
   (much / many)

1. *are you doing*

2. *do you go*

3. *I don't smoke*

4. *are you going*

5. *Is*

6. *is*

7. *work*

8. *to learn*

9. *much*

5 Write the contractions.

I am *I'm* .... she will ....

I have .... will not ....

had not .... we are ....

they have .... cannot ....

does not ....

she'll

I've   won't

hadn't   we're

they've   can't

doesn't

6 Complete the table.

I	me	my	myself	mine
you	....	....	....	....
he	him	....	....	....
she	....	her	....	....
it	....	....	....	–
we	....	....	....	....
you	....	....	yourselves	....
they	....	....	....	....

I	me	my	myself	mine
you	*you*	*your*	*yourself*	*yours*
he	*him*	*his*	*himself*	*his*
she	*her*	*her*	*herself*	*hers*
it	*it*	*its*	*itself*	*–*
we	*us*	*our*	*ourselves*	*ours*
you	*you*	*your*	*yourselves*	*yours*
they	*them*	*their*	*themselves*	*theirs*

7 Give the adverbs.

slow *slowly* .... happy ....

cold .... nice ....

angry ....

comfortable ....

happily

coldly   nicely

angrily

comfortably

fast .... good ....   *fast   well*

careful ....   *carefully*

8 Put in *a, an, the* or no article.

Examples: What's *the*. time?

                She comes from ...–... London.

                She lives in ..*a*... small flat.

1. My brother's .... doctor.   *1. a*

2. Do you like .... music?   *2. –*

3. 'What are you eating?' '........ orange.'   *3. An*

4. 'Where's .... nearest toilet?'   *4. the*

5. 'At .... top of .... stairs, on .... right.'   *5. the, the, the*

6. Can I see .... manager, please? I wish to make   *6. the*

     .... complaint.   *a*

7. Tomorrow will be cold, and there will be ....   *7. –*
   snow.

8. Do you know, ... tomatoes are £1.50 a kilo?   *8. –*

9 Put in the correct preposition where
necessary.

Examples: I usually get up *at*... eight o'clock.

                Where are you *from*?

                I feel tired ...–... this morning.

1. Come back again .... Tuesday.   *1. on*

2. Come back again .... ten minutes – I'm not   *2. in*
   free now.

3. I work well .... the morning. I don't like   *3. in*

     working .... night.   *at*

4. .... the top   .... the middle   *4. at   in*

     .... the bottom   *at*

5. Where were you .... yesterday afternoon?   *5. –*

6. 'I bought these flowers .... you.' 'Oh, thank   *6. for*
   you.'

7. 'How long are you going to stay here?' '...........   *7. Until (Till)*
   March.'

8. Would you like a piece .... bread?   *8. of*

9. No, but could I have a little .... cheese,   *9. –*
   please?

10 Put the words in the right order.

1. open office what does post time the ?

....   *1. What time does the post office open?*

174

2. much I father like mother very and your .

....
....

2. I like your father and mother (mother and father) very much.

3. are people going where those all ?

....

3. *Where are all those people going?*

4. badly Spanish speak I .

....

4. *I speak Spanish badly.*

5. 'arrive boss your did when ?'
   'ago an hour half .'

....
....

5. *'When did your boss arrive?'*
   'Half an hour ago.'

11 Write sentences with *whose, who, where, when, why.*

(various possible answers)

....
....
....
....
....

Vocabulary and language use

1 Give the opposites of these words.

white *black* .... tall *short* ....

loud	happy	*soft/quiet unhappy*
high	fat	*low thin/slim*
polite	easy	*rude/impolite difficult/hard*
expensive	heavy	*cheap light*
well	better	*badly/ill worse*
more	export	*less/fewer import*
hard	wide	*soft/easy narrow*
useful	clean	*useless dirty*
put down	always	*pick up never*
off	out of	*on/on to into/in*
up	top	*down bottom*
rise	back	*fall front*
before	interesting	*after boring*
north	past	*south future*
left		*right*

2 **Put more words in these lists.**   *(various possible answers)*

Example: uncle, aunt, *Cousin* ......

father ......

1. arm, nose, ...

....

2. breakfast, dinner, ...

3. triangle, cross, ...

4. knife, cup, ...

5. fly, walk, ...

....

6. Mr, Mrs, ...

7. dog, gorilla, ...

....

8. post office, bank, ...

....

9. blouse, trousers, ...

....

3 **Write these fractions in words.**

Example: ⅓ *a third* ...... or *one third* ......

⅖	3/7	*two fifths three sevenths*
⅔	¼	*two thirds a quarter/one quarter*
5/9	3/10	*five ninths three tenths*
⅙	1/9	*a sixth/one sixth a ninth/one ninth*

4 2.05 = five past two

3.15 = a quarter past three   **What are:**

4.30 ....   *half past four*

6.45 ....   *a quarter to seven*

9.20 ....   *twenty past nine*

7.55 ....   *five to eight*

10.10 ....   *ten past ten*

5 **Write sentences with these words.**   *(various possible answers)*

Example: sorry *I'm sorry I'm late.* ....

bedroom ....

....

look like ....

....

176

borrow ....

....

lend ....

....

hungry ....

....

winter ....

....

favourite ....

....

manager ....

....

writer ....

....

hurt ....

....

flight ....

....

by cheque ....

....

born ....

....

each other ....

....

else ....

....

I'm sure ....

....

certainly ....

....

get ....

....

6 **Complete these conversational exchanges.**

1. 'Here you are.' '.........................'   *1. Thank you.*

2. 'That was a great film!' 'I .... agree. I   *2. don't*
   .... it was terrible.'   *think/thought*

3. 'Agresti, kunsti sifnit?' 'I'm sorry, I don't
   ....'   *3. understand*

➡

4. 'What's that girl's name?' 'I'm sorry, I don't
........................'

5. 'What does *shut* ....?' 'The same as
closed.'

6. '........................ do?' 'I'm a
photographer.'

7. '........................ do?' 'How do you do?'

8. 'Could I ....?' 'Speaking.'

9. 'What a nice dress.' '........................'

10. 'I *am* sorry.' '........................'

11. '........................ you?' 'I'm 27.'

12. '........................ you?' 'One metre
eighty-five.'

13. '........................ you?' 'Fine, thanks.'

4. *know/remember*

5. *mean*

6. *What do you*

7. *How do you*

8. *speak to ...*

9. *Thank you.*

10. *That's all right.*

11. *How old are*

12. *How tall are*

13. *How are*

7 Answer the questions.

1. If you want to complain in a shop, who do you
ask for? ....

2. What do you use to open a tin with?
....

3. What do you wear if you have bad eyes?
....

4. Where do people buy shoes?
....

5. Where do people buy books?
....

6. Where do people go to read or borrow books?
....

7. What is a window made of?
....

8. John is 20, Alice is 30 and Paul is 40. What is
their average age? ....

9. Give examples of: a noun, a verb, an adjective,
an adverb.
....
....

1. *the manager*

2. *a tin-opener*

3. *glasses*

4. *in (at) a shoe-shop*

5. *in (at) a bookshop*

6. *to a library*

7. *glass (and wood or metal)*

8. *thirty*

9. *(various answers possible)*

Listening

🔊 Ⓐ

Listen to the recording and answer the following questions.

1. At the beginning, does the speaker say that her childhood was happy or unhappy? ....
2. Did she like school? ....
3. At what age did she first go to school? ....
4. Complete this sentence: 'They were the .... years of my life.'
5. Did she work hard at school? ....
6. At what age did she go to boarding school?

   ....
7. At what age did she leave school?

   ....
8. Was she good at French? ....
9. Did she like English? ....
10. Was she good at sport? ....
11. Does she say that she had a lot of friends?

    ....

1. happy

2. no

3. five

4. worst

5. no

6. fourteen

7. sixteen

8. no

9. yes

10. no

11. no

Suggested procedure: play the recording once through without stopping. Then play it again, pausing at the places marked // so that students can write their answers. Finally, play it once again without stopping.

Tapescript
I had a happy childhood from the point of view of being loved and looked after but I was very glad to grow up. // I hated school – and in some respects it wasn't happy. School I hated. // From the age of five to the age of sixteen they were the worst years of my life, something I never ever wish to repeat. // I now regret that I didn't enjoy them, that I didn't work or learn. // I went to school in Purley, which was close to Croydon, and then I went to boarding school when I was fourteen until I left when I was sixteen, and they were the most – they were really miserable years, awful. // I wasn't very good at anything, in fact I was very bad at everything. // I suppose I liked French and English, the only two subjects that appealed; // I was hopeless at sport, I was introverted, I was ugly, I was tall, I had frizzy hair and not a lot going for me, // I didn't have a lot of friends. I tried desperately to make friends but if you're not good at sports and you're not good at work when you're at school, especially then, when you don't have any confidence, you don't stand a lot of chance.

Additional tapescripts

Lesson 5B, Exercise 5

LESLIE: Excuse me, John. What's your address?
JOHN: A hundred and sixteen Market Street.
LESLIE: Thanks. And your phone number?
JOHN: What?
LESLIE: Your phone number.
JOHN: Oh, er, 314 6829.

OFFICER: Name, please.
ANN: ⎫ Ann Webber.
ROBERT: ⎭ Robert Webber.
OFFICER: And where do you live, Mr and Mrs Webber?
ANN: At number 60 Hamilton Road, Gloucester.
OFFICER: I see. And are you on the phone?
ROBERT: Yes, we are.
OFFICER: Could you tell me your number?
ANN: Our number? Yes, it's Gloucester 41785.

FLO: Hello, Alice. How are you?
ALICE: Not too bad, thanks. And you?
FLO: Oh, OK. Mustn't grumble. How's your mother?
ALICE: She's all right, considering. Yes, very well, really.
FLO: She lives in Oxford now, doesn't she?
ALICE: No, in Birmingham.

(Doorbell. Door opens.)
PETER: Excuse me.
SALLY: Yes?
PETER: My name's Peter Matthews. I live on the fourth floor. My telephone isn't working, and I was wondering if I could use yours.
SALLY: Yes, of course. Come in. The phone's over there, in the living room.
PETER: Thanks.

CHAIRMAN: Good morning, everybody. I'd like to introduce Mr Steven Billows, from New York. Mr Billows is going to talk to us about computer software delivery date problems...

MRS SIMON: Hello, Bedford 41632... Yes... Yes, Mrs Simon speaking... Yes... No... No, my address is 16 Norris Road. N, O, double R, I, S, ... Norris *Road*, not Norris *Street*... Yes, that's right. 16 Norris Road.

Lesson 8C, Exercise 3

MARY: Abingdon 31220.
JIM: Hello, Mary. This is Jim. Could I speak to Nelly, please?
MARY: Hi, Jim. I'm sorry. She's gone to the bank. I'm expecting her back in about half an hour.
JIM: Oh, thanks. I'll ring back later. Bye.
MARY: Bye.

MR JACKSON: Hello. Carlisle 71773..
MR ROBERTS: Hello. Mr Jackson?
MR JACKSON: Yes.
MR ROBERTS: My name's Eric Roberts. I wonder if I could speak to Mrs Jackson, if she's at home?
MR JACKSON: Yes, one moment, please. I'll get her. Darling, it's for you...

A: Hello.
B: Hello, is Jane in?
A: No, she's at the swimming pool.
B: Do you know what time she'll be back?
A: No, sorry, I don't.
B: OK, thanks. Bye.

ALICE: Hello.
JOHN: Alice...
ALICE: John! Hello! Where are you?
JOHN: At the station. Listen, Alice, I've got to see you. Now. At once.
ALICE: But John – Peter's here...

Lesson 10A, Exercise 6

STEVE: 'She's about 5ft 8, about 9 stone, fair hair and a fairly thin face, slender figure, a slightly turned-up nose and a little double chin. And that's about it. And that's my wife. I don't know the colour of her eyes.'

LORNA: 'I'm going to describe my mum. She's 5ft 5, long wavy dark brown hair, dark brown eyes, fairly pretty – wearing well, I think – fairly slim, fairly pale complexion. That's about it.'

RUTH: 'I'm going to describe my best friend Dan, whom I grew up with. He's about 5ft 11, 5 10, 5 11, he's, um, dark brown hair, blue eyes I think, yeah, they are blue eyes. He's, um, quite slender build, nice legs (laughter), very nice face, lovely face, very nice face, in fact he's pretty good-looking, and I'm going to marry him. No –' 'Does he know?' 'No, he doesn't know.'

KATY: 'OK. My son is about 105 cm tall. He's got fair hair, blue eyes, is fairly slim. I think he's very good-looking.'

SUE: 'My husband has fair hair going white, he's got lots of white hairs, greying rapidly; a beard and moustache – full beard and moustache – his eyes are blue, his height is around about 5 8, I think, 5 8, 5 9, and he's slightly overweight, and he's got a very round face. That's about it.'

Lesson 12D, Exercise 1

STEVE DIXON
My name's Steve Dixon. I'm quite elderly – I'm 40 years of age. I was born in a little town in the north country of England called Darlington, County Durham. As far as I can remember, my childhood I quite enjoyed. No real problems there. Like all little boys, I dug up the garden, played with worms, played in the sandpit, and this sort of thing. I had for a family, obviously my mother and father; I had a sister and a brother who was older than me, but unfortunately he died when he was about two or three.

ADRIAN WEBBER
My name is Adrian Webber. My age is 42 years, and I was born in Delhi, India. This was due to the fact that my father had spent most of his adult life in India in the Indian police up to that time. I have a sister who's eight years older than myself. She was also born in India. And my childhood was very varied and quite happy as I remember.

LORNA HIGGS
My name's Lorna Higgs. I'm 19 years old, was born in Oxford and (have) lived here all my life. As far as childhood goes it's

180

been quite mixed really. As far as family goes I've two brothers both younger than me. One's left school and has got a job, one of the lucky ones. The other one's still attending school.

SUE WARD

My name is Sue Ward. I was born in Tadcaster in Yorkshire. My father was in the Air Force and when I was seven months old we moved to Hong Kong and spent three years in the Far East, Hong Kong and Singapore. After that we moved every three years, back to England and around England, various places. When I was thirteen my parents went to Africa and I had to go to boarding school. My family consisted of three brothers and one sister, and I had a very happy childhood.

Lesson 13C, Exercise 4

The train now standing at platform 2 is for London Paddington only. Passengers for Reading travel from Platform 4. Platform 4 for Reading. The opposite platform, Platform 3 for Oxford. The opposite platform, Platform 3 for Oxford. London Paddington train only.

Didcot. Train now standing at platform 3 is the 9:25 departure, calling at Appleford, Culham, Radley and Oxford. Passengers for Appleford travel in the first three coaches of this train. Platform 3 for Appleford, Culham, Radley and Oxford.

Train now standing at Platform 4 is for Cholsey, Goring, Pangbourne, Tilehurst, Reading and London Paddington. Passengers for Swindon and the Bristol line travel from Platform 1. Platform 1 for Swindon and the Bristol line. Platform 4 for Cholsey, Goring, Pangbourne, Tilehurst, Reading and London Paddington.

Lesson 14A, Exercise 4

1. Well, Mr Alexander, I'd like to help, but I'm afraid I can't manage it at the moment.
2. 'What are you doing?' 'It's all right, dear, I can explain everything.'
3. Jane's eight years old. I'm surprised that she can't swim.
4. You can borrow my car this evening, but there isn't any petrol in it.
5. I can't understand what she wants.
6. That little Robert can't talk very well.
7. 'Do you have any problems with your digestion?' 'I can eat anything I like.'

Lesson 27B, Exercise 5

'... Carterton 3, Milltown 2.
   Bolario 2, San Pedro 4.
   Allington 1, San Fantastico Town 1.
And now, for some news from the third day of the Fantasian National Games, we go over to our commentator Simon Rask. Over to you, Simon.'

'Thank you, John. Well, it's been a really sensational day here in the National Stadium, with records falling right and left. In the final of the men's 100 metres we had a very fine performance from Arnaldo Higgins, with a time of exactly ten seconds for a national record. You may be interested to know that that corresponds to a speed of just 36 kilometres an hour, so Arnaldo was really travelling.

   Another national record in the women's marathon. Grete White, who led most of the way, finished looking remarkably fresh in the splendid time of two hours 38 minutes and 3 seconds. My colleague informs me that Grete ran the 42 kilometres at an average speed of around 16 kilometres an hour, which is a good deal faster than I could do it on a bicycle.

   Another women's record in the 100 metres freestyle swimming event, which was won by Lucy Pollaro in the amazing time of 51.4 seconds. That's seven kilometres an hour – faster than some of us can walk.'

'Certainly faster than I can walk, Simon. Thank you. Now we have one result in from the international skiing championship at Monte Tremendo. In the downhill Alpine event, the Englishman Harold Collins was a clear winner. He completed the 2 kilometre course in just 74.6 seconds, which means he was skiing at nearly 100 kilometres an hour, believe it or not – 96.3, to be exact.

   And now some more football results...'

Lesson 30A, Exercise 4

(| indicates that two things are said at the same time.)
'What are your two most treasured possessions – is it possible to answer that?'
(sigh) 'Do they have to be single things, or do they – can they be...'
'Not necessarily, no.'
'Mm.'
['My family...'
['Two thing(s)...'
'Yeah' (unintelligible)
'my family,'
'Yeah.'
'... and my health.'
'My family and my life.' (general chuckles)
'Just exactly what I was going to say. My family and my car, OK?'
'My family and my friends.'
['Mm.'
['Yeah.'
'Friendship and happiness.'
'Friendship and ...?'
'Happiness.'
'Happiness.'
'Mm.'
'Yeah.'
(Pause; unintelligible general mumbling)
'I'll go along with that. That's a difficult thing to say, because there's, definitely family (someone else unintelligible), certainly not anything material.'
'Mm.'
'I was going to include my rugby boots, because, uh, ...'
(General laughter)
[(Unintelligible comments)
['I thought you'd come out with two *objects*; but...'
'No, I, I, I include my car, no, that really is ...'
'I think the car actually is pretty ... not *my* car, though, *a* car.'
'*A* car.'
['What's wrong with your car?'
['It's just a heap!'
'But you could still get on without a car, if you had friends ...'
'Yes.'
'But it has character.'
'And I spend more time with that than I do with practically anything else.'
'My work, I think, ...'
'Oh God!'
'... at the moment.'
'Good health and happiness.'
'Yeah! because I went *crazy* not working.'
'Are you working?'
'Part-time, mm.'

Lesson 31A, Exercise 5

'Adrian. Ironing.'
'My wife does it all, except for trousers, which I iron. That's mine and my son's.'
'Yeah, OK. Is that your army training?'
'Yes I should think he (mumble)' 'Must be.'
'Yes.' 'My father's the same...'
'Home decorating. Do you do it yourself or do you get somebody else to do it?'
'I cannot do anything myself; my wife has to help me and therefore keep me at it, 'cause as soon as she down(s) tools, so do I.' (Laughter)
'Cooking – who does the cooking?'
'My wife does it all.'
'Yeah. Washing?'
'She does it all.'
'Yeah. Cleaning?'
'I sometimes help, but she does most of it.'
'Yeah. Washing-up?'
'I do... my fair bit, but, uh, ...'
'Yeah.' (unintelligible remark)
'And who does the shopping?'
'Well, as I'm the only driver, I have to take her down to town, and we both do it together.'
'Oh, well done.'

Lesson 31B, Exercise 2

1. 'Can I take your coat?'
   'Oh, thank you. Here you are.'
   'No, thanks. I'll keep it on. I'm cold.'

2. 'Shall I make you a cup of tea?'
   'Thank you very much. I'd love one.'
   'Not just now, thanks, I'm not thirsty.'
   'I'd prefer coffee, if you've got some.'

3. 'Would you like some toast?'
   'No, nothing for me, thanks.'
   'Yes, I'd love some. Thank you.'
   'No, I've just had breakfast, thanks.'

4. 'Would you like to go and see a film this evening?'
   'That would be very nice.'
   'I'd love to. What time?'
   'Not this evening, thanks. Perhaps another time?'

5. 'Would you like to dance?'
   'Thanks. I'd love to.'
   'Not just now, thanks. I'm a bit tired.'

6. 'Shall I help you to carry that?'
   'That's very kind of you. Thank you.'
   'No, thanks. I can do it myself.'

Lesson 31C, Exercise 5

1. 'Hello, George. Want a lift?'
   'Hi, Keith, Thanks. New car?'
   'Not mine, old boy. Borrowed it from Jane for the day. Mine's in the garage.'

2. 'Pat!' 'Jane!' 'My dear, you look lovely. And what divine trousers! Did you make them yourself?'

3. 'George, dear, what's the matter?'
   'I've lost my glasses again. It's stupid – when you lose your glasses you can't see to look for them.'
   'Here they are, darling, on your chair.'

4. 'Excuse me, Edna. Could I borrow your dictionary?'
   'Yes, of course.'

5. 'I say, Jane, what a lovely plate.'
   'Yes, it belonged to Keith's mother. She gave it to me for my birthday. It's very old.'

6. 'Good heavens, Studying history?'
   'What? – Oh, this book. No, it's Keith's. He left it here yesterday.'

Drawings for Lesson 17D, Optional activity

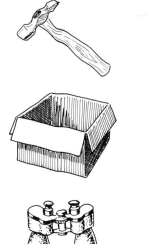

Acknowledgements

The authors and publishers would like to thank the following institutions for their help in testing the material and for the invaluable feedback which they provided:

ILC, Paris, France; Sociedade Brasileira de Cultura Inglesa, Curitiba, Brazil; International Language Centre, Athens, Greece; Adult Migrant Education Service, Australia; Ecole Nationale des Pontes et Chaussées, Paris, France; Communications in Business, Paris, France; Audiovisuelles Sprachinstitut, Zürich, Switzerland; Institut Supérieur de Langues Vivantes, University of Liège, Belgium; Studio School of English, Cambridge; The Cambridge School of English, London; English International, London; International Language Centre, Kuwait; Instituto Anglo-Mexicano de Cultura (Centro and Sur), Mexico; The British Institute of Rome, Italy; Englisches Institut, Köln, West Germany; The Gulf Polytechnic, Bahrain; Institut de Linguistique Appliquée, Strasbourg; Université Lyon 2, France; Abteilung für Angewandte Linguistik, Universität Bern, Switzerland; The British Council, Milan, Italy; International House, Hastings; English Language Centre, Hove, Sussex; Newnham Language Centre, Cambridge; The British Centre, Venice, Italy; Glostrup Pædagogisk Central, Denmark; Kochi Women's University, Kochi-shi, Japan; Institut Français de Gestion, Paris, France; The British Institute, Paris, France; The British School, Florence, Italy; Helmonds Avondcollege, Netherlands; Kodak Pathé, Paris, France; Bell School, Cambridge; Oxford Language Centre, Oxford.

The authors and publishers are grateful to the following copyright owners for permission to reproduce photographs, illustrations, texts and music in the Student's Book:

page 26: *tl* The Tate Gallery, London; *c* Reprinted by permission of Ekdotike Athenon, S.A.; *tr* Reprinted by permission of Royal Gallery of Paintings: Mauritshuis; *br* Copyright © Trustees of the British Museum. The excerpt on the cassette from *Eine Kleine Nachtmusik* by Mozart is from a Decca recording and is used with permission. page 29: *bl* Copyright © 1954 by Ronald Searle; *br* Copyright © Associated Newspapers Group plc. page 41: *br* Copyright © 1956 by Ronald Searle. page 51: *t* Ms. Auct. D. inf. 2.11, Folios 3,7 & 10 recto. By permission of The Bodleian Library, Oxford. page 53: *c,cr* Copyright © Associated Newspapers Group plc; *br* Reproduced by permission of *Punch*. page 61: Reproduced by permission of *Punch*. page 65: *Musical Swag* by Pierre Ranson, Copyright © Tony Bingham. page 80: *tr, bl* Reproduced by permission of *Punch*. page 86: The words of *Why, Oh Why* are copyright © 1960, 1964 and 1972 Ludlow Music Inc. New York, assigned to Tro Essex Music Limited at 85 Gower Street, London WC1. International copyright secured. All rights reserved. Used by permission. page 88: By permission of Rolls-Royce Motors Limited. page 90: *l* Courtesy of the Prado Museum, Madrid; *r* Cliché des Musées Nationaux, Paris. page 96: The lyrics of *Pick it up* are copyright © 1954 Folkways Music Publishers Inc. New York, assigned to Kensington Music Limited at 85 Gower Street, London WC1. International copyright secured. All rights reserved. Used by permission. page 97: *t* copyright © Penguin Books 1973. page 98: *br*, Courtesy of Hilton International, London. page 99: *t* Reproduced by permission of London Transport (Registered User No. 83/200). page 100: *c* Courtesy of British Airways. page 117: *t* Reproduced by permission of *Punch*. page 122: Reproduced by permission of *Punch*. page 126: *ct, tr* By Lucy Bowden. page 130: *t* Copyright © Garsmanda Limited. page 132: *tl, tr, c* Reproduced by permission of *Punch*; *bl* Reproduced by permission of Express Newspapers; *br* From *The Thurber Carnival* by James Thurber. © 1943 James Thurber © 1963 Hamish Hamilton Limited. © 1971 Helen W. Thurber and Rosemary T. Sauers. From *Men, Women and Dogs* published by Harcourt Brace Jovanovich.

BBC Hulton Picture Library: p63 *cr, br*. Brenard Photo Services Limited: p79. Colorific Photo Library Limited: p7 *no. 4*, p19 *ct*, inset *bl, cr*, p21, p38 *cr*, p63 *cl*, p107 *nos. 1, 3, 5, 6*. Colour Library International (Keystone Press Agency Limited): p7 *no. 3*, p9 *no. 2*, p107 *no. 2*, p109 *c*. Daily Telegraph Colour Library: p19 inset *cl*. The Image Bank of

Photography: p66 *Thomas, Mike*, p67 *c B, D, F*, p109 *B, D, E, F*. Alan Philip: p10 *nos. 1-6*, p17, p30 *t*, p35, p50 *r*, p71 *t*, p104 *t*, p115 *t*, p126 *br*. Pictor International Limited: p9 *cr*, p11 *cr*, p14, p66 *Kate, Stuart, Ann*, p67 *A-E, c A, C, E*, p108 *cl, br*, p109 *A*. Scala Istituto Fotografico Editoriale s.p.a: p63 *t*. Sporting Pictures (UK) Limited: p78 Stockphotos International: p66 *Mark*, p107 *no.4*. Tony Stone Associates: p19 *cr*, p108 *tr*. Syndication International Limited: p7 *nos. 1, 5, 7, 8, 9*, p9 *nos. 5, 6*. John Topham Picture Library: p7 *nos. 2, 6, 10*, p9 *nos. 1, 3, 4, 7, 8*, p19 *tl, ct, cb*, inset *tr, br*, p38 *tr*.

John Craddock: Malcolm Barter, Suzanne Lihou, Alexa Rutherford, Kate Simunek. Ian Fleming and Associates Limited: Terry Burton. Davis Lewis Management: Richard Dunn, Bob Harvey, Barry Thorpe. Linden Artists Limited: David Astin, Jon Davies, Tim Marwood, Val Sangster, Malcolm Stokes, Linda Worrell. Temple Art Agency: Mark Bergin, John James, John Marshall, Alan Philpot, Mike Whittlesea. Richard Baldwin, Richard Child, Kaye Hodges, Chris Rawlings, Malcolm Ward, Mike Woodhatch, Youé and Spooner.

Teacher's Book:

the lyrics of Beatles' songs in 30A and 32C are reprinted by permission of ATV Music Ltd, 19 Upper Brook Street, London W1 on behalf of Lennon and McCartney and Northern Songs Limited.

(*t* = top *b* = bottom *c* = centre *r* = right *l* = left)

[handwritten notes:]
uchikin
maekin (deposit of money)
personality = sensai / jinkaku
sensitive: kanji yasui
vegetarian: diet sai-shoku 英食